LAW AND RELIGION IN THE LIBERAL STATE

The relationship between law and religion is evident throughout history. They have never been completely independent from each other. There is no doubt that religion has played an important role in providing the underlying values of modern laws, in setting the terms of the relationship between the individual and the state, and in demanding a space for the variety of intermediate institutions which stand between individuals and the state. However, the relationships between law and religion, and the state and religious institutions differ significantly from one modern state to another. There is not one liberalism but many. This work brings together reflections upon the relationship between religion and the law from the perspectives of different sub-traditions within the broader liberal project and in light of some contemporary problems in the accommodation of religious and secular authority.

Law and Religion in the Liberal State

Edited by
Md Jahid Hossain Bhuiyan
and
Darryn Jensen

•HART•
OXFORD • LONDON • NEW YORK • NEW DELHI • SYDNEY

HART PUBLISHING

Bloomsbury Publishing Plc

Kemp House, Chawley Park, Cumnor Hill, Oxford, OX2 9PH, UK

1385 Broadway, New York, NY 10018, USA

HART PUBLISHING, the Hart/Stag logo, BLOOMSBURY and the Diana logo are trademarks of Bloomsbury Publishing Plc

First published in Great Britain 2020

A catalogue record for this book is available from the British Library.

Library of Congress Cataloging-in-Publication data

Names: Bhuiyan, Jahid Hossain, editor. | Jensen, Darryn, editor.

Title: Law and religion in the liberal state / edited by Md Jahid Hossain Bhuiyan and Darryn Jensen.

Description: Oxford ; New York : Hart, 2020. | Includes bibliographical references and index.

Identifiers: LCCN 2020002498 (print) | LCCN 2020002499 (ebook) | ISBN 9781509926336 (hardback) | ISBN 9781509926343 (Epub)

Subjects: LCSH: Religion and state. | Freedom of religion. | Religious minorities—Legal status, laws, etc..

Classification: LCC K3280 .L3935 2020 (print) | LCC K3280 (ebook) | DDC 342.08/52—dc23

LC record available at https://lccn.loc.gov/2020002498

LC ebook record available at https://lccn.loc.gov/2020002499

ISBN: HB: 978-1-50992-633-6
ePDF: 978-1-50992-635-0
ePub: 978-1-50992-634-3

Typeset by Compuscript Ltd, Shannon
Printed and bound in Great Britain by CPI Group (UK) Ltd, Croydon CR0 4YY

FSC www.fsc.org MIX Paper from responsible sources FSC® C013604

To find out more about our authors and books visit www.hartpublishing.co.uk. Here you will find extracts, author information, details of forthcoming events and the option to sign up for our newsletters.

ACKNOWLEDGEMENTS

The editors acknowledge the assistance of Michael Tarlowski in proofreading the manuscript, and the financial support of the Australian National University College of Law.

CONTENTS

LIST OF CONTRIBUTORS

Md Jahid Hossain Bhuiyan is Associate Professor of Law at Southeast University, Bangladesh and a postdoctoral fellow at the Faculty of Law, North-West University, Republic of South Africa.

Anthony Bradney is Emeritus Professor of Law at Keele University.

Zachary Calo is Professor of Law at Hamad Bin Khalifa University, Qatar, and Professor of Law (adjunct), University of Notre Dame Australia.

Charlotte Carrington-Farmer is Associate Professor of History at Roger Williams University, Bristol, Rhode Island.

Peter Edge is Professor of Law at Oxford Brookes University.

Chad Flanders is Professor of Law at St Louis University.

Javier García Oliva is a Senior Lecturer in Law at the University of Manchester.

Helen Hall is a Senior Lecturer in Law at Nottingham Trent University.

Darryn Jensen is a Senior Lecturer in the Law School at the Australian National University.

Daniela Kalkandjieva is an independent Bulgarian scholar who works in the fields of history, religious studies, archival studies and sociology of scientific knowledge.

Sean Oliveira is Associate Attorney at Ogletree Deakins Nash Smoak and Stewart PC, St Louis, Missouri.

Rafael Palomino is Professor of Law at Complutense University of Madrid.

Carlo Panara is Professor of Comparative Public Law at Liverpool John Moores University.

MC Rajan is a Roman Catholic priest, Practising Advocate, Chennai High Court and Secretary, Diocesan Arbitration Tribunal.

Dorothy Rogers is Associate Professor and Chair of the Department of Religion at Montclair State University, New Jersey.

Maimon Schwarzschild is Professor of Law at the University of San Diego and Affiliated Professor at the University of Haifa.

Carla Zoethout is Professor of Constitutional Law at the Open University in the Netherlands and Associate Professor of Comparative Constitutional Law at the University of Amsterdam.

1

Introduction: Law and Religion in the Liberal State

MD JAHID HOSSAIN BHUIYAN AND DARRYN JENSEN

I. Modernity as Pluralising

Peter Berger said that modernity was 'not necessarily secularizing' but 'necessarily pluralizing'.[1] An outstanding feature of modernity is not the absence of strong religious beliefs but 'an increasing plurality, within the same society, of different beliefs, values, and worldviews'.[2] This certainly poses a challenge to religious traditions, in the sense that the plausibility of any single religious worldview is challenged by visible competing traditions,[3] but it seems not to have led to the decline of religion generally in favour of a pervasive 'enlightened' rationality. Rather, as Berger observed, 'religious communities have survived and even flourished to the degree that they have *not* tried to adapt themselves to the alleged requirements of a secularized world'.[4]

Berger's rejection of the conventional secularisation thesis that modernity is associated with a decline of religion was preceded by the work of Roger Finke and Rodney Stark.[5] Finke and Stark suggested that the religious pluralism associated with modernity was 'stimulus for religious growth'.[6] The core of their argument is captured in the following passage:

> [T]he natural state of religious economies is one in which a variety of religious groups successfully cater to the special interests of specific market segments. This arises because of the inherent inability of a single religious organization to be at once worldly and other-worldly, while the market will always contain distinct consumer segments

[1] PL Berger, 'Secularization Falsified' (2008) (February) *First Things* 23, 23.
[2] ibid.
[3] As Berger said, there is not an 'absence of God' but 'the presence of many gods' (ibid 24).
[4] PL Berger, 'The Desecularization of the World: A Global Overview' in PL Berger (ed), *The Desecularization of the World: Resurgent Religion and World Politics* (Grand Rapids, MI, William B Eerdmans Publishing Co, 1999) 4.
[5] R Finke and R Stark, 'Religious Economies and Sacred Canopies: Religious Mobilization in American Cities' (1988) 53 *American Sociological Review* 41.
[6] ibid 42.

> seeking more and less worldly versions of faith. Indeed, because of this underlying differentiation of consumer preferences, religious economies never can be successfully monopolized, even when a religious organization is backed by the state. Even at the height of its temporal power, the medieval church was surrounded by heresy and dissent.[7]

According to Finke and Stark, then, 'the more highly specialized and aggressive the churches are, the greater the odds that any given individual will be activated'.[8] In a more recent paper, Stark referred to evidence that 'subjective religiousness remains high', even in western European countries where traditional Christian religious *practice* had fallen to a very low level,[9] and that 'among American academics, the proportion who regard themselves as religious is higher the more scientific their field'.[10] To be clear, the supposed religious decline of the West in the late twentieth century was not a decline in religiosity as such but a decline of traditional practice of religion within the institutional framework of monopolistic or oligopolistic 'established' or 'mainline' churches.

Of course, we should not be surprised to find that a pluralising, and consequent energising, of expressions of religion is accompanied by the emergence of much more strident expressions of hostility to religion. We shall return to that point shortly.

II. Tensions within Liberalism

An understanding of modernity as pluralising, rather than as secularising of society generally, exposes a tension within liberal political settlements. In its essence, the tension is between, on the one hand, a view of the state as accommodating and supportive of the plurality of religious expressions and, on the other hand, a view of the state (and the public sphere) as non-religious, however much religion might be allowed to flourish away from public spaces. Berger spoke of the first view in terms of 'institutional differentiation'.[11] On this view, the state 'is not hostile to religion but draws back from direct involvement in religious matters and recognizes the autonomy of religious institutions'.[12] The second view is, for Berger, 'characterized precisely by antireligious animus'.[13] Where this view is taken – Berger gave the example of France – '[r]eligious symbols or actions are rigorously barred from political life, but privatized religion is protected by law'.[14]

[7] ibid.
[8] ibid 43.
[9] R Stark, 'Secularization RIP' (1999) 60 *Sociology of Religion* 249, 264.
[10] ibid.
[11] Berger (n 1) 24.
[12] ibid.
[13] ibid.
[14] ibid.

These two views of the state can be seen to correspond with two branches of the broader liberal political tradition. The first branch might be labelled *liberalism as a truce*. Liberalism as a truce recognises the dangers of a situation in which competing religious worldviews are tempted to fight for political hegemony. Christian Europe, in fact, saw several iterations of such conflict, and memories of this seem to have informed the modern political settlements of many European nations as well as the former British colonies of North America and Australasia. The state, as far as possible, maintains a neutral stance as between religious traditions and accommodates religious differences. It takes care not to coerce people in ways that are contrary to their religious beliefs or which prevent them from performing their religious duties. Moreover, religious communities are 'sovereign' in respect of their internal affairs. Indeed, it might be argued that the state ought to provide a framework within which religious communities can govern their own affairs. Lord Acton, in stating that 'religious liberty is not the negative right of being without any particular religion' but 'the right of religious communities to the practice of their own duties, the enjoyment of their own constitution, and the protection of law',[15] showed an adherence to this way of thinking. A more systematically developed and generalised version of the same idea is found in the 'sphere sovereignty' of the Dutch theologian, Abraham Kuyper. For Kuyper, the state is 'a special sphere of authority' that provides for 'a felicitous interaction' among the various spheres of human life and 'to keep them within the pale of justice'.[16] Accordingly, the state 'may indeed recognize the family and grant it legal status, but in so doing it is neither the author nor authorizer of family'.[17] Two matters stand out here. First, the state is not the only, or even the primary, source of authority to which individuals owe allegiance. Secondly, the state's authority is limited to 'the mutual relations of these spheres' and 'does not obtain within any of these spheres'.[18] Liberalism as a truce is not necessarily grounded in scepticism about religion. Christianity, in particular, might be seen as having affirmed the separation of religious authority and secular authority from its own theological standpoint, although the precise terms of the truce have been the subject of periodic renegotiation in the light of fresh demarcation disputes.[19]

Of course, liberalism as a truce, in recognising the state's authority as to relations between the spheres, is not logically bound to tolerate every religiously-motivated activity. The question of whether Roman Catholics were to be tolerated

[15] JEE Dalberg-Acton, 'The Protestant Theory of Persecution' in JN Figgis and R Vere Laurence (eds), *The History of Freedom and Other Essays* (London, MacMillan & Co, 1907) 150, 151–52.

[16] A Kuyper, 'Sphere Sovereignty', tr G Kamps, *A Public Address Delivered at the Inauguration of the Free University* (20 October 1880) at www.reformationalpublishingproject.com/pdf_books/Scanned_Books_PDF/SphereSovereignty_English.pdf, 6.

[17] KA Van Til, 'Subsidiarity and Sphere-Sovereignty: A Match Made in …?' (2008) 69 *Theological Studies* 610, 633.

[18] Kuyper (n 16) 7; See also Van Til (n 17) 622.

[19] See, eg, R Mohr, 'The Christian Origins of secularism and the rule of law' in N Hosen and R Mohr (eds), *Law and Religion in Public Life: The Contemporary Debate* (London, Routledge, 2011) 34, 40–42.

in seventeenth-century England serves as an illustration. It has commonly been understood that John Locke refused to extend toleration to Roman Catholics on the basis that they were 'ready upon any occasion to seise the Government, and possess themselves of the Estates and Fortunes of their Fellow-Subjects; and that they only ask leave to be tolerated by the Magistrate so long, until they find themselves strong enough to effect it'.[20] Of course, Locke's application of this principle to a particular religious community was contingent upon members of that community, in fact, continuing to hold the belief that they did not owe allegiance to the government and being committed to overthrowing it. To the extent that Roman Catholics did not hold that belief, they could be tolerated. What was not to be tolerated were '[o]pinions contrary to human Society, or to those moral Rules which are necessary to the preservation of Civil Society'.[21] Locke conceded that '[e]xamples in any Church are rare'.[22] Whether the beliefs or practices of any particular religious community are a threat to the peace of the greater community can be a matter of fine judgement in each case. A danger is that Locke's argument as to the limits of toleration might be twisted to provide a pretext for silencing groups with unpopular or unfashionable views. Even where there are genuine public order or public welfare considerations at stake that provide a neutral rationale for state action of some sort, law and public policy justified by reference to those considerations will not necessarily be neutral in terms of its effects upon religious communities.[23] Nevertheless, liberalism as a truce has the virtue of removing the promotion of 'the true faith' from the role of the state, establishing an 'institutional differentiation'[24] between state authority and religious authority and founding a claim that the state ought to respect religious freedom to the extent that the exercise of such freedom does not threaten the common good that the state must advance.

The second branch of the liberal tradition might be labelled *comprehensive liberalism*.[25] Comprehensive liberalism is founded on a set of 'enlightened' values and asserts them as the state's values. Sectional or sub-national values must give way where there is a conflict with the state's values. The difference between the two interpretations might be illustrated using the example of anti-discrimination law.

[20] J Locke, *A Letter Concerning Toleration*, ed with an introduction by M Goldie (Indianapolis, IN, Liberty Fund, 2010) 51.

[21] ibid 50.

[22] ibid. For an argument that Locke did, in fact, advocate toleration of Roman Catholicism, see R Mortensen, 'Specious Delusions: John Locke, Knowledge and Religious Toleration' (2014) 33 *University of Queensland Law Journal* 335, 344–45.

[23] As to the impossibility of complete neutrality between different religious traditions, see RP George, *The Clash of Orthodoxies: Law, Religion, and Morality in Crisis* (Wilmington, DE, ISI Books, 2001) 86–87.

[24] Berger (n 1) 24.

[25] The use of the adjective 'comprehensive' here is intended to invoke John Rawls' distinction between a political conception of justice and a comprehensive doctrine, which 'extend[s] beyond the political and include[s] non-political values and virtues' (J Rawls, *Political Liberalism* (New York, Columbia University Press, 1993) 175). While 'comprehensive liberalism' is to be understood as a comprehensive doctrine in the Rawlsian sense, it is not suggested that comprehensive liberalism should always correspond precisely with the particular political conception of justice preferred by Rawls.

Under liberalism as a truce, the state might see the elimination or reduction of discrimination between people on the basis of race, religion, sex or sexual orientation as part of the state's role as protector of the common good, but it would exercise prudential judgement as to the scope of any prohibition of discrimination so as to avoid unnecessarily interfering with freedom of religious exercise and the sovereignty of religious communities in respect of their internal affairs. Setting the precise scope of state coercion might involve a delicate balancing exercise between the state's interests and the sensibilities of affected religious groups and individuals, but the notions of compromise and proportionality in pursuit of the common good are necessarily implicit in liberalism as a truce. Comprehensive liberalism, by contrast, is more likely to see religious belief and the state's values as locked in a 'winner takes all' game, because the state's role *is* to promote 'enlightened' values. Religious communities that have objections to complying with aspects of anti-discrimination law are seen as seeking exemption from compliance with norms of general application. Consequently, it is the claim for different treatment, rather than the state's extension of coercion, that is questioned and has to be justified. Comprehensive liberalism, to the extent that it prioritises the state's values over religious sensibilities, involves a 'dogmatic secularism' that 'aims to privatize religion altogether, to render religiously informed moral judgment irrelevant to public affairs and public life, and to establish itself, secularist ideology, as the nation's public philosophy'.[26] Where this is so, comprehensive liberalism is 'a sectarian doctrine with its own metaphysical and moral presuppositions and foundations, with its own myths, and … its own rituals'.[27]

Berger identified what we have called comprehensive liberalism with 'an international subculture composed of people with Western-type higher education, especially in the humanities and social sciences, that is indeed secularized' and noted that such people 'control the institutions that provide the "official" definitions of reality, notably the education system, the media of mass communication, and the higher reaches of the legal system'.[28] Such people are 'remarkably similar all over the world today'[29] and, since their travels abroad consist mainly of interactions with people like themselves, they 'easily fall into the misconception that these people reflect the overall visited society'.[30] Therefore, it is not surprising that modern (theistic) religious movements should have a populist character. As Berger observed, they are 'movements of protest and resistance *against* a secular elite'.[31] Modernity has led not to a pervasive secularism but to a heightened tension between religious and dogmatic secularist outlooks. In any event, the atmosphere

[26] George (n 23) 6.
[27] ibid 7–8. It appears that Berger, in stating that 'there are secularist as well as religious fundamentalists' (Berger (n 1) 27), was of the same mind as George on this matter.
[28] Berger (n 4) 10.
[29] ibid.
[30] ibid 11.
[31] ibid.

of contestation with respect to the place of religion in the life of liberal nation states makes an exploration of when and how liberal legal systems should accommodate religious beliefs, symbols, institutions and practices all the more important and urgent. That is the object of this book.

III. The Content of this Book

The essays in this collection are presented in two parts. Part I is concerned with the different traditions of thought concerning the relationship between religious authority and civil authority that have evolved within the Christian (or post-Christian) world. This part of the book illustrates how freedom of religion and separation of religious and civil authority are not monolithic ideas but have evolved along different paths in different national and religious communities on account of different historical conditions.

Charlotte Carrington-Farmer addresses the contribution of the founder of the Rhode Island colony, Roger Williams, to the development of the idea of separation of church and state. It is significant that Williams was not religiously indifferent. He was a fervent Protestant Christian who was theologically opposed to Quakerism and took care to avoid witnessing Native American religious practices. Despite this, he supported everyone's liberty to practise their religion without interference from the state and opposed the idea that the state should mandate a particular religious observance. Carrington-Farmer observes that Williams suffered greatly for his experiment and that the 'lived reality' of religious freedom in the Rhode Island colony involved many practical difficulties. Nevertheless, Williams is a significant historical figure, because he was the first person to have a degree of success in putting the abstract idea of religious freedom into practice.

Zachary Calo traces the development of Roman Catholic thought about religious freedom and liberalism from the 1832 encyclical of Gregory XVI, *Mirari Vos*, to the present time. Calo gives particular attention to the Declaration of Religious Liberty (*Dignitatis Humanae*) and the work of the US theologian, John Courtney Murray. Calo observes that there continues to be a tension between secular liberalism's view of freedom in terms of choice and self-actualisation – and, consequently, its view of religion as 'subjective and interiorised preference' – and Catholicism's view that freedom 'stands in the service of truth'. The logic of secular liberalism tends to prioritise equality and anti-discrimination norms over religious expression and the freedom of religious communities to govern their internal affairs.

Daniela Kalkandjieva considers the distinct case of Orthodox Christianity in the former communist states of Eastern Europe. Former communist states with Roman Catholic and Protestant populations, such as Poland and Hungary, had well-developed traditions of thought and practices to draw upon. The Orthodox countries, by contrast, had experienced a pre-communist 'Caesaropapism', in which the church did not possess an identity that was distinct from that of the nation or state, followed by a particularly rigorous form of secularism under communist rule.[32] Kalkandjieva identifies the characteristic Orthodox contribution to church–state relations as that of 'symphony'. Symphony, in the words of Ecumenical Patriarch Bartholomew cited by Kalkandjieva, involves 'active collaboration' that is 'dynamic and creative'. Kalkandjieva notes that the symphony that is actually being played is one of 'soft and asymmetric separation', in which the Orthodox churches have been able to influence government policies 'while zealously defending their own church autonomy'.

Each of the essays in Part II explores a particular point of contact or area of tension between religious authority and secular authority, usually within one nation state or group of states. Anthony Bradney's contribution begins and ends with the observation that, in Great Britain, very few people experience discrimination by reason of their religious beliefs, but identifies education policies as an area in which tensions have arisen. The ostensibly benevolent or, at worst, innocuous government objective of 'preparing students for life in modern Britain' is not, in practice, as neutral and uncontentious as it may at first seem. Bradney, while conceding that the extent of religious discrimination in Britain is not great, points to 'a prevailing lack of appreciation of the position of those who ground their lives on revealed religious truths'.

Bradney's contribution is followed by three chapters that consider the European experience more broadly. Rafael Palomino considers the question of whether there is a 'soul' to Europe that operates as a unifying and legitimating idea for the European Union. Palomino sees the integration of religion into this soul as a matter of importance, as the dogmas of liberal democracy and human rights provide too narrow a discourse about the common good and are threatening to become an 'illiberal pseudo-religion'.

Carla Zoethout and Carlo Panara survey the European scene at the level of particular legal disputes concerning religious expression. Zoethout's survey of recent decisions by the European Court of Human Rights in religious freedom cases highlights the tension between asserting a European state's duty to remain impartial among religions and recognising scope for the democratic institutions of a nation state to make choices how best to maintain the peaceful coexistence of persons and groups within a society. This tension is perhaps illustrated most sharply by the last matter mentioned by Zoethout, namely, attempts by some states to criminalise the disparaging of particular religious beliefs. Panara's focus is upon the Italian case law concerning the display of the crucifix in schools and other public places. As Panara explains, disputes concerning the display of crucifixes are especially complex because crucifixes remain potent representations of the Christian doctrine of atonement while being pressed into service as supposed neutral symbols of national identity.

[32] Berger described the practice of the Soviet Union and its satellites as a much less benign version of the *laïcité* of France (Berger (n 1) 24).

The focus then shifts from Europe to the United States and the tension between freedom of religious exercise and certain types of laws and government policies. Cases concerning government-mandated employee health insurance[33] and anti-discrimination law[34] have raised the profile of this tension. Maimon Schwarzschild observes that, for religious believers, reliance upon exemptions from anti-discrimination law is 'an unwise and ultimately perhaps a futile strategy'. More attention should be given to the sources of the tension, which are the expansion of the state's sphere of authority so as to cover more and more areas of life and the consequent proliferation of rules and policies that might interfere with freedom of religious exercise. Chad Flanders and Sean Oliveira observe that neither those who claim nor those who oppose religious exemptions from these laws may truly be advancing a pluralist agenda. Both are 'evangelists'. The problem with resolving these disputes by Bill of Rights litigation is that usually one side must win and the other must lose. Flanders and Oliveira suggest that, in those circumstances, it is important to get the process right, so that harm to religious sensibilities or to state interests, as the case may be, is recognised, even if those sensibilities or interests do not win in the case at hand.

Dorothy Rogers, by contrast, examines how religiously-motivated individuals and groups might, by refraining from cooperation with the state, carve out spaces in which their values prevail. Her focus is upon the movement in the United States that provides 'sanctuary' for undocumented immigrants. Rogers comments upon the tradition of *jus asyli* or 'safe haven' within Christianity, which, although it lacks legal standing, provides a space within which religiously-motivated individuals and groups can act according to their own lights and which the state is reluctant to invade.

A matter that is seldom considered in collections of this type is how private law disputes can involve (or cloak) issues of religious freedom. The next two chapters in this collection provide contrasting examples of how religious freedom questions have played themselves out in private law disputes. Javier García Oliva and Helen Hall consider the various ways in which private law touches upon the practice of exorcism and the provision of spiritual advice in England and Wales. They note how English and Welsh private law, in a number of distinct areas, prioritises individual choice over paternalism and so minimises the scope for private law actions against ministers of religion who perform exorcisms or provide spiritual advice. Peter Edge and MC Rajan consider the long-running dispute concerning the Babri Masjid/Ram temple in Ayodhya, India. This dispute was ostensibly a property law dispute, but that seems to have been merely the means by which a conflict between opposing religious claims was fought out. Edge and Rajan suggest that this litigation demonstrates state failures both as to securing enforcement of the court orders in the property law matter and as to providing mechanisms for the freedom

[33] *Burwell v Hobby Lobby Stores Inc* 573 US __; 134 S Ct 2751 (2014).
[34] *Masterpiece Cakeshop Ltd v Colorado Civil Rights Commission* 584 US __; 138 S Ct 1719 (2018).

of religious exercise question to be played out openly. Moreover, the decision in favour of the Hindu community represented a departure from secularism understood as impartiality between religious groups.

Finally, Md Jahid Hossain Bhuiyan discusses the scope for the accommodation of Shari'a law in Australia, noting that government policy seems to be opposed to accommodating Shari'a law in the family law context but looks favourably upon Islamic finance. Bhuiyan observes, against the background of a discussion of 'neoliberal multiculturalism', that this difference in attitude is in need of further explanation and that members of Muslim communities in Australia deserve such an explanation.

It is not the object of this book to propose a single recipe for the accommodation of religious beliefs and practices in liberal legal systems. A simple appeal to 'liberalism' certainly cannot provide any such recipe, because liberalism is not a monolithic tradition. Indeed, the place of religion in a liberal polity is, more than perhaps any other matter, a matter of deep disagreement within that tradition of political thought. It is hoped that the essays in this book will shed at least a little light on the benefits and challenges that religious differences present for contemporary societies and the conditions under which religious beliefs and civil authority can co-exist happily.

PART I

Religious Freedom and Particular Traditions

2

Roger Williams and the Architecture of Religious Liberty

CHARLOTTE CARRINGTON-FARMER

In the spring of 1638, Roger Williams had a problem. His neighbours, Joshua and Jane Verin, were fighting, again. The Verins were amongst the first settlers in Providence in 1636, and they built their house right next door to Williams'. Whilst Joshua did not attend the religious meetings held in Williams' house, Jane did; directly against her husband's wishes. Williams recorded how Joshua 'refused to heare the word with us'.[1] In line with Rhode Island's policy of religious freedom, the colony 'molested him not' for his beliefs.[2] In turn, Joshua refused to offer his wife the same liberty. Williams described how Joshua, a 'boisterous and desperate' man, had 'trodden her [Jane] under foote tyrannically and brutishly' for her disobedience.[3] Joshua's 'furious blowes' meant that Jane a 'gracious and modest woman … went in danger of Life'.[4] The Verin case posed a number of problems for Williams. He had founded Providence on the basis of freedom of conscience, and Joshua's behaviour prevented his wife from freely worshipping as she chose. Moreover, on both sides of the Atlantic, husbands were punished by the courts for 'excessively' correcting their wives.[5] On the other hand, if the town intervened, it challenged God's ordinance that wives were subordinate to their husbands.

Williams and his fellow townsmen debated the Verin case at length. Providence resident, William Arnold, declared that any intervention from the town would

[1] Roger Williams, Letter to John Winthrop (22 May 1638) in GW LaFantasie, *The Correspondence of Roger Williams*, vol 1: *1629–1653* (Hanover, NH, and London, Brown University Press/University Press of New England, 1988) 156.

[2] ibid.

[3] ibid.

[4] ibid.

[5] For example, in 1641, *The Body of Liberties of Massachusetts Bay* ruled that 'Everie marryed woman shall be free from bodilie correction or stripes by her husband unless it be in his owne defence upon her assault.' W Whitmore, (ed), *A Bibliographical Sketch of the Laws of the Massachusetts Colony from 1630 to 1686* (Boston, MA, Rockwell and Churchill, 1890) 51. For a reassessment of the Verin case, see M Murányi Manchester, *Puritan Family and Community in the English Atlantic World: Being 'Much Afflicted with Conscience'* (New York and Oxford, Routledge, 2019).

breach an 'ordinance of God, the subjection of wives to their husbands'.[6] Arnold's comments reflected the widely held belief that intelligence and understanding were given to men, not women. Even though women were a key part of the seventeenth-century household, they were viewed as intellectually and morally weak. After much debate, the town voted to disenfranchise Joshua and 'discard him from our Civill Freedome'.[7] However, this was no *typical* case of spousal abuse. Joshua was not prosecuted for violently beating his wife; his punishment was for challenging her freedom of worship. The ruling held that Joshua would 'be withheld from the liberty of voting … for restraining of the liberty of conscience'.[8] The Verin case highlights the lived reality of Williams' experiment in soul liberty, which separated church and state and allowed religious freedom. In a time when state religion ruled and dissenters faced banishment, corporal and capital punishment, the small colony of Rhode Island and Providence Plantations was arguably one of the freest places in the western world.

I. The Backdrop

The story of how Williams founded a colony based on religious freedom starts in England. Williams grew up in a world of religious turmoil, where the 'official' state religion changed on the whim of a monarch. Following King Henry VIII's break with Rome, England switched back and forth between being a Protestant country and a Catholic country. Williams reflected on the upheaval (and resulting 'false' conversions) in his 1645 work, *Christenings make not Christians*:

> When England was all Popish under Henry the seveneth, how easie is conversion wrought to half Papist half-Protestant under Henry the eight? … From halfe-Protestantisme halfe-Popery under Henry the eight, to absolute Protestanisme under Edward the sixth: from absoluer Protestation under Edward the sixt to absolute popery undet Quegne Mary (just like the Weather-cocke, with the breaty of every Prince) to absolute Protestanisme under Queen Elizabeth &c.[9]

Against this backdrop, Williams witnessed first-hand how the state could pollute the church. Across the Atlantic, in the small colony of Rhode Island on the east coast of North America, Williams wanted to create something different.

Williams grew up within the Church of England under King James I, in the Smithfield district of London. Close to his home on Cowes Lane there was livestock market, a bustling hub of Dutch traders, but also Newgate Prison. Williams' parish church, St Sepulchre without Newgate, was the closest church to the prison and

[6] LaFantasie (n 1) 156.

[7] ibid.

[8] Joshua Verin returned to Salem and he compelled his wife to accompany him. Williams noted (ibid), 'He will hale his wife with ropes to Salem, where she must needes be troubled and troublesome as differences yet stand. She is willing to stay and live with him or elsewhere, where she may not offend.'

[9] R Williams, *Christenings make not Christians* (London, 1645) 11–12.

execution site. Williams was well aware of the long history of persecution in the area. In *The Bloody Tenent Yet More Bloody* (1652), Williams reflected on the death of John Lambert, who was burned at Smithfield in 1538. Although Williams had not been born at the time of the execution, Williams described Lambert as 'a true Follower of the Lambe of God', who cried out in the midst of the flames 'None but Christ, None but Christ'.[10] Smithfield gained further notoriety not only when many Protestants were burned alive there under Queen Mary I, but also because it was the site of the final burning of a religious heretic in 1612. The final burning happened when Williams was approximately eight years old and a 'vast Conflux' of people watched Bartholomew Legate, who was branded an 'incorrigible Heretick' (for being a Separatist), 'burned to ashes' in Smithfield.[11] Thomas Fuller reflected on the irony of the location in his 1656 publication, *Church History of Britain*:

> To Smithfield he was brought to be burned … In this very Smithfield how many Saints in the Marian daies, suffered for the testimony of Jesus Christ? Whereas now one therin dyeth in his own bloody for denying him.[12]

Whilst others were not burned alive for their views at Smithfield, they rotted in Newgate Prison, a stone's throw from Williams' house. Thomas Helwys met his demise in Newgate in 1616 (when Williams was approximately 13 years old) for arguing for the very thing that Williams eventually went on to create in Rhode Island: a place where religion was separate from the state. Helwys argued that 'the Magistrate is not to meddle with religion or matters of conscience, nor to compel men to this or that form or religion'.[13] Williams' childhood neighbourhood revealed the long and bloody history of state persecution for religion's sake. In contrast, Williams created one of the only places in the Western world where religious freedom ruled.[14]

Williams' first steps in his journey away from Smithfield came from the patronage of Sir Edward Coke, Chief Justice of England. Coke, impressed with Williams' flair for short-hand, employed Williams when he was a teenager to take notes on important legal cases.[15] With Coke's backing, Williams was able to

[10] R Williams, *The Bloody Tenent Yet More Bloody* (1652) in SL Caldwell (ed), *The Complete Writings of Roger Williams* (New York, Russell & Russell, 1963) vol IV, 464.

[11] T Fuller, *Church History of Britain* (London, 1656) book X, 63–64.

[12] ibid. Williams' age is an approximation, as St Sepulchre's records were destroyed in the Great Fire of London in 1666.

[13] J Barry, *Roger Williams and the Creation of the American Soul: Church, State, and the Birth of Liberty* (London and New York, Viking, 2012) 319.

[14] Writing to John Winthrop many years later, Williams reflected when 'Myself a child' he had been 'in Christ called and persecuted in and out of my father's house'. Roger Williams, Letter to John Winthrop (between July and December 1632) in LaFantasie (n 1) 8.

[15] Williams later reflected that Sir Edward Coke was a 'Man of Honour and Wisdom and pietie' who was 'often pleased to call me his Son'. Williams acknowledged the impact that Coke had on him as a young boy: 'I may truly say that beside my natural Inclination to stuidie and Activitie, His [Coke's] Example Instruction and Incowragemt have spurd me on a more than ordanarie industrious and patient Course, in my whole Course'. Roger Williams, Letter to Anne Sadlier (ca April 1652), LaFantasie (n 1) 358.

study at Charterhouse and then Cambridge University. Williams graduated from Cambridge in 1627 and took a job as chaplain to a wealthy Puritan family in High Laver, Essex.[16] By this point, Williams had turned his back on the Anglican Church of England for being too Catholic. Williams became a 'hotter sort of Protestant', wanting to purify the Church of England. Williams and his fellow Puritans sought simple worship and personal intimacy with God. However, under Archbishop Laud, Puritan ministers were compelled to use the *Book of Common Prayer*, wear the surplice and lead congregations in what they deemed rote worship. Those who refused faced imprisonment and worse. Williams decided that England's religious climate was too dangerous, and he and his new wife, Mary, decided to move to a 'New' England across the Atlantic. Williams later reflected that Bishop Laud pursued him 'out of this Land', and his 'Conscience was perswaded' not only against Bishops but also against 'the Nationall Church and Ceremonies'.[17]

Williams' decision to move to New England made sense in many respects. In 1620, a group of Separatists, headed by William Bradford, left England (after a stint in Holland) on board the *Mayflower* and founded Plymouth Colony on the east coast of North America. The Separatists believed that the Church of England was too corrupt to save and wanted to separate themselves entirely from it. A decade later, they were joined by a group of Puritans, headed by John Winthrop.[18] As Puritans they wanted to purify the Church of England, rather than separate away from it like the Separatists in Plymouth. Winthrop and company hoped to set an example to England and the rest of the world with their 'city upon a hill'.[19] However, Winthrop and company had no intention of offering religious freedom for all, and they set up their own version of an established church based on congregationalism. Their goal was to build a holy commonwealth that reflected the religious and moral standards they held true.

II. Building a Colony

Roger and Mary Williams arrived in Boston, the nucleus of the Massachusetts Bay Colony, on 5 February 1631 on board the *Lyon*. Upon arrival in Boston, Williams was offered the ministry of the Boston Church, one of the most prestigious jobs in

[16] For more on Williams' early life in England, see OE Winslow, *Master Roger Williams: A Biography* (New York, Macmillan, 1957) and Barry (n 13).

[17] Roger Williams, Letter to Anne Sadlier (ca April 1652), LaFantasie (n 1) 358.

[18] J Winthrop, 'A Model of Christian Charity' in RS Dunn and L Yeandle (eds), *The Journal of John Winthrop, 1630–1649* (Cambridge, MA, Harvard University Press, 1996) 8–9.

[19] Winthrop's *Model of Christian Charity*, where he declared that Massachusetts would be a 'city upon a hill', has received much scholarly analysis. Most notably, Abram C Van Engen has overturned many of the traditional interpretations, especially Perry Miller's analysis. See AC Van Engen, 'Origins and Last Farewells: Bible Wars, Textual Form, and the Making of American History' (2013) 86(4) *The New England Quarterly* 543–92; and P Miller, *Errand into the Wilderness* (Cambridge, MA and London, The Belknap Press of Harvard University Press, 1956).

the entire colony. However, Williams turned the position down and headed north to Salem, where the Church mirrored his religious beliefs more closely. Between 1631 and 1635, Williams was unable to settle in one place, both geographically and spiritually. As his views moved towards Separatist theology, he moved south to Plymouth Colony. However, Williams' views fell out of favour in Plymouth, and he moved back to Salem. By 1635, Williams' opinions on a number of issues had caused problems with the authorities in both Plymouth and Massachusetts. Most notably, he believed that their charters were void, as they had not purchased the land from the natives who inhabited it.[20] Winthrop reviewed the charges laid against Williams in his journal, noting that Williams was 'judged a great contempt of authority' and that his ideas were 'erroneous, and very dangerous'.[21] Williams laid bare how Winthrop's dream for a city upon a hill had failed, in both its legal and religious aims. Williams charged the magistrate with injustice and extreme oppression, and 'all the churches' with being 'full of antichristian pollution'.[22] The Bay colonists, who had founded their colony to be a Christian example to the rest of the world, were appalled by Williams' criticisms.

In October 1635, Massachusetts Bay banished Williams from the colony for his 'newe & dangerous opinions'.[23] Initially, the implementation was deferred to the spring, as Williams was ill and winter was approaching. However, when Williams continued to meet with other like-minded individuals in his home and share his ideas, the magistrates ruled to seize him immediately and banish him to England. Williams got a tip off about the arrest and he escaped in the midst of a blizzard in January 1636. Williams later reflected 'That ever honrd Govr Mr Wintrop privately wrote to me to steer my Course to the Nahigonset Bay and Indians'.[24] Williams took Winthrop's 'prudent Motion as a Hint and voice from God … I steered my Course from Salem'. Members of the Wampanoag tribe, including Massasoit, helped Williams and provided him with shelter. Williams reflected many years later that he still remembered the cold and 'the snow wch I feele yet'.[25] For 14 weeks, 'in bitter Winter Season', he did not know 'what Bread or Bed did meane'.[26] Writing 35 years after his banishment, Williams still believed he had been 'unkindly and unchristianly (as I believe) driven from my howse and land,

[20] The past 500 years have seen a myriad of terms used as referents to the Indigenous Peoples of the Americas. This chapter will use specific tribal names when possible and then use the following terms interchangeably: Indigenous Peoples, Native Americans, and Indians.

[21] J Winthrop, *History of New England, 1630–1649*, ed JK Hosmer (New York, Scribner, 1908) 154, 162–63.

[22] ibid.

[23] NB Shurtleff (ed), *Records of the Governor and Company of the Massachusetts Bay in New England*, vol 1, *1628–1641* (Boston, MA, William White, 1853) 160–61.

[24] Roger Williams, Letter to Major John Wilson and Governor Thomas Prence (22 June 1670) in GW LaFantasie, *The Correspondence of Roger Williams*, vol 2: *1654–1682* (Hanover, NH, and London, Brown University Press/University Press of New England, 1988) 610.

[25] ibid.

[26] ibid.

and wife and children (in the midst of N. Engl. winter.)'[27] Obviously, Williams did not think that his 'new and dangerous' opinions justified this unchristian treatment from his supposedly Christian brethren.

By spring of 1636, Williams and his followers from Salem had started to build a settlement along the Seekonk River, in present-day Rumford, Rhode Island. Williams, in keeping with his views on the land rights of Indigenous Peoples, bought the land from Massasoit. However, Plymouth asserted that the land was within their jurisdiction, which meant that Williams could be arrested. Even though Williams and his followers had already begun to build houses and plant crops, they decided to cross the Seekonk River and settle in a place that lay beyond Plymouth's boundaries. After rounding the river, Williams crossed into Narragansett land, and accordingly he purchased land from the Narragansett Sachems, Canonicus and Miantonomi. He named the settlement Providence, as he believed that it was God's providence that had carried them to safety. The earliest surviving land deed is dated 1638 and confirms earlier verbal and written agreements. The deed bears the date 'the 24th of the first month, commonly called March in ye second year of our plantation', and it was signed by both English colonists (including Williams) and Narragansett Sachems, Canonicus and Miantonomi.[28] Moreover, two more tribal members, Sotaash and Assotemeweit, witnessed the transaction.

The deed represented the first step in Williams' plan to put his 'new and dangerous' ideas into action through building a radical new settlement.[29] One of the reasons Williams was banished from Massachusetts Bay was for asserting the original rights of Indigenous Peoples to their land. By offering a written record that demonstrated that he had purchased the land from Canonicus and Miantonomi, Williams was able to put theory into practice. The deed established Williams' right to settle and defined Providence's settlement as separate from the neighbouring English colonies. Williams' settlement quickly started to grow as a home for those distressed of conscience, and more people who faced banishment from Massachusetts joined him. As the colony expanded off of the mainland, Williams negotiated fair purchase of the land. He later reflected that 'It was not price nor Money that could have purchased Rode Iland. Rode Iland was obtained by Love'.[30] From a Native perspective, the land was most likely gifted with the expectation that Williams would return the favour on a yearly basis by trading with them. In Salem, Williams had theorised that the land belonged to Native Peoples; in Rhode Island and Providence Plantations he lived it.

[27] ibid.

[28] *Deed for Providence from Canonicus and Miantonomi* (1638), original from Providence City Archives held at the Rhode Island State House, Providence, RI. Transcription in *Records of the Colony of Rhode Island and Providence Plantations in New England*, vol 1: *1636–1663*, ed JR Bartlett (Providence, RI, A Crawford Greene and Brother, State Printers, 1856).

[29] Shurtleff (ed) (n 23) 160–61.

[30] Roger Williams, Letter to [General Court of Commissioners of Providence Plantations?] (25 August 1658), LaFantasie (n 24) 485.

III. Governing a Colony

Williams quickly got to work in governing the new colony. Williams was committed to ensuring the separation of church and state. Unlike England and the rest of New England, Rhode Island had no established church. People were free to worship as they chose, which included not worshipping at all if they so desired. The colony's civil compact, which was adopted in August 1637, included the mandate that matters concerning the 'public good' were made by 'major consent' and government had authority 'only in civil things'.[31] Williams' decision to omit any reference to God was deliberate. It demonstrated not only his deep piety, but also his belief that it was profane for humans to arrogantly assume that God embraced any other state than ancient Israel.[32] As the colony grew, Williams renewed the colony's commitment 'still, to hould forth liberty of Conscience' in the 1640 *Report of Arbitrators at Providence containing proposals for a form of government*.[33] The colony's government structure was 'Democraticall; that is to say, a government held by ye free and voluntarie consent of all, or the greater parte of the free inhabitants'.[34] Williams elaborated that governments 'have no more power … than the civil power or people consenting and agreeing shall entrust them with'.[35] Williams went on to reject the idea that God lent His authority to government. Williams' bold vision played out in reality in Rhode Island, and the government got its power from the consent of the people and the majority ruled. Officeholders did not have to pass any religious or social test, as Williams was determined to prove that a person's religious beliefs had no bearing on his ability to serve in public office. Within *The Bloudy Tenent* (1644), Williams summarised his vision: 'The government of the civill Magistrate extendeth no further then over the bodies and goods of their subjects, not over their soules'.[36] Williams had effectively separated church and state.

Rhode Island's commitment to democracy stood in contrast to policy in both England and the rest of New England. As civil war with Parliament brewed in 1642, King Charles I evaluated the 'three kinds of government among men (absolute monarchy, aristocracy, and democracy)', which all had 'their particular conveniences and inconveniences'. Charles rejected democracy to reaffirm the monarchy, concluding that the 'ills of democracy are tumults, violence and licentiousness'.[37] John Winthrop, Governor of Massachusetts Bay, agreed, and

[31] *Records of the Colony of Rhode Island*, ed Bartlett (n 28) 14.

[32] For more on Williams' religious beliefs, see WC Gilpin, *The Millenarian Piety of Roger Williams* (Chicago, IL, University of Chicago Press, 1979) and E Morgan, *Roger Williams: The Church and the State*, 2nd edn (New York, WW Norton & Company, 2007).

[33] *Records of the Colony of Rhode Island*, ed Bartlett (n 28) 22–28.

[34] ibid 156.

[35] R Williams, *The Bloudy Tenent, of Persecution, for cause of Conscience, Discussed, in A Conference betweene Truth and Peace* (London, 1644).

[36] ibid.

[37] King Charles I, *His Maiesties Answer to the XIX Propositions of Both Houses of Parliament* (London, 1642).

declared that 'Democracy is, amongst most civil nations, accounted the meanest and worst form of government'.[38] John Cotton, Teacher of the Boston Church, also agreed: 'Democracy, I do not conceyve that ever God did ordeyne as a fit government eyther from church or commonwealth'.[39] Cotton posed the question 'If the people be governors who shall be governed?'[40] Williams' answer was clear: 'the sovereign, original, and foundation of civil power lies in the people'.[41] Williams knew first hand that the quest for religious uniformity did not ensure social stability and peace. He demonstrated the fallacy of trying to have only 'true' Christians serve as magistrates. Williams' logic held that churches were tasked with nurturing religion, thus it was impossible for mere mortals (representing the state) to do the same job as they could easily err. For Williams, the church could be successful only if it distanced itself from coercive politics.

Conflict between Rhode Island and the other New England colonies was not restricted to governmental structure. As the New England colonies grew in the 1640s, so too did their imperialist desire for land. Rhode Island's prime position along the shores of Narragansett Bay made it a desirable hub for trade and export. Whilst Williams had a deed for Providence from Canonicus and Miantonomi, the other New England colonies did not respect his right to the land. Thus, Williams sailed to England in 1643 to retrospectively get an English charter and to spread his 'new and dangerous' opinions on liberty. Williams arrived in England in the midst of civil war as King Charles I fought against Parliament. Williams drew on his influential connections, including Oliver Cromwell, in order to share his ideas wherever he could, whether it was in Parliament's lobbies, taverns or private homes.[42] On 14 March 1644, Parliament's Committee on Foreign Plantations granted Rhode Island a charter. Whilst Rhode Island had to adhere to English laws, 'so far as the Nature and Constitution of the place will admit', the Committee authorised Rhode Island to continue with its experiment in democracy.[43] Rhode Islanders had 'full Powre & Authority to Governe & rule themselves … by such a form of Civil Government, as by voluntary consent of all, or the greater Part of them shall find most suteable'.[44] By leaving decisions to majority rule, the Committee effectively allowed soul liberty to rule in Rhode Island.

The 1644 charter was revolutionary; however, its long-term impact was hampered by turmoil on both sides of the Atlantic. Amidst this tumult, Williams sailed back to England with John Clarke of Newport in 1651 to try to secure a

[38] Cited in FJ Bremmer, *John Winthrop: America's Forgotten Founding Father* (Oxford, Oxford University Press, 2003).

[39] John Cotton, Letter to Lord Say and Sele (1636) in Thomas Hutchinson, *History of the Massachusetts Bay Colony*, 2nd edn (London, 1765) vol 1, app 3.

[40] ibid.

[41] Williams (n 35).

[42] For more on Williams' time in England, see Barry (n 13).

[43] Bartlett (n 28).

[44] ibid.

stronger charter for the colony.[45] Following the execution of King Charles I in 1649, England had bigger governing issues to resolve than dealing with a small colony of radicals across the Atlantic. Whilst Williams returned to Rhode Island in 1654, Clarke diligently remained in England for another decade to fulfil this work.[46] During this time, Clarke witnessed England's bloody transformation from monarchy to commonwealth and back again. Rhode Island was clearly not at the forefront of England's concerns during the 1650s. Following the restoration of the monarchy in 1660, the issue was finally resolved when King Charles II approved the charter for Rhode Island and Providence Plantations in July 1663. King Charles II's royal authority dominated the opening of the charter, both physically and in the text. In addition to a large portrait of Charles II in the top left hand corner, the charter opened with 'Charles the second by Grace of God, King of England, Scotland, France and Ireland, Defender of the Faith etc.' King Charles II, whose own father had been executed by a Parliament headed by Puritans in 1649, allowed Rhode Island to be a testing ground. For the King, the colony was far enough away and small enough to experiment with the lived reality of religious freedom. The Charter signified that the colony was a 'lively experiment … with a full liberty in religious concernments'.[47] The charter endorsed Williams' vision for soul liberty and separation of church and state:

> no person within the said colony, at any time hereafter shall be any wise molested, punished, disquieted, or called in question, for any differences in opinion in matters of religion, and do not actually disturb the civil peace of our said colony; but that all and every person and persons may, from time to time, and at all times hereafter, freely and fully have and enjoy his and their own judgements and consciences, in matters of religious concernments … they behaving themselves peaceably and quietly, and not using this liberty to licentious and profaneness, nor to the civil injury or outward disturbance of others, any law, statutes, or clause.[48]

The language from Rhode Island's 1663 charter, that nobody could be 'molested, punished, disquieted, or called in question, for any differences in opinion, in matters of religion', was used in other colonial charters. In 1664, 'The Lord Proprietors' of New Jersey agreed that no person would in any way be 'molested, punished, disquieted, or called in question' for any differences in opinion, in matters of religion. The New Jersey document added 'practice'. The following year, King Charles II granted a charter for Carolina that demonstrated that the words of the Rhode Island Charter had acquired a special status of their own.

[45] For more on Clarke's role, see SV James, *John Clarke and His Legacies: Religion and Law in Colonial Rhode Island, 1638–1730*, ed TD Bozeman (University Park, PA, Penn State Press, 2008).

[46] Before returning to Rhode Island, Williams anonymously published, *The Fourth Paper, Presented by Major Butler* (London, 1652) and *The Examiner Defended in a Fair and Sober answer* (London, 1652). He also published an attack on mandatory public support of clergy in *The Hirelings Ministry None of Christs* (London, 1652).

[47] *Rhode Island Charter* (1663), original held at the Rhode Island State House, Providence, RI. Transcription in *Records of the Colony of Rhode Island*, ed Bartlett (n 28).

[48] ibid.

The proprietors were assured that nobody would be 'molested, punished, disquieted, or called in question, for any differences in opinion of practice in matters of religious concernments'.[49]

Writing in 1670, Williams still held onto the legal and symbolic importance of the 1663 Charter and the 'King's extraordinary favour to this Colony'. Williams knew how important the King's endorsement was when 'his Matie [majesty] declar'd himself that he would experimnt whether Civill Govermnt Could consist with such a Liberite of Conscience'.[50] Though only a small corner of the English Atlantic world, Rhode Island was 'a shelter for the poor and persecuted'.[51] The King's approval allowed 'all the World' to 'see by His Maties [majesty's] Declaration' that the King had vouchsafed 'his Royal promise under his Hand and Broad Seal, that no person in this Colony shall be molested or questioned for the Matters of his Conscience to God so he be loyall and keepe the civil peace'.[52] The year before he died, Williams reflected that 'Our Charter Excells all in N. Engl. or the World, as to the Souls of Men'.[53] Williams was right; the 1663 Charter was nothing short of revolutionary. Williams' greatest contribution to religious freedom was not that he simply espoused the theory of liberty but that he created a geographical space where those principles could be lived. Without an instrument of civil government for Rhode Island and Providence Plantations, Williams' laudable opinions would have remained simply theoretical.[54]

IV. Soul Liberty

Williams' journey to make his vision for soul liberty a reality had been long and complicated. In between the 1644 and 1663 charters, Williams wrote extensively on the idea of religious freedom in both published works and private letters. One of his most powerful and direct defences was in the open letter to the town of Providence in 1655, which was written in response to the political discord that rocked Providence.[55] Using the analogy of a ship, Williams argued for religious freedom:

> There goes many a ship to sea, with many hundred souls in one ship, whose weal and woe is common, and is a true picture of a commonwealth, or a human combination or

[49] E Gaustad, *Liberty of Conscience: Roger Williams in America* (Valley Forge, PA, Judson Press, 1999) 194.

[50] Roger Williams, Letter to Major John Wilson and Governor Thomas Prence (22 June 1670), LaFantasie (n 24) 616.

[51] ibid.

[52] ibid.

[53] Roger Williams, Letter to the Town of Providence (15 January 1681/82), LaFantasie (n 24) 775.

[54] For a detailed analysis of Williams' time in London in the 1640s, see J Beecher Field, 'A Key for the Gate: Roger Williams, Parliament, and Providence' (2007) 80(3) *The New England Quarterly* 353.

[55] The town voted to establish a citizen militia and impose fines on those who refused to serve. There was significant opposition to the militia, including by Williams' brother, Robert. Williams wrote how

> society. It hath fallen out sometimes, that both papists and protestants, Jews and Turks, may be embarked in one ship … I affirm, that all the liberty of conscience, that ever I pleaded for, turns upon these two hinges – that none of the papists, protestants, Jews, or Turks, be forced to come to the ship's prayers of worship, nor compelled from their own particular prayers or worship, if they practice any.[56]

However, religious freedom did not mean that citizens could shy away from civil law and responsibilities:

> I further add, that I never denied, that notwithstanding this liberty, the commander of this ship ought to command the ship's course, yea, and also command that justice, peace and sobriety, be kept and practiced, both among the seamen and all the passengers … [I]f any refuse to obey the common laws and orders of the ship … the commander … may judge, resist, compel and punish such transgressors.[57]

The letter to the town of Providence shows that soul liberty had enormous political and secular implications.[58] In reality, balancing religious liberty whilst maintaining a flourishing commonwealth was not so straightforward.

Williams also used his time in England in the 1640s to formally gather his thoughts on religious freedom and the separation of church and state. Williams weighed in on the fierce debates between Independents and Presbyterians with his anonymously published *Queries of Highest Consideration* (1643). In it, Williams outlined how and why he rejected the idea of an official religion, and how religious persecution was inconsistent with Christ's way and a desire for civil peace. Williams declared that 'the Common-weale cannot without a spiritual rape force the consciences of all to one Worship'.[59] Following hot on the heels of *Queries*, Williams published one of the most significant defences of religious liberty in western history: *The Bloudy Tenent, of Persecution, for cause of Conscience, Discussed, in A Conference betweene Truth and Peace* (1644). Scholars have long noted the importance of Williams' seminal work on soul liberty.[60] John Barry avers that it is '[o]ne of the most comprehensive treatises not just on freedom of religion but on the freedom of thought, political freedom, and the foundation of democracy ever written'.[61]

Like *Queries*, the *Bloudy Tenent* was not submitted to the censor for approval, nor was it licensed. The book sold rapidly, and a second edition appeared within a few weeks. Williams left for Rhode Island before his book had come off of the

he remained 'studious of our common peace and liberty', arguing that liberty of conscience does not permit freedom from social obligation. Roger Williams, Letter to the Town of Providence (ca January 1654/55), LaFantasie (n 24) 423–24.

[56] ibid.

[57] ibid.

[58] JC Davis, 'Introduction: Roger Williams and the Birth of an American Ideal' in JC Davis (ed), *On Religious Liberty: Selections from the Works of Roger Williams* (Cambridge, MA, and London, The Belknap Press of Harvard University Press, 2008) 1.

[59] R Williams, *Queries of the Highest Consideration* (London, 1644) 3.

[60] For the importance of *The Bloudy Tenent*, see Davis, 'Introduction' (n 58) 17.

[61] Barry (n 13) 312.

printing press, leaving those who read it outraged. Even those who had been persecuted for their religion themselves could not stomach Williams' bold treatise. In August 1644, Edmund Calany ordered the public hangman to burn Williams' book because it advocated for 'Tolerating of All Sorts of Religion'.[62] Burning a book was not just a symbolic act of disapproval; it was a concerted attempt to extirpate the thought which that book contained. The following month, when Lazarus Seaman preached before Parliament on Fast Day, he averred that the *Bloudy Tenent* was one of the most dangerous books of the time. The sermon acknowledged that Williams' work had been 'burnt by Order', but warned that the 'shell is sometimes throwne into the fire, when the kernell is eaten as a sweet morsell'.[63] Between 1644 and 1649, at least 60 pamphlets directly addressed Williams, and at least 120 more quoted him.[64]

Indeed the kernel that Williams planted in *The Bloudy Tenent* was bold from start to finish. Williams unflinchingly addressed both Houses of Parliament in the dedication, and cited reason, religion and experience to advocate for the separation of church and state throughout the book's 400 pages. The book clearly reflected Williams' personal connection with Francis Bacon's work on the scientific method and Sir Edward Coke's work on liberty, as he cited both of them in the opening pages.[65] In the first page and a half of the book, Williams laid out 12 specific points on religious liberty. Williams' first point was '[t]hat the blood of so many hundred thousand souls of protestants and papists, split in the wars of present and former ages, for their representative consciences, is not required nor accepted by Jesus Christ the Prince of Peace'. In his fifth point, Williams advocated for separation of church and state:

> All civil states with their officers of justice, in their respective constitutions and administrations, are proved essentially civil, and therefore not judges, governors, or defenders of the spiritual, or Christian, state and worship.

Williams did not mince his words in his eighth point, stating plainly that God 'requireth not an uniformity of religion to be enacted and enforced in any civil state'. His twelfth and final point in the opening noted that Christianity could flourish anywhere, 'notwithstanding the permission of divers and contrary consciences'.[66]

Williams used politics, economics, practical application and theology to justify his views. Politically, Williams rejected the prevalent view that religious uniformity was necessary for a good society. He argued that intolerance is 'destructive to the civil peace and welfare of all kingdoms, countries, and commonwealths'. Williams cited lessons from 'the lamentable experiences of former and present slaughters' and specific case studies to bolster his theories. For example, he examined how

[62] Cited ibid 338.
[63] L Seaman, *Solomons choice: or, A president for kings and princes, and all that are in authority* (London, 1644).
[64] Barry (n 13) 339–40.
[65] For more on Coke and Bacon, see ibid, especially 320–23.
[66] Williams (n 35).

Amsterdam had been a poor fishing town until it became a haven for dissenters and transformed into a trading hub. Moreover, the religious wars in Europe and the religious upheaval in England demonstrated clearly that persecution produced false converts, who simply sought to evade punishment. Even those who stayed true to their faith and died for their dedication simply became martyrs, which only served to hardened their followers' resolve.

Williams did not publish *The Bloudy Tenent* in a vacuum; the book was issued as part of a broader publication war between Williams and Massachusetts Bay minister, John Cotton.[67] Williams published *The Bloudy Tenent* in response to Cotton's *A Letter of Mr John Cotton, Teacher of the Church in Boston in New-England, to Mr Williams* (1643). Upon reading *The Bloudy Tenent*, John Cotton wrote *The Bloudy Tenent, Washed, and Made White in the Bloud of the Lamb* in 1647. Cotton made it clear '[w]hat persecution the Lord Jesus if he were on earth, would practise against those who would not receive him'. For Cotton, '[t]he Answer is neere at hand, and is written for the warning of all gain-sayers: Those mine enemies which would not that I should reigne over them, bring them hither, and slay them before my face, *Luk. 19. 27.*'[68] For Cotton, the dual responsibility of the magistrate was to protect the church from heretics and other enemies, and to enforce the 'perpetuall' laws. This meant that coercion was legitimate when Christians went astray, which in turn warranted the civil state to override religious freedom.[69]

Williams disagreed and responded again in print in 1652 with *The Bloody Tenent Yet More Bloody by Mr Cotton's Endeavour to Wash it White in the Blood of the Lamb*. In the pamphlet wars, the two combatants examined key scriptural justifications for persecution, including verse 8 of Psalm 101: 'I will early destroy all the wicked of the land; that I may cut off all wicked doers from the city of the Lord.' *In the Bloudy Tenent*, Williams interpreted many passages in the Old and New Testaments as limiting government interference in any religious matters. For Williams, it was abominable for people to interpret God's law, as they would inexorably err. Williams believed that Ancient Israel was not a blueprint for modern society, and he honed in on Jesus' example of teaching and exhortation. Williams made it clear that whilst the kings of Israel used violence and force to spread their message, Jesus did not. Jesus embodied the distinction between the types of the Old Testament and the antitypes of the New. Williams turned Puritan theology on itself from within.[70] Williams was able to do this because he, like Cotton, worshipped the God of Calvin, saw God in everything, respected the pre-eminent

[67] For more on John Cotton and civil and religious liberty, see D Hall, *A Reforming People: Puritanism and the Transformation of Public Life in New England* (New York, Alfred A Knopf, 2011). For more on pamphlet wars between Roger Williams and John Cotton, see Davis, 'Introduction' (n 58) 27–28.

[68] J Cotton, *The Bloudy Tenent Washed and Made White in the Bloud of the Lamb* (London, 1647).

[69] Hall (n 67) 112–13.

[70] See John Calvin's *Institutes of the Christian Religion*, book XX, paras 1–2, 9–10 for where Williams departs from the tradition. J Calvin, *Institutes of the Christian Religion*, ed JT McNeill, tr F Lewis Battles (Philadelphia, PA, Westminster Press, 1960).

authority of the Bible, and sought to advance the kingdom of God. Their conflict centred on *how* to do this.

As Williams discovered, living with and within the reality of religious freedom was easier said than done. It is no exaggeration to say that Williams despised the Quaker faith. He believed that 'their Religion is not only an Heresy in the matter of Worship, but also in the Doctrines of Repentance Faith'. He held that the Quakers were the 'most obstructive and destructive' religion to conversion and salvation than 'most of the Religions this day extant in the world'. He loathed their writings too: 'their many Books and writings are extremely Poor, Lame, Naked, and sweld up only with high Titles and words of Boastings and Vapour'.[71] Williams' hatred of the Quaker faith came from their belief that they were guided by an inner light, which compelled them to spread their message to others (no matter what the consequence). In the seventeenth century, Quakers were known for the dramatic speeches, which they gave anywhere from the courthouse to the church. They routinely ignored common social conventions, ranging from refusing to doff their caps to superiors to refusing to fully clothe themselves in public. Quakers were widely seen as dangerous religious heretics, as they preached that everyone (male and female, free and unfree) was of equal worth before God. Moreover, they stressed that everyone had direct access to God and that churches were obsolete. Quakers were so determined to spread their beliefs that Massachusetts Bay ordered the jail cell windows to be boarded up to prevent the imprisoned Quakers from preaching to those outside. In spite of the harsh penalties, including banishment, beatings, fines, whippings, imprisonment and mutilation, many Quakers continued to return to Massachusetts to spread their message. Some Quakers, including Mary Dyer, went to the gallows for their beliefs. They faced intense persecution in both England and New England. However, even though Roger Williams was deeply troubled by the Quaker faith, Rhode Island was the only New England colony to offer sanctuary to Quakers.

Williams remained committed to living what he theorised about. Thus, when Quaker leader, George Fox, visited Rhode Island in 1672, Williams invited him to a public theological debate. Williams believed that debate and the pen (rather than the sword) formed the way forward, and he 'resolved to try another way, and to offer a fair and full Dispute'. In preparation, Williams wrote 14 propositions that challenged the core Quaker beliefs. Whilst Fox left the colony and did not rise to Williams' challenge, three of his followers, John Stubbs, John Burnyeat and William Edmundson, debated with Williams. The first part of the debate centred on the first seven of Williams' propositions and took place in at the Quaker meetinghouse in Newport on 9 August 1672. Williams rowed all the way to Newport from Providence in a canoe, no small feat for someone who had suffered from ill-health and was most likely approaching 70 years old at the time. A large crowd gathered and an intense and spirited debate ensued, which lasted for four days.

[71] R Williams, *George Fox Digg'd out of his Burrowes* (Boston, MA, 1676).

The final seven propositions were debated for a full day in Providence shortly after. In 1676, Williams published an account of the debate, entitled *George Fox Digg'd out of his Burrows*, and the following year Fox and Burnyeat responded with *A New-England Fire-Brand Quenched.* Williams' commitment to arguing points of scripture with the Quakers, both in person and in print, suggests that he believed their uncivil practice was the result of a genuine spiritual error. Williams hoped to offer salvation to them through showing them their mistakes. Williams' animosity towards the Quaker faith did not dissipate after he allowed the Quakers to settle within the colony.[72] However, in allowing them to settle in Rhode Island and having a theological debate with them (rather than imprisoning, banishing or hanging them), Williams put his own personal views of the Quakers aside and allowed soul liberty to flourish in the colony.

Williams' experiment in religious freedom had particular implications for his interactions with Indigenous Peoples. Writing to John Winthrop Jr in 1632, Williams acknowledged that 'what I long after [is] the natives Soules'.[73] However, Williams also knew that 'forc't Worshpp stincks in Gods Nostrills'.[74] Williams did not believe in imposing Christian beliefs or English culture upon the Indians against their will. Williams believed that nobody nor any earthly church had a monopoly on religious truth, and he exhorted the Indians to 'seek the truth'.[75] Williams simultaneously believed that Indians conjured the devil and 'labored in spiritual darkness … and their behaviour was at times "barbarous"', whilst also trying to learn all he could about their spiritual and temporal worlds.[76] In *A Key into the Language of America* (1643), Williams noted that the Narragansett 'have a modest Religious perswasion not to disturb any man, either themselves *English, Dutch*, or any in their Conscience, and worship, and therefore say: Aquiewopwaũwash. Peace, hold your peace'.[77] Williams pushed the idea of equality in the eyes of God further in *A Key*: 'Nature knowes no difference between *Europe* and *Americans* in blood, birth, bodies, &c.'[78] He exhorted his countrymen, 'Boast not proud Euglish, of thy birth & blood, Thy brother Indian is by birth as Good. Of one blood God made Him, and Thee & All, as wise, as faire, as strong, as personal.'[79]

Williams consolidated his views in *Christenings make not Christians* (1645).[80] By this point, following his own believer's baptism, Williams had become increasingly

[72] TM Bejan, *Mere Civility: Disagreement and the Limits of Toleration* (Cambridge, MA, and London, Harvard University Press, 2017) 76, 81.

[73] Roger Williams, Letter to John Winthrop, Jr (July and December 1632), LaFantasie (n 1) 8.

[74] Roger Williams, Letter to Major John Wilson and Governor Thomas Prence (22 June 1670), LaFantasie (n 24) 671.

[75] J Warren, *God, War, and Providence: The Epic Struggle of Roger Williams and the Narragansett Indians against the Puritans of New England*, (New York, Scribner, 2018) 46–47.

[76] ibid 46.

[77] R Williams, *A Key into the Language of America* (London, 1643).

[78] ibid.

[79] ibid.

[80] Williams (n 9).

convinced that a valid baptism needed knowing consent.[81] Thus he questioned not only the validity of infant baptism, but also increasingly the missionary efforts to convert Natives. Williams argued that baptising Native Americans was false as they did not truly understand the scripture, and thus relied on another person's translation and interpretation. Despite his 'desires and endeavours … to attaine a propriety of Language', he lamented that conversion was not possible and 'it is out of question to me, that I may not pretend a false conversion'.[82] In light of Williams' views on false conversions, it is unsurprising that he objected to the work of the Bay Colony's chief missionary, John Eliot. Eliot had no qualms about leading efforts to translate the Bible into Wôpanâak and set up praying towns to help with conversion efforts.[83] Williams' lived political reality also influenced his thoughts on conversion. Williams did not want to force the issue of conversion, given that to do so might risk alienating his Narragansett hosts. He saw how much the sachems despised conversion efforts, and he was well aware that the Narragansetts vastly outnumbered the colonists in Rhode Island.

It would be easy to paint an oversimplified hagiography of Williams as a friend to the Indians. Williams was certainly closer to the Native Peoples of New England than most other colonists of his time. He worked hard to mediate conflict between the colonists and Indians in order to keep peace in the region. However, Williams was not the only colonist to learn Narragansett, nor the only one offering services such as writing letters and petitions on behalf of Indigenous Peoples.[84] Moreover, Williams' diplomatic efforts ultimately failed in the midst of King Philip's War in 1675–76. The war, which was the deadliest war in American history in terms of loss to population ratio, was a turning point for Williams.[85] Williams' efforts to live peaceably with his native neighbours ultimately failed. He spent his final years in poverty, after his house and town were burned to the ground in King Philip's War. Following the war, Rhode Islanders, including Williams, agreed to sell Native American captives into slavery in the Caribbean in 1676.[86] Once again, the lived reality of Williams' experiment in liberty was harder to fulfil in practice than in theory.

[81] For more on Williams' own religious views, see JS Lemons, 'Roger Williams was not a Seeker but a "Witness in Sackcloth"' (2015) 88(4) *New England Quarterly* 693.

[82] Williams (n 9).

[83] J Eliot, *The Holy Bible: Containing the Old Testament and the New Translated into the Indian Language* (Cambridge, MA, 1663). For information on how the Eliot Bible has been used to revive the spoken Wôpanâak language, see 'Wôpanâak Language Reclamation Project' at http://www.wlrp.org, accessed 21 September 2019.

[84] J Fisher, 'What is Roger Williams?', paper presented at the Early American History Workshop at Providence College (Providence, RI, March 2018).

[85] J Lepore, *In the Name of War: King Philip's War and the Origins of American Identity* (New York, Vintage, 1999).

[86] For more on slavery in 17th-century New England, see W Warren, *New England Bound: Slavery and Colonization in Early America* (New York, Liveright, 2016); L Fisher, '"Dangerous Designes": The 1676 Barbados Act to Prohibit New England Indian Slave Importation' (2014) 71(1) *The William and Mary Quarterly* 99.

V. Legacy

Traditional biographies of Williams are prone to depicting him as being ahead of his time, both in his dealings with the Indians and in his calls for religious liberty. This was not the case. Williams was not a man out of his time, nor indeed ahead of his day. Whilst he had many remarkable ideas (and did his best to live them), his feet were very firmly on the Narragansett earth.[87] Debates about religious toleration had been raging for centuries when Williams founded Providence in 1636. For example, Sebastian Castellio, a French preacher and theologian, steadfastly advocated for religious toleration in the sixteenth century, and Hugo Grotius, a Dutch legal scholar and philosopher, pushed for toleration of dissent and individual rights in the seventeenth century. Other places also experimented with the lived reality of religious toleration. In 1555, the Peace of Augsburg allowed subjects within different territories of the Holy Roman Empire to emigrate to another territory if they objected to the religion their local leader adhered to. However, this applied only to Catholics and Lutherans. The Dutch moved consistently towards toleration, but only because they had to. Calvinists lived alongside Catholics following a fracturing from Spain in 1570, thus the United Provinces chose *de facto* toleration. However, each Dutch province still had a state church, and the Dutch persecuted Arminians after 1609.[88] These efforts were no match for Rhode Island's bold experiment in religious freedom for all. Williams did not simply advocate for religious toleration; he went further and created a place where religious freedom (not simply toleration) ruled. John Barry notes that Williams 'was not the first person to call for religious freedom, but he was certainly the first to link that call to individual liberty in a political sense and to create a government and society informed by those beliefs'.[89] According to Barry, Williams' writings on freedom were 'remarkable and revolutionary' in their originality.[90]

Williams clearly went against the grain of mainstream European and political traditions and universal public opinion from the thirteenth to the seventeenth century, which demanded death for heretics.[91] Williams' lively experiment and his *magnus opus* on toleration, *The Bloudy Tenent*, also went beyond what his famed contemporaries, John Milton, Thomas Hobbes and John Locke, called for.[92]

[87] For the historiography on Williams' being a man of his time, see Winslow (n 16); E Morgan, *Roger Williams the Church and the State* (New York, WW Norton & Company, 1967) 5; and Barry (n 13) 6.

[88] Barry (n 13) 317.

[89] ibid 6.

[90] ibid 301.

[91] ibid 319. The intellectual and public opinion went back to Augustine, who justified death for unyielding heretics. Aquinas also argued that the sin of heresy was so great that heretics deserved to be separated from the church by excommunication, but also shut off from the world by death. Once in power, neither Luther nor Calvin disputed this.

[92] The International Monument to the Reformation, built to commemorate the 400th anniversary of Calvin's birth, has statues of just 10 men deemed important enough to justify their inclusion. Calvin stands at the centre, and Roger Williams stands to the right. As fate would have it, John Locke is buried in the same church, All Saints High Laver in Essex, where Williams married his wife, Mary.

Williams, unlike Locke, argued not just for toleration but for liberty; he recognised that religious freedom must be understood as a fundamental human right and not just legislative.[93] Williams welcomed atheists in Rhode Island and he desired religious liberty for all, even the religions he personally despised.[94] Most importantly, Williams went beyond Milton, Locke and Hobbes as he put theory into practice; living out his lively experiment in soul liberty.

Williams' experiment in separating church and state came a century and a half before Thomas Jefferson's call for the same thing. Long before James Madison averred that religious freedom was in the interest of civil peace, Williams had managed to put that idea into reality. As James Calvin Davis notes, 'Even now, Williams does not receive the kind of popular attention reserved for the architects of the First Amendment … and the near rock-star status … Revolutionary War heroes enjoy.'[95] Teresa Bejan argues that scholars inspired by the breadth and liberty of Williams toleration like to (incorrectly) portray him as a kind of enlightened proto-liberal running around the New England wilderness. Bejan makes it clear that Williams did not support religious freedom because he was open-minded or 'Enlightened'. He was a religious fanatic by both modern and early modern standards.[96] Williams was not a multiculturalist *avant la letter*. But his 'mere civility' permitted much of what Williams' modern-day revivers want to rule out. All must be tolerated because all were potential converts.[97] Rhode Island was able to accommodate more and deeper kinds of difference, whilst sustaining a commitment to fundamental disagreement *despite* its inherent disagreeableness. Bejan concludes that Williams is the unlikely hero in the story of religious freedom, as he challenges our assumptions about what a tolerant society (or a civil society) should and can look like.

VI. The Lived Reality of Religious Freedom

Ultimately, what made Roger Williams different from the others who called for religious freedom was that he succeeded in actually putting theory in the practice. He crafted a colony built upon *de jure* freedom and separation of church and state.

[93] Scholars have debated the extent and nature of Locke's views on toleration. The traditional scholarship posits that Locke simply argued for toleration for Protestant Christians, not Catholics or Muslims. Scholars have also argued that Locke's view of toleration was also limited because he believed that atheists could not be trusted as citizens, as 'promises, covenants, and oaths, which are the bonds of human society, can have no hold upon an atheist'. See J Locke, *A Letter Concerning Toleration: Humbly Submitted &c* (London, 1689) 63–64. However, Reid Mortensen argues that Locke may have been open to the toleration of Catholics (at least) under certain conditions. See R Mortensen, 'Specious Delusions: John Locke, Knowledge and Religious Toleration' (2014) 33 *University of Queensland Law Journal* 335.

[94] Davis, 'Introduction' (n 58) 40.

[95] ibid 38.

[96] Bejan (n 72) 54.

[97] ibid 64, 13–14.

Williams was not ahead of his time, but his colony was indeed one of the most forward-thinking experiments of the time. Williams advocated for religious freedom from the standpoint of a deeply religious believer, using theology to argue for the right of others to worship freely. Williams did not defend religious liberty in spite of his own dogmatism, but because of it.[98] Williams despised the Quaker theology, and thought that Catholics served the Antichrist. He also refused to watch Indigenous religious rituals for fear of being 'an eyewitness, Spectator, or looker on', in case he was mistaken for 'a partaker of Satans Inventions and Worships'.[99] He considered all these religions false, but he defended others' right to hold and practise their religion without state interference.[100]

Williams' lively experiment in liberty was not a happy-ever-after story of success. On the ground, Williams' experimental system of governance led to chronic dysfunction, internal dispute and chaos. Liberty and licence triumphed over order and discipline. Men elected to office refused to serve, towns refused to pay taxes and land ownership disputes rocked the colony.[101] Contemporaries described how Rhode Islanders were 'brawling continually in Mr Williams medow'.[102] Outsiders insulted Rhode Island with a colourful plethora of slurs, ranging from 'Rogues Island', to the 'receptacle for all sorts of riff-raff' and even 'the sewers (*latrina*) of New England'. Even the Dutch in New Amsterdam referred to Rhode Islanders as 'scumme'.[103] Williams had to find a way to coexist with people with whom he fundamentally disagreed, and the Quakers hammered home the difficulty of Williams' experiment of balancing religious freedom whilst maintaining civil order. Williams also had to deal with the fall out when people such as Samuel Gorton, who seemed intent on causing discord and strife, settled in the colony. Gorton, who had been ousted from Plymouth in 1638 due to his religious beliefs and insubordination towards the civil authorities, eventually made his way to Rhode Island and Providence Plantations. After causing discord in Portsmouth on Aquidneck Island, he moved to Providence. Writing to John Winthrop in March 1641, Williams bemoaned how Gorton was 'now bewitching and bemading poor Providence'.[104] Gorton's actions challenged the civil stability of the town, and he eventually moved out of Providence (much to Williams' relief) and settled in Shawomet.[105]

[98] Davis, 'Introduction' (n 58) 3.
[99] Williams (n 77).
[100] Davis, 'Introduction' (n 58) 45.
[101] Warren (n 75) 172.
[102] Cited in editorial note 'Samuel Gorton in Providence' in LaFantasie (n 1) 211.
[103] Cited in Barry (n 13) 309.
[104] Cited in Gaustad (n 49) 55.
[105] For more on Gorton, see PF Gura, 'Samuel Gorton and Religious Radicalism in England, 1644–1648' (1983) 40(1) *The William and Mary Quarterly* 121; M Burnham, 'Samuel Gorton's Leveller Aesthetics and the Economics of Colonial Dissent' (2010) 67(3) *The William and Mary Quarterly* 433; J Donoghue, '"Out of the Land of Bondage": The English Revolutions and the Origins of Abolition' (2010) 115(3) *The American Historical Review* 943.

Williams was well aware of the price he paid for his experiment, and even those who had known him since childhood turned against him as his radical publications gained traction. Writing to his mentor, Sir Edward Coke's daughter, Anne Sadleir in 1652, Williams lamented that he would be 'a Foole in relating' what he had 'done and Suffred' in both Old and New England.[106] Williams, presumably hoping for a sympathetic ear from a long-term acquaintance, acknowledged how he had recently 'published 2 or 3 things … tis Controversiall'.[107] Williams enclosed a copy of his recent publication, *Experiments of Spiritual Life & Health* (1652), for Sadleir to read.[108] Paper was scarce in the seventeenth century and, as was customary, Williams deftly folded up the letter to make an envelope. When Sadleir received the letter, she used the spare space on the paper to pen her thoughts. Thus, right next to where Williams addressed his letter, 'For my much honoured kind friend Mistres Sadler at Standon neere Puckridge', Sadleir scrawled that Williams was 'a reble to god the king and his country', and if Williams had 'the face to return into his native cuntry Tyborn may give his welcome'.[109] Sadleir's message was clear: Williams' views on religious freedom were so troubling that she wanted him dead. Specifically, as a rebel, she wanted him to join the many Catholics who had met their maker at the infamous Tyburn gallows in London.

Williams' hopes for a sympathetic ear were unsurprisingly dashed when Sadleir wrote back to him warning that his beliefs were 'soe much cri'd up … they will prove but darke'.[110] Sadleir made it clear that she had no interest in reading Williams' *Experiments of Spiritual Life & Health*, and promptly returned it with the letter. Williams was not put off, and he promptly wrote to his 'much honoured kind friend Mrs Sadleir' once more.[111] He acknowledged that her 'last letter' was 'a Bitter-Sweeting … Sweete in that I heare from you … Bitter, in that we differ'.[112] In her previous letter, Sadleir had recommended that Williams procure some books that advocated for the Church of England and for religious conformity. Williams noted that he had 'carefully endeavoured to get them'.[113] After Sadleir had refused to read his *Experiments of Spiritual Life & Health*, Williams decided to send a copy of another of his works, *The Bloody Tenent Yet More Bloody* (1652). After Sadleir had refused to read his previous work, Williams lowered his expectations that Sadleir would comply in reading his latest work. In the accompanying letter to Sadleir he noted 'I cannot but Expect Your Distast of it', yet he 'humbly bold' asked her to cast her 'Judicious and Loving Eye' on the book.[114] Williams was

[106] Roger Williams, Letter to Anne Sadleir (ca April 1652), LaFantasie (n 1) 356–59.
[107] ibid.
[108] R Williams, *Experiments of Spiritual Life & Health* (London, 1652).
[109] 'Roger Williams Letter to Anne Sadleir' R55, Letter 30 and 31, R55, Sadleir Collection, Wren Library, Trinity College, Cambridge University.
[110] Anne Sadleir, Letter to Roger Williams (after April 1652), LaFantasie (n 1) 360–61.
[111] Roger Williams, Letter to Anne Sadleir (ca Summer 1652), LaFantasie (n 1) 363–65.
[112] ibid.
[113] ibid.
[114] ibid.

right; Sadleir had no interest in even opening his book. She lambasted him with her reply: 'When I cast mine eie upon the frontispice of your booke, and saw it intituled the bloody tenent I durst not adventure to looke into.'[115] Sadleir promptly returned the book to Williams, ending the letter with a clear message to leave her alone: 'Thus intreating you to troble me no more in this kind and wishing you a good jorny to your charge in new providence.'[116]

Williams did not take the hint. He promptly wrote back to Sadleir suggesting that she should read Jeremy Taylor, one of her 'owne Authours', who 'excellently asserted, the Tolleracion of differing Religions'.[117] Williams was obnoxiously persistent in his quest to get Sadleir to consider the merits of religious freedom. For Williams, it did not matter *how* Sadleir came to understand the importance of religious freedom, just that she *did*. In spite (or because) of Williams' persistence, Sadleir vehemently did *not* come round to his way of thinking. Sadleir promptly wrote back to Williams explaining that he was shameless and had a 'face of brass' so that he 'cannot blush'.[118] She had hoped that her 'first letter would have given you soe much more Satisfaction, that in that kind I should never have heard of you any more'.[119] Sadleir laid into Williams, calling him a 'villin' and 'rebell', arguing that she had 'the law, with the old and new testament' on her side, whilst all Williams had was 'foule and falce aspertions'.[120] She ended the letter bluntly with two requests. First, that Williams would stop writing to her: 'Howsoever troble me no more with your letters for they are verie troublesum'.[121] Second, that Williams would go back to Providence, the 'place from whence you came'.[122] From the extant correspondence it looks as if Williams got the message and left Sadleir alone. Roger Williams' efforts to persuade his long-term acquaintance, Anne Sadleir, to consider the merits of religious freedom had failed spectacularly.

***

Putting theory into practice is never easy, especially when the odds are stacked against you. Williams' lively experiment cost him dearly. His views made him 'many Adversaries'.[123] He was banished. His masterpiece, *The Bloudy Tenet*, was burned. His neighbours fought. He had to live alongside those he despised. His colony was viewed with contempt. His long-term acquaintances wished him dead.

[115] Anne Sadleir, Letter to Roger Williams (ca Summer or Fall 1652), LaFantasie (n 1) 365–66.
[116] ibid.
[117] Williams suggested that Sadleir read Jeremy Taylor, *A discourse of the liberty of prophesying* (London, 1647). Roger Williams, Letter to Anne Sadleir (ca Winter 1652/53), LaFantasie (n 1) 373–77.
[118] Anne Sadleir to Roger Williams (ca Winter 1652/53), LaFantasie (n 1) 377–79.
[119] ibid.
[120] ibid.
[121] ibid.
[122] ibid.
[123] Roger Williams, Letter to Anne Sadleir (ca April 1652), LaFantasie (n 1) 356–59.

His house and town were burned down in the midst of King Philip's War. He lived his final years in poverty. But Williams *was* successful. In the face of opposition and hardship, Williams ultimately succeeded in crafting the architecture of religious liberty. His *de jure* experiment in soul liberty created the freest place the western world had ever seen. Roger Williams not only theorised about religious freedom, he lived it; whatever the cost.

3

Orthodox Churches in the Post-Communist Countries and the Separation between Religion and State

DANIELA KALKANDJIEVA

I. Introduction

The fall of the totalitarian regimes in Eastern Europe triggered profound political and societal transformations in this part of the world. Leaving no space for the previous monopoly of militant atheism, they called for new relations between religion and the state. While the former communist states with Catholic and Protestant majorities (eg Poland, Hungary, etc) were able to benefit from patterns already developed by western democracies, those with Orthodox majorities (Bulgaria, Romania, Russia, Belarus, Ukraine, Moldova, Georgia, Serbia, Montenegro and North Macedonia[1]) lacked such an opportunity. In the second case, the models of Greece and Cyprus, that is Orthodox countries that had escaped communism, did not fit well into the liberal vision of freedom of religion; for example, their legislation is silent on the separation between religion and state. Especially problematic is the prohibition of proselytism in the Greek Constitution (Article 13) and in ordinary laws that have no parallel in any other European country.[2] As a result, the post-communist states with Orthodox majorities needed to invent a new model of church–state relations that would allow them to join in the club of Western democracies. This task has raised difficult questions with no ready-made answers. Therefore, the case of this group of states calls for special attention.

Furthermore, the Orthodox churches in the former atheist countries have already experienced a specific type of separation from the state. Its grounds were

[1] Until 2019, North Macedonia was known as the Former Yugoslav Republic of Macedonia (FYROM).

[2] S Ferrari, 'The Strasbourg Court and Article 9 of the European Convention on Human Rights: A Quantitative Analysis of the Case Law' in J Temperman (ed), *The Lautsi Papers: Multidisciplinary Reflections on Religious Symbols in the Public School Classroom, Studies in Religion, Secular Beliefs and Human Rights* (Nijhoff, Brill, 2012) 11, 24.

laid down in 1918 by Lenin's Decree on the separation of church from state and school from church in Bolshevik Russia. After the Second World War, the Soviets imposed this model on the Eastern European societies in their zone of influence. From this perspective, the collapse of communism had a twofold effect on the religious sphere: it left no space for the communist-pattern of church–state separation, and it allowed the religious communities to exercise their beliefs without state intervention on an equal footing. This is a novel development in the history of traditionally Orthodox societies, where religious minorities have never experienced such equal treatment.

This chapter shifts the focus from the role of the political factor in shaping the relations between religion and the state to that of the Orthodox churches. In this regard, it takes into consideration the fact that the equal opportunities, granted to the majority and the minority religions in Eastern Europe in the first years after the fall of communism, do not result in equal influence on the debate about the interaction between religion and the state. According to the national censuses and various sociological surveys held since 1989, the percentage of the population in each of Bulgaria, Romania, Russia, Belarus, Ukraine, Moldova, Georgia, Serbia and Montenegro that is affiliated with Orthodoxy varies between 71 and 92 per cent.[3] Only North Macedonia shows a slight deviation, with 65 per cent Orthodox Macedonians and 32 per cent Muslims (mostly ethnic Albanians).[4] No political party or coalition that has come to power in these 10 countries since the end of the Cold War has been able to achieve and maintain such a number of supporters. At the same time, the relatively low proportion of regular Orthodox church-goers, which varies between 21 per cent (Romania) and 5 per cent (Bulgaria), has no significant impact on the favourable attitude of the Orthodox Eastern Europeans to their churches.

This favourable attitude to Orthodoxy is rooted in the strong correlation of religious and national identity in the traditionally Orthodox countries. A factor that is no less important is the historical link between many Eastern European nation states and their local Orthodox churches. It is especially strong in Bulgaria, Romania, Serbia, Georgia and Russia, where the majority of citizens view the local Orthodox churches as guardians of their national sovereignty throughout the centuries. Similar attitudes can be also traced in Montenegro and North Macedonia, where many people associate their national and religious identity with such medieval churches as the Metropolinate of Zeta and the old Archbishopric of Ohrid (abolished in 1767). More complicated are the cases of Ukraine, Belarus and Moldova, where the Orthodox population has almost never experienced ecclesiastical independence. In this regard, the Pew Research Center has registered a very

[3] Religious Belief and National Belonging in Central and Eastern Europe Pew Research Center, 10 May 2017, at www.pewforum.org. See also Sociological and legal data on religions in Europe and beyond at www.eurel.info.

[4] A Jahangir, *Report of the Special Rapporteur on freedom of religion or belief*, A/HRC/13/40/Add.2, UN Human Rights Council, 28 December 2009, 8, at www2.ohchr.org.

high correlation between national and religious identity in Georgia (81 per cent) and a quite low one in Belarus (45 per cent).[5] Despite these fluctuations, the (above-)described historical link allows the Orthodox ecclesiastical leaderships to play a key role in shaping public opinion in the group of countries discussed, especially on religion-related issues.

Finally, this chapter approaches the relations between the Orthodox churches and the post-communist states in Eastern Europe from the perspective of the debate on the compatibility of Orthodoxy with the principle of separation between religion and the state. This issue is of special significance for the post-communist societies, as the implementation of the separation principle has been widely considered as a guarantee of their advancement towards democracy.[6] While most studies place their focus on the political or the theological aspects of church–state relations in Orthodoxy, this chapter pays special attention to history. It employs a comparative overview of church–state relations in Orthodoxy in different epochs and countries to demonstrate their complexity. It also discusses the issue of church–state separation in Christianity from the perspective of the different patterns adopted in the West and in the East. From this perspective, it investigates the response of the Orthodox ecclesiastical elites to the post-communist policies of separation of religion and state in their countries. In this way, it takes into consideration the double challenge faced by the Orthodox churches in the former totalitarian states. On the one hand, they have to overcome the burden of militant atheism and to find a new boundary in their relations with the post-atheist, but still secular, state. On the other hand, they take an active part in the creation of the new pattern of relations with the state.

II. Church–State Relations in Orthodoxy: Between Theory and History

The researchers of church–state relations in Orthodoxy have not come to an agreement on their nature. This diversity is a product of the researchers' different academic backgrounds and expertise. Scholars who study Byzantium and Muscovite Russia prefer the term 'theocracy' to describe the specific nature of church–state relations in both polities.[7] At the same time, this term is entirely

[5] *Religious Belief and National Belonging in Central and Eastern Europe* Pew Research Center, at http://www.pewforum.org/2017/05/10/religious-belief-and-national-belonging-in-central-and-eastern-europe.

[6] S Huntington, 'The Clash of Civilizations?' (1993) 72 *Foreign Affairs* 22, 30–31.

[7] S Runciman, *The Byzantine Theocracy* (London, Cambridge University Press, 1977); A Papadakis, 'The Historical Tradition of Church-State Relations under Orthodoxy' in P Ramet (ed), *Eastern Christianity and Politics in the Twentieth Century, Christianity Under Stress* (Durham, NC, Duke University Press, 1988) 1, 36–40; IE Karayanopoulos, *The Byzantines' Political Theory*, tr Kiril Pavliyanov, from Greek to Bulgarian (Sofia, Universitetsko izdatelstvo 'Sv. Kliment Ohridski', 1992).

inappropriate in analyses of the persecution of religion under communism.[8] In their turn, theologians have adopted the term 'symphony' (Gr *symphonia*) to define the nature of church–state relations in Orthodoxy. It is rooted in a concept promoted by the Byzantine emperor Justinian I in his famous *Sixth Novella* of 535, which reads:

> The greatest blessings of mankind are the gifts of God which have been granted to us by the mercy on high: the priesthood and the imperial authority. The priesthood ministers to the things divine; the imperial authority is set over, and shows diligence, in things human; but both proceed from the same source and both adorn the life of man.[9]

The concept cited refers to a different historical reality and system of worldviews. Moreover, it is not about the relations of the imperial authority of the Byzantine ruler with the priestly authority of the Patriarch of Constantinople, but with that of the Christian Church as a whole, that is, a body that has consisted of several ecclesiastical structures, the most important of which were the Churches of Rome, Constantinople, Alexandria, Antioch and Jerusalem. When applying this sixth-century concept to the relations between the contemporary Orthodox Church(es) and secular state(s), theologians often interpret it as a harmonious interaction between the religious and the political that is based on their mutual recognition and respect. Besides, the leaders of the different Orthodox churches diverge in their approach to this issue.

The Ecumenical Patriarch Bartholomew of Constantinople has placed the emphasis on the relationship of the Orthodox Church with society. He states:

> Whether we are living in a confessional or a non-confessional system – and as Christians we can accept either situation – it is our hope that there will exist between religion and the state a symphonia of active collaboration. We should not think only of separation, neutrality or mutual tolerance, but of a relationship that is far more dynamic and creative. Our Christian attitude towards the total society in which we live is expressed exactly in the statement of Saint Paul (he was speaking, it is true, of membership within the Church, but we are justified in giving his words a wider application): 'If one member of the body suffers, all suffer together with it; if one member is honoured, all rejoice together with it' (I Cor 12:26).[10]

In their turn, the leaders of national Orthodox churches tend to narrow their focus on relations with their particular states. In this regard, the observation of Patriarch Daniel of Romania about the asymmetric and irregular character of symphony in terms of similar powers deserves special attention. He states, 'The Church *constantly prayed for the State*, and often it also *pleaded to the State* for

[8] AA Valentinov, *Chernaya kniga ('Shturm nebes')* [Black book ('Storm of the Heavens')] (Paris, Izd. Russkago natsional'nago studentcheskago ob"edineniya, 1925); P Ramet, 'Autocephaly and National Identity in Church-State Relations in Eastern Christianity: An Introduction' in Ramet (ed) (n 7) 18–19.

[9] Karayannopoulos (n 7) 67.

[10] Bartholomew, Patriarch of Constantinople, *The Role of Religion in a Changing Europe*, Speech of His All Holiness Ecumenical Patriarch Bartholomew at the London School of Economics for the London Hellenic Society (3 November 2005) at www.patriarchate.org.

help. The State in its turn, *supported* the Church, yet, it often tended to subjugate the Church.'[11]

A similar attitude can be also traced in the case of the Orthodox churches that have obtained a transnational character following the dissolution of the Soviet Union and Tito's Yugoslavia. As a result, the contemporary leaderships of the Russian and the Serbian Orthodox Church exercise their ecclesiastical authority not only within the borders of present Russia and Serbia, but also in most independent states established in their Near Abroad.[12] When Patriarch Kirill of Moscow was enthroned in 2009, he mentioned that symphony is 'a dream rather than a real project'.[13] Nevertheless, he stressed that some parameters of this concept were achievable in the contemporary world. In particular, the church must keep its autonomy from the state. It also should avoid being involved in political projects or in the struggle of one political party against another, because such behaviour will divide its adherents. At the same time, although Patriarch Kirill admits that the church–state relations in the Russian Orthodox Church's case cannot be limited to those with the Russian Federation, he tends to discuss symphony mostly in relation to this particular state, and fails to comment on the ways in which symphony can be implemented in the Near-Abroad independent states.

Another group of scholars employ the term 'caesaropapism', which was introduced at the beginning of the eighteenth century by Justius Henning Böhmer, a German expert on Protestant ecclesiastical law.[14] In his writings, this word was used to define the relations between the Byzantine emperor and the Christian Church before the Great Schism (1054), when the See of Rome and Orthodoxy were both part of an undivided church. Later on, however, scholars began to link caesaropapism exclusively with Orthodoxy. During the Cold War, its usage was also influenced by the ideological polarisation of the word. As a result, it placed Catholicism in opposition to Orthodoxy not only in religious but also in political terms. This development is illustrated in the writings of Cyril Toumanoff, a Russian-born US scholar who converted to Roman Catholicism upon his emigration from Bolshevik Russia. In 1946, he wrote that 'Catholicism alone establishes

[11] Daniel Ciobotea, Patriarch of Romania, 'State–Church Relations in Romania: Tradition and Present-Day Experience, Past and Present, Tradition and Current Context' in I Marga, GG Sander and D Sandu (eds), *Religion zwischen Kirche, Staat und Gesellschaft – Religion between Church, State and Society* (Hamburg, Verlag Dr Kovac, 2007) 117.

[12] Originally the term 'Near Abroad' appeared after the collapse of the Soviet Union. It is used in reference to the new independent states established within the framework of the former Soviet borders but outside the post-1991 Russian Federation. In this sense, there is a parallel between post-Soviet Russia and post-Yugoslavian Serbia that permits the use of the term 'Near Abroad' in this particular case.

[13] Svyateyshii Patriarkh Kirill: Model' tserkovno-gosudarstvennykh otnoshenii ne svoditsya isklyuchitel'no k otnosheniyam Russkoy Tsekvi i Pravitel'stva RF [His Holiness Patriarch Kirill: The Model of church–state relations is not limited to the relations of the Russian Orthodox Church with the Government of the Russian Federation] (24 July 2009) at www.patriarchia.ru.

[14] H de Wall, 'Caesaropapism' in HD Betz et al (eds), *Religion Past and Present, vol 2: Bia–Chr* (Boston, MA, Brill, 2007).

the harmonious correlation of the spiritual and the material, of soul and body, of form and matter, of Church and State.'[15] Although Orthodox theologians, as well as many researchers from other fields of humanities and social sciences, can provide sound arguments against such statements, they need to give credit to Toumanoff's approach to caesaropapism as a process. In his view, it began with the 'caesaropapistic diarchy' in Byzantium, but reached its full development with 'the absorption of Church by State' in imperial Russia.[16] In this regard, especially valuable is Toumanoff's understanding of the *church–state relations in Orthodoxy as dynamic and a subject of change*.

Since the end of the Cold War, however, some alternative visions have appeared. According to Alfred Stepan, 'Orthodoxy's caesaropapist structures and quietist culture' hide an opportunity to make the national Orthodox churches more supportive of democracy upon the end of communism.[17] Stepan has also suggested that the weaker resistance of these religious bodies to state authority has been caused not by their specific religious teaching, but rather by Orthodoxy's organisational forms. In addition, he hinted that the 'caesaropapist' state control on religion is not a unique feature of Orthodoxy but was also widespread in Lutheranism.[18] At the same time, many experts in Byzantine Studies disagree with the use of the term caesaropapism, as it does not reflect the church–state relations in Byzantium but those in the German Protestant principalities. Therefore, to distinguish the two types of interaction, they prefer to speak about 'eastern caesaropapism' in Byzantium as well as in Russia.[19]

Furthermore, neither of the concepts and definitions outlined is able to embrace the complexity and variety of church–state relations in Orthodoxy as well as their dynamics across time and space. Instead, they tend to present specific episodes or developments in Byzantine and Russian history as inherited and eternal features of Orthodoxy or of all states and societies where this Christian tradition prevails. One of the neglected forms of interaction of the Orthodox church(es) with the corresponding political formation is the custom of Orthodox hierarchs to act as regents during the infancy of the heirs to the throne: for example, the Patriarch of Constantinople, Nicholas Mystikos (852–925), during the childhood of the Byzantine Emperor Constantine VII Porphyrogenitus (905–959); Metropolitan Alexii of Moscow (1353–1378), during that of the Grand Prince Dmitry II Donskoy (1350–1389); and the Romanian Patriarch Miron Cristea (1919–1939) during that of Prince Michael (1921–2017). On a series of occasions, churchmen bore personal responsibility for the government of their states: for example, between

[15] C Toumanoff, 'Caesaropapism in Byzantium and Russia' (1946) 7 *Theological Studies* 213, 240.
[16] ibid 241.
[17] A Stepan, 'Religion, Democracy and the 'Twin Tolerations' (2000) 11 *Journal of Democracy* 37, 53.
[18] ibid 44.
[19] G Dagron, *Empereur et prêtre: Étude sur le césaropapisme byzantin* (Paris, Editions Gallimard, 1996); DJ Geanakoplos, 'Church and State in the Byzantine Empire: A Reconsideration of the Problem of Caesaropapism' (1965) 34 *Church History* 381, 385.

1516 and 1735, the Metropolitans of Zeta (present Montenegro) combined their religious duties with political ones; in 1886, Metropolitan Kliment of Tarnovo was Prime Minister of Bulgaria; in 1938, Patriarch Miron Cristea became Prime Minister of Romania; between 1960 and 1977, Archbishop Makarios III of Cyprus was the President of Cyprus. Moreover, there were Orthodox hierarchs who secured military victories as commanders-in-chief, for example Metropolitan Daniil of Zeta (1697–1735) defeated the Ottomans in 1712, as did Metropolitan Peter I of Zeta (1781–1830) in 1796.

After the fall of communism, Samuel Huntington expressed concerns that Orthodox societies 'seem[ed] much less likely to develop stable democratic political systems'.[20] One of his key arguments was that they are alien to the western idea of separation between religion and the state.[21] This thesis provoked intensive debates among Orthodox theologians.[22] Some of them associated the principle of separation with French *laïcité*, and feared that its adoption would exclude religion from public life.[23] Others pointed to the Orthodox religious teaching on the different nature of church and state as a feature that allows common ground to be found within the liberal concept of separation between religion and the state. In this regard, they advanced a new reading of symphony, which takes into account the different missions of church and state, namely that 'The one God assigns to each institution, church and state, its own sphere of influence: church is responsible for spiritual matters, while the state is responsible for worldly needs.'[24] In parallel, some theologians suggest that 'religion' as a private matter should be distinguished from 'church' – as a public one. According to Pantelis Kalaitzidis, this situation 'implies a tripartite distinction (between state, public, and private), instead of bipartite (state and private)'.[25]

Taking advantage of the aforementioned vision of the Ecumenical Patriarch Bartholomew, who associates the Orthodox Church with civil society rather than with the state, Kalaitzidis continues:

> The church can be involved in the public sphere, provided that it is aware of the boundaries and conditions of that sphere (its neutrality in regard to ideology, religion, and values) and to the extent that it respects the values established in that sphere. Central to these values is respect for the fundamental achievements of modernity and above all for human rights, religious freedom and tolerance of difference and the distinct role of church and state.[26]

[20] Huntington (n 6) 30–31.
[21] ibid 40.
[22] See the discussion between Stanley Harakas and Vigen Guroian on the Orthodox model of church–state relations in A Papanikolaou, 'Byzantium Orthodoxy and Democracy' (2003) 71 *Journal of the American Academy of Religion* 77, 77–98.
[23] ibid 92.
[24] ibid 85.
[25] P Kalaitzidis, *Orthodoxy & Political Theology* (Geneva, World Council of Churches Publications, 2012) 82.
[26] ibid.

Kalaitizdis also distinguishes between the presence and the authority of the Orthodox Church in the public sphere. The Church can act within that sphere, but its contemporary public role is no longer all-encompassing as it used to be in the Middle Ages, for example it cannot intervene by force in the public and private life of citizens. At first glance, it may appear that the modern principle of separation works 'against the holistic vision of Orthodoxy, which looks to a catholic transformation of the life of the world and of humankind, a radical change and renewal of every aspects of life'.[27] At the same time, Kalaitzidis reminds us that the eschatological nature of the Church offers a different perspective that allows it to continue its mission despite its separation from the state. In his view, the liberalisation of the public space and citizens from previous ecclesiastical tutelage has simply 'reminded the churches of the voluntary character of Christian communities'.[28] In this way, Kalaitzidis comes close to Peter Berger's suggestion that a transformation of the Orthodox churches into voluntary associations will allow them to sustain democracy, despite their limited historical experience in this form of social governance.[29]

At the same time, a historical overview of church–state relations in the Christian world calls for some refinement of Huntington's statement that Orthodox societies are not familiar with the principle of separation. More specifically, it seems inaccurate to neglect the autonomous functioning of the Orthodox church(es) in the Ottoman Empire – a practice that lasted about five centuries. Although the non-Muslim subjects of the sultan were in an disadvantaged position in comparison with the Muslim ones, the former enjoyed an internal religious autonomy with no parallels in the then existing Christian empires, kingdoms and principalities. In this regard, the status of *Millet bashi*, the chief administrator of all Orthodox subjects in the Ottoman Empire, was especially important. Granted by Sultan Mehmed II to Patriarch Gennadios II Scholarios after the conquest of Constantinople (1453), this privilege was preserved until the fall of the Empire. It was accompanied by a series of rights, described in detail by Steven Runciman:

> Though the Sultan's government had to confirm Episcopal appointments, no bishop could be appointed or dismissed except on the recommendation of the Patriarch and the Holy Synod. The Patriarchal law-courts alone had penal jurisdiction over the clergy; the Turkish authorities could not arrest or judge anyone of Episcopal rank without the permission of the Patriarch. … The Patriarch could tax the Orthodox on his own authority to raise money for the needs of the Church.[30]

Furthermore, this custom of church autonomy had also an effect on the other Orthodox churches in the Ottoman Empire, especially the Patriarchate of Peć

[27] ibid.

[28] ibid.

[29] PL Berger, 'Orthodoxy and Global Pluralism' (2001) 9 *Democratizatsiya, The Journal of Post-Soviet Democratization* 437, 441.

[30] S Runciman, *The Great Church in Captivity: A Study of the Patriarchate of Constantinople from the Eve of the Turkish Conquest to the Greek War of Independence*, 10th edn (Cambridge, Cambridge University Press, 2006) 171–72.

(between 1558 and 1766), the Archbishopric of Ohird (until 1767), the Church of Cyprus and the Bulgarian Exarchate (between 1870 and 1912).

At the same time, the Russian Orthodox Church has never experienced such internal autonomy and religion-based separation from the state. From this perspective, the analysis of the Orthodox patterns of church–state relations should take into account not only the division between the Orthodox East and Western Christianity, but also the internal one – between Orthodox Russia and the Muslim policy of the Ottomans. The neglect of the second development blurs the difference between the Russian pattern of church–state relations, which is characterised by a total absence of church autonomy, and those of the Balkan Slavs, thus leading to an artificial view of Russia as 'the leader of a distinct Slavic-Orthodox civilization'.[31]

Another flaw in the assessment of the capacity of Orthodox societies to embrace the principle of separation between religion and the state stems from the tendency to view it as something unified and fixed, even in the West. Meanwhile, the more careful analyses of the church–state relations reveal significant differences and dynamics in the ways they have been understood and practised throughout history. In this regard, especially valuable is John Witte's cogent evidence that the development of separation between church and state has been a process lasting centuries. He convincingly demonstrates that this separation has varied from country to country and from one epoch to another under the influence of the concrete historical circumstances, as well as of the philosophical worldviews of the local political elites and/or the theological visions of the contemporary religious leaders.[32]

In the case of the post-communist societies, another source of confusion is Lenin's formula for the 'separation of the church from the state'. In particular, it obscures the difference in the ways in which former atheist states and western democracies have understood and practised this separation. Therefore, it is necessary to outline its deviation from such classical western models as Thomas Jefferson's wall of separation and the French *laïcité*. The first of these was inspired by an understanding of the divine nature of religious liberty and rights, and aimed to keep religion free from state intervention.[33] In its turn, the 1905 French Law on the Separation of the Churches and the State introduced a more restrictive separation that praised the secular state, but which showed respect to religion as a private affair. As a result, the major difference between these two models was that the American model did not affect the public presence of religion, while the French one imposed a ban on it. From this perspective, it becomes clear that the communist regimes introduced a third type of separation. Driven by a militant atheist ideology and with the aim of creating an entirely godless society, the communist

[31] Huntington (n 6) 43.

[32] J Witte, Jr, 'Facts and Functions about the History of Separation of Church and State' (2006) 48 *Journal of Church and State* 15, 15–45.

[33] MD Peterson, 'Jefferson and Religious Freedom' (1994) 274 *The Atlantic Monthly* 112, 112–24.

states envisioned wiping out religion not only from the public arena, but also from the minds of the people. Therefore, this model presupposes not only full-scale repression of religious organisations, but also the persecution, and even physical extermination, of their ministers and adherents. After the fall of communism, however, this perception of the term 'separation' has not disappeared in Eastern Europe, and it provokes negative reactions among many Orthodox churchmen and believers. As a result, they are inclined to regard the principle of separation of religion and the state in the post-Cold War constitutions of their countries as a threat to their Orthodox Church, rather than as a guarantee of religious liberty.

III. Power Dimensions of the Post-Communist Church–State Relations

In the case of Orthodox majority nations, the institutional aspects of this religious denomination, rather than the spiritual ones, empower the leadership of a given Orthodox Church to undertake and effectively pursue specific policies regarding the state(s), where the former has structures and communities under its jurisdiction. In this regard, the fall of communism in Eastern Europe and the new religious liberty have allowed local Orthodox churches to function as *bodies of power*. In particular, these ecclesiastical institutions have obtained the opportunity not simply to perform religious activities publicly, but to exert influence on state authorities by employing such human resources as the Orthodox hierarchy, clergy and laity, as well as such specific networks as their dioceses, parishes, monasteries and religious non-governmental organisations. No less important is the tremendous growth of the church economy in the former communist lands, following on from the restoration of profitable properties such as arable land, forests, etc,[34] the expansion of the candle industry, the boom in religious rites (baptisms, weddings, funerals), the rise of religious tourism, etc. The income from these assets and activities has changed the role of the Orthodox Church in the domestic economy. In the meantime, however, a shortage of information about church income and the ways in which it is spent impedes a more precise analysis of the effect of this new development on church–state relations.

The changed economic profile of the Orthodox churches in the post-communist lands has provoked some tension with the state authorities. In 2018, a draft law on the amendment of the Bulgarian Religious Denomination Act proposed that religious institutions would report their income to the state.

[34] After 1989, the Bulgarian state restored all economic assets of the Bulgarian Orthodox Church, which used to be national property under communism. See D Kalkandjieva, 'The Economic Development of the Bulgarian Orthodox Church before and after Communism' in *Archives de Sciences Sociales des Religions*, janvier–mars 2019, 185 [Dossier thématique: Christianisme orthodoxe et économie dans le sud-est européen contemporain, VN Makrides and K Seraïdari (eds)] 125–44.

The Holy Synod of the Bulgarian Orthodox Church (BOC) immediately argued that these requirements contradicted 'the millennial internal ecclesiastical and canonical convention on the immunity of the Church's property', as well as the exclusive authority of bishops over church properties and finances, which had been guaranteed by canon law.[35] It also claimed that the Church's possessions had been received mostly through donations and testimonials, that is through deeply personal acts, and thus the benefactors should remain anonymous. At the same time, the Synod linked the Church's right of possession and ownership with its divine mission. As the former guarantees the fulfilment of the latter, an allusion was made to the fact that the requirement that the Church must report its finances and other assets would be not simply an act of state intervention in the religious sphere but an act of persecution of the Church. In addition, the Bulgarian Synod emphasised that the proposed amendment contradicted Orthodox canon law, the statutes of religious institutions in Bulgaria and the constitutional principle of the separation of these institutions from the state (Article 13, paragraph 2).[36] On these grounds, Orthodox hierarchs categorically rejected the right of the state to require the Church to submit such reports, except regarding the amounts received as state subsidies. The objection had an effect, and the National Assembly of Bulgaria did not support the criticised draft.

Another key aspect of the power dimensions of the relations between Orthodox churches and post-communist states concerns the role of the former in shaping the boundary between the religious and the secular in society. After 1989, the states discussed had adopted constitutions in which the principle of separation was preserved. At the same time, they coupled it with a new understanding of religious liberty. More specifically, the Stalinist formula of 'freedom of worship' was replaced with definitions inspired by the European Convention for the Protection of Human Rights and Fundamental Freedoms (ECHR).[37] In this way, freedom of religion began to be approached as a complex of rights that allows every citizen to change his religion and 'either alone or in community with others and in public or in private, to manifest his religion or belief, in worship, teaching, practice and observance'.[38]

This liberal vision, however, has not been welcomed by many Orthodox hierarchs. They are especially hesitant regarding the conversion of individuals who themselves, or whose families, used to be members of the Orthodox Church.

[35] Stanovishte na Svetiya Sinod na Balgarskata pravoslavna tsarkva otnosno zakonoproekti za izmenenie i dopalnenie na Zakona za Veroizpovedaniyata [The statement of the Holy of Synod of the Bulgarian Orthodox Church on the draft laws on the amendment of the Religious Denominations Act] (3 October 2018) at www.bg-patriarchia.bg.

[36] *Constitution of the Republic of Bulgaria*, 13 July 1991, at www.parliament.bg.

[37] Council of Europe, Convention for the Protection of Human Rights and Fundamental Freedoms 1950, *ETS* 5, available at https://www.europeansources.info/record/convention-for-the-protection-of-human-rights-and-fundamental-freedoms/.

[38] Art 9 ECHR.

In such cases, Orthodox churchmen accuse those faith communities that have accepted such people of proselytism. Moreover, there is a strong tendency to regard these acts as threats to national identity, and even to state security. This attitude finds fertile soil in countries in which nation states have arisen as ethno-religious entities. It even used to influence some acts of the state administration. For example, the instructions for collecting demographic data for the Bulgarian censuses of 1992 and 2001 defined religious affiliation as 'the historically determined adherence of the individual or of his/her parents and forefathers to a certain group with concrete religious views'.[39] When Bulgaria joined the European Union, however, this approach was abandoned. As a result, during the 2011 census, Bulgarian citizens were free to choose whether to provide information about their religious, ethnic and linguistic background or not.

In 2018, however, an amendment to the Bulgarian Religious Denominations Act again raised the question of the freedom of citizens to declare or not declare their religious identity. More specifically, it introduced a differentiation between the religious communities on the grounds of their results in the national censuses (§9).[40] Enacted at the end of the year, it changed the rules for estimating the 2019 annual state subsidy for the religious communities in Bulgaria. Now the key criterion is the number of people who declared themselves as members of a particular religion during the 2011 census, that is, when nobody had been aware of the consequences of his or her decision to announce or not announce his or her religious affiliation. Under these conditions, citizens have lost one of the advantages of declaring or not declaring their religious affiliation. Furthermore, the new law introduced a threshold of 1 per cent, which is passed by two religious organisations – the Orthodox Church and the Muslim community.[41] According to the new rules, their leaderships will receive 10 levs (about €5) per member. In the case of the BOC, this means that its Holy Synod will get a subsidy of 43,741,359 levs in total (about €22,000,000). In parallel, it receives additional financial support for the Bulgarian Orthodox dioceses and parishes abroad. Although the amendment envisions subsidies for small religious communities, it does not clarify the criteria to be used for their estimation. It is possible to expect that the new rules will stimulate competitiveness on the religious market in Bulgaria, thus leading either to its restructuring or to a more rigid bond between the religious and the ethnic identities. Such developments may provoke tensions between the two major ethno-religious communities in the country, or between the Orthodox majority and the minority religions.

[39] *Religious Structure of the Population* (Summary of the results of the 2001 Bulgaria Census), Bulgarian National Statistical Institute, at www.nsi.bg.

[40] Decree No 319 of the President of the Republic of Bulgaria, 28 December 2019 for the publication of the amendment of the Religious Denominations Act in the State Gazette, National Assembly of Bulgaria, at www.parliament.bg.

[41] *Religious Structure of the Population* (n 39). According to the 2011 Census, 4,374,135 Bulgarian citizens or 59.4% of the population of the country self-identified themselves as Orthodox, and another 577,139 citizens or 7% as Muslims.

Another source of discontent for the Orthodox churches in the former communist states stems from 'the right to freedom of peaceful assembly and to freedom of association with others' under Article 11 ECHR, as it allows their adherents to move to another church jurisdiction or to establish their own. While the European Court of Human Rights considers that in such cases the freedom of religion (Article 9 ECHR) must be interpreted in the light of freedom of association (Article 11 ECHR),[42] the leaderships of the Orthodox churches insist that this group of cases belong to the sphere of canon law. In the view of the latter, only a canonically recognised autocephalous Orthodox Church has the right and competence to grant autocephaly, that is canonical independence, as well as various levels of administrative autonomy to one or another of its parts.[43] Besides, in these cases, Orthodox hierarchs are more concerned about the authority and unity of their local Orthodox Church than the right of citizens to exercise the collective dimension of their religious freedoms. According to the Russian Metropolitan Hilarion (Alfeyev), the 'calls to establish an autocephalous Church are actually calls to tear away the Ukrainian Orthodox faithful from the united Russian Orthodox Church'.[44] In practice, Orthodox churches place emphasis on their right to grant or to refuse to grant autonomy or autocephaly to their branches. In addition, the exercise of this right is not limited to the territory and citizens of the state where a particular Orthodox Church has its headquarters, but embraces the territories and citizens of foreign states under its jurisdiction. After the dissolution of the Soviet Union and Tito's Yugoslavia, this approach has been demonstrated many times by the leaderships of the Russian and the Serbian Orthodox Church, who refuse to recognise the self-declared autocephalies of Orthodox communities in Ukraine and North Macedonia. In such cases, the Orthodox churches also demonstrate a selective attitude to the role of the state(s) in their resolution; for example, their hierarchs insist on a strict separation between religion and the state when civil authorities act against their interests, but welcome any state support that enhances their position. From a broader perspective, the opposition of Orthodox churches to the attempts of their former adherents to leave their jurisdiction have not only domestic dimensions,[45] but also international ones.[46]

[42] See, eg, *Metropolitan Church of Bessarabia and Others v Moldova* App no 45701/99 (ECHR, 27 March 2002) para 118; *Svyato-Mykhaylivska Parafiya v Ukraine* App no 77703/01 (ECHR, 14 September 2007) para 112.

[43] The contemporary Orthodox Church consists of 14 canonically recognised autocephalous bodies. Their list includes the four ancient patriarchates of Constantinople, Alexandria, Antioch and Jerusalem; the five younger patriarchates of the Russian, the Serbian, the Romanian, the Bulgarian and the Georgian Orthodox Churches; the Orthodox churches in Greece, Cyprus, Albania and Poland, as well as that in the former Czechoslovakia, now operating under the name 'Orthodox Church in the Czech Lands and Slovakia'.

[44] Cited from LN Leustean, 'Preface' in A Curanović, *The Guardians of Traditional Values: Russia and the Russian Orthodox Church in the Quest for Status, Transatlantic Academy Paper Series* 1 (Washington, DC, Transatlantic Academy, 2015) 1, at www.transatlanticacademy.org.

[45] See especially *Holy Synod of the Bulgarian Orthodox Church (Metropolitan Inokentiy) and Others v Bulgaria* App nos 412/03 and 35677/04 (ECHR, 22 January 2009).

[46] See especially *Orthodox Ohrid Archdiocese (Greek-Orthodox Ohrid Archdiocese of the Peć Patriarchy) v The Former Yugoslav Republic of Macedonia* App no 3532/07 (ECHR, 16 November 2017).

Furthermore, the Orthodox churches in the former communist states, where the former represent the majority religion, emphasise their role as key factors in the survival of the corresponding nations and/or states throughout the centuries. In the case of religious minorities, however, the Orthodox churches have adopted double standards. They agree that the so-called historical faiths should be tolerated by the state but call for restrictions on western evangelical denominations and new religious movements that have gained access to their countries in the course of their post-Cold War liberalisation. An analogous approach can be also traced in the post-Cold War legislation of many former totalitarian states. The 1997 Russian Law on Freedom of Conscience and Religious Associations introduces three categories of faith communities: 'centralized religious organisations'; 'local religious organisations'; and 'religious groups.' Only those religious communities that have existed in Russia for over 50 years, namely Orthodoxy, Islam, Buddhism and Judaism, are eligible to obtain the highest status as centralised religious organisations and to enjoy such privileges as state subsidies and various tax exemptions.[47]

In a similar manner, the Serbian Act on Churches and Religious Communities distinguishes between seven 'traditional churches and religious communities' that 'have had a historical continuity within Serbia for many centuries and which have acquired the status of a legal person in accordance with particular acts' issued before the establishment of Tito's regime and the so-called 'confessional communities'.[48] The legal position of the latter continues to be regulated in accordance with religion-related acts of the former Federal National Republic of Yugoslavia.[49] In its turn, Article 13, paragraph 3 of the 1991 Bulgarian Constitution singles out Orthodoxy as the traditional religion in the country.[50] In 1998, Judgment No 2 of the Constitutional Court clarified that 'the traditional nature of Eastern Orthodoxy expresses its cultural and historical role for the Bulgarian state, as well as its present significance for the state life and especially its impact on the system of official holidays'.[51] The 2002 Religious Denominations Act, however, undermined this understanding of the traditional character of Orthodoxy by associating the notion of tradition with a particular national religious institution. Its preamble emphasises 'the special and traditional role of the Bulgarian Orthodox Church in the history of Bulgaria to establish and develop its spirituality and culture'.[52] On these grounds, the law justified the *ex lege* recognition of this church (Article 10), while requiring the other religious communities to undergo court registration (Articles 14–20).

[47] Religlaw Database, *Russian Federation: Law and Religion Framework Overview* (2016) (International Center for Law and Religious Studies) 3–4, at www.religlaw.org.

[48] 'Zakon o crkvama i verskim zajednicama' [Act on Churches and Religious Communities], *Sluzhbeni Glasni* [Official Gazette of the Republic of Serbia], no 36/2006, 27 April 2006, 3–8.

[49] ibid.

[50] Constitution of the Republic of Bulgaria (1991).

[51] Constitutional Court of the Republic of Bulgaria, *Reshenie no 2 ot 18 fevruari 1998 g.* [Judgment no 2 of 18 February 1998] at www.constcourt.bg.

[52] Religlaw Database, *Religious Denominations Act* [adopted by the National Assembly of the Republic of Bulgaria on 20 December 2002], *Darzhaven Vestnik* [State Gazette] no 120 (29 December 2002).

Finally, the Orthodox churches in the post-communist states have achieved a more relaxed implementation of the principle of separation than religious minorities. As a rule, the former enjoy wider access to various social and cultural institutes in their countries, for example to public schools, prisons, hospitals. The privileges of the Orthodox majorities are especially visible in the sphere of education. In contrast to religious minorities, which often have to use their own resources to organise religious lessons for the children of their adherents, Orthodox churches rely on courses organised at public schools. As a rule, they are covered by the state budget and taught by lay graduates of Orthodox theological faculties. In Romania, Orthodox priests are also allowed to teach such lessons. This state support does not always guarantee high attendance, however; for example, the religious classes in the Bulgarian public schools are attended by less than 1 per cent of all students.[53]

An understudied area of collaboration between the Orthodox Church and the state concerns the presence of the former in national military forces. This option is directly addressed in the 2001 Romanian Constitution (Article 29, paragraph 5).[54] Although the fundamental laws of the other post-communist countries do not include such texts, many local Orthodox churches have signed cooperation agreements with the corresponding national military forces, for example in Russia, Georgia, Serbia, Ukraine, etc.[55] The major outcome has been the restoration of the pre-communist institute of military chaplains. In countries with significant non-Orthodox minorities, however, this move requires some innovations. In contrast to the entirely Orthodox military chaplaincy in imperial Russia, the one in post-Soviet Russia includes not only Orthodox priests, but also Muslim, Buddhist and Jewish chaplains. Still, the leadership of the new institute remains in the hands of Orthodox clergy, presenting over 80 per cent of the army staff.[56] In March 2013, 19 Orthodox priests and a Muslim imam were enrolled in courses at the Military University of the Ministry of Defence of the Russian Federation.[57] In December 2013, the Holy Synod of the Russian Orthodox Church adopted a special statute on military chaplains.[58] In 2011, the chaplaincy service was also introduced in the Serbian Armed Forces in accordance with the Act on

[53] Mitropolit Gavriil, 'Sv Sinod na BPTs ima kontseptsiya za religioznoto obuchenie v balgarskite uchilishta' [Metropolitan Gavriil: 'The Holy Synod of the Bulgarian Orthodox Church has a concept on teaching religion in the Bulgarian public schools], 8 December 2018, at www.diakonia.bg.

[54] See Religlaw Database at www.religlaw.org.

[55] Y Karamikhalev, 'Pravoslavnata tsarkva i armiyata' [Orthodox Church and Army] *Dveri* (7 June 2008) at www.dveri.bg; I Ponomarenko, 'Ukraine Launches Chaplaincy for Armed Forces' *Kyiv Post* (21 April 2017) at www.kyivpost.com.

[56] S Mozgovoy, 'K voprosu o vvedenii instituta voennogo dukhovenstva v Rossiiskoy Armii' [Concerning the introduction of the institute of millitant chaplaincy], *Voenno-yuridicheskii zhurnal*, 2010, No 11, at www.portal-credo.ru.

[57] 'Shtatnykh voennykh svyashtennikov obyazhut proyti special'nuyu podgotovku' [Salaried military chaplains will receive special training], Moscow Patriarchate of the Russian Orthodox Church (28 March 2013) at www.patriarchia.ru.

[58] 'Polozhenie o voennom dukhovenstve Rossiyskoy Pravoslavnoy Tserkvi v Rossiyskoy Federatsii' [Statute of the Russian Orthodox Church on military chaplaincy in the Russian Federation, adopted by the Russian Holy Synod during its session held on 23–25 December 2013, at www.patriarchia.ru.

the Serbian Armed Forces.[59] For this purpose, the Serbian Ministry of Defence signed special agreements with the Holy Synod of the Serbian Orthodox Church and six other traditional religious communities.

More recently, Ukraine also adopted a multi-confessional model of military chaplaincy, where the Ukrainian Greek Catholic Church is also present.[60] In this case, however, the issue of chaplaincy has been also influenced by the objections of the Russian Orthodox Church to the negotiations of the Government of Petro Poroshenko with the Ecumenical Patriarch Bartholomew of Constantinople, for the establishment of a new autocephalous Orthodox Church in Ukraine. On 20 December 2018, on the eve of this act, the Parliament of Ukraine amended the Law on Freedom of Conscience and Religious Organisations. It required the autonomous branch of the Russian Orthodox Church, known as the Ukrainian Orthodox Church of the Moscow Patriarchate (UOC-MP) to modify its name by reproducing in its own name the full statutory name of the foreign religious organisation to which it belongs. The change was justified by the fact that this particular religious body was subordinate to a foreign church administration, located in a state that 'was carrying out military aggression against Ukraine and/or temporarily occupying part of the territory of Ukraine'.[61] On the same grounds, the amendments imposed a ban on the UOC-MP's military chaplains.[62] In response, the Chair of the Legal Department of the UOC-MP declared that the new law 'violates the right to freedom of religion and discriminates on religious grounds millions of believers who are Ukrainian citizens'. He also warned that his Church will contest the law at the Constitutional Court, as an act that 'does not comply with the Constitution of Ukraine and violates the international obligations' undertaken by this state.[63]

Although Orthodox churches define their relations with the state as symphony, collaboration or partnership, they apply double standards to their own autonomy and to that of the state. As a rule, Orthodox hierarchs justify such behaviour as a defence of the so-called traditional values, 'usually defined in contrast to modern or post-modern values'.[64] In this regard, the Russian and other Orthodox churches attempt to act as an ultimate authority, which has the potential to determine the attitude of society to such issues as religion, family and gender.[65]

[59] B Barovac, 'Serbian Military to Get Chaplains in June' *Balkan Insight* (17 January 2011) at www.balkaninsight.com; Serbian Armed Forces, *Chaplaincy Service in the SAF*, no date, at www.vs.rs.

[60] J Kisyk, 'On the Spiritual Battlefront with Ukraine's Military Chaplains' *The Catholic World Report* (26 April 2016) at www.catholicworldreport.com.

[61] 'Ukraine's Parliament passes bill on renaming UOC-MP', UNIAN Information Agency (20 December 2018) at www.unian.info.

[62] Parliament Obliged the UOC (MP) to change the name and restricted its chaplains' access to the army, Institute for Religious Freedom, Ukraine (20 December 2018) at https://www.irf.in.ua/eng/index.php?option=com_content&view=article&id=458:1&catid=34:ua&Itemid=61.

[63] 'UOC-MP set to appeal to Constitutional Court to retain its name', RISU [Religious Information Service in Ukraine] (27 December 2018) at www.risu.org.ua.

[64] Curanović (n 44) 1.

[65] ibid.

They have been especially successful in opposing the attempts of the post-communist states to adopt laws recognising same-sex marriages. In 2018, protests, initiated by the Bulgarian Orthodox Church against the ratification of the Council of Europe Convention on preventing and combating violence against women and domestic violence (Istanbul Convention), led to Judgment No 13/2018 of the Constitutional Court, which declares the Convention incompatible with the Bulgarian Constitution.[66]

IV. Conclusions

This overview of the debates on church–state relations in Orthodoxy, and the responses of the Orthodox churches to the changed modes of separation between religion and the state in the former communist lands, challenges some traditional concepts and visions. In particular, it reveals the dynamic character of this relationship, and the ability of the Orthodox churches to act as power institutions. In this regard, the soft and asymmetric separation achieved by the Orthodox churches in those post-communist states where they represent the majority religion deserves special attention. They have succeeded in establishing closer relations with the respective states than have the religious minorities, and have been more successful in influencing some policies and acts of the corresponding civil authorities, while zealously defending their own church autonomy.

At the same time, the analysis presented here calls for a revision of the view of church–state relations in Orthodoxy as a purely domestic issue. This feature needs the special attention not only of scholars from the fields of the humanities and social sciences, but also that of policy-makers: the power dimension of the relations of the Orthodox churches with their state(s) has a direct effect not only on the society in one country or another, but on international affairs too. Finally, the power dimension of this relationship raises important questions about the tensions between civil law and Orthodox canons, which the principle of separation between religion and state raises in the countries where Orthodoxy is the majority religion.

[66] Constitutional Court of the Republic of Bulgaria, *Reshenie no 13 ot 27 yuli 2018 g* [Judgment no 13 of 27 July 2018] at www.constcourt.bg.

4

Catholic Social Thought, Religious Liberty and Liberal Order

ZACHARY R CALO

I. The Problem of Religious Freedom

At the heart of Catholic social thought during the past century has been the project of developing a liberal tradition. It was through development of a Catholic liberalism that the Church sought to establish a critical voice within modernity, able to speak the language of modernity while advancing an account of modernity uniquely informed by the Catholic worldview. The longstanding problem of religious freedom played a central role in the formation of this liberal tradition. Church–state separation and liberal religious freedom were long thought to undermine the authority of the Church and the moral structure of society. Reimagining the relationship between law and religion was thus essential to shaping the Catholic Church's more constructive engagement with modernity.

The Church had long resisted the normative idea of liberal religious freedom in both its individual and societal expressions. Indeed, more than simply resisting, the Church defined its own social and political vision against liberalism. Freeing the state from cooperating with the Church was thought to invite barbarism and moral chaos. As Pope Gregory XVI wrote in the 1832 encyclical *Mirari Vos*, removing the 'restraints of religion' through separation of church and state would bring 'the destruction of public order' and 'ruin in sacred and civil affairs'.[1] Moreover, it is 'insanity', Gregory argued, to permit citizens 'liberty of conscience and worship' that is 'restrained by no authority whether ecclesiastic or civil'.[2]

The *Syllabus of Errors*, issued by Pope Pius IX in 1864, captures most bluntly the antagonistic posture papal thought adopted towards political modernity in general, and the liberal separation of church and state in particular. The *Syllabus* lists 80 propositions deemed anathema to Catholic teaching, including proposition 55 ('The Church ought to be separated from the State, and the State

[1] Gregory XVI, *Mirari Vos* (1832) §§5, 14.
[2] Piux IX, *Quanta Cura* (1864) §3.

from the Church'), proposition 77 ('In the present day it is no longer expedient that the Catholic religion should be held as the only religion of the State, to the exclusion of all other forms of worship') and proposition 80 ('The Roman Pontiff can, and ought to, reconcile himself, and come to terms with progress, liberalism, and modern civilization'). The *Syllabus* was a hyperbolic document, criticised even by some Catholics at the time of publication for its reactionary excess. Yet the document nevertheless revealed how central the church–state question was to the Church's broader encounter with the modern age. At stake in the debate about church–state relations and religious freedom was the question of the more basic relationship between law, politics and truth. What modernity's apostles defended as 'liberty', Pius warned, was an invitation for people to become 'slaves' trapped in the 'snares of error'.[3]

While the *Syllabus of Errors* was particularly aggressive in its denunciations of liberalism, it was by no means unrepresentative of broader patterns of papal thought at the time. For instance, while Pope Leo XIII defended church–state union in a more nuanced way than his predecessor, Pius, he remained wed to the basic conviction that Christian culture was incompatible with liberal politics. The state and the church must work collaboratively to uphold the moral order of society, and this collaboration must be reflected in the legal status of the Church. Leo makes this point vividly in *Longinqua Oceani*, an 1895 encyclical addressed to the Catholic Church in the United States, in which he proposes that

> without morality the State cannot endure … But the best and strongest support of morality is religion. She, by her very nature, guards and defends all the principles on which duties are founded, and setting before us the motives most powerful to influence us, commands us to live virtuously, and forbids us to transgress. Now what is the Church other than a legitimate society, founded by the will and ordinance of Jesus Christ for the preservation of morality and the defense of religion? For this reason have We repeatedly endeavored, from the summit of the pontifical dignity, to inculcate that the Church, whilst directly and immediately aiming at the salvation of souls and the beatitude which is to be attained in heaven, is yet, even in the order of temporal things, the fountain of blessings so numerous and great that they could not have been greater or more numerous had the original purpose of her institution been the pursuit of happiness during the life which is spent on earth.[4]

In Leo's formulation, the Church could best advance 'the order of temporal things' by directly acting through law. The Church is not one society among others that might indirectly influence law through soft cultural suasion. It is the society of societies, which alone renders political order coherent. By contrast, the separation of church and state as envisaged in liberal thought, particularly its continental variations, was premised on severing politics from church and religion. The liberalism of France, in particular, drove Leo's critique, but even the more pragmatic

[3] *Quanta Cura* §1.
[4] Leo XIII, *Longinqua Oceani* (1895) §4.

and less doctrinaire liberal order in the United States did not persuade the Pontiff to deviate from his general condemnation. In the end, there were not meaningful distinctions to made between forms of liberalism. In fact, the Pope urged the Church in the United States to avoid complacency and to reject 'the conclusion that in America is to be sought the type of the most desirable status of the Church'. The Church 'would bring forth more abundant fruits if, in addition to liberty, she enjoyed the favor of the laws and the patronage of the public authority'.[5] A political order that rejected granting formal legal recognition to the Church remained in a basic way disordered.

Leo offered similar lines of argument in *Testem Benevolentiae*, his 1899 encyclical addressed to James Cardinal Gibbons of Baltimore and the hierarchy of the American Church. This letter primarily addressed what historians have termed the Americanist controversy, a movement among certain ecclesial leaders to synchronise Catholicism with the vitality and liberty of the United States.[6] John Tracy Ellis would label Americanism a 'phantom heresy', but it caused acute alarm among European conservatives at the time.[7] It was the tendency of Americanising prelates to look favourably on the nation's approach to religious liberty that attracted particular papal rebuke. In a blunt passage, Leo warned Cardinal Gibbons that the 'civil freedom which is now the right and the foundation of almost every secular state' undermines the Church's ability 'to impart the truth of the gospel and to widen the bounds of civilization'.

There was pushback, to be sure, particularly among American Catholic commentators.[8] One response was to creatively interpret these papal admonitions in a way that rendered them largely inapplicable to the American situation. A Cambridge, Massachusetts, parish newspaper, for instance, rejected the view that the 'encyclicals aim at effecting a close union between Church and State, or gaining the supremacy for the Church over the State'. Far from collapsing church and state, papal teaching 'upholds and defines the rights of Church and State' within their proper spheres of authority.[9] Leo, so this line of argument went, wanted to protect the Church from the secular state, not have the secular state bestow privileges on the Church. Insofar as the American liberal order preserved the freedom of the Church, it was not running afoul of the encyclical tradition.

Finally, Leo's 1885 encyclical *Immortale Dei* is important in linking the church–state question to broader concerns about the moral ordering of politics. The

[5] ibid §6.

[6] See generally, T McAvoy, *The Great Crisis in American Catholic History, 1895–1900* (Chicago, IL, Henry Regnery, 1957) and R Scott Appleby, *'Church and Age Unite!' The Modernist Impulse in American Catholicism* (Notre Dame, IN, University of Notre Dame Press, 1992).

[7] See J Tracy Ellis, *The Life of James Cardinal Gibbons* (Milwaukee, Wis, Bruce Publishing Company, 1952) 25.

[8] See generally ZR Calo, '"The Indispensable Basis of Democracy": American Catholicism, the Church–State Question, and the Soul of American Liberalism, 1900–1920' (2005) 91 *Virginia Law Review* 1037.

[9] 'Leo XIII on the Jurisdiction of Church and State' *The Sacred Heart Review* (26 July 1890).

encyclical is more nuanced in its critique of separationism than other papal writings. *Immortale* is not a simple broadside against the liberal state, nor a defence of a particular form of political order. Government 'may take this or that form', Leo proposes, provided that rulers 'bear in mind that God is paramount ruler of the world'.[10] *Immortale* was thus an attempt to provide a deeper structural account of the place of the Church within the modern political order. It was not a rejection of liberalism as such but a statement against certain tendencies that Leo saw as endemic to modern understandings of the state's relationship to religion.

Leo was particularly troubled by the manner in which the modern liberal state interfered with the authority and jurisdiction of the Church. Under the guise of promoting freedom, Leo argued, the secular state arrogated to itself an ever more totalising scope of authority. The jurisdiction of the state especially grows at the expense of the Church. Once the Church is placed under control of the civil law, matters properly within the Church's jurisdiction come under the control of the state. Those who exercise civil power, Leo charged, 'claim jurisdiction over the marriages of Catholics, even over the bond as well as the unity and the indissolubility of matrimony. They lay hands on the goods of the clergy, contending that the Church cannot possess property'.[11]

Against this tendency, Leo defended the traditional notion of state and church as distinct but concurrent loci of authority – what Leo called the 'twofold jurisdiction'.[12] In summarising the idea of twofold jurisdiction, Leo wrote, '[t]he Almighty, therefore, has given the charge of the human race to two powers, the ecclesiastical and the civil, the one being set over divine, and the other over human, things' and both are 'supreme' within fixed limits.[13] In this respect, the Pope was not proposing a theological subsumption of secular politics into the Church, but the preservation of space for the Church to freely pursue its work.

Of course, Leo did not want the Church simply to be given jurisdictional freedom within a pluralistic and differentiated social order. The Church is a unique society, and it would be folly, the Pope emphasises, to think it 'differs in no respect from other societies in the State'.[14] The state and the Church are more than coequal spheres of authority operating within their respective spaces. The Church is a society whose very life and logic renders coherent the 'twofold jurisdiction' by which state and Church collectively uphold the common good. The Church can offer an account of political order in which it shares jurisdiction with the state. The state, by contrast, seeks to colonise space properly due to the Church. As such, the Church is not simply to be afforded space alongside other social bodies; it must be afforded a pre-eminence of place so as to uphold true jurisdictional differentiation. It is in light of such considerations that Leo rejects liberalism as 'pernicious'.[15]

[10] Leo XIII, *Immortale Dei* (1885), §4.
[11] ibid §27.
[12] ibid §27.
[13] ibid §13.
[14] ibid §27.
[15] *Longinqua Oceani* §15.

True liberty cannot, in the end, be realised within a liberal order that fails to recognise the unique vocation of the Church in sustaining the social order.

Leo XIII opened the Church to a constructive engagement with modernity but remained too wed to the ancien régime to fully escape the Church's well-established resistance to liberalism. Leo was a transitional figure who moved beyond some of the more excessive illiberal vitriol of Pius and the *Syllabus of Errors*, but who still could not be fully at peace with the place afforded religion within the liberal order. At the same time, Leo's thought did set the stage in subtle ways for the emergence of a new approach to religious freedom and church–state relations. It would fall on later Catholics to examine how certain Leonine premises could be understood in a way that opened the door to a more meaningful rapprochement with forms of liberal religious freedom.

II. The Vision of *Dignitatis Humanae*

The Church's critique of liberalism, as embodied in the writings of Leo XIII, set the terms of debate by which Catholic thinkers later moved to develop a new understanding of religious freedom. Two of the most critical contributions to this process were the promulgation of *Dignitatis Humanae*, the Second Vatican Council's Declaration on Religious Freedom, and the constructive theoretical work of the American Jesuit John Courtney Murray. The account of liberal order developed in these works established the basic terms by which Catholic social thought entered into a more constructive engagement with liberal religious freedom. *Dignitatis* is helpful in seeing the development of an account of individual religious freedom. Murray, while also concerned with individual rights, is helpful in seeing the application of Catholic social doctrine to structural matters of constitutional order, and especially the freedom of the Church. More than a half century on, lines of argument developed in *Dignitiatis* and by Murray continue to influence the basic orientation of the Church towards questions of law and religion. Returning to these sources provides a way to appreciate not only the foundational disposition of Catholic liberalism, but also the limits and possibilities of this tradition going forward.

Dignitiatis Humanae is often, and not incorrectly, identified as having inaugurated a new moment in Catholic thought about religious freedom. In its opening section, *Dignitatis* announces 'that constitutional limits should be set to the powers of government, in order that there may be no encroachment on the rightful freedom of the person and of associations'.[16] With these words the Church, in the words of one commentator, 'broke traditional linkages between Catholicism and the state' that had defined Catholic social thought.[17] However, *Dignitatis* not

[16] *Dignitatis Humanae* (1965) §1.

[17] PC Manuel, et al, *The Catholic Church and the Nation State: Comparative Perspectives* (Washington, DC, Georgetown University Press, 2006) 25.

only altered the Church's basic posture towards matters of law and religion, but also effected a more basic shift in its orientation towards political modernity. While *Gaudium et Spes* systematically addressed the position of 'the Church in the modern world', *Dignitatis* brought about a definitive re-evaluation of the anti-modern impulse that had undergirded Catholic social thought. Writing during the Vatican Council debate, John Courtney Murray summarised the aspirations of the new text as the 'simple and straightforward affirmation' that government should exercise no coercion in matters of religion.[18]

The narrative of *Dignitatis*' historical significance is relatively straightforward, but there remains room for debate about the terms on which it approached religious freedom. By one reading, *Dignitatis* offered a residually illiberal perspective. The shift from condemning to endorsing religious freedom occurred not through adopting a liberal posture but by drawing on longstanding themes found in such thinkers as Augustine and Aquinas concerning coercion and religious belief. Points of intersection between *Dignitatis* and liberal constitutionalism are, in this reading, largely accidental and do not indicate an endorsement of liberalism. Along these lines, it is notable that *Dignitatis*, unlike other documents in the Catholic social tradition, does not directly engage matters of political order. In fact, it offers very little in terms of political theology. The vision of *Dignitatis* rather consists largely of general comments about 'the constitutional order of society' preserving 'the right of all citizens and religious communities to religious freedom'.[19] *Dignitatis* has political implications, of course, but the document did not aim to develop a detailed normative account of politics as such.

The reason *Dignitatis* largely bypasses matters of political order is that it aims to reframe the issue of religious freedom. The enduring innovation of *Dignitatis* was to locate structural issues concerning religion and law within an anthropological framework, thereby turning away from the notion that matters of religious freedom are primarily political in nature. The title of the document – 'Of the Dignity of the Human Person' – signals this methodological shift. It is not that politics are rendered unimportant, but rather that the focus of Catholic social thought is moved from top-down structural issues of church and state to bottom-up questions of human personhood. The task of politics is to sustain institutions and norms that support human flourishing. Thus, even as human flourishing in community is inseparable from law, *Dignitatis* boldly proposes that the personal precedes the political. In other words, political order exists to serve the person, and therefore properly assessing the relationship between religion and law should begin with anthropology. Get the human person right and the politics will follow.[20] In this respect, approaching *Dignitatis* in terms of the categories of liberal and illiberal

[18] J Courtney Murray, 'This Matter of Religious Freedom' *America* 112 (9 January 1965) 40.

[19] *Dignitatis* §6.

[20] Along these lines, Jacques Maritain argues that there are no 'rights of man' unless 'a certain order … is inviolably required by what things are in their intelligible type or their essence, or by what the nature of man is, and is cut out for': J Maritain, *Man and the State* (Chicago, IL, University of Chicago Press, 1951) 96.

might be to impose a category mistake. Although *Dignitatis* does aim to effect a reconciliation with forms of liberal politics, it upends expectations by turning to personhood as the source of common ground.

The Declaration on Religious Freedom approaches the human person primarily through the category of dignity. 'The right to religious freedom', the Declaration announces, 'has its foundation in the very dignity of the human person as this dignity is known through the revealed word of God and by reason itself'.[21] Yet while dignity provides a framework for the Declaration's account of religious freedom, the meaning of this dignity is elusive. Dignity is sometimes associated with 'with reason and free will'.[22] It is also linked with the divinely created nature of the person.[23] However, the Declaration makes no sustained effort to define the meaning and grounds of dignity, leaving its reliance on dignitarian language subject to critique that it is vague and indeterminate.

What Stephen Pinker notably said of dignity as used in contemporary bioethical debate – that '"dignity" is a squishy, subjective notion, hardly up to the heavyweight moral demands assigned to it' – could perhaps also be levelled against its use in *Dignitatis*.[24] However, *Dignitatis* is less concerned with defining dignity than invoking the term to describe the experience of what it termed 'responsible freedom'.[25] The language of freedom is littered throughout the document, invoked on nearly 50 occasions. Many of these references to freedom occur in the context of grounding a political right to religious freedom. The 'right of man to religious freedom has its foundation in the dignity of the person'.[26] Yet what *Dignitiatis* describes as the right to 'freedom or immunity from coercion in matters religious' is based fundamentally on an understanding of human freedom.[27] The anthropological precedes the political. In this respect, dignity speaks mainly to the ways in which freedom is exercised and experienced under the unique conditions of modernity. No longer is it possible for freedom to be 'driven by coercion'. It must rather be 'motivated by a sense of duty'.[28] Freedom is a moral vocation that is characterised as 'proper to the human spirit'[29] and grounded in the 'very nature' of personhood.[30] There is a mutually enriching quality between dignity and freedom, especially religious freedom, that represents an opportunity for the person to affirm that which is ultimately true. Human dignity makes religious freedom necessary.[31]

[21] *Dignitatis* §2

[22] ibid §2.

[23] ibid §11.

[24] S Pinker, 'The Stupidity of Dignity' *The New Republic* (27 May 2008).

[25] *Dignitatis* §1.

[26] ibid §9.

[27] ibid §4.

[28] ibid §1.

[29] ibid §1.

[30] ibid §2.

[31] Catholic thought continues to give primacy to the connection between dignity and religious freedom. For instance, Archbishop Giovani Lajolo, Secretary for the Holy See's Relations with States,

By defining freedom as constitutive of human nature, *Dignitatis* creates a point of contact between Catholic social thought and the experience of life in modernity. *Dignitatis* initiates an encounter with the dynamic reality of freedom in modernity, and makes this encounter central to the Catholic political witness. It sees in modernity the disclosure of something that is fundamentally true about the human person, even if the freedom modernity offers is often distorted. Freedom thus becomes the conceptual mechanism by which the Church both finds a voice within modernity and simultaneously critiques the tilt of modern freedom towards aimlessness. The experience of radical freedom is offered as something that cannot merely be rejected but must be engaged. To be human, to be dignified, is to encounter the world from a fundamental posture of freedom. The issue, then, is not freedom versus unfreedom, but the disposition one adopts towards the use of this freedom within the arc of human life.

Just as dignity affirms freedom as a constitutive aspect of human nature, dignity also shapes the meaning and ends of freedom. Freedom, in particular, cannot be dissociated from truth. Against the idea that freedom should exhibit an agnosticism towards human goods, *Dignitiatis* proposes that freedom must be conceptually linked to an account of truth. Freedom is teleological. The freedom endorsed in *Dignitatis* is not a licence 'to define one's own concept of existence, of meaning, of the universe, and of the mystery of human life', as the United States Supreme Court famously stated.[32] Freedom is rather an opportunity to orient oneself towards goods temporal and eternal, and to exercise the 'responsibility' to embrace that which is true.[33] Recognition of religious freedom in law, by extension, establishes 'an environment in which men can without hindrance be invited to the Christian faith, embrace it of their own free will, and profess it effectively in their whole manner of life'.[34] The state does not impose matters of ultimate truth, but instead creates the conditions within which the human person can freely receive or reject it. As Archbishop Charles Chaput writes, '[e]rror has no rights, but persons *do* have rights – even when they choose falsehood over truth'.[35] The state simply provides a zone of 'immunity from external coercion' within which the free conscience can guide.[36]

Dignitatis develops the connection between freedom and truth by invoking the same language of 'true freedom' that was so central to Leo's critique of modernity.[37]

spoke recently of 'religious freedom as the cornerstore of human dignity'. It is in this sense that Lajolo can present religious freedom as having an architectonic role in the Holy See's international diplomacy. Lajolo, who served as the Vatican's foreign minister, observed that '[i]n the realm of human rights, the Holy See, understandably, gives special attention to religious freedom'. See *Address of Archibishop Giovani Lajolo*, Gregorian University of Rome (3 December 2004), at http://www.vatican.va/roman_curia/secretariat_state/2004/documents/rc_seg-st_20041203_lajolo-gregorian-univ_en.html.

[32] *Planned Parenthood of Southeastern Pennsylvania v Casey*, 505 US 833, 851 (1992).

[33] *Dignitatis* §1.

[34] ibid §10.

[35] C Chaput, 'Religious Liberty 50 Years after *Dignitatis Humanae*' *Crisis Magazine* (24 March 2015).

[36] *Dignitatis* §2.

[37] ibid §§8, 11.

In this way, the document is able to offer a positive gloss on freedom, even as it maintains a point of contact with the traditional concerns of Catholic social thought. *Dignitatis* pulled the Church more fully into the life of the modern world, but not by means of a radical rupture with the tradition that preceded it. *Dignitatis* declares in its opening that it 'leaves untouched traditional Catholic doctrine on the moral duty of men and societies toward the true religion and toward the one Church of Christ'.[38] However, by shifting from an oppositional framing of freedom and truth to one in which they are mutually reinforcing, the document opened the door to the idea that modernity is not incompatible with the advancement of Christian truth. True freedom for Leo was something unrealisable within the confines of a liberal order, whereas *Dignitatis* maintains the contrary. In this way, *Dignitatis* nudged Catholic social thought from an either/or to a both/and understanding of the relationship between liberal freedom and truth.

The shift to dignity and freedom in *Dignitiats* allowed the Church to move beyond its traditional suspicion of liberalism, while simultaneously sharpening aspects of its critique of liberalism. The 'true freedom' *Digniatis* invoked captures the complex and often tension-filled relationship with liberalism that has animated modern Catholic social thought. *Dignitatis* offers a simultaneous yes and no to liberal accounts of religious freedom. At base, *Dignitatis* sought to preserve the claims about dignity and truth that had animated Leo's critique of modernity, while moving past the political architecture Leo thought a necessary corollary. Leo XIII wrote in his 1888 encyclical *Libertas* that a full account of Christian dignity reveals the 'absurdity' of separating church and state. It is the state, working in cooperation with the Church, that enables a community 'to live properly, that is to say, according to the laws of God'.[39] For Leo, a critique of liberal anthropology cannot be dissociated from a critique of liberal politics. The two go hand in hand as part of a comprehensive critique of modernity. *Dignitas*, by contrast, redefined the relationship between the vocation of persons and the vocation of politics, by severing the Leonine connection between true freedom and the Christian state. Yet it did not do so in an absolute sense. Shared moral truths were still to inform public life. It remained the role of the state 'to help create conditions favorable to the fostering of religious life, in order that the people may be truly enabled to exercise their religious rights and to fulfill their religious duties'.[40] Yet rather than emphasising the centrality of law in upholding true freedom, *Dignitatis* shifted the focus of Catholic social though to the primacy of culture. As Thomas Curry observes, the resources to sustain an authentic humanism would, after Vatican II, 'be based on a turn to culture' and 'no longer be a product of power'.[41] In its account of Christian culture, *Dignitatis* offered a new way to combine freedom, politics and moral order.

[38] ibid §1.
[39] *Libertas* §18.
[40] *Dignitatis* §6.
[41] TJ Curry, *Farewell to Christendom: The Future of Church and State in America* (Oxford, Oxford University Press, 2001) 63.

By so doing, did *Dignitatis* give the Church's imprimatur to an account of religious freedom fundamentally consonant with political liberalism? This has been a prevailing narrative among Catholics and non-Catholics alike. In *Political Liberalism*, for instance, John Rawls speaks of how the Catholic Church 'radically changed' at Vatican II and embraced 'the principle of religious freedom'.[42] It is commonly proposed that Vatican II 'resolved' the matter of Catholicism's relationship to liberalism, in the phrasing of another commentator.[43] But *Dignitatis* did not resolve the relationship between the Church and liberalism so much as reframe it. Interpreting *Dignitatis* on straightforwardly liberal or illiberal terms misses the subversive creativity of its attempts to move beyond these categories.

In the end, *Dignitatis* rested on the sanguine proposition that modernity could both be embraced and transformed. Leo had sought to upend modernity, identifying its understanding of freedom as fundamentally disordered. The freedom of modernity could not, in his assessment, sustain Christian culture. *Dignitatis*, by contrast, saw in modernity's freedom certain aspects of a fundamentally Christian nature that could provide a point of contact for constructive encounter. Catholicism did not need to sweep liberalism away but could work within it, to shape a political order reflective of Christian understandings of personhood and freedom. As Patrick Deneen proposed, '*Dignitatis humanae* reflected great confidence in the capacities of liberal democracy not only to accommodate, but robustly support the basic commitments of religion generally, and Catholic belief in particular'.[44] It was this sanguinity that modernity could hold together freedom and truth and Catholicism and liberalism, that defined the work of *Dignitatis* and much of the Catholic liberal tradition that followed. It is this same sanguinity that represents a major challenge for the contemporary Catholic Church in its ongoing engagement with an evolving liberal order.

III. John Courtney Murray

The writings of the American Jesuit John Courtney are particularly helpful in understanding the tensions and ambiguities that have defined the Catholic encounter with religious freedom. No twentieth-century figure was more influential in shaping the Church's thought on this topic than Murray. Of Murray, Joseph Cardinal Bernardin wrote, '[n]o single figure in American history has had greater impact on how Catholics conceive of the relationship between religion

[42] J Rawls, 'The Idea of Public Reason Revisited' in *Political Liberalism* (New York, Columbia University Press, 2005) 477.

[43] R Bruce Douglass and D Hollenbach, 'Introduction' in *Catholicism and Liberalism* (Cambridge, Cambridge University Press, 1994) 10.

[44] PJ Deneen, 'Religious Liberty after Liberalism: Re-Thinking *Dignitatis Humanae* in an Age of Illiberal Liberalism' (2013) 40 (Summer-Fall) *Communio* 6.

and politics'.[45] Murray, so the dominant narrative goes, helped lead the American and, eventually, the worldwide Church into a new understanding of the possibilities of democratic liberalism.

By one measure, this is a proper reading of Murray's intellectual project and influence. He was indeed a transformative thinker, who saw an opportunity to redefine the Church's relationship to liberal religious freedom. Murray consulted extensively with the 'reformers' seeking to realise a shift in the Church's approach to church and state questions.[46] At the debate over the religious freedom text at the Second Vatican Council, during which American bishops spoke in support of the document, one bishop commented that 'The voices are the voices of the United States bishops; but the thoughts are the thoughts of John Courtney Murray!'[47] Murray's intellectual footprint was all over *Dignitatis*.

Yet, as Kenneth Grasso points out, Murray's work is 'more often invoked than carefully read and seriously engaged'.[48] This is no more apparent than in the tendency to pigeonhole Murray as a sanguine apologist for liberalism. While it might well be the case that Murray maintained qualified optimism about the prospects for American politics and the role of the Catholic Church within it, he was equally aware of dangers that liberalism posed to the Church. Even as Murray advanced a Catholic defence of religious freedom, he acknowledged the fragility of his position. At times, one even glimpses Murray wavering in his convictions, fearful that modern liberal order lacks the cultural resources needed to sustain the very account of religious freedom he endorses.

In a 1965 essay published in the Jesuit journal *America*, Murray summarised *Dignitatis* in the following terms:

> The Declaration made a simple and straightforward affirmation, namely, that coercion in religious matters, worship, observance, practice, witness is, in principle, to be repudiated as offensive to the dignity of man. Primarily in view was legal coercion exercised by government; also in view were other forms of compulsion, direct or indirect, brought to bear by institutions or forces within society. In positive terms, the Declaration affirmed the free exercise of religion in society to be a basic human right that, in any society pretending to be well-ordered, should be furnished with a juridical guarantee so as to become a civil or constitutional right. Religious freedom, therefore, was clearly stated to be a juridical notion. Moreover, freedom here has the sense of 'freedom from'. It is an immunity in a twofold sense. First, no man is to be forcibly constrained to act against his conscience. Second, no man is to be forcibly restrained from acting according to his conscience.[49]

[45] Joseph Cardinal Bernardin, *A Moral Vision for America* (Washington, DC, Georgetown University Press, 1998) 38.

[46] B Hudock, 'The Fight for Religious Freedom: John Courtney Murray's Role in "Dignitatis Humanae"' *America* (30 November 2015).

[47] ibid (quoted by Hudock).

[48] KL Grasso, 'Getting Murray Right' (2011) 16 *The Catholic Social Science Review* 85.

[49] Murray (n 18) 40.

In these straightforward terms, Murray captures both the anthropological and political dimensions of the Declaration. Human dignity demands respect for conscience in the sphere of religious belief, and laws should therefore be organised in such a way as to protect religious freedom. Yet this account of religious freedom belies Murray's deeper ambivalence about whether a robust regime of religious freedom, properly understood, could endure 'in an industrial society to which religion has become largely irrelevant and even insipid'.[50] Murray's particular concern was with whether western modernity could give expression to the framework in *Dignitatis*.

One issue Murray explored is the way in which the freedom that modernity makes possible also tends to undermine itself. Dignity demands freedom, but freedom is also corrosive of dignity. He argued that 'the central problem' of the modern age is the 'horrid vision' in which man becomes the 'master of nature but not of himself, the possessor of nature who has lost his own identity'.[51] The radical freedom unleashed reveals something about the human person that had been previously occluded, something that Christianity can affirm as true. At the same time, this freedom corrodes the very resources needed to properly order and control itself. The problem of the emerging 'post-modern era', Murray writes bluntly, is 'the problem of freedom'.[52] Freedom always exists on a knife's edge, teetering between liberty and chaos. The greatest threat to freedom is freedom itself.

This tension within modernity's experience of freedom is the by-product of Christianity's historical influence in the West. Murray observes that 'Christianity freed man from nature by teaching him that he has an immortal soul, which is related to matter but not immersed in it or enslaved to its laws'.[53] The transcendent impulse within Christianity guides the person out of the self and beyond the boundaries and limits of history. Yet this experience of transcendence also leads people to deny the limits and ends of their nature. There is always an unstable balance between freedom and order, legality and antinomianism. At its best, this tension can be animating. Modernity, however, has unleashed dynamics that are ultimately difficult to contain. The question that Christians need to consider is thus whether true freedom can hold under such conditions? As Murray mused, seemingly uncertain of the answer, can one 'live as a man and a Christian, in the enjoyment of his birthright of freedom and in the discharge of the responsibility this birthright imposed on him'?[54]

The problem of freedom is linked in Murray's assessment to a loss of faith in reason. More specifically, Murray saw modernity as fostering an 'autonomous

[50] ibid.

[51] J Courtney Murray, *We Hold These Truths: Catholic Reflections on the American Proposition* (Kansas City, KS, Sheed and Ward, 1960) 200.

[52] ibid 198.

[53] ibid 192.

[54] ibid.

reason' divorced from nature.[55] The 'barbarism' of modernity comes from its 'open and explicit rejection of the traditional role of reason and logic in human affairs'.[56] That is, the elevation of an autonomous reason frees humanity from the limits of nature and spawns a spurious freedom. The denial of reason feeds, in turn, a political order divorced from an overarching ontological system.[57] Surveying a political landscape in which democratic liberalism was under attack from both right and left, Murray argued that the 'imperatives of the universal moral law' served as the 'inner architecture' of a free society.[58] Freedom of self and society must be ordered in deference to these eternal verities. Without reason and nature as guides, the free person and the free society to which modernity gave birth will not remain truly free.

In a 1957 essay, 'Are There Two or One', Murray used Romano Guardini's description of the 'interior disloyalty of modern times' to express concern about the future of religious freedom.[59] While the principle of religious freedom is 'derived from Christian concepts of man's sacredness', modernity lacks cultural resources to nurture it.[60] Modernity exhausts itself – the 'modern era runs out', Murray wrote – as it becomes increasingly separated from the Christian concepts that once undergirded it.[61] What results is a radical 'experiment in human freedom' in which the meaning and ends of freedom are 'based on a denial or disregard of the essential Christian contribution'.[62] Can the freedom of *Dignitatis* be realised and sustained under these conditions? Murray fears it cannot, for modernity has spawned a ' horrid vision of man' without 'identity'.[63] This seductive freedom beckons the person to move beyond the bounds of the self, but ultimately offers only a 'myopic individualism' that destroys authentic selfhood.[64]

IV. Catholic Liberalism and the Future of Religious Freedom

Catholic thought about religious freedom found a voice during the mid-twentieth century through a critical yet constructive engagement with liberalism. As encapsulated in *Dignitatis Humanae*, this tradition was based on a tension. Its operating assumption was that the Church could transform liberal modernity while retaining basic aspects of the world to which it had given rise.

[55] ibid 28.
[56] ibid 12.
[57] ibid 198–99.
[58] ibid 36.
[59] ibid 214–15.
[60] ibid 198–99.
[61] ibid 208.
[62] ibid 210–11.
[63] ibid 200.
[64] ibid.

The challenge for this tradition is that it rested on the idea that liberal culture has resources to receive and sustain the Church's distinctive account of freedom. In other words, the governing assumption was that liberalism contained basically Christian understandings of society and the human person, however distorted these had become. Thus *Dignitatis* sought, at base, to re-tether the modern experience of human freedom to a theological account of the human person. The trouble, as Murray recognised, is that these resources might be inadequate and increasingly depleted within modernity, producing a liberal culture that not only fails to receive the Catholic vision but actively resists it.

In many respects, this would appear to characterise the present state of affairs. Rather than shaping debate, the Catholic account of religious freedom in *Dignitatis* appears ever more marginal. The Church tried to save modernity but has found itself outstripped by that which it aimed to subvert and transform. Legal developments in the field of religious freedom reveal how the logic of modernity has increasingly taken shape at odds with the Catholic vision. More than a half century following the issuance of *Dignitatis*, contemporary jurisprudence shows the acceleration of an account of religious freedom to which the Declaration has little to offer beyond rejection and critique.

There has been a notable convergence in the law of religious freedom across legal systems, revealing the ways in which post-Christian societies have adopted forms of moral order in tension with Catholic social thought. With respect to individual religious freedom, a survey of legal developments in the United States and Europe reveals an animating anthropology that emphasises the primacy of autonomy, self-creation and self-fulfilment. It is the case that the retrenchment of law from advancing strong accounts of normative meaning has generated a body of case law that affords space for religious freedom.[65] However, the underlying account of freedom rejects the idea at the heart of Catholic social thought, which is that freedom has an order and end. As *Dignitatis* proposes, the end of the person is to 'participate' in the divine law, and it is the duty of persons 'to seek the truth in matters religious'.[66] Religious freedom, within this framework, is a right that facilitates fulfilment of a duty. Freedom stands in the service of truth. By contrast, the liberal freedom that finds sanction in law advances a consumerist approach to religious preference. The end of freedom is choice. Choice in matters of religion, like choice in other spheres of life, promotes a search for meaning, satisfaction and authenticity. Points of contact between this account of freedom and the freedom of Catholic social thought are accidental rather than reflective of any jurisprudential symmetry.[67]

Because legal liberalism resists connecting freedom to a particular account of human goods, law has difficulty resolving disputes in which competing preferences

[65] ZR Calo, 'Law, Religion and Secular Order' (2019) 7 *Journal of Law, Religion and State* 104, 107.
[66] *Dignitatis* §3.
[67] ibid §2.

come into conflict. No issue has proved more contentious in recent years than balancing the relationship between religious freedom and gay rights. The Supreme Courts of Canada, the United States, and the United Kingdom have all recently heard major cases in this area, while the Ruddock Commission in Australia issued a report on religious freedom in the wake of a national survey on same-sex marriage. While the status of law varies within and across legal systems, there is a transnational legal settlement taking shape that deems limitations on religious expression as appropriate to preserve antidiscrimination norms and to advance the status of gay rights. Equality has repeatedly trumped religious freedom when the two values come into conflict. These legal developments reveal not only something about the current cultural landscape with respect to sexuality, but also the unfolding logic of liberalism in relation to religion across similarly situated legal systems. The treatment of religion as a subjective and interiorised preference makes it difficult to warrant elevating this right above legal protections for sexual orientation, all the more so given the importance of sexual identity in shaping contemporary understandings of authenticity and selfhood.

Similar developments are occurring in the area of institutional religious freedom. Often at issue here is the question of whether religious organisations should be exempt from neutral laws of general applicability in order to maintain autonomy as self-governing institutions. Legal cases concerning freedom of the church or the ministerial exception implicate constitutional structure in a way that individual religious freedom does not. The legal status granted religious institutions thus offers a window into the underlying liberal order and its relationship to religion, particularly the extent to which law permits religious traditions to enact and sustain strong forms of collective moral identity.

Catholic engagement with religious freedom has long been concerned with institutional religious freedom. *Gaudium et Spes*, for instance, stressed that '[i]t is very important, especially where a pluralistic society prevails, that there be a correct notion of the relationship between the political community and the Church'.[68] Law should create space within which the Church can fulfil its vocation. This space is needed so that Catholic institutions can maintain particular forms of identity and be a presence within the social body. Freedom of the Church is also a measure of a healthy liberal order that preserves space for religious institutions to be vibrant carriers of moral tradition. Does law recognise this principle, or is it slipping into the monistic form that Murray feared?

From one perspective, recent legal developments would seem to be broadly consonant with a Catholic understanding of religious freedom. Significant decisions in a number of jurisdictions have found that there are circumstances in which the authority of law should not impinge on the autonomy due to religious institutions. For instance, the United States Supreme Court, in the 2012 case *Hosanna-Tabor v EEOC*,[69] unanimously endorsed the doctrine of the ministerial

[68] *Gaudium et Spes* (1965) §76.
[69] *Hosanna-Tabor v EEOC* 565 US 171 (2012).

exception in finding that federal disability laws did not apply to a teacher in a Lutheran school. According to the logic of the decision, the state lacks jurisdictional authority to regulate matters pertaining to the internal governance of a religious institutions. Preserving this autonomy is part of upholding religious freedom. There have been similar legal developments in recent years at the European Court of Human Rights. A number of cases, including *Obst v Germany*,[70] *Schüth v Germany*,[71] *Siebenhaar v Germany*[72] and *Fernández Martinez v Spain*,[73] have given shape to European law in this area. These decisions are varied but, taken together, establish a legal basis for religious autonomy and the ministerial exception. European Court of Human Rights case law has relied more on a balancing approach to different rights claims, whereas the American approach embodied in *Hosanna-Tabor* is grounded more in constitutional structure. As such, the doctrine is arguably more stable in its American variation. All the same, both legal systems have endorsed a basic norm, broadly consonant with Catholic thought, that protection for religious liberty requires not only freedom for individuals but also collective forms of religious expression.

In spite of these legal developments, the Church has remained outspoken in warning of threats to institutional religious freedom. The United States Conference of Catholic Bishops, addressing a legal requirement that employers provide contraceptive coverage, claimed that 'in an unprecedented way, the federal government will both force religious institutions to facilitate and fund a product contrary to their own moral teaching and purport to define which religious institutions are "religious enough" to merit protection of their religious liberty'.[74] Pope Benedict XVI expressed similar concerns in criticising initiatives that would deny the right of conscientious objection to religious institutions. Benedict described this as a threat 'to the Church's public moral witness presented by a radical secularism'.[75] A refusal to grant the Church 'proper independence', Benedict argued, is an affront to religious freedom and an act of injustice by which the state fails to 'recognize' limits to its jurisdiction and authority.[76] Pope Francis has likewise warned that freedom of conscience is under attack in 'Christian countries', and that this freedom needs to go beyond 'freedom to worship alone' to encompass the capacity to live individually and collectively in accord with moral convictions.[77]

[70] *Obst v Germany* App no 425/03 (ECHR, 23 September 2010).

[71] *Schüth v Germany* App no 1620/03 (ECHR, 23 September 2010).

[72] *Siebenhaar v Germany* App no 18136/02 (ECHR, 3 February 2011).

[73] *Fernández Martinez v Spain* App no 56030/07 (ECHR, 12 June 2014).

[74] United States Conference of Catholic Bishops, *Our First, Most Cherished Liberty: A Statement on Religious Liberty* at http://www.usccb.org/issues-and-action/religious-liberty/our-first-most-cherished-liberty.cfm.

[75] *Address of His Holiness Benedict XVI to the Bishops of the United States of America on the 'Ad Limina' Visit*, 19 January 2012 at http://w2.vatican.va/content/benedict-xvi/en/speeches/2012/january/documents/hf_ben-xvi_spe_20120119_bishops-usa.html.

[76] Benedict XVI, *Deus Caritas Est* (2012) §28.

[77] 'Pope Francis: Freedom of conscience in danger in "Christian Countries"' at https://www.catholicnewsagency.com/news/pope-francis-freedom-of-conscience-in-danger-in-christian-countries-17941.

The concern expressed by Benedict, Francis and the American bishops is that liberal order in the secular West is no longer capable of preserving a full account of freedom of the church. These concerns echo Murray's from decades earlier. In blunt terms, Murray had argued that 'the political experiment of modernity has essentially consisted in an effort to find and install in the world a secular substitute for all that the Christian tradition has meant by the pregnant phrase, the "freedom of the church"'.[78] The recognition of freedom of the church is an achievement that was made possible by 'Christianity's basic contribution to the political order'.[79] Can this understanding endure within a liberal order premised on a fundamentally different social ontology, particular a liberal order in which Christianity is increasingly privatised and culturally marginalised? Murray's most compelling insight was to identify within modernity a 'socio-juridical monism that is always basic to the secularist position'.[80] Murray argues that 'there can be only one society, one law, one power, and one faith, a civic faith that is the "unifying" bond of the community, whereby it withstands the assaults of the assorted pluralisms'.[81] The logic of modernity, in other words, seeks to impose a monopoly over moral meaning. Granting space to the church as an ongoing community of moral meaning entails the secular state ceding its authority, contrary to the impulse to control and suffocate rivals. For Murray, the freedom of the church is a fragile and tenuous proposition always prone to collapse. Whether contemporary liberal order has the capacity to uphold a strong version of it remains a question for Catholic social thought.

The gap between *Dignitatis* and the current legal state of religious freedom reveals the increasingly tenuous nature of the Catholic liberal project. *Dignitiatis* marked a new moment in the Catholic Church's engagement with liberalism and religious freedom. It was a statement defined by optimism, both about the moral possibilities of modern politics as well as the Church's capacity to shape a liberal order broadly consonant with Catholic principles. The impulse to achieve a rapprochement between Catholicism and liberal modernity marked a departure from the illiberalism that had defined Catholic social thought from the late nineteenth century onward. Yet this optimism has increasingly given way to a more critical and even pessimistic posture. The United States Bishops Conference issued 'an urgent summons to our fellow Catholics and fellow Americans to be on guard, for religious liberty is under attack, both at home and abroad'.[82] Pope Benedict spoke of there being 'grave threats' to freedom of religion.[83]

[78] Murray (n 51) 201.
[79] ibid.
[80] ibid 21.
[81] ibid 21.
[82] United States Conference of Catholic Bishops, *Our First, Most Cherished Liberty: A Statement on Religious Liberty* at http://www.usccb.org/issues-and-action/religious-liberty/our-first-most-cherished-liberty.cfm.
[83] 'Pope warns of "grave threat" to religious freedom in US' *Catholic News Agency* (19 January 2012) at http://www.catholicnewsagency.com/news/pope-warns-of-grave-threat-to-religious-freedom-in-us/.

Religious freedom, for both the individual and the church, seems unstable and the dominant liberal order increasingly irredeemable. Anxiety abounds, fed by a sense that Christianity is losing cultural and legal ground.

Is this an instance of Catholic thought about liberalism going back to the future? Is Catholic social thought returning to illiberal impulses present at its Leonine genesis? It is probably the case that a certain discomfort with liberalism has always remained within Catholic social thought. Yet what appears in the current engagement with religious freedom is less outright rejection of liberalism than an emerging concern that contemporary law and culture lacks the capacity to support the sort of liberal order endorsed in the Church's social tradition. We are not seeing retrenchment from the normative vision developed in *Dignitas* so much as a reconfiguration in how the Church approaches contested issues in law and religion. The aims now seem both more modest and more defensive, focused more on preserving space within liberal society than transforming its basic nature. Catholic social thought still has much to offer debate, but it will perhaps need to return more to the critical diagnostic roots that shaped its earlier encounter with western liberalism. While the vision for religious freedom set out in *Dignitatis* seems more distant, Catholic social thought possesses unique resources for understanding the cultural dynamics needed to animate and sustain religious freedom. This is something Murray understood well.

PART II

Contested Issues

5

The Right to be Different: Religious Life in Twenty-First Century Great Britain

ANTHONY BRADNEY

'I know to assert, 'I can only love those who are like me,' reflects a blighted soul.'[1]

'[F]rom Jerusalem to Mumbai those who pray to different gods find it difficult to live in the same place.'[2]

I. Introduction

In 2012, the Equality and Human Rights Commission observed that 'The overwhelming majority of people in Britain do not experience discrimination because of their religion or beliefs.'[3] Given the contemporary legislation that relates to religious belief and practice in the United Kingdom, this statement might seem unsurprising. One of the rights that the Human Rights Act 1998 is intended to protect is the right to 'freedom of thought, conscience and religion'.[4] Religion is also a 'protected characteristic' under the Equality Act 2010.[5] Religious belief has received at best spasmodic and intermittent legal protection for most of British history.[6] However, following the enactment of these two provisions, the converse currently seems to be the case. The right of those who are religious to be different in Great Britain, now a secular society, is, it appears, established in law and, according

[1] G Steiner with L Adler, *A Long Saturday* (London, University of Chicago Press, 2017) 16.

[2] R Sennett, *Building and Dwelling: Ethics for the City* (London, Allen Lane, 2018) 3.

[3] Equality and Human Rights Commission, *Human Rights Review 2012: How Fair is Britain? An Assessment of how well Public Authorities Protect Human Rights* (London, Equality and Human Rights Review, 2012) 319.

[4] Human Rights Act 1998 (UK), sch 1, para 1.

[5] Equality Act 2010 (UK), s 10.

[6] On this spasmodic protection, see further A Bradney, *Religions, Rights and Laws* (Leicester, Leicester University Press, 1993) 5–7.

to the Equality and Human Rights Commission, in fact.[7] In turn, it might then be argued that this protection afforded to those who are religious exemplifies a new wider tolerance in British society, whereby differences such as those of sex, race or sexual orientation, themselves also protected characteristics under the Equality Act 2010, are no longer seen as being of consequence for a person's place in society. British society, which once imagined itself as being homogeneous, now accepts and even valorises variation amongst its members.[8]

It is undoubtedly the case that there have been major improvements to the legal position of various previously marginalised groups in British society in recent decades. To take one obvious example, male homosexuality was criminalised until the Sexual Offences Act of 1967. In 2016, Sir Terence Etherton, who is openly gay, became Master of the Rolls, the second most important judge in the British legal system.[9] The Marriage (Same Sex Couples) Act 2013 now facilitates both gay and lesbian marriages in England and Wales, whilst the Marriage and Civil Partnership (Scotland) Act 2014 does the same thing in Scotland. The change to the way that the law treats gay men could hardly be greater. Equally, more specifically for the focus of this chapter, some religious believers are clearly now afforded much better legal treatment than they once were. Thus, for example, in 1973 in *Buckley v Buckley*,[10] a mother who was a Jehovah's Witness was denied custody of her children by a court specifically because she was a Jehovah's Witness, who would

[7] On Great Britain as a secular society, see further A Bradney, *Law and Faith in a Sceptical Age* (Abingdon, Routledge, 2009) 3–9 and references therein; and A Bradney, 'The United Kingdom, The Prevalence of Secularism' in J Nelis, C Sägesser and J Schreiber (eds), *Religion and Secularisms in the European Union: State of Affairs and Current Debates* (Brussels, Peter Lang, 2017) 187. In the main, the arguments in this chapter pertain to Great Britain and not to the United Kingdom taken as a whole. The place of religion in Northern Ireland has long been said to be different from the place of religion in other parts of the United Kingdom (see, for example, G Davie, *Religion in Britain Since 1994* (Oxford, Basil Blackwell, 1994) 14). It might be true to say that the place of religion in Northern Ireland society is beginning to change (C Mitchell, 'Is Northern Ireland Abnormal? An Extension of the Sociological Debate on Religion in Northern Ireland' (2004) 38 *Sociology* 237). However, the significance of religion in Northern Ireland society is still much greater than elsewhere in the United Kingdom (C Mitchell, *Religion, Identity and Politics in Northern Ireland: Boundaries of Belonging and Belief* (Aldershot, Ashgate, 2006)). At the time of the 2011 census, 82.7% of people in Northern Ireland claimed a religious identity (see at https://www.statista.com/statistics/384634/religion-of-northern-ireland-residents-census-uk/). In England and Wales, 25% of the population said that they had no religion (see at https://www.ons.gov.uk/peoplepopulationandcommunity/culturalidentity/religion/articles/fullstorywhatdoesthecensustellusaboutreligionin2011/2013-05-16), whilst in Scotland 37% of the population in 2011 said that they had no religion (see at https://www2.gov.scot/Topics/People/Equality/Equalities/DataGrid/Religion/RelPopMig).

[8] Anderson argues that all nations are 'imagined communities' (B Anderson, *Imagined Communities* (London, Verso, 2006) 6. On the idea of Great Britain as a homogeneous society, see, for example, L Tabili 'A homogeneous society? British internal "others", 1800–present' in C Hall and S Rose (eds), *At Home with the Empire: Metropolitan Culture and the Imperial World* (Cambridge, Cambridge University Press, 2006) 53. There is a voluminous literature on the myth of 'Britishness', which includes a myth of homogeneity. My argument is not that Great Britain was ever homogeneous but that it once imagined that it was.

[9] *The Guardian* (26 May 2016) at https://www.theguardian.com/law/2016/may/26/britain-first-openly-gay-judge-master-of-the-rolls-terence-etherton.

[10] *Buckley v Buckley* (1973) 3 Fam Law 106.

therefore bring her children up to live separately from those around them; 'the children … would be different from the children around them' and being different was, in itself, wrong.[11] It is now no longer the case that being a Jehovah's Witness will necessarily prevent a person from succeeding in a custody battle for his or her children. In *Re T (Minors) (Custody: Religious Upbringing)*, Scarman LJ, as he then was, opined that 'it is [not] wrong … that life [for Jehovah's Witnesses] should be in a narrower sphere'.[12] Nevertheless, despite genuine improvements in the way that the law treats the religious, this chapter will argue that being religious in modern-day Britain and attempting to live a religious life can cause great difficulties for believers. Further, the law sometimes compounds these difficulties. Some religious lives take believers unequivocally outside mainstream British mores, and when this happens the law will not necessarily side with the religious, putting in doubt whether this particular legal right to be different really exists.[13] If this is so, this, in turn, notwithstanding advances in the treatment of minority groups, raises questions about how much Great Britain now facilitates or even permits genuine deviance from its norms.

The arguments in this chapter seek to show that the right to be different for religious believers continues to be severely restricted in Great Britain. At one level the existence of restrictions on difference is unsurprising. Some forms of difference are plainly unacceptable. Seeking to enslave others, for example, or to physically harm them without their consent in pursuit of a different way of life, clearly could not be condoned in a democratic, liberal society where the rule of law prevails. Nevertheless, actual limitations on difference that are found in the law are more debateable. Pursuing sadomasochistic practices will, even when they are consensual, give rise to criminal liability in Great Britain.[14] This particular restriction on how one should live one's life raises problems similar to those analysed in this chapter because of its impact on those who are, on one view, merely 'differently pleasured' from the majority, wishing to purse their minority beliefs and practices with like-minded fellows.[15] The problem with justifying this restriction is

[11] ibid 107. On Jehovah's Witnesses and their way of life, see J Beckford, *The Trumpet of Prophecy: A Sociological Study of Jehovah's Witnesses* (Oxford, Basil Blackwell, 1975).

[12] *Re T (Minors) (Custody: Religious Upbringing)* (1981) 2 FLR 239, 245.

[13] The notion of the right to be different has been put forward in many different contexts: see, eg, J Reedman, 'Secularism as a Barrier to Integration? The French Dilemma' (2004) 42 *International Migration* 5, discussing the French Government attitudes towards school girls who wear Islamic headscarves; and K Nash, 'Human Rights Culture: Solidarity, Diversity and the Right to be Different' (2005) 9 *Citizenship Studies* 335, discussing media and activist representations of lesbian, gay, bisexual and transgender people. For a general analysis of the right to be different as a human right, see F Hassan, 'The Right to be Different: An Exploratory Proposal for the Creation of a New Human Right' (1982) 5 *Loyola of Los Angeles International and Comparative Law Review* 62.

[14] *R v Brown* [1994] 1 AC 212.

[15] L Bibbings and P Alldridge 'Sexual Expression, Body Alteration and the Defence of Consent' (1993) 20 *Journal of Law and Society* 356, 356. The reasoning in the decision has been the subject of much criticism. In addition to Bibbings and Alldridge, see, eg, M Weait, 'Fleshing it Out' in L Bently and L Flynn (eds), *Law and the Senses: Sensational Jurisprudence* (London, Pluto Press, 1996); and C Stychin, *Law's Desire: Sexuality and the limits of justice* (London, Routledge, 1995) ch 7. It has also

exacerbated by the fact that boxing, by contrast, even though violent, is an acceptable and even a vaunted activity within British society.[16] Exploring the appropriate legal and ethical limitations to permissible differences in life choices involves complex and difficult arguments. Religious believers are not alone in finding their right to be different put into question. Nevertheless, this chapter will argue that it is significant that some ways of life preferred by many thousands of people in Great Britain, ways of life chosen because of religious beliefs, are either unacceptable under, or at least not facilitated by, British law.

The precise number of religious believers who are affected by this treatment in British law cannot be stated with any degree of precision. People within a variety of religious traditions are involved. In all of these traditions there are variations in beliefs and practice. Even if subsets within these traditions are examined, variance is still the pattern. Thus, for example, the ultra-orthodox haredi Jews in Great Britain, who will be referred to in section II, do not have just one set of beliefs and practices.[17] Moreover, beliefs and practices change over time. Thus, to be sure how many people in how many communities are put at disadvantage at any one time is impossible to determine. The fact, however, that it is not just individuals but communities that are affected, whatever their precise size, is of particular significance for this chapter.[18]

If the state denies the legitimacy of a way of life lived by communities within its borders, it excludes those communities from the polity. This has consequences not only for the excluded communities, but also for the state that does the excluding. In his *Letter on Toleration*, Locke wrote that

> [i]t is not the diversity of opinions (which cannot be avoided), but the refusal of toleration to those that are of different opinions (which might have been granted), that has produced all the bustles and wars that have been in the Christian world upon account of religion.[19]

The violence and wars that have resulted from conflict between religious communities are now largely a matter of history within most European states, but that does not make them any less real. It does not need war or even violence for conflict with a religious community to become a problem for a state. The need to acknowledge and accommodate the needs of religious communities is a matter of political expediency, as well as an ethical imperative. Writers from Laski to Shachar have

been argued that the House of Lords misunderstood the nature of the practices that they criminalised: see C White, 'The Spanner Trials and the Changing Law on Sadomasochism in the UK' (2006) 50 *Journal of Homosexuality* 167.

[16] On the law relating to boxing, see J Anderson, *The Legality of Boxing* (London, Birkbeck Law Press, 2007). For an account of boxing that is in part laudatory, see N Mailer, *The Fight* (London, Penguin Books, 1991).

[17] S Baumel, *Sacred Speakers: Language and Culture among the Haredim in Israel* (New York, Berghahn Books, 2006) 166–78.

[18] Individuals should be protected even if their situation is unique to them. The reasons for this are, however, different from those arguments that are developed here.

[19] J Locke, *A Letter Concerning Toleration* (The Hague, Martinus Nijhoff, 1963) 105.

queried how far and in what way the state is justified in exercising jurisdiction over those individuals and communities that are within it.[20] For some, perhaps most, religious communities, the rightful limitation to the state's authority over them is a matter of pressing concern. Moreover, it is their answer to that question that is of primary interest for them, not the state's answer. As this chapter will seek to show, if the state's authority comes into conflict with the authority that a religious community exercises over itself, it is not necessarily that state's authority that will prevail. As Laski noted,

> [a] society like the Presbyterian Church, which recognises only the leadership of Christ, will resist to the uttermost any external attempt at the definition of its life; and experience seems to suggest that the state will lose far more than it can gain by the effort.[21]

Resisting, indeed not even acknowledging state authority, is, it might be argued, the default position for religious communities, whether Christian or not.

II. 'Preparing Students for Life in Modern Britain'

Education is a good place to focus on, in an examination of whether it is possible to live a genuinely different religious life in modern Britain. Education is of special significance both for the religious and for the state. Religious communities in general and religious parents in particular will want to educate their children in the ways of their faith. The state, on the other hand, has an interest in how children who live in the state are socialised. Children can be 'understood as mini-citizens, citizens-in-training, or the future of a particular religious or cultural "sub-community"'.[22] These two sets of understandings can come into conflict.[23] When this happens, the question is which of these understandings is to prevail.

In her 2016/17 Annual Report, Amanda Spielman, Her Majesty's Chief Inspector at Ofsted, the state body charged with regulating schools, observed that 'there are schools spreading beliefs that are widely shared within the community that the school serves but that clash with British values or equalities law'.[24]

[20] H Laski, *Studies in the Problem of Sovereignty* (New Haven, CT, Yale University Press, 1917); H Laski, *Authority in the Modern State* (New Haven, CT, Yale University Press, 1919); and A Shachar, *Multicultural Jurisdictions: Cultural Differences and Women's Rights* (Cambridge, Cambridge University Press, 2001).

[21] Laski, *Authority in the Modern State* (n 20) 56.

[22] S van Praagh 'The Education of Religious Children: Families, Communities and Constitutions' (1999) 47 *Buffalo Law Review* 1343 T P 1345.

[23] Both understandings can be seen to ignore children themselves as a focus of concern and analysis. For an article that seeks to correct this, see B Miller-Melemore, 'Whither the Children? Childhood in Religious Education' (2006) 86 *The Journal of Religion* 635.

[24] *The Annual Report of Her Majesty's Chief Inspector of Education, Children's Services and Skills 2016/17* (London, Ofsted, HC 618) 15. These remarks are an established point of view on the part of Spielman. See also her speech to the Church of England Foundation for Educational Leadership at https://www.gov.uk/government/speeches/amanda-spielmans-speech-at-the-church-of-england-foundation-for-education-leadership. In her second annual report, Spielman was critical of schools

Such schools, she said, 'seek to isolate young people from the mainstream, do not prepare them for life in Britain or, worse, actively undermine fundamental British values'. Spielman included Christian, Jewish and Muslim schools in her remarks, which reflect longstanding and widespread attitudes amongst regulatory bodies to some faith schools.[25] As long ago as 1983, the Talmud Torah Machzikei Hadass school, an ultra-orthodox Jewish school, was served with a notice of complaint, the beginning of the process of deregistration so that the school would not be legally allowed to offer a full-time education.[26] Since then, there have been highly critical reports on a number of faith schools that serve a range of religious communities.[27]

In a secular society such as Great Britain, it is not surprising to find faith schools:

> Strongly religious parents will inevitably chafe at an educational environment that, in its quite proper adherence to secular standards of reasoning, implicitly or explicitly denies the transcendental truths around which these parents believe life ought to be organized.[28]

Faith schools, defined as in the contemporary sense in Great Britain, have a long history. Cohen writes that the first Jewish Talmud Torah school was established

run by 'fundamentalist religious beliefs' whose pupils, she asserted, could be 'at risk of radicalisation' (*The Annual Report of Her Majesty's Chief Inspector of Education, Children's Services and Skills 2017/18* (London, Ofsted, HC 1701, 20). She was also critical of 'faith settings such as yeshivas and madrasas, providing religious instruction for five and sometimes six days a week', saying that '[t]hese settings have a significant and negative impact on the children who attend them, who do not have the opportunities other children have to develop academically, personally and socially so that they are ready and able to take their place in British society' (ibid 21). Spielman has also expressed strong views on Muslim dress for pupils in schools (see, eg, S Weale, 'Ofsted chief accuses minority groups of "entitlement" in hijab row' *The Guardian* (9 July 2018)).

[25] On the history of such criticisms, see N Meer, 'Muslim Schools in Britain' (2007) 27 *Asia Pacific Journal of Education* 55. Spielman's position, speaking in an official capacity, is not unique to her. Meer notes that in 2005 David Bell, then Chief Inspector of Schools and head of the Office for Standards in Education, had written that Muslim schools did 'not fit pupils for their lives as Muslims in modern Britain' (ibid 55). More recently, Sir Michael Wilshaw, formerly Chief Inspector at Ofsted, has been reported as saying that lessons on LGBT rights that had been suspended at some primary schools after objections by mainly Muslim parents, should be reinstated because parents should understand that they lived in a 'liberal society': *The Guardian* (25 March 2019). Whilst Chief Inspector of Ofsted, Wilshaw had observed in an Advice Note to the Secrterary of State for Education that four schools, previously inspected the Bridge Schools Inspectorate, when re-inspected by Ofsted were not promoting 'the fundamental British values of democracy, the rule of law, individual liberty and mutual respect, and tolerance of those with different faiths and beliefs' (Advice Note to Secretary of State for Education, 24 November 2015, at https://assets.publishing.service.gov.uk/government/uploads/system/uploads/attachment_data/file/479122/HMCI__advice_note_BSI.pdf).

[26] The notice was subsequently withdrawn following an action for judicial review, *R v Secretary of State for Education and Science, ex parte Talmud Torah Machzikei Haddass School* [1985] *The Times*, 12 April. A full report of this judgment is only available on the LEXIS database. (On this judgment and the subsequent legal action, see further A Bradney, 'Separate Schools, Ethnic Minorities and the Law' in *New Community* XIII (1987) 412). Reports can be found at https://reports.ofsted.gov.uk/. On the process of producing Ofsted reports, see N Roberts and L Abreu, *School Inspections in England: Ofsted* (2019) London, House of Commons Briefing Paper 07091.

[27] See, eg, Ofsted, *Al-Mizan School* (2014) and Ofsted, *Grindon Hall Christian School* (2014).

[28] S Burtt, 'Religious Parents, Secular Schools: A Defense of an Illiberal Education' (1994) 56 *The Review of Politics* 51, 64. See further E McCreery, L Jones and R Holmes, 'Why do Muslim parents want Muslim Schools?' (2002) 27 *Early Years* 203.

in 1770.[29] Indeed education in Great Britain at primary and secondary level grew out of what might, in a broader sense, be termed faith schools, both the Church of England and the Roman Catholic Church having played a significant part in establishing early schools.[30] Contemporary faith schools do not constitute a uniform group, partly because what makes something a 'faith school' is a matter for debate: 'in law there is no such thing as a "faith school"'.[31] In contemporary times, references to faith schools are generally references to schools whose religious ethos dominates what they do, and where that ethos is seen as being outside of mainstream mores.[32] What they seek to do for their pupils, what they teach and what their relationship is with their parent faith community are different in different schools.

Censure of faith schools in reports on them has ranged over a variety of matters.[33] However, the criticism that is both central to such reports and most germane to this chapter is the suggestion, repeated by Spielman, that some faith schools do not 'prepare students for life in modern Britain'.[34] Whilst individual reports on schools rarely elaborate on what this means, the Ofsted *School Inspection Handbook* does contain more detail about what currently is expected of schools.[35] Schools are, for example, required both to teach their pupils knowledge about and inculcate into them values that relate to British life. Pupils must be able

[29] I Cohen, *Contemporary Jewry: A Survey of Social, Cultural, Economic and Political Conditions* (London, Methuen, 1950) 53.

[30] 'Historically, faith schools have been at the centre of the English Educational system': G Walford, 'Faith-based schools in England after ten years of Tony Blair' in R Gardner, J Cairns and D Lawton (eds), *Faith Schools: Consensus or Conflict?* (Abingdon, Routledge Falmer, 2005) 69. See further B Gates, 'Faith schools and colleges of education since 1800' in Gardner, Cairns and Lawton (eds), ibid 14–35; and J Murphy, *Church, State and Schools in Britain, 1800–1970* (London, Routledge & Kegan Paul, 1971).

[31] R Barker and J Anderson, 'Segregation or Cohesion: Church of England Schools in Bradford' in Gardner, Cairns and Lawton (eds) (n 30) 122.

[32] Church of England schools are commonly regarded as being, and perhaps as paradigmatically being, faith schools (see, eg, S McKinney, 'The faith-based schools debate: challenging assumptions and stereotypes' (2006) 35 *Journal of Moral Education* 105, 106), but this definition would arguably exclude such schools since they are usually 'faith inclusive' (C King, 'Faith Schools in Pluralistic Britain: Debate, Discussion and Considerations' (2010) 25 *Journal of Contemporary Religion* 281, 287; and McCreery, Jones and Holmes (n 28) 204). The imprecision inherent in the term can be seen when one considers whether a contemporary state-sponsored Quaker school whose antecedents are clearly rooted in the Quaker faith, a faith group that 'derive[s] much of our identity from our tradition' (J Punshon, 'The End of (Quaker) History? Some Reflections on the Process' in P Dandelion (ed), *The Creation of Quaker Theology* (Abingdon, Ashgate, 2004) 37), but whose present practices have only some connections with that faith, is in fact a faith school. (On such a school, see H Johnson, 'Living Your Values: Exploring the "Hidden" Culture of a Voluntary-Controlled Quaker School' (2001) 22 *Journal of Beliefs and Values* 197.)

[33] This has been true since the first critical reports. Concerns about the qualifications of teachers in the schools and the physical conditions of buildings have, for example, been expressed (Bradney (n 26) 414–15, 418).

[34] Ofsted, *Ebrahim Academy* (2014) 1.

[35] The current Ofsted *Handbook* was drafted following a change in government policy (J Arthurs, 'Extremism and Neo-Liberal Educational Policy: A Contextual Critique of the Trojan Horse Affair in Birmingham Schools' (2015) 63 *British Journal of Educational Policies* 311, 323).

to 'participate fully in and contribute positively to life in modern Britain'. Equally, they must, amongst other things, be able to 'recognise legal boundaries and, in so doing, respect the civil and criminal law of England'.[36] The tone of the *Handbook* implies that the matters referred to are uncontentious as educational objectives. The resultant adverse reports on some faith schools make it clear that this is not the case.

One report on a Muslim school commented that '[w]hen discussing Sharia law and English law, they [the pupils] were unable to tell inspectors which laws they should follow, and which were more important'.[37] From the perspective of the Ofsted *Handbook*, this indicates a clear failing on the part of the school. Nevertheless, the pupils' confusion is in fact understandable. A number of commentators have written about the ways in which Muslim communities in England and Wales navigate the complexities of their relationship with Islamic law and British state law.[38] Ofsted may think that it is clear that state law should always have priority over Islamic law, but some – probably many – Muslims will disagree.[39] Nor are Muslims the only religious group in the United Kingdom that is faced with this problem or who take this position. Thus, for example, the Religious Society of Friends text 'Quaker Faith & Practice' advises Quakers to '[r]espect the laws of the state but let your first loyalty be to God's purposes'.[40] For many believers in many faiths, the relationship between the dictates of their religion and their relationship with the state in which they live is a fraught matter.[41] Indeed, if an

[36] Ofsted, *School Inspection Handbook* (London, Ofsted, 2017) 39–41. On teaching 'British values', see also *Training from the Citizenship Foundation* at http://www.doingsmsc.org.uk/training/. It has been argued that the Ofsted policy is illegal, since it is incompatible with the ruling in *R v Secretary of State for Education and Science, ex parte Talmud Torah Machzikei Haddass School*, noted at n 26, where it was held that a school curriculum would be lawful 'if it primarily equips a child for life within the community of which he is a member, rather than the way of the country as a whole, as long as it does not foreclose the child's options in later years to adopt some other forms of life if he wishes to do so' (U Siddiqui, *Losing Faith in Ofsted: Importing Narrow Values into Faith Schools* (London, Claystone, 2018) 14–15). See also A Struthers, 'Teaching British Values in our Schools: But Why not Human Rights Values?' (2017) 26 *Social & Legal Studies* 89.

[37] Ofsted, *Mazahirul Uloom School* (2014) 1.

[38] See, eg, D Pearl and W Menski, *Muslim Family Law* (London, Sweet & Maxwell, 1998) 56–68; and I Yilmaz, *Muslim Laws, Politics and Society in Modern Nation States* (Aldershot, Ashgate, 2005) 59–66.

[39] For a survey of different Islamic approaches to this topic, see K Abou El Fadl 'Legal Debates on Muslim Minorities: Between Rejection and Accommodation' (1994) 22 *Journal of Religious Ethics* 127, 146–51. For a detailed individual analysis of the problem, see A Ahmed An-Naim, 'The Compatability Dialectic: Mediating the Legitimate Coexistence of Islamic Law and State Law' (2000) 73 *Modern Law Review* 1.

[40] The Yearly Meeting of the Religious Society of Friends, *Quaker Faith & Practice* (London, 1995) 1.02 35. An actual willingness to disobey state law has been integral to Quaker actions over the centuries. See, eg, R Byrd, *Quaker Ways in Foreign Policy* (Toronto, University of Toronto Press, 1960) 36; and H Freeman, 'Moral Preemption Part I: The Case for the Disobedient' (1966) 17 *Hastings Law Journal* 435, 437. This reflects a wider understanding of the relationship between the citizen and the state. See, eg, J Calvert, 'The Quaker Theory of a Civil Constitution' (2006) 27 *History of Political Thought* 586.

[41] Nor is this problem one that is restricted to religious believers. Laski observed that '[w]hatever the requirements of legal theory, in actual fact no man surrenders his whole being to the state. He has a sense of right and wrong. If the state, or its instruments, goes too consistently against that sense, he is

individual's religion is not an established church, where politics and theology may be conjoined, this will almost necessarily be the case.[42] 'Faith-based schools are challenged to reconcile the laws and practices accepted by society with those set out by their respective faith traditions.'[43] However, notwithstanding what Ofsted appears to believe, it is not obvious to all of those responsible for faith schools or the communities for which they work that such reconciliation should involve changes to their practices.[44] In the context of these debates, it would be more worrying to find pupils who were wholly convinced that state law ought always to have priority over religious beliefs or ethical values, thus ignoring centuries of philosophical and theological argument, than to find them regarding the relationship as being potentially problematic.

The relationship between state law and religious belief raises particular problems, but underlying it is a more fundamental question about the place of faith schools and Ofsted's view of their role. What precisely does it mean to say, in Ofsted's words quoted above, that schools should teach their pupils to 'participate fully in … life in modern Britain'? Pupils from faith schools will grow up to live an adult life in Britain; in one sense they thus have no choice but to live a 'life in modern Britain' however they are educated.[45] None the less, Ofsted seems to set clear parameters to how those pupils should live that life. The key to Ofsted's view may lie in the phrase 'participate fully' in modern Britain. One inspection report on a haredi school observed that

> [t]he secular curriculum (*Chol*) is inadequate. Limited time is allocated to the teaching of literacy and numeracy in English and without a clear curriculum map and schemes of work to guide teachers, pupils make inadequate progress. Other subjects such as science, physical education (PE), design technology, art and music are not taught, thus the curriculum does not provide appropriate experiences for pupils in the scientific, technological, physical, and aesthetic and creative areas of learning.[46]

Elsewhere, the report said that

> [t]he Kodesh [religious studies] curriculum is good. It is varied and exciting and ensures that pupils gain the necessary skills upon which to build as they progress in

pricked into antagonism. The state, that is to say, is for him sovereign only where his conscience is not stirred against its performance' (Laski, *Authority in the Modern State* (n 20) 42–43).

[42] In this context, establishment is not a necessarily a binary matter. The degree to which the Church of England, for example, is established in England is clearly waning. See further Bradney, *Law and Faith in a Sceptical Age* (n 7) ch 3.

[43] King (n 32) 284.

[44] Nor is this position confined to religious believers. Civil disobedience when fundamental mores and the views of the state clash is a longstanding political tradition within many political cultures.

[45] An exception to this will be when state requirements about the education that faith schools can provide mean that parents move their children to other jurisdictions. Proposed Ofsted guidance on what pupils will have to be taught about same-sex relationships has led some Haredi parents to state that they would move their children abroad rather than allow them to be schooled in such a way (*The Guardian* (20 January 2018)).

[46] TTMH Belz Day School, *Inspection Report* (2007) 2.

> their Jewish religious education and future lives as observant Jews within the Belz's [haredi] community.[47]

Later the report commented that

> [t]he best teaching was seen in the Kodesh lessons where it is good overall. The relationship between staff and pupils is excellent. Pupils' response to the teachers' high expectations is outstanding particularly with regard to middos (good character traits including behaviour and respect). They display remarkable respect towards their teachers and visitors and they stand up immediately when an adult enters their classroom. Most teachers are extremely secure in their subject knowledge and are very successful in imbuing pupils with a love of Torah and mitzvos (commandments).
>
> All teachers, including the non-Jewish staff, demonstrate their full understanding of, and respect for, the orthodox ethos of the school and they are excellent role models to the pupils.[48]

The essence of this criticism is that pupils are taught to live in the haredi world but are not taught about things that will allow them to live in the non-haredi world. Neither teachers nor pupils in the school put the same value on secular studies as they do on religious studies. The report observed that, in secular studies, the teachers 'lack good subject knowledge'.[49] Nonetheless the pupils 'said they loved the learning [of religious studies] and the inspector believed them'.[50] Perhaps because of this, the '[s]piritual development [of the pupils] is outstanding'.[51]

Haredi schools vary, and the degree to which the curricula in them are focussed solely on the haredi world also varies. Valins, Kosmin and Goldberg note that some haredi schools achieve 'some of the best academic results [in state tests] of all Jewish day schools'.[52] Nevertheless, as a generalisation, it is true to say that 'strictly Orthodox [haredi] children attend Jewish schools especially designed to meet the religious needs of this community'.[53] Teaching pupils little if anything about the non-haredi world is a matter of deliberate policy. For the haredim the world outside their community is 'in a process of moral decay'.[54] 'There is a sense among haredim of their living an alternative world from the one shared by those who do not live by the same rules and proscriptions.'[55] '[M]ost people born into this [haredi] community remain within it throughout their lifetime'.[56]

[47] ibid 1.
[48] ibid 2.
[49] ibid.
[50] ibid 3.
[51] ibid.
[52] O Valins, B Kosmin and J Goldberg, *The Future of Jewish Schooling in the United Kingdom* (London, Institute for Jewish Policy Research, 2002) 103.
[53] L Daniel Staetsky and J Boyd, *The rise and rise of Jewish schools in the United Kingdom* (London, Institute for Jewish Policy Research, 2016) 25.
[54] S Heilman, *Defenders of the Faith: Inside Ultra-Orthodox Jewry* (Berkeley, CA University of California Press, 1992) 170.
[55] H Rabinowicz, *A World Apart: The Story of the Chasidim in Britain* (London, Valentine Mitchell, 1997) 214.
[56] Daniel Streatsky and Boyd (n 53).

Secular studies aimed at the outside world are, for the haredim, thus both an irrelevance and also a possible distraction from the pursuit of an appropriate way of life.[57] For the haredim, to participate fully in life in modern Britain would, literally, be anathema.

Haredi schools are not unique in educating their pupils in a way that will allow them to live their lives within their religious communities. The concept of teaching pupils to live a life that is spent more in a Muslim community than it is in the wider world is also to be found in some Muslim schools. As with Jewish schools, it is not difficult to find Muslim schools that have received the very highest ratings by Ofsted.[58] However, Muslim parents do not necessarily choose Muslim schools because their teaching and curricula are things that would appeal to Ofsted: '[W]hat is seen as a good Islamic education does not necessarily coincide with what is considered to be a good Western liberal education.'[59] Promoting Islamic values may, for example, be a priority for Muslim schools and for parents who send their children to such schools.[60] Teaching a child to live within a religious community is not always seen as being consistent with teaching the child to live in the wider world, and it is the former that is more important for parents, children and schools.

Living a life withdrawn from modern Britain and to some extent separate from it is not unique to Jewish and Muslim communities in this century. It could instead be regarded as a not infrequent feature of religious lives. Those who are religious sometimes prefer to step outside of mainstream society in order to better pursue their religious lives. Orders of monks and nuns, some enclosed or cloistered and some not, have long been a part of Christian churches.[61] Within the Hindu religion there are both sadhus, traditionally wandering ascetics, and monks.[62]

[57] J Lupu, *New Directions in Haredi Society: Vocational Training and Academic Studies* (Jerusalem, The Floersheimer Institute for Policy Studies, 2005) 19–20. For a more detailed development of these points, see A Bradney, 'The Inspection of Ultra-Orthodox Jewish Schools: "The Audit Society" and "The Society of Scholars"' (2009) 21 *Child and Family Law Quarterly* 133, 136–43.

[58] See, eg, Ofsted, Preston Muslim Girls High School (2016). See similarly Ofsted, *Tauheedul Islam Girls' High School and Sixth Form College* (2014).

[59] McCreery, Jones and Holmes (n 28) 211.

[60] See further Meer (n 25) 59; and McCreery, Jones and Holmes (n 28) 209–213.

[61] The phenomenon has received comparatively little attention in sociology (H Goddijn, 'The Sociology of religious orders and congregations' (1960) 7 *Social Compass* 431). It is relevant to the themes in this chapter that historically the phenomenon has sometimes been the subject of hostile comment (see, eg, R Kollar, *A Foreign and Wicked Institution? The Campaign Against Convents in Victorian England* (Eugene, OR, Pickwick Publications, 2011).

[62] The distinction between the two is not always clear. Van der Veer writes of 'the taming of the wild, free-moving ascetic and the success of the temple-dwelling, law-abiding devotee' (P van der Veer, 'Taming Ascetic: Devotionalism in a Hindu Monastic Order' (1987) 22 *Man, New Series* 680, 683). Both have figured in legal actions in Great Britain. For the former, see *Chauhan v Ford Motor Company*, an Employment Appeal Tribunal case, judgment in which is to be found only on the LEXIS database. (For a discussion of this judgment, see A Bradney, 'Faced by Faith' in P Oliver, S Douglas-Scott and V Tadros (eds), *Faith in Law* (Oxford, Hart Publishing, 2000) 92–94). On the legal problems of a Hindu monastery, see M Warries, 'The Temple Bull Controversy at Skanda Vale and the Constraints of Hindu Identity in Great Britain' (2010) 13 *International Journal of Hindu Studies* 261.

Buddhism has similar figures.[63] Moreover, it is not only the religious who have been attracted to the benefits of a life lived withdrawn from the wider community. Thus, for example, Thoreau famously wrote about his life on Walden Pond once he was 'a sojourner in civilized life again'.[64] Nothing in his book, however, suggests that he preferred his 'civilized life' to Walden; instead the contrary seems to have been the case.[65] It is not difficult to find others, religious and secular, who are also sceptical about the virtues of fully living life in modern Britain.

Writing about Christian faith schools, Pike has argued that 'Christians do not want to be treated as if they are the same as everyone else; they want the freedom to be different'.[66] Pike's observation is equally applicable to a number of Muslim and Jewish schools. However, various official regulatory regimes over the past decades have sought to deny, or at the very least restrict, that right to be different with respect to education.[67] In doing so, this has put in question how far religious freedom is acknowledged within Great Britain where religious communities and schools question mainstream mores within British society.

III. The Impact of Adverse Reports on Faith Schools

The fact that religious freedom is not facilitated by legal regimes does not mean that religious freedom does not exist. Official reports on faith schools, even when adverse, may have little impact on those schools. The history of the Talmud Torah Machzikei Hadddas School illustrates this phenomenon. After the 1985 decision in *R v Secretary of State for Education and Science, ex parte Talmud Torah Machzikei Haddass School*, the school has subsequently been inspected on a number of occasions, receiving various ratings. Its latest inspection reported it as 'Inadequate'.[68] In this report, whilst the school's teaching of Judaism and Hebrew was said to be a strength, the school was not thought to 'adequately prepare pupils for their future lives in modern Britain'. Somewhat surprisingly, given that 'leaders' of the school said that the pupils unanimously said that they wanted to continue their religious

[63] See, eg, S Butt, *Buddhist Monks and Monasteries of India: Their History and Their Contribution to Indian Culture* (London, George Allen & Unwin, 1962).

[64] H Thoreau, *Walden; or Life in the Woods* (New York, Rinehart & Co, 1948) 1.

[65] On Thoreau's time at Walden Pond, see L Dassow Walls, *Henry David Thoreau: A Life* (Chicago, IL, University of Chicago Press, 2017) ch 5.

[66] M Pike, 'Citizenship Education and Faith Schools: What should children in Christian schools understand about a liberal and secular society?' (2005) 9 *Journal of Education and Christian Belief* 35, 42.

[67] In seeking to educate their children in their own values, these communities are not seeking to impose those values on others. On an attempt to do this by creating sharia-compliant areas, see Z Pieri, 'Identifying Counter Radical Narratives from Within British Muslim Communities: The Case of "Muslim Patrol" and Muslim Community Schools' (2018) 38 *Journal of Muslim Minority Affairs* 39.

[68] Ofsted, *Talmud Torah Machzikei Hadass School* (2018). In 2007 the school was also rated as 'Inadequate', whilst in 2010 it was rated as 'Satisfactory' and in 2014 as 'Good': see at https://reports.ofsted.gov.uk/provider/27/100294.

studies in Israel, the school report felt that the pupils were 'poorly prepared for the next stage of their education'.[69] The report concluded by noting that 'leaders and governors declined the opportunity to receive feedback about the inspection judgements and refused to engage further with inspectors'.[70] This lack of interest by the school in the reporting process may be explained in part by the previous 2007 report that had also judged the school to be 'Inadequate'. In that report it had been noted that 'Parents and pupils are overwhelmingly positive about the school. Pupils are well prepared for life within their community'.[71] In 2007, the school had 283 pupils, whilst in 2018 it had 649 pupils.[72] What leads parents to send their children to faith schools may have nothing to do with Ofsted reports. Thus, for example, the 2018 report commented on what it saw as the poor standard of English amongst pupils, but also noted that the school had said that no parent had requested that their child be taught English in those years when it was optional in the curriculum.[73] Similarly, whilst the report considered that pupils' lack of exposure to the use of computers disadvantaged them in relation to future employment and education, it also noted that the school reported that it was acting on the wishes of parents in this matter.[74] Critical reports may seem, in this context, to be an irrelevance to both schools and the communities they serve. The fact that the reporting process itself has recently been described as being 'arbitrary and ad hoc' may further diminish the impact that the reports have.[75]

IV. The Law and Religious Difference in Great Britain

There is a long history of legal accommodation to religious difference in Great Britain. Lord Hardwicke's Act of 1753, which made it compulsory for marriage in England to be a public ceremony in a church of the Church of England but exempted Jews and Quakers from this requirement, is an early illustration of this phenomenon. However, there is also a long history of the state's seeking to restrict religious difference and failing in that attempt. Thus, for example, prosecuting and

[69] Ofsted, *Talmud Torah Machzikei Hadass School* (2018) 1, 3, 5 and 6.

[70] ibid 10.

[71] Ofsted, *TTMH Belz Day School* (2007) 1.

[72] ibid 7; Ofsted *Talmud Torah Machzikei Hadass School* (2018) 8. On the general reaction of Muslim communities to regulation and inspection of Islamic schools, see I Mogra, 'Religious Education at the Crossroads in the United Kingdom: Muslims Perspectives to Registration and Inspection' (2018) 38 *Journal of Muslim Minority Affairs* 198.

[73] Ofsted, *Talmud Torah Machzikei Hadass School* (2018) 3.

[74] ibid 5.

[75] Arthurs (n 35) 323. See similarly I Mogra, 'The "Trojan Horse" affair and radicalisation: an analysis of Ofsted reports' (2016) 60 *Educational Review* 444, 460. For an argument that there are inconsistencies in Ofsted reports on the teaching of spirituality in state secondary schools in Norfolk, see J Watson, 'OFSTED's Spiritual Dimension: and analytical audit of inspection reports' (2001) 31 *Cambridge Journal of Education* 205. For a more radical critique of the Ofsted inspection process, see M Fielding, 'OFSTED, Inspection and the Betrayal of Democracy' (2001) 35 *Journal of Philosophy of Education* 695.

imprisoning members of the Peculiar People in the nineteenth and early twentieth centuries, because they used spiritual healing rather than conventional medicine when their children fell ill, had no impact on either the sect's beliefs or its practices.[76] Both of these histories are found in the contemporary British legal position. On the one hand, for example, there have been recent legislative changes to enable commercial transactions to be compliant with both the sharia and British state law.[77] On the other hand, a series of high-profile cases, where believers sought accommodation for their religious beliefs in a number of different areas of life, have failed.[78] It seems unlikely that these failures will result in changes of religious belief or practice.[79] Indeed, notwithstanding the failure to establish a legal right to accommodation, in some instances factual accommodations were or could have been made. Thus, for example, in *Eweida v British Airways*,[80] Eweida sought openly to wear a Christian cross in contravention of British Airways uniform policies. By the time her case came to court, those policies had been amended to make this possible.[81] Similarly, in *Ladele v Islington LBC*, whilst Islington London Borough Council insisted on Ladele's, a registrar, officiating at civil partnership ceremonies, in contravention of her Christian beliefs, arranging her schedule so that she was not involved with such ceremonies would, it seems, not have impaired the work of the Council.[82] Nevertheless, it is difficult not to sympathise with those commentators who have expressed doubts about the value of legislation in this area, with Sandberg, for example, suggesting that in British domestic courts 'litigants will argue anything *but* Article 9 [protecting freedom of religion]'.[83] Law continues to do little to facilitate the lives of some believers.

[76] On the Peculiar People, see M Sorrell, *The Peculiar People* (Exeter, The Paternoster Press, 1979). For a detailed account of these prosecutions, see S Peters, *When Prayer Fails: Faith Healing, Children, and the Law* (Oxford, Oxford University Press, 2008) ch 2.

[77] See, eg, J Ercanbrack, 'The Regulation of Islamic Finance in the United Kingdom' (2011) 13 *Ecclesiastical Law Journal* 69, 70–71.

[78] These cases include *Eweida v British Airways* [2010] ICR 890; *Ladele v Islington LBC* [2010] 1 WLR 955; *McFarlane v Relate Avon* [2010] WL 3256201; *Preddy v Bull* [2013] 1 WLR 3741; *R (on the application of Begum) v Governors of Denbigh High School* [2007] 1 AC 100; and *R (on the application of Playfoot) v Millais School* [2007] HRLR 34.

[79] One example of this is the decision in *Preddy v Bull* (n 78), where the Supreme Court held that it was illegal for a hotel to refuse accommodation in a double-bedded room to a gay couple on the grounds of the owners' Christian beliefs about the sanctity of marriage. Six years later, the hotel's current booking terms say that the hotel 'prefers to let double-bedded accommodation to heterosexual married couples'. See at https://www.chymorvah.org/booking-and-terms/.

[80] *Eweida v British Airways* [2010] ICR 890.

[81] ibid 893.

[82] *Ladele v Islington LBC* [2010] 1 WLR 955, 968. On the desirability of considering such an accommodation see C Stychin, 'Faith in the Future: Sexuality, Religion and the Public Sphere' (2009) 29 *Oxford Journal of Legal Studies* 729, 749–50.

[83] R Sandberg, 'The Right to Discriminate' (2011) 13 *Ecclesiastical Law Journal* 157, 162. For similar doubts about the effectiveness of legislation with relation to religious discrimination, see L Vickers, 'Religious Discrimination in the Workplace; An Emerging Hierarchy?' (2010) 12 *Ecclesiastical Law Journal* 280.

The Equality and Human Rights Commission is right to say that very few people in Great Britain currently experience religious discrimination.[84] Given the low level of religious belief in Great Britain, it could scarcely be otherwise.[85] But for that minority that is religious, and particularly for that minority that is part of a revealed religion where precepts are seen to be the literal word of god, the situation is very different. In *McFarlane v Relate Avon*, Lord Carey, a former Archbishop of the established Church of England, submitted a witness statement in which he argued that recent court judgments had shown 'a lack of sensitivity to [Christian] religious belief'.[86] Later in his statement, Lord Carey went on to argue that, if the judiciary failed to understand basic Christian beliefs, they were still less likely to understand religious beliefs 'where the practices are further removed from our traditions'. Whilst the Court of Appeal, seemingly taking Lord Carey's statement to be a plea for the priority of the Christian message, rejected his statement, the arguments above suggest that Lord Carey's basic premise was correct.[87] There is a prevailing lack of appreciation of the position of those who ground their lives on revealed religious truths. Framing the issues that result as being about the question of the validity or desirability of these professed truths, as some official sources have done, ignores the more important question. That question is whether what Shachar, in a slightly different context, has called 'a secular absolutist approach' to these matters, which refuses to grant any recognition to the religious distinctiveness of these communities, is a productive path for the state?[88] Instead, might it be better politics to accept the fact of 'joint governance'; to acknowledge that, as has been shown, the state, religious communities and individuals all have – and whatever any of them individually wish, will necessarily have – a continuing role in decisions about future developments in this area?[89]

[84] See n 3.

[85] See n 7 and the references therein.

[86] *McFarlane v Relate Avon* [2010] WL 3256201. The full statement is not quoted in *McFarlane* but nothing turns on those matters in the statement that are omitted in the judgment. I am grateful to Professor Russell Sandberg who supplied me with a copy of the full statement.

[87] ibid para 23.

[88] Shachar (n 20) 72–78.

[89] ibid ch 5.

6

Law, Religion and States: Searching for a Soul for Europe

RAFAEL PALOMINO

'The European cannot live unless embarked upon some great unifying enterprise. When this is lacking, he becomes degraded, grows slack, his soul is paralysed.'

José Ortega y Gasset, *The Revolt of the Masses* (1930)

I. Introduction

The Europe of the mid-twentieth century and the beginning of the twenty-first century is a consolidated political reality. It was born of the desire to overcome confrontations, wars and anti-human ideologies. From the initial notion based on a common economic strategy, Europe has reached ever-higher levels of integration (European Union (EU)) and political and legal cooperation (Council of Europe). In 1951, six countries constituted the European Coal and Steel Community; in 1973 there were nine members of the European Communities; 10 in 1981 (Greece); and 12 in 1986 (Spain and Portugal). After the new annexations of 1995, 2007 and 2013, the European Union consisted of 28 Members States and more than 500 million people. It is a progressive, peaceful and unprecedented political union.

From 1990 onwards, the then President of the European Commission, Jacques Delors, spoke of the need for a soul for Europe. In his address of 5 November 1990, Delors pointed out, '*We need a heart and a soul. The door is open for whoever can offer a heart and a soul.*'[1] Two years later, Delors himself insisted '*If in the next ten years we haven't managed to give a soul to Europe, to give it spirituality and meaning, the game will be up*.'[2] His successor, Jacques Santer, maintained the same idea,[3]

[1] L Hogebrink, *Europe's Heart and Soul: Jacques Delors' Appeal to the Churches* (Geneva, Globethics.net, 2015) 11 (original emphasis).

[2] ibid 16 (original emphasis).

[3] M Ventura, *La laicità dell'Unione Europea: Diritti, Mercato, Religione* (Turin, G Giappichelli, 2001) 198–99.

encouraging the participation of churches and belief groups to give meaning to the constitutional process in which the European Union was engaged.[4]

The request for a soul for Europe was framed in a unique historical, economic and legal project. However, two decades later it seems that the European project has reached a dead end: in Western Europe, Brexit represents a failure of integration, which could be repeated in other states; in Eastern Europe, newly incorporated countries claim their own initiatives, sovereignty and identity, in front of what they consider the Brussels diktat.[5] Europe seems to be threatened by populism instead of driven by major political projects.[6] Economic neo-functionalism joins European bureaucracy and reduces the motto 'unity in diversity' to an empty rhetoric,[7] giving way to the worst face of liberalism: the reinforcement of the sense of autonomy of the individual at the cost of increasingly empowering the state.[8] Europe is at an unprecedented crossroads and its future depends on a vocation, an inspiration. If the EU fails to create an interconnection of persons, of cultural links that unite its citizens, it will be little more than a group of countries united with shared economic rights, a single market or political mechanism of supranational institutions. However, a policy based on mass consumption and the cooperation of political elites without a shared social imagery cannot achieve the enthusiasm and fervour necessary in hard times.[9]

What was the meaning of giving a soul to Europe? Is it a failed project in light of the current times? What was the role that religion would have played in giving a soul to Europe? In this chapter, I shall give answers to these questions.

II. What is Europe? Past, Present, Future

A. The 'Soul' of Europe

The concept of a soul referred to by Delors is linked to the philosophical and spiritual traditions of Europe,[10] not necessarily as a specifically religious concept.[11] The metaphor of the soul for Europe may include several meanings:[12]

[4] J Barnett, *A Theology for Europe: The Churches and the European Institutions* (Oxford, Peter Lang, 2005) 80.

[5] J Diamant and S Gardner, 'In EU, There's an East-West Divide over Religious Minorities, Gay Marriage, National Identity' (Pew Research Center) at http://www.pewresearch.org/fact-tank/2018/10/29/east-west-divide-within-the-eu-on-issues-including-minorities-gay-marriage-and-national-identity/, accessed 30 October 2018.

[6] Slawomir Sierakowski, 'In Europe, the Only Choice Is Right or Far-Right' *Foreign Policy*, at https://foreignpolicy.com/2018/05/21/in-europe-the-only-choice-is-right-or-far-right/, accessed 14 November 2018.

[7] A Pabst, 'Market-State or Commonwealth?' in J Chaplin and G Wilton (eds), *God and the EU. Faith in the European Union* (London, Routledge, 2016) 109, 112–13.

[8] PJ Deneen, *Why Liberalism Failed* (New Haven, CT, Yale University Press, 2018) 46–49.

[9] Pabst (n 7) 117.

[10] M Matlak, 'Jacques Delors : The Single Market and the Failed Attempt to Give "a Soul to Europe"' (Robert Schuman Centre for Advanced Studies, 2018) Working Paper 6, 6–7, at http://cadmus.eui.eu//handle/1814/52005, accessed 28 August 2018.

- The soul is the spiritual or immaterial part of a human being or animal, regarded as immortal. In this sense, giving a Soul for Europe is giving life to the legal and political structures with something spiritual or immaterial.
- The soul is an emotional or intellectual energy or intensity, especially as something revealed as part of a work of art or an artistic performance. In this sense, a Soul for Europe is an impulse that warms the cold legal, economic and political structure and gives life and a unique character to Europe.
- The soul is a spiritual or moral force. In this sense, a Soul for Europe is a moving leading idea or principle that encourages state members and/or citizens to contribute to the Union, brings forth a sense of pride for being part of this common project; something worth living and dying for; something important to love.
- The soul is the essence or embodiment of a specified quality. In this sense, the Soul of Europe is the essence, the unique and different patterns that construct Europe's specific identity.

In a way, all these meanings are mixed into the idea of a soul for Europe, because all of them seem to respond to the need of a reality that is both simple and complex, a driving force shared by both European institutions and citizens.

B. Not Simply a Continent

I must admit the difficulty of giving a definition (marking the borders or limits) of Europe. Europe is not only an entity or geographical unit, but it is also (by and large) a historical and cultural entity.[13]

Europe belongs to Western culture and shares with America a number of constituent elements of civilisation, such as a predominant political regime (democracy), the rule of law, human rights and the market economy, with different nuances. However, when attempting to give a soul to Europe, I also tried to delimit to some extent the distinctive character of Europe with respect to America. I am aware that there is a danger of oversimplification in establishing this distinctive character and that it is impossible to treat Europe as a single entity. However, there are several elements that differentiate Europe from the United States of America (Canada being, in a certain way, a mixture of both). In the context of Western civilisation, America has a relatively short history, characterised (especially in the United States of America) by a new beginning (*Novus Ordo Seclorum*) in

[11] C Garcimartín Montero, *La Religión En El Espacio Público* (Cizur Menor, Thomson Reuters Aranzadi 2016) 92.

[12] *Oxford Living Dictionaries* – 'soul', at https://en.oxforddictionaries.com/definition/soul, accessed 20 November 2018; *Merriam-Webster Dictionary* – 'soul' at https://www.merriam-webster.com/dictionary/soul, accessed 20 November 2018.

[13] M Pera and J Ratzinger, *Sin Raíces: Europa, Relativismo, Cristianismo, Islam* (Barcelona, Ediciones Península, 2006) 53.

opposition (politically) to the old Continent. The United States was initially built by Europeans from different countries, while in Europe the separate national identities were maintained, without prejudice to an ideal unit, *In varietate concordia*, united in diversity, as the EU's 2000 motto states. The United States of America aspires to have unity (*E pluribus unum*), while Europe has no plans to consolidate into a federal state,[14] but it has followed a successful path to constitute a peculiar supranational political-legal entity. The United States of America is characterised in its official public life by ceremonial deism,[15] while Europe (I am thinking of the European Union, but also of the Council of Europe) is characterised by a 'default' ceremonial secularism[16]

TS Eliot said, 'European culture has an area but not definite frontiers: and you cannot build Chinese walls'.[17] It influences other cultures and is simultaneously influenced. The main peculiarity of European culture (regarding its identity and definition) lies in its eccentric character:[18] it rests on three symbolic hills, scattered across and beyond the Continent – the Acropolis in Greece, the Capitol in Rome and Golgotha in Jerusalem.[19] Each of these hills provides a peculiar and distinctive element: a philosophy and a way of thinking from Greek culture, legal tradition from Rome and ethics from the Judeo-Christian school of thought.

But let us go back to the idea of a soul for Europe. In its complexity, we have seen that the soul refers to an identity, to something immaterial and spiritual; a guiding idea that moves Europeans. Interestingly, the idea of the soul is not new in the history of Europe. In fact, in medieval Western Christianity the idea of the soul was present, insofar as the 'body' of temporal political power was animated (and completed) by the soul that represented the Church.[20] The transnational community of Christian believers transcended the borders of the kingdoms and

[14] JHH Weiler, 'European Democracy and the Principle of Constitutional Tolerance: The Soul of Europe' in F Cerutti and E Rudolph (eds), *A Soul for Europe: A Reader* (Leuven, Peeters Publishers, 2001) 33, 33–35.

[15] RN Bellah, 'Civil Religion in America' (2005) 134 *Daedalus* 40; RV Pierard, 'Civil Religion: A Global Phenomenon with a Uniquely American Character' [2011] *Derecho y Religión* 11; S Cañamares Arribas, 'Religión Civil y Deísmo Ceremonial En Los Estados Unidos de América' (2013) *XXIX Anuario de Derecho Eclesiástico del Estado* 199; *Elk Grove Unified School District v Newdow*, 542 US 1, 37 (2004) (O'Connor J concurring in judgment).

[16] G Weigel, *The Cube and the Cathedral* (New York, Basic Books, 2008).

[17] TS Eliot, *Christianity and Culture* (New York, Harcourt, Brace, 1949) 136.

[18] R Brague, *Eccentric Culture: A Theory of Western Civilization*, tr S Lester (South Bend Ind, St Augustines Press, 2009).

[19] Eliot (n 17) 200; G Davie, 'Religion in Europe in the 21st Century: The Factors to Take into Account' (2007) 47 *European Journal of Sociology* 271, 273; G Davie, *Religion in Modern Europe: A Memory Mutates* (Oxford, Oxford University Press, 2000); I Sánchez Cámara, *El Crepúsculo de Europa. El Espíritu de La Cultura Europea* (Madrid, Fundación Iberdrola 2006) 63–146; 'The Paris Statement. A Europe We Can Believe In' *A Europe We Can Believe In* (4 October 2017) paras 10–11 https://thetrueeurope.eu/a-europe-we-can-believe-in/, accessed 16 February 2018.

[20] B Tierney, *The Crisis of Church and State*, 1050–1300 (Toronto, University of Toronto Press, 1988) 41; F Prieto, *Historia de las Ideas y de las Formas Políticas*, vol 2: *Edad Media* (Madrid, Unión Editorial, 1998) 18.

was ultimately governed (*Potestas Ecclesiae in temporalibus*) by the Pope, defining their unity as opposed to other religions.

Political Europe today is configured similarly to 'secularised Christianity', that is, a transnational community of individuals belonging to different states in a space without religion: instead of Rome the centre is Brussels, the common element is not religion but the currency (the Euro) and football (the UEFA Champions League), the supreme arbitrator is no longer the Pope but a court in Luxembourg (the Court of Justice of the European Union) and another in Strasbourg (the European Court of Human Rights) that converge in the defence of new dogmas: liberal democracy, progressive human rights and market economy.

Does religion have anything to do with the soul of Europe? Absolutely. To demonstrate this, let us stop to observe the 'body' which that 'soul' animates in its current configuration, both in its demography and in its religious affiliation as realities connected to each other.[21]

C. Europe as a Body

The old Continent is an ageing body. According to diverse global statistics, Europe is the only continent that progressively decreases in population.[22] It is projected that between 2018 and 2050, Europe will lose 26,926,996 inhabitants.[23] For some this is not a problem, it is simply another phase of the global evolution of the world's population; Europe will maintain its population thanks to the immigration that comes from other over-populated continents. But these immigrants who come with their own culture and religion, will they then be the right body for the soul of Europe? Will there be a process of assimilation, or one of substitution? The syndrome attributable to the novel by Houellebecq, *Submission*[24] (a Europe ruled by an Islamic political majority, ultimately due to the greater fertility of Muslims with respect to European Christians), leads many to think of a cultural collapse[25] in the context of a 'cultural climate change' that also affects individuals' beliefs and religions.[26]

[21] I Furseth et al, *The Changing Soul of Europe: Religions and Migrations in Northern and Southern Europe* (Oxford, Ashgate Publishing Ltd, 2014).

[22] Population Division of the Department of and Economic and Social Affairs, *Integrating Population Issues into Sustainable Development, Including the Post-2015 Development Agenda. A Concise Report* (New York, United Nations, 2015) 3; '2018 World Population Data Sheet With Focus on Changing Age Structures – Population Reference Bureau' at https://www.prb.org/2018-world-population-data-sheet-with-focus-on-changing-age-structures/, accessed 26 October 2018.

[23] United Nations, Department of Economic and Social Affairs, Population Division, *World Population Prospects: The 2017 Revision*, custom data acquired via website at https://population.un.org/wpp/DataQuery/.

[24] M Houellebecq, *Submission: A Novel*, tr L Stein (New York, Picador, 2016).

[25] J Bethke Elshtain, 'While Europe Slept' [2009] (March) *First Things* 33, 35.

[26] '"Cultural Climate Change" – Rabbi Sacks at The Chautauqua Institution – Rabbi Sacks' at http://rabbisacks.org/cultural-climate-change/, accessed 24 October 2018.

Not all European countries agree that immigration is a solution to demographic decline. The Visegrád group, composed of Slovakia, Poland, Hungary and Czechia, seems to follow a different double pattern: accepting selective immigration and promoting demographic change from within the country itself. When referring to the decline of the European demographic, some make the following point:

> [T]here are more sensitive policies than importing the next generation of Europeans from Africa. They might conceive that while diversity may be advantageous in small numbers it would irrevocably end society as we know it.[27]

Besides, keep in mind that for a significant number of Eastern European citizens', religion is part of their national identity and continues to play an important role in social cohesion: religion cannot be privatised as in Western Europe.[28] The political spectrum has been radicalised in some way. On the one hand there are those who equate Muslim immigration with the import of terrorism; on the other are those who simply welcome any type of immigration and brand those who oppose them as fascists. Meanwhile, the underlying problem remains: demography should be a primary concern, but no effective and decisive reaction has been produced so far, since tackling the problem head-on seems alarmist.

It is true that religious beliefs can be related to demography.[29] From an intuitive point of view, it is almost evident that an observant and fervent Muslim population will surpass a Christian or Western population of weak belief and practice. On a global scale, perhaps this conclusion is acceptable according to reliable statistics.[30] However, the issue is a little more complex in the actual European scenario, in which it seems that the Muslim population will decrease in the coming years.[31]

For centuries, Europe has been the home of Christianity. In 1910, 66.3 per cent of Christians lived in Europe, while in 2010 only 25.9 per cent of Christians lived in Europe whilst 36.8 per cent lived in America.[32] However, despite Western Europe's being a secularised region, the majority of its inhabitants still declare themselves

[27] D Murray, *The Strange Death of Europe: Immigration, Identity, Islam* (London, Bloomsbury Publishing, 2017) 300–01.

[28] S Jakelić, *Collectivistic Religions: Religion, Choice, and Identity in Late Modernity* (Farnham, Ashgate Gower, 2010); Pew Research Center, *Eastern and Western Europeans Differ on Importance of Religion, Views of Minorities, and Key Social Issues* (2018) ahttp://www.pewforum.org/2018/10/29/eastern-and-western-europeans-differ-on-importance-of-religion-views-of-minorities-and-key-social-issues/, accessed 3 November 2018.

[29] EP Kaufmann, *Shall the Religious Inherit the Earth?: Demography and Politics in the Twenty-First Century* (London, Profile Books, 2010).

[30] M Lipka, 'Muslims and Islam: Key Findings in the US and around the World' (Pew Research Center) at http://www.pewresearch.org/fact-tank/2017/08/09/muslims-and-islam-key-findings-in-the-u-s-and-around-the-world/, accessed 24 October 2018.

[31] R Puyol, 'Una Europa Musulmana?' *The Conversation* at http://theconversation.com/una-europa-musulmana-104066, accessed 26 October 2018.

[32] 'The Size and Distribution of the World's Christian Population', Pew Forum on Religion & Public Life (19 December 2011) at http://www.pewforum.org/2011/12/19/global-christianity-exec/, accessed 26 October 2018.

to be Christians (median of 71 per cent).[33] Christian identity in Europe remains a cultural, social and religious marker: it is therefore surprising that a number of scholars understand the Christian presence as a physical reality (ancient religious buildings[34]), although they simultaneously argue that Europe is Christian in a negative sense because it is not Buddhist, nor Muslim or Shinto.[35] Religious affiliation is polarised between religious believers and non-religious believers: the mobility of individuals between different denominations or religions, as is common in the United States of America, is not common in Europe.[36]

The changing religious landscape of Europe at the beginning of the twenty-first century was in some ways marked by factors that demonstrated a continuity-discontinuity pattern:[37] the legacy of the historic Christian churches in the configuration of European culture, the awareness of those same churches of having a special role at specific moments in the lives of Europeans (rites of passage), even though they do not reflect the beliefs and behaviour of the majority of the population; the progressive replacement of a model of compulsory religious practice for an optional one; the arrival of immigrants from the south with other religious creeds; the protective reaction of the secularised cultural elites before the new relevance of religion in the public and private sphere; and the growing awareness that Europe is certainly exceptional with respect to the rest of the world as far as the presence of religion in society is concerned.

D. An Inner or an Outer European Soul?

Previous reflections could lead academics to think that Europe peacefully presupposes religion's playing an important role in the soul of Europe; however, this does not reflect the reality of the situation. The role of religion is a debated issue; debated in a double sense. On the one hand, because the same concept of religion is ambiguous, and on the other because it is debated whether the soul of Europe should be a principle intrinsic or extrinsic to the political community. I shall begin by expanding on the latter issue.

[33] Pew Research Center, 'Most Western Europeans Continue to identify as Christians, though few regularly attend church' (2018) ahttps://www.pewforum.org/2018/05/29/being-christian-in-western-europe/pf_05-29-18_religion-western-europe-00-00-1/, accessed 17 June 2019: 15 countries surveyed, ie Austria, Belgium, Denmark, Finland, France, Germany, Ireland, Italy, Netherlands, Norway, Portugal, Spain, Sweden, Switzerland, United Kingdom. As this report explains, the median 'is the middle number in a list of figures sorted in ascending or descending order. In a survey of 15 countries, the median result is the eighth on a list of country-level findings ranked in order.'

[34] L Zucca, *A Secular Europe: Law and Religion in the European Constitutional Landscape* (Oxford, Oxford University Press, 2012) 69.

[35] ibid 78–79.

[36] Pew Research Center, *Being Christian in Western Europe* (2018) at http://www.pewforum.org/2018/05/29/being-christian-in-western-europe/, accessed 26 October 2018.

[37] Davie, 'Religion in Europe in the 21st Century' (n 19) 271–72; P Jenkins, *God's Continent: Christianity, Islam, and Europe's Religious Crisis* (New York, Oxford University Press, 2007) 19.

According to the Böckenförde dilemma, so called because it was formulated by the famous German scholar:

> [T]he liberal, secularised state is nourished by presuppositions that it cannot itself guarantee ... On the one hand, it can only survive as a liberal state if the liberty it allows its citizens regulates itself from within on the basis of the moral substance of the individual and the homogeneity of society. On the other hand, it cannot attempt to guarantee those inner regulatory forces by its own efforts – that is to say, with the instruments of legal coercion and authoritative command – without abandoning its liberalness and, at a secularised level, lapsing into the pretension to totality out of which it led the way into the denominational civil wars.[38]

The liberal state does not emerge from nothing. It has a long history behind it and its deepest foundations (freedom and equality) are the aftermath of the Christian thought.[39] The European political community, the EU, is inspired in an imperceptible way in a horizon of significance.[40] If that horizon is abandoned or forgotten, its orientation is permanently lost: the most recent economic crises might be the evidence of this.[41]

For other commentators, there is no outer origin that sustains the great foundations of the political community; it is wrong to refer to a kind of religious monopoly surrounding the origins of the current liberal state, 'we should urgently stop talking about religion in general or in the abstract, because religions then and now certainly have not done all these beneficial things but have done and do serious wrong and evil'.[42] Consequently, the soul of Europe is outside its origins: it is in its immediate legal and political manifestations – the welfare state[43] and certain political principles (adherence to democracy, rule of law, respect for human rights, freedom and equality).[44] The soul of Europe is a way of creating a political community, which must end up penetrating the conscience and way of life of all citizens.

[38] EW Böckenförde, *State, Society, and Liberty: Studies in Political Theory and Constitutional Law* (Providence, RI, Berg, 1991) 45. See also K-H Ladeur, 'The Myth of the Neutral State and the Individualization of Religion: The Relationship Between State and Religion in the Face of Fundamentalism' (2009) 30 *Cardozo Law Review* 2445.

[39] L Siedentop, *Inventing The Individual. The Origins of Western Liberalism* (London, Penguin Books, 2015).

[40] C Taylor, *The Ethics of Authenticity* (Cambridge, MA, Harvard University Press, 1991) 38–40.

[41] Sir Jonathan Sacks, '"Has Europe Lost Its Soul?" – Lecture at The Pontifical Gregorian University, Rome' (Pontifical Gregorian University, Rome, 12 December 2011) at http://rabbisacks.org/has-europe-lost-its-soul-transcript-of-lecture-delivered-at-the-pontifical-gregorian-university-rome/, accessed 27 October 2018.

[42] V Bader, 'Excluded, Included or Foundational? Religion in Liberal-Democratic States' in G D'Costa et al (eds), *Religion in a Liberal State* (Cambridge, Cambridge University Press, 2013) 158.

[43] D Vaughan-Whitehead, *The European Social Model in Crisis: Is Europe Losing Its Soul?* (Geneva, Edward Elgar Publishing, 2015).

[44] A López Rovira, 'El Futuro de La UE, Una Cuestión de Valores' *Política Exterior* (26 July 2018) at https://www.politicaexterior.com/actualidad/el-futuro-de-la-ue-una-cuestion-de-valores/, accessed 19 August 2018.

The concept of religion, as I mentioned earlier, is ambiguous. In the legal domain, up to three major meanings have been specified, though they are not necessarily concurrent or cumulative: belief, identity and lifestyle.[45]

Belief deals with the *forum internum*, the freedom of choice of beliefs, and personal and collective adherence to dogmas or explanations. Identity refers to adherence to a group, similar to adherence to a clan or a nationality; a sense of belonging or identification that may be distinct or separate from what each individual believes or fails to do, though it refers more specifically to a shared history, culture or tradition. Lifestyle refers to religion as actions and rites; these facilitate an individual's ability to distinguish one religion from another, and lifestyle is expressed not only in religious symbols but also in cultural traits.

Despite that ambiguity and richness of meaning, by the influence of Protestantism the concept of religion has been reduced to belief and, consequently, to freedom of choice and protection of individual autonomy. This is the main perspective under which religion is currently considered in the law and in politics.[46] The social presence of the other two aspects of religion (identity and lifestyle) have been submitted to the same regime (freedom of choice), so that the traditional, cultural and historical manifestations impregnated with Christianity (how could it be otherwise in Europe!) are excluded from the public sphere because they involve an imposition (ie something *not chosen*) on the backs or on the minds of non-Christian European citizens.

I think that this confusion of meanings about religion lies in the rejection of the mention of Christianity in the ill-fated European Constitution.[47] Zucca thinks that nothing militates in favour of entrenching Christian values in the preamble to the European Constitution to preserve their disappearance in society.[48] The most evident proof of its importance, though, has been that, once that mention disappeared, the constitutional project simply failed. The mention of Christianity would transfer to the legal-political structure of Europe a historical fact, not a value. At any rate, Christian values were already incorporated where the rights of the person, freedom, equality, the rule of law (Treaty of Lisbon), human dignity or solidarity are mentioned (Charter of Fundamental Rights of the European Union). Moreover, as recently recognised, the movement of human rights and the consecration of human dignity as Europe's foundation after the Second World War, a movement parallel with the beginning of the European Union, had a proven Christian impulse.[49]

[45] TJ Gunn, 'The Complexity of Religion and the Definition of "Religion" in International Law' (2003) 16 *Harvard Human Rights Journal* 189.

[46] MJ Sandel, 'Freedom of Conscience or Freedom of Choice' in J Davison Hunter and O Guinness (eds), *Articles of Faith, Articles of Peace: The Religious Liberty Clauses and the American Public Philosophy* (Washington, DC, Brookings Institution Press, 1990) 74, 87–92.

[47] R Navarro-Valls, 'Le basi della cultura giuridica europea' (2002) 18 *Anuario de Derecho Eclesiástico del Estado* 19, 20–23; JHH Weiler, *Una Europa Cristiana: Ensayo Exploratorio* (Madrid, Encuentro 2003) 51–80; G Milton, 'God and the Constitution' in Chaplin and Wilton (eds) (n 7) 191.

[48] Zucca (n 34) 69.

[49] S Moyn, *Christian Human Rights* (Philadelphia, PA, University of Pennsylvania Press, 2015).

Like national Constitutions – but also somewhat distanced from them, since it was a supranational structure norm – the European Constitution could have fulfilled three objectives:[50] (i) regulation of the structure of the EU; (ii) the enshrinement of fundamental rights; and (iii) the proclamation of values, ideals and symbols of European identity. The last is the objective connected with the soul of Europe, and this has been the abandoned issue that has ultimately led to the failure of the constitutional project. That confusion of meanings concerning religion is present too in the debate about the presence of the cross in Italian schools and in European public spaces:[51] a cross in a public space is interpreted in terms of adhesion, profession of belief and coercion … but its linkage with collective identity, a history or a culture is lost from sight.[52]

Mentioning Christianity in the European Constitution, in the Treaty of Lisbon or in the Charter of Fundamental Rights was in no way meant to be a confessional declaration of the EU or a hypothetical exclusion or marginalisation of other religions or beliefs. The affirmation of the intellectual, ethical or legal origins of Europe would have been an opportunity for reconciliation and encounter. In this light, I return to the thoughts of Eliot:

> The dominant force in creating a common culture between peoples each of which has its distinct culture, is religion. Please do not, at this point, make a mistake in anticipating my meaning. This is not a religious talk, and I am not setting out to convert anybody. I am simply stating a fact … An individual European may not believe that the Christian Faith is true, and yet what he says, and makes, and does, will all spring out of his heritage of Christian culture and depend upon that culture for its meaning.[53]

Not even the mention of God in the European Constitution could be considered to be a manifestation of confessionalism, since such a mention can be considered a meta-legal concept that serves precisely to put limits to the totalitarian temptations of the state through law, recalls the centrality of the human person, of their dignity and equality, and appeals to the responsibility and freedom of the human being.[54]

[50] IC Ibán, 'God in Constitutions and Godless Constitutions' in C Cianitto et al (eds), *Law, Religion, Constitution: Freedom of Religion, Equal Treatment, and the Law* (Farnham, Routledge, 2013) 53; F Felice, 'Thinking Europe in a New Way' in G Kugler and M Kugler (eds), *Exiting a Dead End Road. A GPS for Christians in Public Discourse* (Vienna, Kairos Publications, 2010) 147.

[51] P Stanitsz, M Zawiślak and M Ordon (eds), *Presence of the Cross in Public Spaces* (Newcastle upon Tyne, Cambridge Scholars Publishing, 2016); J Temperman, *The Lautsi Papers Multidisciplinary Reflections on Religious Symbols in the Public School Classroom* (Leiden, Martinus Nijhoff Publishers, 2012).

[52] C Panara, 'Another Defeat for the Principle of Secularism: Recent Developments on the Display of the Crucifix in Italian Courtrooms' (2011) 6 *Religion and Human Rights* 259; CM Zoethout, 'Religious Symbols in the Public School Classroom: A New Way to Tackle a Knotty Problem' (2011) 6 *Religion and Human Rights* 285.

[53] Eliot (n 17) 199–200.

[54] R Domingo, *God and the Secular Legal System* (New York, Cambridge University Press, 2016) 23–71.

However, the 'secularist prejudice' prevailed.[55] The final result has had a perverse effect: on the one hand, direct references to Christianity have been avoided, its being argued that those who do not belong to that religion might feel marginalised; but, on the other hand, this marginalisation of citizens of other religions is inflicted under the guise of a hypothetical neutrality,[56] or under the pretence of guaranteeing social conventions that presumably facilitate co-existence (*vivre ensemble*) as part of the fundamental rights of other citizens.[57] Paradoxically, Europe thus becomes a space to live together, but only as long as citizens comply with certain rules that reflect a kind of new meta-positive-secularist law (*ordre public immatériel*).[58] Perhaps the attitude that would decisively widen this path is to count on religions as social agents of promotion of living together, to promote a secularity of recognition, driving away the ghost of extremism.[59]

III. Spirits in a Material World: The Soul in the European Flesh

The Peace of Westphalia of 1648 put an end to the political project of Western Christendom, to the Christian empire and to the supremacy of the Pope as the great arbiter of international disputes. A new regime emerged with it, adopting the nation state as its basic unit. The political mythology that was slowly created after the Peace of Westphalia argues that when religion is brought into public life, the result is intolerance, war, devastation and even the collapse of the international order. Overcoming these evils would require the marginalisation of the religious factor. The emergence and development of the modern state entailed secularisation, the disenchantment of the world and, most notably, the disappearance of religion from the political scene.[60] Progressively, religion manifests itself through a subjective right and religious freedom is consecrated. Religious freedom became a legal channel through which the unpredictable current of religion, capable of

[55] J Casanova, 'The Problem of Religion and the Anxieties of European Secular Democracy' in G Motzkin and Y Fischer (eds), *Religion and Democracy in Contemporary Europe* (London, Alliance Publishing Trust, 2008) 73.

[56] Case C-157/15 *G4S Secure Solutions*, EU:C:2017:203 (Judgment of 14 March 2017); Case C-188/15 *Bougnaoui y ADDH*, EU:C:2017:204 (Judgment of 14 March 2017).

[57] *SAS v France* App no 43835/11 (ECHR GC, 1 July 2014); *Osmanoğlu and Kocabaş v Switzerland* App no 29086/12 (ECHR, 10 January 2017). P Norris, '"Le Vivre Ensemble": Intercultural Dialogue and Religion in the European Union' in M Fethi (ed), *Interculturalism at the Crossroads: Comparative Perspectives on Concepts, Policies and Practices* (Paris, UNESCO Publishing, 2017) 145.

[58] M-O Peyroux-Sissoko, 'L'ordre Public Immatériel En Droit Public Français' (2018) thése no 01 *Revue des Droits et Libertés Fondamentaux* at http://www.revuedlf.com/theses/lordre-public-immateriel-en-droit-public-francais/, accessed 2 November 2018.

[59] Parliamentary Assembly, Council of Europe, Resolution 2076 (2015) 'Freedom of religion and living together in a democratic society' at http://assembly.coe.int/nw/xml/Xref/Xref-XML2HTML-en.asp?fileid=22199&lang=en, accessed 3 November 2018.

[60] S Thomas, *The Global Resurgence of Religion and the Transformation of International Relations: The Struggle for the Soul of the Twenty-First Century* (New York, Palgrave Macmillan, 2005) 54–58.

flooding the peace and prosperity of the peoples with its 'irrational' waters, is recognised and protected. Simultaneously, in Western societies – and European ones in particular – religions were subjected to a process of formatting or standardisation,[61] which yielded a societal area (the religious area) that expresses itself in an institutional way (religious denominations, religious communities, worship associations, etc).

This is critical because it influences two features of the presence of religion in Europe that have made it difficult for religion, and more particularly Christianity, to have some kind of role in the soul of Europe.

On the one hand, religion has been legally expressed as a fundamental right and a ground of unlawful discrimination. As is well known, since 1993 the European Court of Human Rights has developed legal principles concerning the content and limits of the fundamental right of religious freedom, starting in particular from Article 9 of the European Convention on Human Rights, so that the Council of Europe appears as the ultimate guarantor of the freedom of citizens vis-à-vis the European states.[62] In recent years, the Court of Justice of the European Union has also joined this goal of developing the content and limits of freedom of religion.[63] If this legal work is possible in Europe, this is because there are a number of related elements of departure, and also some common principles, that inspire European politics and law.[64]

In general, scholars and experts welcome the performance of both courts (though not always without strong criticism), not only because they are instruments to enforce Communitarian law and fundamental rights, but also because they generate European cohesion with respect to the fundamental principles of coexistence within the Continent. Both the Court of Strasbourg, perhaps more popular in its mission, and the Court of Luxembourg determine the law on very controversial issues in Europe.

[61] O Roy, *Holy Ignorance: When Religion and Culture Part Ways* (New York, Oxford University Press, 2010) 187; S Rossano, 'Ruolo Delle Religioni e Libertà Religiosa Nell'Unione Europea' in JA Araña y Mesa (ed), *Libertà religiosa e reciprocità* (Milan, Giuffrè, 2009) 359, 361.

[62] J Martínez-Torrón, 'European Convention on Human Rights' in *Encyclopedia of Law and Religion* (Leiden, Martinus Nijhoff Brill 2016); C Evans, *Freedom of Religion under the European Convention on Human Rights* (Oxford, Oxford University Press, 2001); R Mazzola (ed), *Diritto e religione in Europa: rapporto sulla giurisprudenza della Corte europea dei diritti dell'uomo in materia di libertà religiosa* (Bologna, Il Mulino, 2012).

[63] K Alidadi and M-C Foblets, 'European Supranational Courts and the Fundamental Right to Freedom of Religion or Belief: Convergence or Competition?' (2016) 5 *Oxford Journal of Law and Religion* 532; E Fokas, 'Comparative Susceptibility and Differential Effects on the Two European Courts: A Study of Grasstops Mobilizations around Religion' (2016) 5 *Oxford Journal of Law and Religion* 541; R McCrea, 'Singing from the Same Hymn Sheet? What the Differences between the Strasbourg and Luxembourg Courts Tell Us about Religious Freedom, Non-Discrimination, and the Secular State' (2016) 5 *Oxford Journal of Law and Religion* 183.

[64] R Carp, 'Religion in the Public Sphere: Is There a Common European Model?' (2011) 10 *Journal for the Study of Religions and Ideologies* 84, 98; N Doe, *Law and Religion in Europe: A Comparative Introduction* (New York, Oxford University Press, 2011) 263–64; S Ferrari, 'The New Wine and the Old Cask. Tolerance, Religion and the Law in Contemporary Europe' (1997) 10 *Ratio Juris* 75.

However, every judgment has winners and losers: it seems to unite, but in the end it provokes division (some have won, others have lost in deep ethical issues) without prior social dialogue, which is particularly important and acute in the case of religion.[65] Consequently, the work of these courts is unifying only in appearance: they have given the last word (*Rome locuta, causa finita* in the secular version), but that last word is odious for an important portion of the European population.

On the other hand, Delors' aspiration to breathe a soul into Europe has ended up being an unspiritual, normative, bureaucratic and institutionalised task. This is nothing but the very denial of what Delors intended;[66] perhaps a more ethereal soul, a human community that thinks, discusses and constructs from a common philosophical, legal and religious tradition, would have been a goal more in keeping with the pretensions of its first promoter.

If, as one might propose, the soul of Europe should have some kind of relationship with the religious, in whole or in part, the truth is that this soul has been reified and standarised. Among the various examples that could be cited here, there are very concrete manifestations contained in Article 17 of the Treaty on the Functioning of the European Union:

1. The Union respects and does not prejudice the status under national law of churches and religious associations or communities in the Member States.
2. The Union equally respects the status under national law of philosophical and non-confessional organisations.
3. Recognising their identity and their specific contribution, the Union shall maintain an open, transparent and regular dialogue with these churches and organisations.[67]

Article 17(1) and (2) aim to reinforce collective religious freedom,[68] placing the EU in a position of subsidiarity in line with the principles that inspire the Union,[69] a deferential position that is also reflected in both equality and non-discrimination,[70] which does not generate an area of privilege but instead

[65] R McCrea, 'Rights, Recourse to the Courts and the Relationship between Religion, Law and State in Europe and the United States' (2015) Working Paper at http://cadmus.eui.eu//handle/1814/38812, accessed 20 April 2016.

[66] Matlak (n 10).

[67] Consolidated version of the Treaty on the Functioning of the European Union [2012] OJ C326/47.

[68] AM Rodrigues Araújo, *Iglesias y organizaciones no confesionales en la Unión Europea: el artículo 17 del TFUE* (Pamplona, EUNSA, 2012); JR Polo Sabau, *El estatuto de las confesiones religiosas en el derecho de la Unión Europea: entre el universalismo y la peculiaridad nacional* (Madrid, Dykinson, 2014).

[69] Doe (n 64) 241–42.

[70] Council Directive 2000/78/EC of 27 November 2000 establishing a general framework for equal treatment in employment and occupation [2000] OJ L303/16. Art 4(2) provides that 'Member States may maintain national legislation in force at the date of adoption of this Directive or provide for future legislation incorporating national practices existing at the date of adoption of this Directive pursuant to which, in the case of occupational activities within churches and other public or private organisations the ethos of which is based on religion or belief, a difference of treatment based on a person's religion or belief shall not constitute discrimination where, by reason of the nature of these activities or of the context in which they are carried out, a person's religion or belief constitute a genuine, legitimate

of singularity.[71] Mentioning philosophical organisations alongside religious organisations, far from being a balanced solution to the equal treatment of religious and non-religious believers, quantitatively privileges European humanist organisations of Masonic inspiration.[72] In this and other issues, the EU has prioritised the French and Belgian perspective.[73] Article 17(3) specifies the EU's relationship with religious groups and non-confessional organisations through open, transparent and regular dialogue. Here, a glimpse of cooperation can be seen, which is discussed later in this chapter.[74]

Further relevant evidence of standardisation is contained in the Charter of Fundamental Rights of the European Union:[75]

> 1. Everyone has the right to freedom of thought, conscience and religion. This right includes freedom to change religion or belief and freedom, either alone or in community with others and in public or in private, to manifest religion or belief, in worship, teaching, practice and observance.
> 2. The right to conscientious objection is recognised, in accordance with the national laws governing the exercise of this right.

To comprehensively understand the recognition in Article 10 of the fundamental right of freedom of thought, conscience and religion, Article 9 of the European Convention on Human Rights must also be taken into account, particularly its second paragraph, which establishes the constituent elements of the legitimate limitations of the fundamental right.[76] Regarding the scope of the right of conscientious objection, Article 10 of the Charter of Fundamental Rights barely brings anything new, with the exception of its express mention, which places us almost in the same line of uncertainty that previously existed.[77]

and justified occupational requirement, having regard to the organisation's ethos. This difference of treatment shall be implemented taking account of Member States' constitutional provisions and principles, as well as the general principles of Community law, and should not justify discrimination on another ground.' See also L Vickers and European Commission, *Religion and Belief Discrimination in Employment: The EU Law* (Luxembourg, Office for Official Publications of the European Communities, 2007); Art 19 of the Treaty on the Functioning of the European Union.

[71] Case C-68/17 *IR v JQ*, EU:C:2018:696 (Judgment of 11 September 2018). Dismissal of a Catholic doctor from a managerial position by a Catholic hospital due to his remarriage after a divorce may constitute unlawful discrimination on grounds of religion. See also Art 13 of the Treaty on the Functioning of the European Union.

[72] Matlak (n 10) 7, 9.

[73] M Pasikowska-Schnass, 'Article 17 TFEU: The EU Institutions' Dialogue with Confessional and Non-Confessional Organizations' (European Parliamentary Research Service 2018) 2 at http://www.europarl.europa.eu/thinktank/en/document.html?reference=EPRS_BRI(2018)614658, accessed 19 November 2018.

[74] Doe (n 64) 251–54.

[75] Charter of Fundamental Rights of the European Union [2007] OJ C303/01.

[76] M López Escudero et al, *Carta de los Derechos Fundamentales de la Unión Europea: Comentario artículo por artículo* (Bilbao, Fundación BBVA 2008) 256–69.

[77] A Power-Forde, 'Freedom of Religion and "Reasonable Accommodation" in the Case Law of the European Court of Human Rights' (2016) 5 *Oxford Journal of Law and Religion* 575.

In recent years, the Court of Justice of the European Union has issued numerous decisions regarding religious communities in connection with labour law,[78] data protection,[79] religious dietary norms and animal slaughter,[80] to mention but a few of the most recent issues. It is probable that in the near future the judicial pronouncements of the Court will be as frequent as those of the European Court of Human Rights. With regard to the issues of those future judgments of the Court of Luxembourg, they would not necessarily be conflicts related to religious freedom, or even religious problems that have arisen in connection with apparently neutral regulation. Rather, a third category arises in the complex framework of EU law: specific issues governed by EU law applicable to religious communities, which occupy a distinct position inside the law of the EU. For example, Article 14 of the Charter of Fundamental Rights of the European Union defines a right to education:

1. Everyone has the right to education and to have access to vocational and continuing training.
2. This right includes the possibility to receive free compulsory education.
3. The freedom to found educational establishments with due respect for democratic principles and the right of parents to ensure the education and teaching of their children in conformity with their religious, philosophical and pedagogical convictions shall be respected, in accordance with the national laws governing the exercise of such freedom and right.

In addition, Article 22 provides that the Union 'shall respect cultural, religious and linguistic diversity'.

These two articles of the Charter guarantee areas of free exchange of ideas – which includes religious ideas – that make up the identity and culture of Europe.

The institutionalisation of the contribution of religious groups to the soul of Europe has been carried out by both parties (EU and religious groups) through liaison groups, forums and activities.[81] The EU placed dialogue with religious and non-religious groups in its organisational chart under the impulse of President Barroso in 2005. It has organised annual meetings at the highest level on issues of ethical-political dimension (human rights, terrorism, the environment, amongst others), and seminars sponsored by the Forward Studies Unit, the Group of Policy Advisors (GOPA) and the Bureau of European Policy Advisors (BEPA). Under

[78] Case C-414/16 *Vera Egenberger v Evangelisches Werk für Diakonie und Entwicklung eV*, EU:C:2018:257 (Judgment of 17 April 2018). The requirement of religious affiliation for a post within the Church must be amenable to effective judicial review.

[79] Case C-25/17 *Jehovan todistajat*, EU:C:2018:551 (Judgment of 10 July 2018). A religious community, such as the Jehovah's Witnesses, is a controller, jointly with its members who engage in preaching, for the processing of personal data carried out by the latter in the context of door-to-door preaching.

[80] Case C-426/16, *Liga van Moskeeën en Islamitische Organisaties Provincie Antwerpen and Others*, EU:C:2018:335 (Judgment of 29 May 2018). The Court confirms that ritual slaughter without stunning may take place only in an approved slaughterhouse.

[81] Leustean (n 2); Hogebrink (n 1).

the presidency of Jean-Claude Junker, dialogue with religious and philosophical organisations was entrusted to the first Vice-President of the Commission and is located organically in the General Direction of Justice. The obstacle to the development of this institutional dialogue is often found in religious groups themselves, because of the difficulty of augmenting a uniform common opinion (as is the case in Protestant churches) or the difficulty of achieving a single representation (in the case of the European Islamic communities).[82]

It may be thought that European politicians have not been able to assess the significance or the impact of religion on the European construction: what threats and opportunities the division between Catholics, Protestants and Orthodox brings about for the EU, or how to manage the link between religion and national identity in Eastern European countries that are in this respect very different from those Western countries in which the national religious identity has disappeared, as in France or Belgium.[83]

The Council of Europe, though, has been able to devote its attention more globally, less compelled by an institutional dimension, when dealing with these issues:

- the role of religion in European democracies and the cultural dimension of religions;[84]
- religion as part of the state education curriculum;[85]
- complex religious issues that shocked a secular mentality and for which a certain dose of understanding is necessary;[86]
- the need to respect the autonomy of religious groups as an important element of the separation between religions and political power;[87] and
- the right to the conscientious objection of health professionals.[88]

[82] Matlak (n 10) 7–9; S In't Veld, 'E Pluribus Unum? A European Community of Values Must Remain Secular' in F de Beaufort, I Hägg and P Van Schie (eds), *Separation of Church and State in Europe* (Brussels, European Liberal Forum, 2008) 21–24.

[83] B Arruñada and M Krapf, 'Religion and the European Union' (Social Science Research Network 2018) SSRN Scholarly Paper ID 3131883 at https://papers.ssrn.com/abstract=3131883, accessed 19 March 2018.

[84] Recommendation 1396 (1999) Religion and democracy, Text adopted by the Assembly on 27 January 1999 (5th Sitting) at http://assembly.coe.int/nw/xml/Xref/Xref-XML2HTML-en.asp?fileid=16672&lang=en, accessed 13 November 2018.

[85] Recommendation 1720 (2005), Education and religion, Text adopted by the Assembly on 4 October 2005 (27th Sitting) at http://assembly.coe.int/nw/xml/Xref/Xref-XML2HTML-en.asp?fileid=17373&lang=en, accessed 13 November 2018.

[86] Resolution 2076 (2015), Freedom of religion and living together in a democratic society, Text adopted by the Assembly on 30 September 2015 (33rd Sitting) at http://assembly.coe.int/nw/xml/XRef/Xref-XML2HTML-en.asp?fileid=22199&lang=en, accessed 13 November 2018.

[87] Recommendation 1804 (2007), State, religion, secularity and human rights, Text adopted by the Assembly on 29 June 2007 (27th Sitting) at http://assembly.coe.int/nw/xml/XRef/Xref-XML2HTML-en.asp?fileid=17568&lang=en, accessed 13 November 2018.

[88] Resolution 1763 (2010) The right to conscientious objection in lawful medical care, Text adopted by the Assembly on 7 October 2010 (35th Sitting) at http://assembly.coe.int/nw/xml/XRef/Xref-XML2HTML-EN.asp?fileid=17909&lang=en, accessed 13 November 2018.

The Council of Europe has analysed all of these issues through soft-law instruments, which involve (or coerce) Member States to a lesser extent.

IV. Concluding Remarks

Insufflating a soul to Europe constituted, at the beginning of the twenty-first century, a necessary task to unify all the citizens of a diverse community and to promote the legitimacy of a supranational political organisation that aspired to achieve greater levels of cohesion and identity on the international stage.

Religions might well have played a role in giving a soul to Europe. The circumstances of a demographic nature, of confusion of meanings or dimensions about religion (the affirmation of the relevance of Christianity could be understood as a form of confessionalism), or the institutionalisation and bureaucratisation of the contribution of religion and beliefs to Europe, seem to hinder the contribution of religion to the construction of the European project. This contribution is not the influence of religion as such but is rather an affirmation of an origin of ideas and values, an identity and an open dialogue; something far removed from the institutionalisation of relationships. As has been noted, religions are not only an opportunity to pray together but also to think together.[89] Instead, religion in Europe appears to be a conflictual issue that, in order to not be dangerous or threatening, is to be reduced to a fundamental right in the private sphere.

The importance of integrating religion into the soul of Europe was not reducible to the affirmation of a social relevant fact in the history of the Continent, or to emphasising the utility religions may provide in the construction of Europe or to the preservation of democratic peace. In my view, the integration of religion in the soul of Europe purports a kind of creative discourse in European public life that is beneficial for the common good, preventing liberal democracy from becoming an illiberal pseudo-religion,[90] something that, it seems to me, is already happening.

[89] M McGuinness, 'Praying and Thinking: The Role of Christians in Ensuring a Human-Centred Europe' *Europeinfos. Christian Perspectives on the EU* (2017) at http://www.europe-infos.eu/the-role-of-christians-in-ensuring-a-human-centred-europe?ts=1513068630, accessed 12 December 2017.

[90] Pabst (n 7) 27.

7

How to Deal with Religion in the Increasingly Pluralistic European Societies?

The European Court of Human Rights on Crucifixes, Face-covering Veils and Disparaging Muhammad

CARLA M ZOETHOUT

At the beginning of the twenty-first century, religion seems to be on the rise again. While western societies have become more secular since the 1950s and membership of official religious denominations is decreasing, religious manifestations of all sorts are more and more present in contemporary societies. Many moral and legal topics concerning religion are being discussed. There is case law, heated debates, moral quandaries – religion is back in the public debate. Often, the debate takes place nationwide, or even worldwide.

A few recent law cases may illustrate the diversity of religious issues these days. One is the *Masterpiece Cakeshop Case*, about a baker in the State of Colorado (USA) who refused – on religious grounds – to bake a cake for a same-sex wedding.[1] Another example is the United Nations Human Rights Committee's view[2] (2018) that France violated the human rights of two women by fining them for wearing the niqab (a face-covering veil[3]).[4] Remarkably, one year earlier, the

[1] *Masterpiece Cakeshop Ltd, et al* v *Colorado Civil Rights Commission et al* 584 US _; 138 S Ct 1719 (2018) (Supreme Court of the United States).

[2] The UN Human Rights Committee is based on the First Optional Protocol to the International Covenant on Civil and Political Rights (ICCPR). It is authorised to consider communications from individuals subject to its jurisdiction who claim to be victims of a violation by a state party of any of the rights set forth in the Covenant (provided the state has recognised the Protocol).

[3] The niqab and burka are both face-covering veils. The niqab is a veil for the face that leaves the area around the eyes clear. It may be worn with a separate eye veil. The burka is a one-piece veil that covers the face and body, often leaving just a mesh screen to see through.

[4] Comité des droits de l'homme, Constatations adoptés par le Comité au titre de l'article 5 (para 4) du Protocole facultatif, concernant la communication no 2747/2016 (with two minority views). It is

European Court of Human Rights (ECtHR) issued a judgment about a similar ban in Belgium, with the opposite outcome. The Court unanimously accepted one of the main reasons for the ban, namely, that wearing a full-face veil impedes living together in society.[5]

When it comes to Europe, it is the European Convention of Human Rights (ECHR), adopted in 1950 within the Council of Europe, that provides a common framework for the freedom of religion in European societies. At the start of its existence, the Council of Europe included 10 politically and culturally homogeneous countries, organised according to the principles of liberal democracy.[6] In the second phase of its existence the Council expanded to 23 states, including almost all Western European countries and Turkey.[7] A third phase began after the fall of the Berlin Wall in 1989 until 2003, when 24 countries (many of which were from Central and Eastern Europe) joined the Council. The Council of Europe now comprises countries as diverse as Turkey in the south, the UK and Iceland in the west, the Scandinavian countries in the north, and Russia in the east.

As an international court for (now) 47 countries, the ECtHR, too, is being confronted with various cases concerning religious issues. This is small wonder, because it is supposed to supervise the position of religion in Member States having an established church (the UK, Denmark), secular regimes (France, Turkey) and many different models in between. This chapter discusses the way the Court interprets the relationship between state and religion, and thus the state's role in regulating religion in contemporary pluralistic societies. The focus is on five recent determinative judgments. Which requirements should the state meet in dealing with religion in general? What are the conditions for a state to regulate religious manifestations and problems related to religion?

I shall start with a brief sketch of the Court's case law[8] concerning the freedom of religion from 1993 until 2011 (*Lautsi v Italy II*[9]). Over this period, the Court's approach may be characterised as a secular one, requiring the Member States to act neutrally and impartially towards all religions (section I). The year 2011, and more in particular the Italian crucifix case (the Grand Chamber judgment in *Lautsi II*), seems to present a break with this approach – not in the interpretation

important to note that the views by the Committee are not judicial decisions, given the composition of the institution. See, on this, Art 28 ICCPR and Art 5(4) Optional Protocol to the ICCPR.

[5] *Dakir v Belgium* App no 4619/12 (ECHR, 11 July 2017); and *Belcacemi and Oussar v Belgium* App no 37798/13 (ECHR, 11 July 2017).

[6] The Council of Europe was founded in 1949 on the initiative of 10 countries (Belgium, Denmark, France, Ireland, Italy, Luxembourg, the Netherlands, Norway, Sweden and the United Kingdom (UK)).

[7] All countries of the Continent, except Belarus and Vatican City (which is not a democratic but a theocratic state).

[8] The first case concerning the freedom of religion was *X v Sweden* App 434/58 (ECmHR, 30 June 1959), decided by the European Commission of Human Rights. The Commission (which used to decide on the admissibility of complaints, was abolished by the 11th Protocol in 1998, when the Court was installed on a permanent basis. I shall focus on the Court's case law concerning Art 9 ECHR.

[9] *Lautsi v Italy (Lautsi II)* App no 30814/06 (ECHR GC, 18 March 2011).

by the proponents of this judgment but certainly by its critics (section II). Recent case law, however (*Metodiev and others v Bulgaria*[10]), demonstrates that the Court again endorses its previous position. Subsequently (section III), the question is to what extent the state is allowed to restrict religious manifestations or issues related to religion in society? Judgments ranging from the ban on face-covering veils to a conviction for disparaging religious doctrines will be discussed (section IV). Finally, some concluding observations are made about the Court's recent case law concerning religious issues (section V).

I. The Court's Case Law from 1993 Until 2009: The Secular State Approach

Despite their prominent role in today's debate, claims based on the freedom of religion took a long time to reach the ECtHR. The first judgment concluding a violation of Article 9 ECHR[11] was issued as late as 1993, that is more than 30 years after the creation of the Court.[12] In this case – the famous judgment in *Kokkinakis v Greece*[13] – the Court for the first time expressed the importance of the freedom of thought, conscience and religion:

> As enshrined in Article 9 … freedom of thought, conscience and religion is one of the foundations of a 'democratic society' within the meaning of the Convention. It is, in its religious dimension, one of the most vital elements that go to make up the identity of believers and their conception of life, but it is also a precious asset for atheists, agnostics, sceptics and the unconcerned. The pluralism indissociable from a democratic society, which has been dearly won over the centuries, depends on it.[14]

Note that the Court interprets the freedom of thought, conscience and religion as including the rights of atheists, agnostics, sceptics and 'the unconcerned'.

Since 1993, the number of decisions dealing with the freedom of religion has increased considerably. All the same, in his quantitative analysis of the Court's

[10] *Metodiev and Others v Bulgaria* App no 58088/08 (ECHR, 15 June 2017) [section V].

[11] Art 9 ECHR (freedom of thought, conscience and religion) provides: '1. Everyone has the right to freedom of thought, conscience and religion; this right includes freedom to change his religion or belief and freedom, either alone or in community with others and in public or private, to manifest his religion or belief, in worship, teaching, practice and observance. 2. Freedom to manifest one's religion or beliefs shall be subject only to such limitations as are prescribed by law and are necessary in a democratic society in the interests of public safety, for the protection of public order, health or morals, or for the protection of the rights and freedoms of others.'

[12] The first case concerning Art 9 ECHR was *X v Sweden* (n. 8). This complaint was admitted and decided by the European Commission of Human Rights, being the first instance before cases were brought before the Court (pre-1998).

[13] *Kokkinakis v Greece* App no 14307/88 (ECHR, 25 May 1993). Mr Kokkinakis was, after becoming a Jehovah's Witness in 1936, arrested for proselytism more than 60 times. He was also interned and imprisoned on several occasions. Before the Court he complained that his conviction for proselytism was contrary to Art 9 ECHR (amongst other rights).

[14] *Kokkinakis v Greece* (n 13) para 31.

case law, Silvio Ferrari demonstrates that, compared to decisions concerning the freedom of expression, the case law about Article 9 is still relatively small.[15] Spread over 50 years, only 100 decisions were handed down, of which 30 found a violation of Article 9 (as against 392 such decisions establishing a violation of Article 10).

Until the year 2000, most claims regarding Article 9 by the ECtHR related to individual religious freedom. There were cases about proselytising activities of Jehovah's Witnesses; about the refusal of parents to allow their children to participate in school activities; about conscientious objections to taking an oath, and so on.[16] The year 2000, however, saw a turning point, represented by the case of *Hasan and Chaush v Bulgaria*.[17] This case was about the unlawful interference by the state with the internal organisation of the Muslim religious community in Bulgaria. As the Grand Chamber put it:

> Indeed, the autonomous existence of religious communities is indispensable for pluralism in a democratic society and is thus an issue at the very heart of the protection which Article 9 affords. It directly concerns not only the organization of the community as such but also the effective enjoyment of the right to freedom of religion by all its active members. Were the organizational life of the community not protected by Article 9 of the Convention, all other aspects of the individual's freedom of religion would become vulnerable.[18]

The decision marked a shift in the cases coming before the Court. From now on, it was not so much the religious freedom of the individual but that of the *entire religious community* that was often at stake.

In this new phase, questions concerning the church–state relationship had to be decided. According to Françoise Tulkens,[19] in its case law, the Court expressed two fundamental principles:

(a) the prohibition of arbitrary interference in the internal organisation of religious communities; and
(b) the duty of the state to maintain an attitude of neutrality and impartiality towards all religions.

Frequently, national laws had to be changed in order to make them conform to the framework of the Convention and the Court's jurisprudence. The newly admitted

[15] S Ferrari, 'The Strasbourg Court and Article 9 of the European Convention of Human Rights: A Quantitative Analysis of the Case Law' in J Temperman (ed), *The Lautsi Papers: Multidisciplinary Reflections on Religious Symbols in the Public School Classroom* (Leiden, Martinus Nijhoff Publishers, 2012) 13, 19. (Ferrari's research deals with the case law from 1959 to 2012.)

[16] ibid 26.

[17] *Hasan and Chaush v Bulgaria* App no 30985/96 (ECHR GC, 26 October 2000).

[18] ibid para 62.

[19] F Tulkens, 'The European Convention and Church–State Relations: Pluralism v Pluralism' (2009) 30 *Cardozo Law Review* 2579, 2580–86. Both principles return in different descriptions: Tulkens refers to *Hasan and Chaush v Bulgaria* (n 17), para 78; *Metropolitan Church of Bessarabia and others v Moldova* App no 45701/99 (ECHR, 13 December 2001) para 116; *Leyla Sahin v Turkey* App no 44774/98 (ECHR, 10 November 2005) para 107; *Church of Scientology Moscow v Russia* App 18147/02 (ECHR, 24 September 2007) para 72. See also Ferrari (n 15) 27.

Member States to the Council of Europe, which, after the demise of communism, accepted a more prominent role for religion in society, had more difficulties with the Court's secular approach.[20] Perhaps the clash between the Court and the Member States after the Chamber decision in *Lautsi v Italy*[21] was therefore to be expected.

II. A Break with the Secular State Approach?

A. The Crucifix Cases

The much-disputed 'crucifix cases' started with a complaint by Mrs Soile Lautsi about the compulsory display of crucifixes in public school classrooms in Italy.[22] Mrs Lautsi regarded this prominence of the Catholic religion as an infringement of her (and her children's) freedom of religion and her right to educate her children according to her philosophical convictions – a right laid down in Article 2 of the First Protocol to the Convention.[23] Before the Italian courts, her claims were rejected.[24] Mrs Lautsi then submitted her case to the Chamber of the ECtHR. In response to the Italian Government's claim that the crucifix has a neutral and even secular meaning, the Chamber declared its recognition of the symbol's predominantly religious (and more specifically Catholic) meaning.

The Court could not see how the display in state-school classrooms of a symbol that it is reasonable to associate with Catholicism (the majority religion in Italy) could serve the educational pluralism that is essential for the preservation of 'democratic society' within the Convention's meaning of that term.[25] In a unanimous decision, the Chamber concluded:

> [T]he compulsory display of a symbol of a particular faith in the exercise of public authority in relation to specific situations subject to governmental supervision, particularly in classrooms, restricts the rights of parents to educate their children in conformity with their convictions and the right of schoolchildren to believe or not believe. It is of

[20] According to Ferrari, the accession of the former communist countries marked 'a significant strengthening of the Orthodox and Catholic component and the simultaneous decline in the percentage of the Protestant countries': Ferrari (n 15) 14.

[21] *Lautsi v Italy (Lautsi I)* App 30814/06 (ECHR, 3 November 2009).

[22] On the origins and legal and political role of the crucifix in Italy, see Carlo Panara's contribution in ch 8 of the present volume: 'Religious Symbol or Something Else? The Legal and Political Signification of the Crucifix in Italy from the Unification of the Country (1861) to the Present Day'.

[23] Art 2, First Protocol to the ECHR provides that 'No person shall be denied the right to education. In the exercise of any functions which it assumes in relation to education and to teaching, the State shall respect the right of parents to ensure such education and teaching in conformity with their own religious and philosophical convictions.'

[24] In the conclusion to his overview of the Italian case law on the display of crucifixes, Carlo Panara writes that 'the case law discussed … reveals a remarkable lack of consistency'. This 'lack of consistency' concerns both the meaning that is attributed to the crucifix and the outcomes of the case law (both in support of the display of the crucifix and against it). See Panara, ch 8 of this volume.

[25] *Lautsi I* (n 21) para 56.

> the opinion that the practice infringes those rights because the restrictions are incompatible with the State's duty to respect neutrality in the exercise of public authority, particularly in the field of education.[26]

The decision caused a storm of protest, both in Italy and abroad. Of the 47 Members of the Council of Europe, 21 criticised the Chamber, although at the same time considerable support for the judgment could be noted.[27] An unprecedented number of 'third parties' filed an *amicus curiae*, asking the Court to reverse the first judgment. In practice, this was the result of a campaign initiated by the Italian Government and supported by the Holy See.[28]

On 18 March 2011, the Grand Chamber repealed the former decision. The crucifix is above all a religious symbol, the Grand Chamber observed.[29] But the crucial matter was that the Italian authorities considered its presence in public school classrooms to be the result of Italy's historical development. Thus, it corresponded to a tradition the authorities wanted to perpetuate. The question of whether or not to perpetuate a tradition, said the Grand Chamber, is an aspect that falls within the margin of appreciation of the respondent state. Moreover, a crucifix on a wall is 'an essentially passive symbol', and 'it cannot be deemed to have an influence on pupils comparable to that of didactic speech or participation in religious activities'.[30] For that reason, the principle of neutrality of the state had been upheld after all, according to the Grand Chamber. It concluded that there had been no violation of the Convention.

Much has been written about *Lautsi* since.[31] Obviously, the Court was confronted with a knotty problem. Had the first decision been sanctioned, the Court's position as the final authoritative judicial institution could have been severely threatened – what if Italy would not comply with the decision? This consequence is even more pressing these days than it was in 2011.[32] The Grand

[26] ibid para 57.

[27] For more detail on this, see P Cliteur, 'The Crucifix and the Ideal of a Religiously Neutral State' in (2019) 61 *Journal of Church and State* 181; and CM Zoethout, 'Rethinking Adjudication under the European Convention' in Temperman (ed) (n 15) 413.

[28] Armenia, Bulgaria, Cyprus, the Russian Federation, Greece, Lithuania, Malta and the Republic of San Marino acted as third-party interveners, while 10 more states expressed their solidarity with Italy (Albania, Austria, Croatia, Hungary, Macedonia, Moldavia, Poland, Serbia, Slovakia and Ukraine): Ferrari (n 15) 29. As Ferrari wryly remarked (ibid 29), 'Such a strong political support could not be ignored by the Strasbourg Court and probably carried some weight on the decision of the Grand Chamber.'

[29] Reacting to the Italian Government, which had tried to downplay its religious meaning and even tried to present it as a 'humanist and secular' symbol: *Lautsi II* (n 9) para 66.

[30] ibid para 72.

[31] See Temperman (ed) (n 15); D McGoldrick, 'Religion in the European Public Square and in European Public Life: Crucifixes in the Classroom' (2011) 11 *Human Rights Law Review* 451; MD Evans, 'From Cartoons to Crucifixes: Current Controversies Concerning the Freedom of Religion and the Freedom of Expression before the European Court of Human Rights' (2010) 26 *Journal of Law and Religion* 345; S Mancini, 'The Crucifix Rage: Supranational Constitutionalism Bumps against the Counter-Majoritarian Difficulty' (2010) 6 *European Constitutional Law Review* 6.

[32] In more or less the same period, the debate in the UK about the *Hirst* case took place. In this case, the ECtHR rejected the general ban on voting rights for prisoners in the UK. The UK reacted furiously.

Chamber in effect gave up the idea of neutrality when it comes to public education. That may be comprehensible from a political point of view, but it is dubious from a legal point of view, to say the least.

The politically sensitive character of the cases and the need of the Court to steer in a course between religion and politics is apparent in later judgments. Four cases, all decided in the years 2017 and 2018, will now be discussed, which demonstrate the diversity of the claims and the difficulties the Court is facing as a 'constitutional court for Europe'.

B. Reaffirmation of State Neutrality

A matter regularly brought before the Court is the registration of (new) religious organisations. One such case is that of *Metodiev and others v Bulgaria*.[33] This case is important for different reasons. First, it is once more a reaffirmation of the principle of state neutrality and impartiality as required by the Convention; and, second, the Court expresses yet another principle underlying the freedom of religion. This principle may prove to be important, particularly when it comes to new religions and philosophical stances.

The case deals with the refusal of the Bulgarian authorities to register an association of the Ahmadyya faith, a religious movement based on Sunni Islam and considered heretical by the mainstream Sunni tradition. The claimants call themselves the 'community of Muslim Ahmadyya'. The Ahmadiyyas derive their name from Muhammad's alternative name, Ahmad, and they are also known as Ahmadi Muslims, Ahmadiyyas or Ahmadis.

The Bulgarian authorities have refused to register the organisation, allegedly owing to the lack of a precise description of its beliefs and rites in its statutes. In practice, that means the community cannot be distinguished from other religious communities, as required by the Bulgarian Religions Act. The Act aims to differentiate between different denominations in order to avoid confrontations between religious communities. As a consequence, new associations with (according to the authorities) the same doctrine as an existing denomination are unable to attain legal status in Bulgaria, meaning that only *one* religious association for each religious movement is allowed. The Court subsequently observed that:

> In a situation of conflict within the religious community, the State has *the duty to remain neutral and impartial* and it should not take measures favoring a particular leader of a

The Court's judgment even prompted the House of Commons to adopt a resolution stating it would not to abide by the Court's decision. *Hirst v United Kingdom* App no 74025/01 (ECHR, 6 October 2005). For more about the consequences of *Hirst* for human rights protection in the UK, see CM Zoethout, 'Should we be worrying about a Brexit from the European Convention on Human Rights now, too?' (2017) 21 *Ancilla Iuris* 22.

[33] *Metodiev and others v Bulgaria* (n 10).

> divided religious community or seeking to compel the community, or part of it, to place itself under a single leadership against its will.[34]

Besides this, the *assessment of the nature* of beliefs (ie whether they are different from those of existing denominations) has become a matter for the Bulgarian courts and not for the religious communities themselves to decide. Such an approach is hard to reconcile with Article 9 ECHR, as interpreted in the light of the freedom of association (Article 11 ECHR). The freedom of religion *excludes any assessment by the State of the legitimacy of religious beliefs or the forms of expression of those beliefs.*[35] That principle holds true even if the aim is to preserve unity within a religious community. The alleged lack of precision in the description of the religious association's beliefs and rites in its constitution, does not justify denial of its registration. The Court concluded that there had indeed been a violation of Article 9 ECHR.

If accepted, the Bulgarian system would lead to consequences entirely at odds with European freedom of religion. Instead of taking a position of religious neutrality, the courts have to decide which current group within a specific religious tradition is the preferred one. Apparently, the Bulgarian authorities do not consider the Ahmadis the rightful heirs of the Islamic creed, but the question as to why remains.

C. Newly Emerging Religions

There is yet another reason why *Metodiev* deserves closer attention. The Court expresses an important principle with regard to newly emerging religions and beliefs. In order to understand this, a much more conspicuous example may be introduced than the case of the Ahmadis. A contemporary issue with which courts are struggling is the American religion of the Church of the Flying Spaghetti Monster. So far, the ECtHR has not been required to consider an application concerning this conviction, but it seems only a matter of time before it will need to do so. Recently, a case was decided by the Council of State of the Netherlands. A Pastafarian (an adherent to the Church) was refused permission to wear a colander as a manifestation of her religion on a photo for an official document.[36]

A short introduction may give some context. In January 2005, the Kansas Board of Education was considering making changes to its 'science standards', and thus to education in the State of Kansas (USA). The Board proposed that 'intelligent

[34] ibid para 46 (emphasis added). The judgment was published in French.

[35] ibid: 'La Cour rappelle en effet que, selon sa jurisprudence, le droit à la liberté de religion tel que l'entend la Convention exclut en principe que l'État apprécie la légitimité des croyances religieuses ou les modalités d'expression de celles-ci, et ce même dans un souci de préserver l'unité au sein d'une communauté religieuse.'

[36] Afdeling Bestuursrechtspraak Raad van State (Council of State, administrative justice section), 15 August 2018, Decision 201707148/1/A, para 8, ECLI:NL:RVS:2018:2715.

design' be presented as an alternative explanation to the scientific evolution theory. 'Intelligent design' is the claim (based on Biblical doctrine) that a conscious being created the universe. The decision did not pass unnoticed. In protest at the Board's proposal, in May 2005, Bobby Henderson, a 25-year-old Oregon University student at the time, posted an open letter to the Kansas School Board on its website. In this letter, Henderson wrote that the idea of intelligent design was no more valid than the belief that a Flying Spaghetti Monster created the universe. That being so, why not teach that theory as well?

The Kansas Board withdrew its plans within two years, but the Church of the Flying Spaghetti Monster has outlasted the dispute, spreading via the Internet to countries around the world. In 2006, Henderson published *The Gospel of the Flying Spaghetti Monster*[37] and continued to be critical of 'intelligent design'. Meanwhile, the Church of the Flying Spaghetti Monster (FSM) or Pastafarians gained many adherents.[38] In Europe, where the evolution theory is fairly uncontroversial, the purpose of the Flying Spaghetti Monster has shifted somewhat.[39] Followers of the Church test the relationship between Church and state in countries ranging from relatively secular France to Catholic Poland.[40]

Pastafarians wear a headcover, just like many religious people do – in this case, a colander. This headgear is considered a sacred object, which adherents wear in public in order to honour the Flying Spaghetti Monster. And that is what was disputed in the Dutch court case. The petitioner wanted to wear a colander in the photograph for her passport.[41] After rejection by the first court (in which the judges found that Pastafarianism does not prescribe the wearing of a colander), the Dutch Council of State focused on the question: 'Is Pastafarianism to be considered a religion in the sense of Article 9 ECHR?'[42] This was an important development, because now the thorny question was put on the table: which set of beliefs can be accepted as 'religious'? Moreover, can the state judge on the nature of religions without losing its status as a neutral arbiter?

The Council of State started with a seemingly uncontroversial approach, following the ECtHR's case law. Accordingly, it stated that a precondition for a set of convictions to be recognised as a religion is that these convictions 'attain a certain level of cogency, seriousness, cohesion and importance'.[43] According to

[37] R Henderson, *The Gospel of the Flying Spaghetti Monster* (New York, Villard, 2006).

[38] There is no official count of Church membership in Europe (or anywhere else), but 'Pastafarian' Facebook pages from countries across the Continent have accumulated thousands of likes, writes Kathy Gilsinan in 'The Church of the Flying Spaghetti Monster' *The Atlantic* (November 2017) 23.

[39] ibid.

[40] ibid.

[41] The Dutch laws regulating the requirements for photographs for driving licences, allows exceptions to the general rule that faces must be uncovered, for religious, philosophical or medical reasons. Afdeling Bestuursrechtspraak Raad van State (n 36) para 2.

[42] ibid para 8.

[43] ECtHR, *Campbell and Cosans v United Kingdom*, 25 February 1982, Series A, No 48, 4 EHHR 293; *Eweida v UK* App nos 48420/10, 59842/10 and 36516/10 (ECHR,15 January 2013) para 81; and *SAS v France* App no 43835/11 (ECHR, 1 July 2014) para 55.

the Council, Pastafarianism does not fulfil these requirements. After – admittedly – a very precise description and weighing by the Council, Pastafarianism was considered a parody. The required 'seriousness' and 'cohesion' were lacking, according to the Council.[44] What seems to have played a major role in the State Council's judgment is that it had difficulties in accepting the serious intentions of the Pastafarians. They were suspected of being engaged in parody. The point is, however, that from the perspective of an individual believer, her own ideas about the transcendental realm might appear entirely cogent and serious, whereas from the perspective of an outsider there may be less cogency.

As long as national courts are inclined to be indulgent and accept a broad range of religions, there seems to be no problem. Of course, even if considered a religion, it is subject to the limitations set out in Article 9(2) ECHR. But the question is, must a phenomenon that some people will consider to be a parody of the Christian faith, and perhaps of any faith, by definition *not* fall within the scope of Article 9? That seems hard to believe. By taking the Pastafarian dogmas less seriously than Christianity, the Dutch Council of State seems to be entering a dangerous zone. The Council becomes a partisan participant in a discussion about what religious ideas are serious, even though the judiciary is supposed to act neutrally. Does not the Strasbourg Court require that the state, or judges for that matter, should refrain from this form of review (*Metodiev v Bulgaria*)? This approach runs the risk of unjustified discrimination against less well-known religions.[45] Most likely, these kinds of cases will shortly be brought before the ECtHR. The question is whether the Court will be able to stick to its criterion of 'seriousness' without being accused of bias.

III. The Neutral State Regulating Religion in Society

A. The Ban on the Face-covering Veil

While the state should take a neutral and impartial stance towards religion, the question is what it means for the state when regulating religious manifestations

[44] The satirical character of Pastafarianism is expressed in the way in which the theist beliefs are parodied in the doctrine of the Flying Spaghetti Monster, according to the Council. The Church has 'holy' books, among which are *The Gospel of the 'Flying Spaghetti Monster* and *The Loose Canon*, which covers 'The Old Pastament', 'The New Pastament' and the 'Official Pastafarian Prayer Book'. The last of these contains the most important prayer: 'Our Pasta, who "Arghh" in heaven, Swallowed by the shame. Thy Midgit come. Thy Sauce be yum, On top some grated Parmesan. Give us this day our garlic bread. And give us our cutlasses, As we swashbuckle, splice the main-brace and cuss. And lead us into temptation, But deliver us some Pizza. For thine are Meatballs, and the beer, and the strippers, for ever and ever. Ramen.' According to the Dutch Court, 'This prayer is unmistakenly deduced from the Christian Tradition's "Our Father" and intends to be a parody.' (Afdeling Bestuursrechtspraak Raad van State (n 36) para 9.2.)

[45] A matter that may come before the ECtHR within a few years is the Santo Daime Church, whose tea ceremony resulted in criminal convictions by the Dutch Court of Appeal (ECLI:NL:GHAMS:2018:689 – Gerechtshof Amsterdam, 28-02-2018/23-003369-16). The Santo Daime Church's religious rituals

in society. The meaning of the limitation clause in Article 9(2) ECHR[46] has been developed further by the Strasbourg Court in some talked-about recent cases.

In 2010, the French National Assembly proclaimed a general ban on the wearing of the face-covering veil – a law that was 'tested and approved' by the ECtHR in the case of *SAS v France*.[47] Since then, Belgium has adopted a similar law, pursuing the aims of public safety, gender equality and a certain conception of 'living together in society'.[48] In 2017, two cases were judged by the Court challenging the Belgian ban on wearing a full-face veil in public: *Dakir v Belgium* and *Belcacemi and Oussar v Belgium*.[49] The Belgian law was very similar to the French law prohibiting the concealing of the face in public, and thus the cases were comparable to *SAS v France*.

Two critical aspects in the judgments deserve to be highlighted. First, in reviewing whether or not the law in question had a 'legitimate aim', the notion of 'living together in society' is accepted by the Court. It repeats the Belgian Government's motive for enacting the law, which was 'to address a practice which it deemed incompatible, in Belgian society, with the ground rules of social communication and more broadly the establishment of human relations that are essential for living together'. Put differently, 'living together' in society means that recognition of the other and being identifiable, are preconditions for social relationships.[50]

Second, the Court explicitly refers to the fact that democratically legitimated institutions adopted the law and thus constituted 'a choice of society'.[51] For that

include a ceremony involving tea containing a drug (DMT) that is prohibited by the Dutch law on opiates. Adherents to the Church invoked their freedom to manifest their religion (and thus the transporting and use of the tea). The Court however, considered the limitation justifiable with a view to national healthcare (the reason why the hard drug was prohibited in the first place).

[46] Art 9(2) ECHR (freedom of thought, conscience and religion) provides: 'Freedom to manifest one's religion or beliefs shall be subject only to such limitations as are prescribed by law and are necessary in a democratic society in the interests of public safety, for the protection of public order, health or morals, or for the protection of the rights and freedoms of others.'

[47] *SAS v France* (n 43).

[48] *Belcacemi and Oussar v Belgium* (n 5) para 49.

[49] *Dakir v Belgium* (n 5); *Belcacemi and Oussar v Belgium* (n 5). The Belgian law of 1 June 2011 differed from its French counterpart in that it provided, in addition to a fine, for a term of imprisonment (up to a maximum of €200 or seven days' imprisonment, respectively, in the event of a repeat offence). Furthermore, the French law made it possible to fine the person who forces a woman to cover her face, too.

[50] See, on the notion of 'living together' in society in the French parliamentary debate on the law prohibiting the wearing of the face-covering veil, CM Zoethout, 'Secularism Stated, Rejected, and Reaffirmed: France, Italy, and Canada and the Dilemmas of Multi-Religious Societies' (2015) 17 *Journal of Religion and Society* 1.

[51] *Dakir v Belgium* (n 5) para 56: 'However, the respondent State, in enacting the provisions in question, sought to address a practice which it deemed incompatible, in Belgian society, with the ground rules of social communication and more broadly the establishment of human relations that are essential for living together (see the judgment of the Constitutional Court of 6 December 2012, paragraph B.21, cited in paragraph 21 above). In doing so, it sought to protect a form of interaction between individuals that was essential, in the respondent State's view, to the functioning of a democratic society (see the above-cited judgment, paragraph B.28, cited in paragraph 21 above). From this perspective, and similarly to the situation which previously arose in France (*SAS v France*, § 153), it seems that the question whether or not it should be permitted to wear the full-face veil in public places in Belgium constitutes a choice of society.'

reason, the Court stated 'it had to show restraint in its scrutiny of Convention compliance'.[52] The decision-making process leading up to the impugned ban took several years and was accompanied by a wide-ranging debate within the House of Representatives, and by a detailed and thorough examination by the Belgian Constitutional Court of all the interests involved. Moreover, since there is no European consensus on the matter, the Belgian authorities must be left a wide margin of appreciation, according to the Court's standing practice. The ECtHR concludes unanimously there has been no violation of Article 9 ECHR. Even though the wearing of these veils is accepted as a manifestation of one's religious beliefs, limitations have been considered justified.

B. Secular Clothing in a Religious Context

A case that deals with the relationship between the freedom of religion and the freedom of expression is *Sekmadienis Ltd v Lithuania*, of January 2018.[53] This case is about 'secular clothing' within a religious context, and once more expresses some important principles. What is at stake?

Sekmadienis Ltd is a clothing company that had been fined. In the city of Vilnius and on its website, the company displayed a series of advertisements deemed by the Lithuanian courts and other bodies to offend against public morals. The advertisements had used models and slogans referring to Jesus and Mary. The first of the three advertisements showed a young man with long hair, a headband, a halo around his head and several tattoos, wearing a pair of jeans. A caption at the bottom of the image read 'Jesus, what trousers!' The second advertisement showed a young woman wearing a white dress and a headdress with white and red flowers in it. She had a halo around her head too, and was holding a string of beads. The caption at the bottom of the image read 'Dear Mary, what a dress!' In the third advertisement Jesus and Mary are both shown wearing 'secular clothes'.[54]

The Strasbourg Court found that, despite having triggered a number of complaints (including from the Roman Catholic Church in Lithuania), the advertisements were not gratuitously offensive and did not incite hatred. Nor had the domestic authorities provided sufficient justifications why such use of religious symbols had been contrary to public morals. Accordingly, the domestic authorities had failed to strike a fair balance between, on the one hand, the protection of public morals and the rights of religious people, and, on the other hand, the applicant company's right to freedom of expression.

[52] *Dakir v Belgium* (n 5) para 57: 'The Court points out, as it emphasized in *SAS v France* (cited above, §§153–55), that in such cases it has to show restraint in its scrutiny of Convention compliance, in this case in assessing a decision taken democratically within Belgian society.'

[53] *Sekmadienis Ltd v Lithuania* App no 69317/14 (ECHR Chamber Judgment, 30 January 2018).

[54] ibid paras 6–8.

In this case, the Court reiterates its key phrase about the freedom of expression in a democratic society. The freedom of expression not only encompasses expressions with which everybody agrees, but it also extends to ideas that offend, shock or disturb. The Court further restates that in a pluralist democratic society, those who choose to exercise the freedom to manifest their religion cannot reasonably expect to be exempt from all criticism. They must tolerate and accept the denial by others of their religious beliefs, and even the propagation by others of doctrines hostile to their faith.[55] Even though the advertisements had a commercial purpose and could not be said to constitute 'criticism' of religious ideas,[56] the applicable principles were nonetheless similar, according to the Court.

Sekmadienis Ltd v Lithuania is important for several reasons. First of all, the decision was an expression of the underlying principle in the Convention system, that religion does not have priority over the freedoms of speech or expression. Second, the case affirmed that there is no such thing as a right not to be insulted. What is more, living in present-day pluralist society means allowing one's cherished convictions (be they religious or not) to be criticised by others. Third, the Court expressly said that the same principles that are valid for the freedom of expression apply to commercial advertisements.

So far, so good. But 10 months later, in the case of *ES v Austria*,[57] the Court weighed the first two principles quite differently. In that case, there is strong emphasis on a principle that might have been casually evoked but which at this time of looming terrorist violence achieves a new meaning – the principle of 'religious peace' (as opposed to religious violence). In this case the state's duty to preserve 'religious peace' prevails over other values. Different though these cases are, the question that comes to the fore is whether there is a difference in the need for protection of religious feelings between Christians and Muslims?

C. Disparaging Religious Doctrines

In the case of *ES v Austria*, the applicant, ES, had been convicted for making statements suggesting that Muhammad had had paedophilic tendencies. The case is primarily about freedom of expression, but since it concerned a conviction in Austria for disparaging religious doctrines, it is relevant in the present context. Moreover, in this case, the preservation of public peace plays an important role. Undoubtedly this value will return for consideration in future case law. For these reasons, a somewhat more detailed discussion of this case follows.

In October and November 2009, Mrs ES (Elisabeth Sabaditsch-Wolff, a well-known anti-Islam activist) held two seminars entitled 'Basic Information on

[55] ibid para 81, para 70. See also *Otto-Preminger Institut v Austria* App no 13470/87 (ECHR, 20 September 1994) para 47 and *İA v Turkey* App no 42571/98 (ECHR, 13 December 2005) para 28; and see the position of the Venice Commission in para 49 of *Sekmadienis* (n 53).

[56] *Sekmadienis Ltd v Lithuania* (n 53) para 76.

[57] *ES v Austria* App no 38450/12 (ECHR Chamber Judgment, 25 October 2018).

Islam', in which she discussed the marriage between the Prophet Muhammad and a 6-year-old girl, Aisha, which allegedly was consummated when she was 9 years old. Inter alia, the applicant stated that Muhammad 'liked to do it with children' and 'A 56-year-old and a six-year-old? … What do we call it, if it is not paedophilia?'[58]

Although the term 'paedophilia' was, of course, not mentioned in Islamic sources, authentic Islamic scriptures attest to the fact that this marriage occurred, and this is uncontested in Islamic tradition. Muhammed had indeed married a girl named Aisha, and the age difference is generally accepted as a historical fact. The only difference is about what to think of this, or how to classify this. In 2011, the Vienna Regional Criminal Court found that Mrs ES's statements implied that Muhammad had had paedophilic tendencies, and convicted her for disparaging religious doctrines (under Article 188 of the Austrian Criminal Code). The higher courts confirmed this decision.

Before the ECtHR, Mrs Sabaditsch-Wolff complained that in her view, her statements were value judgements based on facts, not contested in official Islamic doctrine and, therefore, not *mere* value judgements (as the national courts classified them). Second, she argued that her criticism of Islam occurred in the framework of an objective and lively discussion that contributed to a public debate, and had not been aimed at defaming Islam. Third, she submitted that religious groups had to tolerate even severe criticism. The Chamber's decision was handed down on 25 October 2018.[59]

The Court, on the basis of Article 9(2) ECHR, now had to review whether there was a legal basis for the limitation on freedom of religion, whether there was a legitimate aim and, if so, whether the limitation was necessary in a democratic society. As far as the legitimate aim of Article 188 of the Criminal Code[60] (the basis for ES's prosecution) was concerned, the Court accepted the assessment that the interference pursued the aim of 'preventing disorder by safeguarding religious peace as well as religious feelings'.[61]

[58] The applicant herself said that she was saying this, quoting a conversation she had had with her sister, who was of the opinion that 'one [had] to paraphrase [the accusation that Muhammad was a paedophile], say it in a more diplomatic way': ibid para 53.

[59] One third party intervener, the European Centre for Law and Justice, also submitted that the statements – though value judgements – were not devoid of any factual basis. Furthermore, the organisation observed that Art 188 of the Austrian Criminal Code, which protects the *belief itself rather than the believer's feelings*, is a prohibition of blasphemy – a criminal charge that, according to international law standards, should be abolished. Finally, it pointed out that Art 188 had a deterrent ('chilling') effect, obstructing free debate: ibid para 38.

[60] Art 188 (Disparagement of religious doctrines): 'Whoever, in circumstances where his or her behaviour is likely to arouse justified indignation, publicly disparages or insults a person who, or an object which, is an object of veneration of a church or religious community established within the country, or a dogma, a lawful custom or a lawful institution of such a church or religious community, shall be liable to up to six months' imprisonment or a day-fine for a period of up to 360 days.'

[61] The aim of protecting 'religious peace and the religious feelings of others' is part of the Court's previous case law. See *ES v Austria* (n 57) para 21, with references to among others *Otto-Preminger v Austria* (n 55).

Subsequently, the Court had to decide about the question whether the interference 'was necessary in a democratic society' (Article 9(2) ECHR). In weighing this matter, the Court has frequently held that states enjoy a margin of appreciation, particularly where there is no uniform European approach. Apart from this, the Chamber reiterated that the Member State had a positive obligation under Article 9 of ensuring the peaceful coexistence of all religions and those not belonging to a religious group by ensuring mutual tolerance.[62] As to the classification of statements of fact and value judgements, this again is a matter for the national authorities to decide.

In applying these principles to the case before it, the Chamber first reiterated the *Sekmadienis* approach, that 'a religious group must tolerate the denial by others of their religious beliefs and even the propagation by others of doctrines hostile to their faith, as long as the statements at issue do not incite hatred or religious intolerance'.[63] It then referred to the explanation of the national courts that 'the applicant's statements had been capable of arousing public indignation', and 'could only be understood as having been aimed at demonstrating that Muhammed was not a worthy subject of worship'.[64] The Court endorsed this assessment. It concluded that the national courts had comprehensively assessed the wider context of the applicant's statements and carefully examined her right to freedom of expression as against the rights of others to have their religious feelings protected and to have religious peace in Austria. In addition, the Court remarked that the impugned statements were not phrased in a neutral manner but amounted to a generalisation without factual basis. Thus, by considering them as going beyond the permissible limits of an objective debate and classifying them as an abusive attack on the Prophet of Islam (which was capable of stirring up prejudice and putting at risk religious peace), the domestic courts had come to the conclusion that the facts contained elements of incitement to religious intolerance. The Court accepted this reasoning.[65]

This was a remarkable case indeed, for many reasons. The Court's overview of relevant international material included reports from four international organisations that contained statements that blasphemy should not be deemed a criminal offence.[66] Oddly enough, in the subsequent reasoning of the Chamber, there was

[62] The Chamber refers among other judgments to *SAS v France* (n 47) paras 123–28.

[63] *ES v Austria* (n 57) para 52.

[64] ibid.

[65] ibid para 53.

[66] ibid para 27 (Council of Europe Parliamentary Assembly), para 28 (the 'Venice Commission') and para 30 (UN Human Rights Committee). Finally, the European Parliament, in its resolution of 27 February 2014 on the situation of fundamental rights in the European Union (2012) (2013/2078(INI)), held that 'The European Parliament, … [r]ecalls that national laws that criminalise blasphemy restrict freedom of expression concerning religious or other beliefs, that they are often applied to persecute, mistreat, or intimidate persons belonging to religious or other minorities, and that they can have a serious inhibiting effect on freedom of expression and on freedom of religion or belief; *recommends that the Member States decriminalise such offenses*.' (emphasis added)

no reference to the statements of these international organisations whatsoever. The Chamber referred only to previous case law. The fact that Article 188 of the Austrian Criminal Code was penalising blasphemy was not discussed at all.

Furthermore, Article 188 of the Austrian Criminal Code requires that there is a situation of 'justified indignation'. A disputable phrase, because the question is: What is 'justified'? Does not the term 'justified' refer to an objective standard? As a consequence of the Austrian provision, it is the believers' approach that is the basis for prosecution, rather than public disorder in general. That in itself is already problematic. But in addition, one may wonder whether the context here does not make the 'justified indignation' (if accepted at all) questionable. The point is that Mrs Sabaditsch-Wolff is an activist of the right-wing Freedom Party of Austria, who made her statements at a semi-public seminar attended by about 30 people, including one undercover journalist.[67] As Greg Taylor puts it in his study on Austria's law against defamation of religion, 'the reputation of the Freedom Party of Austria is such that it could hardly be expected that the seminar would be one long hymn in praise of Islam'.[68] Neither the Court nor the national courts considered this point, which is certainly a justified criticism of the case.

IV. Concluding Remarks

The freedom of religion is a much-disputed phenomenon in twenty-first-century societies. As has been demonstrated by the preceding selection of ECtHR case law, the cases touch upon sensitive issues, more often than not concerning the role of the state in regulating religion. In line with previous case law, with one exception, the Court has once more been expressing the state's duty to remain neutral and impartial towards religions.

The case law discussed in the previous paragraphs raises many questions the Court will most likely have to answer in the near future. One of these questions is whether the preconditions for recognising a religion (namely that convictions attain 'a certain level of cogency, seriousness, cohesion and importance') can be maintained. Is it possible to uphold the principle of neutrality of the state authorities, while at the same time having the courts assess these notions? Much will depend on the Court's interpretation of these preconditions when confronted with newly emerging sets of religious beliefs.

In reviewing the Belgian ban on face-covering veils, the Court accepted the law's aim to ensure the observance of the minimum requirements of life in society. In addition to this, it considered the parliamentary debate that preceded the

[67] See G Taylor, 'Austria's law against defamation of religion: a case study' (2005) 30 *Journal of Law and Religion* 80. According to Taylor, Art 188's principal concern is with the public standing of religions as quasi-public institutions – that is, with their honour. It is a law against defamation of religion.

[68] ibid 95.

adoption of the law. It concluded that the law constituted a 'choice of society'. For that reason, the Court stated it had to show restraint in its scrutiny of Convention compliance. This is a fundamental point the Court is making here. But the question remains: under what conditions will the Court give priority to the national democratic institutions?

Then the Chamber's judgment in the Austrian case on disparaging religious doctrines – a judgment that affects freedom of religion, freedom of speech and even freedom of association. In a semi-public gathering, a question was raised concerning an element that is uncontested in Islamic doctrine – the marriage between the Islamic Prophet and a young girl of the age indicated. This question ended up in a conviction for disparaging a religious doctrine and disturbing the religious peace. Now one may seriously wonder about what this implies: if it is no longer possible to raise these questions about a religious doctrine in a gathering of about 30 people, would not this be a very alarming message indeed for the scope of both freedom of speech and freedom of religion?

8

Religious Symbol or Something Else?

The Legal and Political Signification of the Crucifix in Italy from the Unification of the Country (1861) to the Present Day

CARLO PANARA

I. Introduction

Catholicism has been historically, and remains, an important marker of the Italian identity despite the significant drop in the number of Italians who identify as Catholic. According to Eurispes, the percentage of Italian citizens who identify as Catholic was 87.8 per cent in 2006, 76.5 per cent in 2010 and 71.1 per cent in 2016, as against 12.2 per cent, 23.5 per cent and 28.9 per cent respectively who identify as non-religious or as belonging to another religious denomination. According to polls conducted by Ipsos, 85.4 per cent of Italians identified themselves as Catholic in 2007, as against 13 per cent as non-religious and 1.6 per cent identifying with other religious denominations. In 2017, 74.4 per cent of Italians identified themselves as Catholic, versus 22.6 per cent as non-religious and 3 per cent identifying with other religious denominations. However, the overwhelming majority of those who declare themselves to be non-believers or agnostics have a family background in Catholicism. According to a study of the Osservatorio socio-religioso della Conferenza Episcopale Italiana, in 2009 nearly 59 million out of 60 million residents in Italy had been christened as Catholic, that is, 97.9 per cent of the resident population.

The notable decrease in the number of Italians who identify as Catholic is the result of the progressive secularisation of Italian society – especially since the 1970s, when divorce and the abortion legislation were introduced – and of the increasing multicultural and multi-religious character of Italian society due to immigration from non-Catholic countries. In 2018, over 5 million foreign citizens, mostly non-Catholic, resided in Italy (8.3 per cent of the overall population). A study by Istat found that in 2011–12, 983,000 foreign residents were Orthodox Christians, 957,000 Muslim and 913,000 Catholic, whilst the remaining 714,000 identified with other religious denominations or as atheist or agnostic, or refused to say.

This chapter seeks to reconstruct the meaning of the presence of the crucifix in public establishments in Italy as this emerges from the case law of the Italian courts. The display of crucifixes in public establishments in Italy has given rise to many important court cases, including the famous *Lautsi v Italy* saga, which was heard by the European Court of Human Rights (ECtHR) in 2009 and 2011. The number of legal disputes concerning the crucifix in Italy is not surprising. Italy is the centre of Roman Catholicism, with the Holy See being based in the Vatican City in Rome. Historically, the country has always had a strong Catholic identity. On the other hand, over the last 20 years the increasing influx of migrants belonging to different faiths, along with the progressive secularisation of the Italian society, has led Italian governments and political parties to rethink national identity. All these features make Italy one of the most interesting case studies concerning the display of religious symbols in schools, courtrooms and other public establishments. In this study, I shall look at the history of the display of crucifixes in public buildings in Italy since the unification of the country in 1861. I shall attempt to show that the crucifix in the context of public establishments, far from having an exclusively or primarily spiritual signification, has always responded to certain political demands, such as legitimising the authority of the state to its 'subjects', or 'defending' Italian identity from the perceived threat from 'newcomers' who belong to different religious denominations and cultures.[1]

II. The Historical Origins of the Compulsory Display of Crucifixes in State Schools and Courtrooms

The obligation to display the crucifix in Italian classrooms dates back to prior to the unification of Italy. It was introduced by a royal decree issued in the Kingdom of Piedmont-Sardinia (Royal Decree No 4336 of 15 September 1860), one of the various kingdoms that existed before the creation of a unitary Italy. This obligation reflected the position of the Albertine Statute of 1848, the constitutional charter that King Carlo Alberto of Savoia had conceded to his subjects in Piedmont-Sardinia in response to the demands of liberal and radical groups. Upon the unification of Italy under the crown of the Savoia family in 1861, the Albertine

[1] Although it builds on some of my previous work, this study has a focus, aim and objectives completely different from those of my earlier publications: C Panara, '*Lautsi v Italy*: The Display of Religious Symbols by the State' (2011) 17 *European Public Law* 139; C Panara, 'Another Defeat for the Principle of Secularism: Recent Developments on the Display of the Crucifix in Italian Courtrooms' (2011) 6 *Religion & Human Rights* 259; C Panara, 'Back to the Basics of Fundamental Rights: An Appraisal of State-Imposed Symbols in Light of the ECHR and of Italian Constitutional Law' in J Temperman (ed), *The Lautsi Papers – Multidisciplinary Reflections on Religious Symbols in the Public-School Classroom* (Leiden/Boston, MA, BRILL/Martinus Nijhoff, 2012) 301.

Statute became the constitutional charter of the new-born Kingdom. Article 1 of the Statute attributed primacy to Catholicism, defined as 'the only religion of the state', whereas the other existing cults were merely 'tolerated'.

Despite this strong constitutional proclamation of allegiance to Catholicism, the predominantly liberal and secular elites that ruled Italy from the unification of the country until the collapse, in 1922, of the liberal parliamentary regime and the rise to power of the fascist dictator Benito Mussolini, endorsed the separation between the State and the Catholic Church. This is due to a number of reasons, including the anti-clerical views of many liberals who identified the Catholic Church with the anti-liberal ideas of the old regimes, but also the existence of the Papal States encompassing the region of Rome, which prevented the new-born Kingdom of Italy from installing its capital in Rome until 1870. That year, following the defeat of the French army by the Prussians in the battle of Sedan and the subsequent fall of Napoleon III, which ended the protection the Pope enjoyed from France, the Italian army invaded the Papal States, capturing Rome in September 1870.

The Kingdom of Italy granted a number of prerogatives to the Pope and the Church, and maintained the palaces in the Vatican under the control of the Pope. Quite understandably, though, the capture of Rome by the Italians caused a significant split between the State and the Church, and led to an interruption of the bilateral relations between the Kingdom of Italy and the Holy See that lasted until the concordat of 1929. The split was further exacerbated by the '*non expedit*' ('it is not expedient') instruction of 1874, whereby Pope Pius IX forbade Italian Catholics from standing as candidates or voting in parliamentary elections, a prohibition that would be expressly revoked only in 1919 by Pope Benedict XV.[2]

The display of crucifixes in classrooms in state schools must have receded particularly in the years after the First World War, possibly due to the rise of anticlerical leftist parties, such as the Socialist Party (which obtained over 32 per cent of the popular vote in the parliamentary election of 1919 and controlled 1,915 Italian municipalities out of 6,647 in 1920) and the Communist Party (founded in 1921). This would explain why Giovanni Gentile, the Minister of Education in the Mussolini Government from 1922 to 1924, addressed this issue during his first month in office and in November 1922 sent the following instruction to the municipalities:

> In recent years the image of Christ and the portrait of the King have been removed from many primary schools of the Kingdom. This is a manifest and unacceptable violation and in particular it damages the dominant religion of the State, as well as the unity of the Nation. For this reason, all the municipalities of the Kingdom shall reinstate the two crowned symbols of [our] faith and [of our] national sentiment in all the schools which do not currently display them.[3]

[2] On the relations between the State and the Catholic Church until the Lateran Pacts of 1929, see C Cardia, *Risorgimento e religione* (Turin, Giappichelli, 2011).

[3] Instruction No 68 of 22 November 1922. All the translations from Italian or other languages are the author's, except where otherwise specified.

In 1926, the Government extended the obligation to display the crucifix to all public schools of any type and level and to the universities:

> The symbol of our religion, sacred to the faith and the national sentiment, shall admonish and inspire young students, who prepare their minds and spirits in the universities and in the high schools for the elevated duties to which they are destined.[4]

These measures were confirmed by two royal decrees issued in 1924 and 1928.[5] The return of the crucifix in the classrooms was a by-product of the fascist Government's policy of rapprochement with the Catholic Church in an attempt to consolidate the grip of the regime on Italian society. On 11 February 1929, this policy culminated in the signature by Italy and the Holy See of a concordat, known as the 'Lateran Pacts' (*Patti Lateranensi*), which would remain in force until 1984. Article 1 of the Lateran Pacts restated the old principle of the Albertine Statute, whereby Catholicism enjoyed a privileged status in Italy as the only religion of the state.

In 1926, the display of crucifixes also became mandatory in courtrooms. This obligation originates from an instruction issued in 1926 by the Minister of Justice, who ordered that the 'venerated symbol of truth and justice' had to be 'reinstated' in the courtrooms 'in accordance with our ancient tradition'. This demonstrates that in previous years crucifixes had often disappeared from public buildings, but also confirms that the fascist regime had set itself the mission of restoring the symbols of Catholicism, clearly as part of a wider policy of rapprochement with the Catholic Church.[6]

The historical and political context surrounding the legal obligation to display crucifixes in state schools and courtrooms, and the stated rationale for their presence in state buildings, evidences that the fascist Government saw the crucifix as more than a mere religious symbol. The 1922 instruction applies both to the crucifix (symbol of faith) and the portrait of the King (symbol of national unity), and clearly implies that, in order to prosper, Italy needs an alliance of faith and national sentiment. The 1926 instruction concerning state schools is even more explicit, in that the crucifix seems to symbolise the religious but also the national sentiment ('sacred to the faith *and* the national sentiment', emphasis added). The progressive blurring of boundaries between State and religion continues also with the 1926 instruction concerning courtrooms, where the crucifix becomes a 'symbol of truth and justice', in this way implying that the truth and justice that shall be achieved in the court ought to be the same truth and justice that stem from God. These legal documents lay out a particular conception of Catholicism as the 'religion of the State'. This goes beyond the mere sociological acknowledgement that Catholicism is the religious denomination of an overwhelming majority of Italians and, as

[4] Instruction No 2134-1867 of 26 May 1926.

[5] Art 118 of Royal Decree No 965 of 30 April 1924 and Art 119 of Royal Decree No 1297 of 26 April 1928. The Council of State in 1988 recognised that these provisions are still in force.

[6] Instruction of the Department of Justice No 2134/1867 of 29 May 1926.

such, the prevalent religion in Italy. They put forward a more intimate connection between the State and the Catholic Church, and – particularly in the case of the instruction of 1926 on the crucifix in the courtrooms – appear to imply that the legitimacy of State decisions, their truth and justice, originates from the Catholic God or – as per the 1926 instruction concerning high schools and universities – that the young Italians can accomplish their 'elevated duties' only if they follow the symbol of 'our faith and national sentiment'. The instructions issued by the early fascist Government also reveal a 'reaction' to modern secularism and atheism, both in their liberal and Marxist declinations (the crucifix has to be 'reinstated' and the 'ancient tradition' has to be restored).

III. Case Law on the Display of the Crucifix

A. The Italian Constitution and the New Concordat

After the Second World War, the democratic Constitution came into effect on 1 January 1948. The Constitution radically changed the landscape in relation to religion by not granting to Roman Catholicism the status of official religion of the state and, unlike the Albertine Statute, by recognising in article 8(1) that religious denominations other than Catholicism are not merely 'tolerated' by the state but equally free before the law. Catholicism is therefore no longer the 'religion of the State', but it is still in a unique position. Due to the fact that it is the religion of the large majority of Italian people, Roman Catholicism is the only religion to have a constitutional article that specifically relates to it. Article 7(1) establishes the principle of separation of the State and Church by saying that '[t]he State and the Catholic Church are independent and sovereign, each within its own sphere', while article 7(2) stipulates that their relations continue to be regulated by the Lateran Pacts. In 1984 the Lateran Pacts were significantly amended by the New Concordat between Italy and the Holy See, which, at article 1, stipulates the mutual independence and sovereignty of the State and the Church. Point 1 of the Additional Protocol to the New Concordat expressly acknowledges that the principle of 'Catholicism as the religion of the state' has been repealed.[7] This constitutional framework explains why Italy can be seen as a *sui generis* secular state, which, however, still acknowledges the particular position of the Catholic Church in the Italian society.

The case law of the Constitutional Court confirms that the Italian Republic is a secular state. For example, in 2000 the Court declared null and void a provision of the Penal Code of 1930 that punished the public defamation of Catholicism given its status of 'religion of the State'. The Court stated that the approach of the state to different religions must be 'equidistant and impartial',[8] and pointed out

[7] The New Concordat was incorporated into Italian law through Law No 121 of 25 March 1984.
[8] See Ruling No 508 of 20 November 2000, para 3 of the Legal Reasoning.

that '[this] position of equidistance and impartiality is a corollary of the principle of secularism … which has the status of "supreme principle" … and characterises our State as pluralist and as a State in which different religions, cultures and traditions are equally free and shall coexist'.[9] The secularism of Italy, therefore, differs profoundly from the French notion of *laicité* in that it does not imply indifference towards religion but rather 'a positive and welcoming attitude towards *all* religions and religious communities'.[10] Some scholars hold the opinion that, along with such 'negative secularism' (*laicità negativa*), which requires equidistance and impartiality by the state as well as the duty for the state to abstain from imposing religious or metaphysical truths on its citizens, Italian constitutional law also recognises a 'positive secularism' (*laicità positiva*). This envisages positive actions by the state to promote religion as a social phenomenon by ensuring that citizens can enjoy their religious freedom (typical examples of state interventions in this field include tax relief for religious organisations and the provision of religious education in state schools).[11]

In the following sections of this chapter, I shall look at cases concerning the display of the crucifix in public establishments decided by the Council of State, the supreme advisory and judicial body on administrative law matters (section III.B), and the Court of Cassation, the court of last instance on civil law and criminal law matters (section III.C). I shall also look at cases decided in lower courts (section III.D) and, albeit briefly, at the ruling of the ECtHR in the landmark case *Lautsi v Italy*, which originated from the display of the crucifix in an Italian classroom (section III.E).[12]

B. Council of State

In 1988, the Council of State issued an Opinion stating that the obligation to hang crucifixes in state schools had not been impliedly repealed by the 1947 Constitution nor by the New Concordat of 1984 between Italy and the Holy See. The Council of State (Second Division) stated:

> This Division holds, in the first place, that the Crucifix or, simply, the Cross, in addition to its [religious] signification for the believers, [also] symbolises Christian civilisation

[9] ibid. On the same wavelength, see also the rulings of the Constitutional Court No 203 of 12 April 1989; 259 of 25 May 1990; 13 of 14 January 1991; 195 of 27 April 1993; 421 of 1 December 1993; 440 of 18 October 1995; 334 of 8 October 1996; 329 of 14 November 1997; 327 of 9 July 2002; and 67 of 7 April 2017.

[10] S Mancini, 'The Crucifix Rage: Supranational Constitutionalism and Counter-Majoritarian Difficulty' (2010) 6 *European Constitutional Law Review* 6, 8–9 (emphasis in original).

[11] See P Lillo, '[Commentary to] Art 7 [Italian Constitution]' in R Bifulco, A Celotto and M Olivetti (eds), *Commentario alla Costituzione*, vol I (Turin, UTET, 2006) 171, 180–81.

[12] I shall not examine cases on the display of crucifixes in the courtrooms, because they do not contain relevant statements concerning the meaning of the crucifix. I have discussed that case law in my journal article 'Another Defeat for the Principle of Secularism: Recent Developments on the Display of the Crucifix in Italian Courtrooms' (n 1).

> and culture, in its historical origin, as a universal value, [and it is] independent of a particular religious denomination.
>
> ...
>
> It also needs to be considered that the republican Constitution, albeit it guarantees equal freedom to all religious denominations, does not prohibit in any way the display of a symbol which, like the Crucifix, for the principles it evokes ... forms part of the historical heritage [of Italy].[13]

These statements downplay the religious meaning of the crucifix for the non-believer. Indeed, the Council of State conveys the view that a non-Catholic would not necessarily see the crucifix as a symbol of Catholicism. At the same time, it concedes that the crucifix must have some religious signification for non-believers too, and recognises that it is a symbol of 'Christian civilisation and culture', which the Council of State identifies as a 'universal value'. The principles it evokes are also seen as part of the 'historical heritage' of Italy. This opinion echoes the close association between the crucifix and the 'national sentiment' that had been typical of the fascist regime, although it emphasises that the crucifix symbolises universal values and the historical heritage of the country rather than specifically one religious denomination. In this way it disempowers or denies altogether the religious signification of the crucifix for Roman Catholicism. The crucifix is therefore secularised and transfigured from the status of religious symbol to that of a civic image that represents the cornerstone values of the Italian Nation.

In a more recent Opinion, the Council of State rejected a request for removal of crucifixes filed by an association, and expressly acknowledged that the crucifix is not only a religious symbol but also 'a historical and cultural landmark' and a 'sign of national identification'.[14] However, according to the Council of State, the crucifix is also a symbol of Christianity rather than specifically of Roman Catholicism. As such, it symbolises more than one Christian denomination, and for this reason it is compliant 'with the principles of secularism' that demand 'pluralism' and a 'non-confessional state'.[15] Whilst Italy is certainly a pluralist and non-confessional state, it appears questionable to say the least that the crucifix could be seen as a neutral symbol as between different Christian denominations. There are Protestant groups, for example, that expressly prohibit graven images of Jesus. Especially when hung above an altar in a church, the crucifix clearly points to a specifically Roman Catholic understanding of the sacrifice of the Eucharist, but it may produce the same effect in other, different contexts, such as in state schools and other public establishments.

In the same Opinion, the Council of State also argues that, thanks to the decisive contribution of Christians to the formation of the republican Constitution (the Catholic party, Christian Democracy, held the relative majority of seats within

[13] Council of State (Second Division), Opinion No 63 of 27 April 1988.
[14] Council of State (Assembly of the Second Division), Opinion of 15 February 2006, para 3.
[15] ibid para 4.

the Constituent Assembly), Christian values such as freedom, equality and human dignity became key constitutional principles of the Italian state. The Council of State traces back the idea of religious freedom to the Christian value of tolerance, which in turn, according to the Council, also originated the principle of secularism of the state. Therefore, the Council of State concludes that the crucifix not only symbolises constitutional principles such as freedom, equality and human dignity, but also religious freedom and the secularism of the state.[16]

The argument that state secularism derives from the Christian tradition, though, in my view, needs to be qualified. Secularism is historically and ideologically in opposition to the idea of the confessional state, and envisages a separation between the State and the Church which the State has historically promoted and enforced against the will of the Church (although nowadays this separation also protects the Church from excessive interference by the State). Catholic politicians, along with the Catholic tradition of Italy, have certainly played a key role in shaping the Constitution and the political developments since its entry into force. Nevertheless, the construction of the crucifix as a symbol of the secular state probably goes too far. Certainly, this interpretation would not be immediately understandable to everyone, especially non-Catholics. On the contrary, the religious meaning of the crucifix and its relationship to one Christian tradition would appear immediately and patently clear to most people, both Catholic and non-Catholic.

In the same Opinion the Council of State also discusses the educational value of the crucifix, and it would appear that the Council of State does not see the crucifix as a mere 'passive' symbol incapable of impressing or indoctrinating the non-Catholic. The Opinion ascribes to the crucifix the high educational value of discouraging any form of 'religious fundamentalism', a term usually evocative of Islamic fundamentalism. The Council of State also indicates another important role of the crucifix as a symbol of 'our identity' in the context of an increasing immigration into Italy of people from non-EU countries, and in doing so it betrays a rather negative view about immigration from non-EU and non-Christian countries, as well as a rather negative view about immigrants and 'their' values. The Council of State uses a terminology that intentionally and strongly brings to mind the 'clash of civilisations' theory of Samuel P Huntington, where it is said that reaffirming 'our' values is key to preventing the current 'tumultuous encounter' with other cultures from turning into a 'clash'. This language appears even more impressive if one considers that the Opinion was delivered in February 2006, when the scars of 9/11 were still fresh and the notion of a 'clash of civilisations' was often used and abused by politicians and political commentators.[17]

[16] ibid para 5.

[17] Council of State (Assembly of the Second Division), Opinion of 15 February 2006, para 6. See SP Huntington, *The Clash of Civilizations and the Remaking of World Order* (London, Simon & Schuster, 1996) and SP Huntington, *Who Are We? America's Great Debate* (London, Simon & Schuster, 2005).

In deciding the *Lautsi* case later in the same year (before it landed in the ECtHR[18]), the Council of State downplays once again the exclusively religious meaning of the crucifix when displayed in state schools, highlights once more its important educational role for both believers and non-believers, and differentiated its meaning according to whether the pupil is Catholic or not. In a series of long and complex statements, the Council of State distinguishes the meaning of the crucifix in a religious context (a place of worship) and in a secular context (a state school). In a church, the crucifix has a religious meaning, but in a state school, whilst it still remains a 'religious symbol' for believers, it has a 'highly educational symbolic function' for both believers and non-believers. Catholicism is the source of the most important values of what the Council of State indicates as 'Italian civilisation'. These are 'tolerance', 'mutual respect', 'valorisation of the person', 'affirmation of one's rights', 'consideration for one's freedom', 'autonomy of one's moral conscience *vis-à-vis* the authority', 'human solidarity' and 'refusal of any form of discrimination'. These values are identified as the foundation of the Italian Constitution and of the 'type of secularism appropriate to the Italian State'. In Italy, according to the Council of State, there is 'autonomy of the temporal power *vis-à-vis* the spiritual power' but no 'opposition' between the two. Given their 'religious origin' and 'their full and complete correspondence with Christian teachings', the above-mentioned values are well symbolised by the crucifix and 'may be endorsed by all', irrespective of their religious creed. In conclusion, the crucifix in a state school should be seen as an 'educational symbol' reflecting the fundamental principles of 'Italian civilisation' and the 'sources of the civil values' of the Italian legal order, including the particular secularism of the Italian state.[19]

Throughout this reasoning the Council of State attempts to refute the argument advanced by the claimant Soile Lautsi that the display of crucifixes in state schools could offend the sentiments of non-Catholic pupils. However, the entire construction of the Council of State appears far from persuasive, in that it assumes, rather than demonstrates, that non-Catholic pupils would actually or potentially be able to understand the civic values symbolised by the crucifix and see these as prevailing over its straightforward religious connotation as a symbol of Roman Catholicism. The mere fact that a symbol *may* have a certain meaning does not suffice in order to determine that it *actually produces* that particular effect on the viewer, nor does it rule out that the religious meaning might still be perceived as its predominant feature by non-Catholic pupils. There is, though, another problematic aspect in the reasoning of the Council of State. Through its argumentation the Council of State appears to have stripped the crucifix of its specifically religious meaning. The Council of State ultimately denies that in the state school context the crucifix is necessarily and universally to be seen as a religious symbol

[18] See section III.E.

[19] Council of State (6th Division), Ruling 13 April 2006 No 556, para 3. The phrases quoted are the English translations used in the *Lautsi* case before the ECtHR, except for minor corrections made by the author.

of a particular denomination. This secular symbolism stands in contrast to the spiritual idea that the crucifix communicates most vividly for Christians, that is, the sacrificial, atoning death of the Son of God. Accordingly, the conclusion of the Council of State has triggered criticism not only from those who oppose the display of crucifixes in the name of a more rigorous concept of secularism, but also from those Catholics who argue that in this way the crucifix has been appropriated by the state as a secular symbol and consequently reduced to a symbol of secular notions that are merely derivative of Christianity.[20]

C. Court of Cassation

In 2000, the Court of Cassation issued an important ruling in *Montagnana*.[21] Marcello Montagnana had been recruited to work as a secretary at a polling station during the 1994 general election. However, he refused to perform his duties as a protest against the presence of crucifixes in polling stations. There is no law specifically imposing the display of crucifixes in polling stations, but these are usually set up in state schools. The Court acquitted the defendant from the charge of unjustified refusal to perform official duties. In this ruling, the Court recognised that the crucifix is a religious symbol[22] and strongly criticised the view that it could be seen as a symbol of 'Italian civilisation', of 'universal values' or of the 'collective ethical conscience', in this way marking a clear difference from the Council of State. Through a reference to the judgment of the German Federal Constitutional Court on the display of the crucifix in school classrooms in Bavaria, the Court of Cassation argued that the denial of the religious meaning of the crucifix might be even seen as a 'profanation' of this symbol.[23]

The Court also held that, in the context of a secular state, the neutrality of the place where voters cast their ballots needs to be ensured. This neutrality would be irremediably compromised by the display of a religious symbol that would trigger an inner conflict between the civil duty to perform a public function and the moral duty to comply with a command of the conscience concerning the need to ensure secularism and impartiality of that function.[24]

The supreme judicial body on civil law and criminal law disputes takes therefore a completely different approach compared to the Council of State. It sees the

[20] See P Farinella, *Crocifisso tra potere e grazia*, Il Segno dei Gabrielli editori, Negarine di S Pietro in Cariano, 2006. Paolo Farinella is a Catholic priest from Genoa, famous for his opposition to the display of the crucifix in school classrooms. This matter is addressed in A Koltay, *The Troubled Relationship between Religions and the State* (Oxford, Whitelocke, 2017) 57–73, esp 73.

[21] Court of Cassation (4th Criminal Division), Ruling No 4273 of 1 March 2000.

[22] ibid, para 6.

[23] ibid para 7. The reference is to the Federal Constitutional Court ruling of 16 May 1995 (published in *Entscheidungen des Bundesverfassungsgerichts* [hereafter *BVerfGE*], vol 93, 1–37. This judgment declared the unconstitutionality of section 13.1 of the Bavarian elementary school regulation of 1983. See further section IV of this chapter.

[24] Ruling No 4273 of 1 March 2000 (n 21) para 8.

crucifix as the symbol of one particular religious denomination, and holds the display of that symbol in polling stations as incompatible with the principle of secularism of the state. A few political parties in Italy at the time of the ruling explicitly identified with Roman Catholicism and had the cross as their symbol. By allowing the crucifix in the polling station, the state would therefore not only have chosen a particular religious denomination but also indicated support for a particular political direction.

D. Cases in Lower Courts

i. Crucifix in the Classroom

Adel Smith, an Italian citizen of the Muslim religion, sent his two children (who were 4 and 6 years old at the time) to the nursery/primary school in Ofena (near L'Aquila). Smith brought a claim to the Tribunal of L'Aquila requesting the immediate removal of the crucifix from the classroom. The Tribunal upheld the claim, with the argument that the display of the crucifix was in breach of the religious freedom of the claimant's children.[25] The Tribunal held that the display of the crucifix was incompatible with the principle of secularism and expressed the old concept that sees Catholicism as the 'religion of the State'. The Tribunal criticised the Council of State's reasoning that essentially views the crucifix as a symbol of national identity. It rejected the argument that Catholicism has the right to a privileged position as the religious denomination of the majority of Italian people and for its deep roots in Italian history and culture. In the view of the Tribunal, the use of these arguments would be tantamount to acknowledging that Catholicism is still the official religion of the Italian state. This, however, would be in breach of the principles of secularism and of equality, which require the equal treatment of all religious denominations and worldviews, as well as the prohibition of discrimination on grounds of faith.[26]

The Tribunal also held that the display of the crucifix seriously infringed on the religious freedom of the pupils and was incompatible with the requirements of an increasingly multicultural society,[27] and also observed that youths and children who 'still lack solid opinions' would 'tend to give that religious symbol the religious meaning which immediately belongs to it'.[28] On the basis that the dispute around the crucifix concerned both the religious freedom of pupils and the neutrality of a public institution, the Tribunal concluded that crucifixes should be removed from state schools.[29] Accordingly, the Tribunal held that the display not only of

[25] Tribunal of L'Aquila (Civil Division), Order of 23 October 2003.
[26] ibid para 5.
[27] ibid.
[28] ibid para 5.1.
[29] ibid para 5.

the crucifix but also of *any* religious symbol would jeopardise the secular nature of the Italian state.[30] An appeal against this judgment was immediately filed by the Minister of Education, who obtained the annulment of the decision on grounds of the lack of jurisdiction of the court that had passed the ruling.[31] Therefore, the ultimate outcome of this litigation was that the crucifix remained in the classroom.

Another case concerned a primary school teacher, Angelo Lazzarini. On a number of occasions, he had removed the crucifix from the classroom during his lessons. The head of school forbade him from doing so. Lazzarini challenged the lawfulness of this instruction before the Administrative Tribunal on the grounds that it infringed his freedom of teaching and the secularism of the state. The Administrative Tribunal dismissed both claims. Departing from the 1988 Opinion of the Council of State, the Tribunal conceded that, after the New Concordat of 1984, the royal decrees imposing the presence of the crucifix in the classrooms in state schools had become 'obsolete'. However, the Tribunal held that the display of the crucifix is a 'longstanding tradition'.[32] On this basis, the Tribunal concluded that any issues concerning the display of religious symbols in state schools' classrooms need to be addressed in each school by the relevant governing body, the school board, which in this case had pronounced by majority in favour of continuing to display the crucifix.[33]

A further case concerns Franco Coppoli, a history teacher of a third-year class (attended by 16–17-year-old pupils) in a high school in Terni. The royal decrees of 1924 and 1928 only apply to primary and middle schools, and there is no legal obligation to display crucifixes in high schools. Despite that, at the beginning of the school year in September 2008, some of the pupils asked the head of school if they might hang a crucifix in the classroom. The head of school allowed them to do so. Coppoli, however, did not accept this decision and removed the crucifix from the wall during his lessons. His action was motivated by a refusal to teach in a school environment marked by a religious symbol. During a class assembly, the pupils discussed this issue, and the *majority* of them voted in favour of the presence of the crucifix in the class, including during history lessons (this decision was later confirmed by the class council – a body composed of teachers and representatives of parents and pupils). Despite the position of the majority of the class and of the class council, Coppoli kept removing the crucifix from the wall during his lessons and hanging it up again before leaving the classroom. The head of school made several attempts to persuade Coppoli to comply with the unequivocal will of the majority of pupils, but once all his attempts had failed, he initiated a disciplinary procedure against the history teacher for his insubordination.

[30] ibid.

[31] Tribunal of L'Aquila (Civil Division), Order of 19 November 2003. Smith appealed the decision to the Court of Cassation, which dismissed the appeal. See Court of Cassation (United Divisions), Order No 15614 of 10 July 2006.

[32] Administrative Tribunal of Lombardy (Division of Brescia), Ruling No 603 of 22 May 2006, para 3.3.

[33] ibid.

In February 2009, Coppoli was found guilty by the National Council of Public Education (the body dealing with disciplinary proceedings against public school teachers) and suspended from work and salary for one month. Coppoli filed a lawsuit with the Tribunal of Terni against the allegedly discriminatory behaviour of the head of school. The Tribunal, though, held that no discrimination had taken place, because the head of school was complying with the will of the majority of the class.[34] It clearly emerges from this reasoning that according to the Tribunal, the principle of secularism justifies the imposition by the *majority* of pupils of a religious symbol on the dissenting pupils and teachers, even when – as in the present case – the hanging of the crucifix is not required by law.

ii. Crucifix in the Polling Station

The Tribunal of Bologna firmly denied that the display of crucifixes in polling stations violates the right to vote and the religious freedom of voters. In its reasoning, the Tribunal downgraded the crucifix to a 'non-symbol' for the non-believer or the non-Christian, and as such it regarded it as incapable of influencing or of creating 'a psychological obstacle' to those voters.[35]

In a similar case, the Tribunal of Naples highlighted that the crucifix in Italy appears everywhere, because it is 'expression of the deeply rooted religious and cultural tradition of the country', and that it is 'not understandable how the mere presence of the symbol could ever prevent the voter … from freely casting his vote'.[36]

Another case was decided by the President of the Tribunal of L'Aquila. The reasoning in this case emphasised the historical and cultural importance of the crucifix in Italy, and the President of the Tribunal stressed that the crucifix is ultimately a 'passive symbol' in that it does not require 'active behaviour (worship or oath) by people with different religious convictions'.[37]

In both the Bologna and L'Aquila rulings, the judges held that the opportunity offered to voters to obtain the temporary removal of the crucifix from the polling station for the time necessary to cast their ballot was an adequate guarantee of respect of their (negative) religious freedom and of the principle of secularism, although voters could obtain the temporary removal of crucifixes only if they actively communicated to the chair at the polling station their opposition to the presence of this religious symbol. In my view, this could create a significant psychological obstacle for some people who may be reluctant to openly voice their unease regarding the crucifix.

[34] Tribunal of Terni (Civil Division), Order of 24 June 2009.

[35] Tribunal of Bologna (1st Civil Division) Order 24 March 2005. The translation from Italian is mine.

[36] Tribunal of Naples (10th Civil Division), Order of 26 March 2005.

[37] Order of the President of Tribunal of L'Aquila, 31 March 2005. This decision was later confirmed by the Tribunal of L'Aquila (Civil Division), Order of 26 May 2005.

In a case of 2006, the Court of Appeal of Perugia, following the precedent set by the Court of Cassation in *Montagnana* (see section III.C), dismissed an application to remove from office the chair of a polling station who had taken the crucifix off the wall for the duration of the ballot operations. The Court stated that the presence of the crucifix in polling stations is not imposed by any law. It is therefore part of the responsibility of the chair to ensure the neutrality of the space, meaning the absence of any symbol that may (even indirectly or involuntarily) influence the voter.[38] However, it is not explained in the judgment *how* the crucifix would actually influence the voter, and the Court seems to take for granted that the crucifix is a symbol capable of producing this effect. In 2016, the Tribunal of Modena confirmed this line of reasoning, and held that the chair of a polling station can lawfully remove the crucifix from a classroom used as a polling station to ensure the neutrality of the space in which the ballots are cast. The judge gave the following explanation of the 'discriminatory effect' of the crucifix:

> [I]t is quite possible that voters face the choice between political groups that are inspired by the religious meaning of the cross and groups that are not inspired by that meaning. … The discriminatory effect [of the crucifix] on the voter who wishes to express a preference for the group that is not inspired by the religious meaning of the symbol is [therefore] self-evident, if he has to cast the ballot in a physical space (specifically organised for the voting operations) that is characterised by the presence of a symbol which inspires the political group he does not choose. … [T]he idea that the religious symbol also has to remain hanging on the walls [of the classroom] on election days, even if it is a mere manifestation of the attachment to a tradition, indicates the need for identity roots, understandable to an extent, which, inevitably, excludes those who do not want or cannot recognise that identity.[39]

E. *Lautsi v Italy*

The most famous 'crucifix litigation', known as *Lautsi v Italy*, started in April 2002, when Soile Lautsi, an Italian citizen of Finnish origin, requested the removal of the crucifix from the classrooms of the middle school in Albano Terme (near Padua) attended by her two children. Lautsi pointed out that the presence of the crucifix conveyed a religious message in breach of the secular character of the Italian state. She argued that the crucifix also infringed her right to bring up her children in accordance with her secular values. Following the refusal of the school to comply with her request, Lautsi brought a case before the Regional Administrative Tribunal of Veneto.

The Tribunal dismissed the claim and held that the crucifix is the symbol not just of Catholicism but also of Italian history and culture, and consequently of

[38] Court of Appeal of Perugia (Civil Division), Decree of 10 April 2006.
[39] Tribunal of Modena, Ruling of 20 December 2016 (Case No 40322/2012).

the identity of the Italian people. The Tribunal also stated that important values embodied by the Italian Constitution are a legacy of Christendom: freedom, equality, human dignity and religious tolerance are all symbolised by the crucifix. According to the Tribunal, even the principle of secularism of the state is a result of Christian tolerance. This makes the crucifix the universal symbol of acceptance and respect for any human being, irrespective of his religious beliefs. As such, the crucifix does not need to be banned from classrooms.[40] The decision of the Administrative Tribunal was upheld on appeal by the Council of State (the supreme judicial body on administrative matters). Once again (as in 1988), the Council of State used the argument that the cross is not just the symbol of one religion and that it symbolises secular values of the Italian Constitution, and for this reason it is not capable of offending anyone.[41]

After exhausting all the available domestic remedies, Lautsi brought the case to the attention of the ECtHR. She submitted that the exposition of the crucifix was an infringement on her right under Article 2 of Protocol No 1 to the European Convention of Human Rights (ECHR), which recognises the right of parents to ensure that their children's education and teaching are in conformity with their religious and philosophical convictions. Lautsi also claimed that the crucifix violated her freedom of religion as protected by Article 9 of the ECHR, which states that everyone has 'the right to freedom of thought, conscience and religion'. The ECtHR initially upheld Lautsi's claim and found that there had been violations of both Article 2 and Article 9.[42] According to the Court, the state should refrain from imposing beliefs, even indirectly, in places such as state school classrooms where people are dependent on it or, like school children, in a particularly vulnerable position. The Court continued as follows:

> The schooling of children is particularly sensitive because in this case, the binding power of the State is imposed on minds that still lack (depending on the level of maturity of the child) the critical capacity to allow them to distance themselves from the message implied by a preferential choice expressed by the State in religious matters.[43]

In the view of the Court, the crucifix is a symbol the religious meaning of which prevails over any other signification. The Court linked this conclusion to the precedent set in *Buscarini v San Marino*,[44] where the Grand Chamber had held the obligation for Sammarinese parliamentarians to take an oath on the Gospel to be in breach of Article 9 of the Convention.[45] At the same time, the crucifix is

[40] Regional Administrative Tribunal of Veneto (3rd Division), Ruling 17 March 2005 No 1110.

[41] Council of State (6th Division), Ruling 13 February 2006 No 556. On the same wavelength, see Council of State (Assembly of the 2nd Division), Opinion of 15 February 2006. This Opinion reaffirmed that the royal decrees on the display of crucifixes in state schools are still in force and that such display does not violate the constitutional principles of secularism or religious freedom. See my discussion in section III.B of the arguments of the Council of State in this case.

[42] *Lautsi v Italy* App No 30814/06 (ECHR (2nd Division), 3 November 2009).

[43] ibid para 48.

[44] *Buscarini and Others v San Marino* App no 24645/94 (ECHR GC, 18 February 1999).

[45] *Lautsi* (n 42) para 52.

necessarily perceived as an integral part of the school environment and can therefore be considered as a 'powerful external symbol', that is, a sign that is immediately visible to everyone and which implies allegiance to a particular faith.[46] By the same token, the display of the crucifix in the classroom may give schoolchildren of all ages the perception of being educated in an environment marked by a given religion. This would be an encouragement for those who belong to that religion, but it could be emotionally disturbing for those who have a different belief (particularly those schoolchildren belonging to religious minorities). This is because the religious freedom of Article 9 of the Convention also entails a 'negative freedom'; that is, the right not to believe in one or any religion. On this point, the Court concluded as follows:

> This negative right deserves special protection if the State expresses a belief and if a person is placed in a situation from which he cannot escape or only by an effort and cost that are disproportionate.[47]

The Court ruled out that the display of any religious symbol could be justified by the request of other parents demanding an education consistent with their beliefs, and rebutted the Italian Government's argument that the presence of the crucifix could be legitimated by the need to achieve a compromise with political parties of Catholic inspiration no matter how prominent they are in the Italian political landscape. The Court continued:

> The Court does not see how display in classrooms of public schools of a symbol that it is reasonable to associate with Catholicism (the majority religion in Italy) could serve the educational pluralism that is essential to the preservation of a 'democratic society' as conceived by the Convention. The State is obliged to religious neutrality in public education where attendance is required irrespective of religion and must seek to instil in students critical thinking.[48]

On these grounds, the Court found Italian legislation ultimately to be in breach of Article 2 of Protocol No 1 taken together with Article 9 of the Convention.

In 2011, the Grand Chamber of the ECtHR overturned the earlier judgment of the 2nd Division. Whilst it found the display of crucifixes in state schools not to be in conflict with the ECHR, and that in the light of the principle of subsidiarity decisions on this matter are to be reserved for the Member States, the Court still conceded that the crucifix is primarily a religious symbol:

> The Court … considers that the crucifix is above all a religious symbol. The domestic courts came to the same conclusion and in any event the [Italian] Government have not contested this. The question whether the crucifix is charged with any other meaning beyond its religious symbolism is not decisive at this stage of the Court's reasoning.[49]

[46] ibid para 54.

[47] ibid 55. The concept of negative freedom (of association) was developed for the first time by the ECtHR in *Young, James and Webster v United Kingdom* App nos 7601/76 and 7806/77 (ECHR, 13 August 1981).

[48] *Lautsi* (n 42) para 56.

[49] *Lautsi v Italy* App No 30814/06 (ECHR GC, 18 March 2011) para 66.

The *Lautsi* ruling of the Grand Chamber marks the end, so far, of the crucifix-in-the-classroom saga in Italy. The crucifix is indeed a religious symbol of Christianity, but it is seen by the Grand Chamber of the ECtHR as a merely 'passive symbol' that does not denote 'a process of indoctrination' of school pupils. It can therefore remain in the classrooms, and it is for each Member State to balance the principle of religious freedom with the display of the symbols of the denomination that, for historical reasons, has achieved a prominent status in its society.[50] This decision has triggered deep controversy among scholars, and some see it as a sign that the Grand Chamber 'gave up the idea of neutrality' of the state that had, until then, been one of its cornerstones.[51]

IV. Similar Crucifix Disputes in Other European Countries

It is valuable to look briefly at analogous disputes in other European countries, to determine how their domestic courts have construed the meaning of the crucifix.

A. Germany

In 1995, the German Federal Constitutional Court (*Bundesverfassungsgericht*) declared invalid a Bavarian elementary school regulation imposing the display of crucifixes in Bavarian public schools.[52] In this judgment – known as the '*Kruzifix-Urteil*' ('crucifix ruling') – the Federal Constitutional Court held that the cross is specifically a symbol of Catholicism and not merely an expression of Western culture marked by Christianity. The Court's view was that interpreting the crucifix as a secular Western tradition or as a religious symbol without specific reference to a particular religious belief would amount to a 'profanation'.[53] The position of the German Court is therefore diametrically opposed to that taken by the Italian Council of State. The German Court would probably not hesitate to label the

[50] ibid paras 71–72.

[51] On this debate, see Temperman (ed) (n 1). See ch 7 of this book by Carla M Zoethout. The precedent set in the *Lautsi* case of 2011 has been expressly referred to and followed in the recent Regional Administrative Tribunal of Sardinia (2nd Division), Ruling 31 May 2017, No 383, concerning the decision by the Mayor of Cagliari to display crucifixes in all the public buildings within the municipal territory. In upholding the decision of the Mayor, the Administrative Tribunal declared that the crucifix is the symbol of the cultural and religious identity of countries of Christian tradition. See FJ Fara 'Il crocifisso quale simbolo dell'identità culturale e religiosa dei Paesi di tradizione cristiana' (2018) 33 *Rivista giuridica sarda* 519.

[52] Federal Constitutional Court Ruling of 16 May 1995, *BVerfGE* vol 93, 1–37. This judgment declared the unconstitutionality of section 13.1 of the Bavarian elementary school regulation of 1983.

[53] *BVerfGE* vol 93, 19–20. On the *Kruzifix-Urteil*, see J Kokott, '[Commentary to] Art 4 GG' in M Sachs (ed), *Grundgesetz Kommentar*, 5th edn (Munich, CH Beck, 2009) 247.

Council of State's construction of the crucifix as a symbol of Italian history and culture a 'profanation' of the cross. The German Federal Constitutional Court's orthodox adherence to the authentic religious signification of the crucifix, almost paradoxically, leads to the invalidation of the Bavarian regulation imposing its mandatory display; whilst in Italy, the secular interpretation of the crucifix by the Council of State as a non-exclusively Roman Catholic sign allows its permanence in the classroom.[54]

B. Switzerland

In 1990, the Federal Tribunal decided an important case on the display of crucifixes in public schools.[55] The case originated from the decision of the Municipality of Cadro to affix crucifixes in the classrooms of the local primary school. The Tribunal held this measure to be unconstitutional for being in breach of the principle of state secularism. The Tribunal argued that the state must not identify with a religion – in this particular case Catholicism – because this could estrange citizens belonging to a different denomination.

The ruling of the Federal Tribunal is more radical than the *Kruzifix-Urteil.* There the German Federal Constitutional Court appeared to deny the non-religious meaning of the crucifix, or to deem it negligible. The Swiss Court argues that even if the crucifix could be seen, hypothetically, as a tribute to the Christian foundations of the Western civilisation and culture, it still remains a *predominantly* religious symbol that may convey the idea that the state adopts one particular religious denomination, with the result of offending, potentially, the religious sentiments of non-Catholic and non-Christian pupils.

C. Spain

In Spain, the display of crucifixes in classrooms is not required by any legal provision. However, crucifixes used to be displayed in a number of schools. In 2008 the Administrative Court of Valladolid ruled on a lawsuit brought by a father against the presence of crucifixes in the classroom of a public school attended by his child. The Court held that the display of crucifixes in public schools violated section 16(3) of the Spanish Constitution ('No religion shall have state character'), as well as the religious freedom of the pupils and of their parents. On this basis, the Court ordered the removal of all the crucifixes from that school, because 'the crucifix

[54] See also on the same wavelength the earlier Ruling of 17 July 1973 (published in *BVerfGE* vol 35, 366–76) concerning the display of crosses in courtrooms.

[55] Federal Tribunal Ruling of 26 September 1990 in the case *Comune di Cadro v Guido Bernasconi.*

has a religious connotation, although it may also have others; ie it did not lose its religious connotation even if it may have acquired others'.[56]

The Spanish crucifix litigation acknowledges the infringement of the negative religious freedom of pupils and parents, even if the crucifix is not only a religious symbol and may also have other meanings. The mere fact that it possesses a religious meaning, as well as others, suffices to trigger the mechanism that may lead to the removal of the crucifix from the classroom. A problem with this mechanism, though, is that parents and pupils who wish to have the crucifix removed would have to come forward and request its removal, in this way exposing themselves to possible negative reactions from other pupils and parents, as well as from the school authorities and teachers.[57]

Whilst not specifically relating to the crucifix, the Spanish Constitutional Court decided an interesting case on secularism. It concerned the claim of a lawyer from Seville who challenged the traditional use by the Seville Bar Association of the Virgin of the Immaculate Conception as its patron. The Court upheld the constitutionality of this image, mainly on the ground that such patronage has nowadays become only a secular tradition and has no religious meaning.[58] This ruling not only downplays but also radically denies the religious meaning of a traditional religious image, and in this manner takes away entirely the potential encroachment on the principle of secularism and the negative religious freedom of the citizens. This operation of stripping an obviously religious symbol of its religious message is certainly more radical, but not entirely dissimilar to the downplaying of the religious meaning of the crucifix by the Italian Council of State.

V. Concluding Remarks

The case law discussed in this chapter reveals a remarkable lack of consistency. The range of meanings ascribed to the crucifix goes from 'religious symbol of Catholicism' or 'symbol of Christianity', to 'symbol of Italian civilisation, culture and history' or even to 'symbol of constitutional principles', including, surprisingly, the principle of state secularism. This lack of consistency is not confined to the meaning of the crucifix; it embraces its alleged impact on schoolchildren or other viewers. So the crucifix has been seen variously as a 'passive symbol', because it lacks the power of 'indoctrination' (Grand Chamber in *Lautsi v Italy*); as a 'powerful external symbol' (2nd Division of the ECtHR in the same case); as a symbol whose display may legitimise the refusal by a public official to comply with his

[56] Administrative Court (No 2) of Valladolid Ruling No 288 of 14 November 2008.

[57] I have argued elsewhere that this cannot be seen as a satisfactory guarantee of the rights of the citizens, and that a failure to display crucifixes and other religious symbols in public establishments would be preferable: C Panara, '*Lautsi v Italy*: The Display of Religious Symbols by the State' (2011) 17 *European Public Law* 139, 163.

[58] Ruling No 34/2011 of 28 March 2011.

official duties (*Montagnana* case, concerning the secretary of a polling station); or as a symbol which a public official could decide to remove, at least temporarily, from the wall (chair of a polling station).

In the face of this multi-faceted case law, the current position of Italian law lacks consistency too. The *Lautsi v Italy* ruling of the Grand Chamber in 2011 legitimises the display of crucifixes in Italian public schools. However, the display of the crucifixes in polling stations lacks a reliable authority in the form, for example, of a judgment of the Court of Cassation. *Montagnana* concerned a secretary who refused to perform his duties, *not* the actual removal of a crucifix from a polling station or from all polling stations. In the light of the more recent case law, though, it seems to be within the discretionary responsibility of the chair of the polling station to keep or remove the crucifix according to the circumstances, should a voter request its removal before casting his or her vote, or should the chair judge that this is appropriate in order to ensure the neutrality of the polling station. As to the display of the crucifix or of other religious symbols in other public places, such as buildings of local councils and courtrooms, the position is still unclear due to the lack, again, of definitive statements or precedents set by the Court of Cassation. In a case concerning an employee of the Sicilian municipality of Paternò, the Tribunal, despite acknowledging that 'the exposition of any religious symbol in a public place … marks a departure from the principle of secularism of the State', held that it lacked jurisdiction and could not order the removal of a statue of the Virgin Mary from the council building.[59] In the case of a judge who refused to hold hearings so long as crucifixes were displayed in Italian courtrooms, the final outcome was the dismissal of the judge, although the Disciplinary Division of the High Council of the Judiciary did not pronounce on the lawfulness of the removal of the crucifix from the wall.[60]

The cases analysed in this chapter evidence at least three tendencies that emerge in the wider case law, despite the many inconsistencies. A first tendency identifies the crucifix primarily, if not exclusively, as a religious symbol of Roman Catholicism. It is paradoxically this rigorous allegiance to the authentic mystical and religious meaning of the crucifix that triggers its removal, on the basis of the argument that, as a religious symbol of one particular denomination, its display would involve the *exclusion* of adherents to other religions or non-believers.[61]

[59] Tribunal of Catania, Order of 12 April 2008, later confirmed by the Court of Cassation, United Divisions, Order No 17789/09 of 30 July 2009.

[60] See Disciplinary Division of the High Council of the Judiciary, Decision of 22 January 2010.

[61] Court of Cassation (4th Criminal Division), Ruling No 4273 of 1 March 2000; Tribunal of L'Aquila (Civil Division), Order of 23 October 2003; Court of Appeal of Perugia (Civil Division), Decree of 10 April 2006; Tribunal of Modena, Ruling of 20 December 2016 (Case No 40322/2012); Tribunal of Catania, Order of 12 April 2008. Among non-Italian case law, see *Lautsi v Italy* App No 30814/06 (ECHR (2nd Division), 3 November 2009); Swiss Federal Tribunal Ruling of 26 September 1990 in the case *Comune di Cadro v Guido Bernasconi*; German Federal Constitutional Court Ruling of 16 May 1995; Administrative Court (No 2) of Valladolid Ruling No 288 of 14 November 2008.

A second tendency downplays the religious signification of the crucifix and *also* ascribes to it other meanings. Often this tendency is accompanied by the claim that the meaning of this symbol depends on the individual viewer, so that the believer in Roman Catholicism would probably understand it as a symbol of his religion, while another would see it as a symbol of constitutional or universal values.[62] A third tendency, which is however virtually non-existent in the Italian context, deprives the religious symbol either almost entirely or entirely of its religious connotation and attempts to construe it as a neutral 'tradition'.[63] The second and third tendencies converge in the sense that both lead to the rescue of the display of the crucifix in public buildings, and in that both attribute to the crucifix an *inclusive* function, especially when the crucifix is seen as possessing the pedagogic function of educating the children of immigrants to 'our' values.

Apart from these three tendencies along the illustrated exclusion-inclusion axis, some of the analysed cases also evidence an ambiguous approach to the question of whether the crucifix is a merely passive symbol, incapable of indoctrination, or an active one, capable of indoctrinating or at least impressing its viewers (particularly schoolchildren) and giving them and their parents the impression that they are taught in an environment marked by allegiance to a particular religion. The Grand Chamber in the *Lautsi* case of 2011 concluded that the crucifix is a passive symbol. One would expect that the cases that downplay the religious meaning of the crucifix in order to justify its permanence in the public space would also argue in favour of the passive nature of the symbol as a further corroboration of its neutrality. Quite surprisingly, though, it is indeed in some of these particular cases that there is a stronger emphasis on the educational and *active* role of the crucifix in teaching Western, Italian and constitutional values to people who come from different cultures.[64]

The ambiguities illustrated reflect those of a constitutional system that is not entirely that of a secular state, and where the notion of secularism reflects a positive interest of the state in facilitating the religion practised by the majority of its citizens in accordance with the notion of *laicità positiva*. However, the active involvement of the state in imposing the presence of crucifixes implies a politicisation of this symbol. It means that the crucifix is not displayed only as a symbol of Catholicism but also for political reasons. For the fascist regime of the 1920s and

[62] Council of State (Second Division), Opinion No 63 of 27 April 1988; Regional Administrative Tribunal of Veneto (3rd Division), Ruling 17 March 2005, No 1110; Order of the President of Tribunal of L'Aquila, 31 March 2005; Tribunal of L'Aquila (Civil Division), Order of 26 May 2005; Council of State (6th Division), Ruling 13 February 2006, No 556; Council of State (Assembly of the Second Division), Opinion of 15 February 2006; Council of State (6th Division), Ruling 13 April 2006, No 556.

[63] See Spanish Constitutional Court Ruling No 34/2011 of 28 March 2011 concerning the use of the image of the Virgin of the Immaculate Conception as the symbol of the Seville Bar Association. A possible example of this tendency in Italy could be the recent Regional Administrative Court of Sardinia (2nd Division), Ruling 31 May 2017, No 383.

[64] Council of State (6th Division), Ruling 13 April 2006 No 556; Council of State (Assembly of the Second Division), Opinion of 15 February 2006.

1930s, this was a way of cementing an alliance between itself and the Catholic Church,[65] and was a reaction against the secular or even atheist views of liberals and Marxists. Today, in a democratic setting and in a more – and increasingly – multicultural and multi-religious society, the crucifix is again seen by some groups not only as the symbol of Catholicism, but also as a symbol of Italian identity in an era when nationalist and religious sentiments are in resurgence in Europe. The crucifix has therefore become the subject of a backward-looking battle in which, frequently and increasingly, it is used by anti-immigration groups to defend a misconceived 'genuine' Italian identity.[66] So it is that this symbol of an ancient religious faith has been progressively politicised to evoke certain political values: the spiritual unity of the Italian Nation during the fascist regime and its communion with the Catholic Church, and today the 'Christian identity' of Italy as a response to the perceived threat posed in particular by non-Christian immigrants.

[65] Following the Lateran Pacts, Pope Pius XI publicly defined Mussolini as the 'Man of Providence' in a speech delivered to the students of the Università cattolica del Sacro Cuore, 13 February 1929.

[66] It is not merely by accident that Matteo Salvini, leader of the anti-immigration party *Lega*, often appears during political rallies with a copy of the Gospel and with a rosary.

9

Religious Exemptions from Civil Laws and Free Exercise of Religion in the USA

MAIMON SCHWARZSCHILD

I. Introduction

The first article of the American Constitution's Bill of Rights guarantees the free exercise of religion, or more precisely forbids any public law 'prohibiting' free exercise.[1] Yet what this should mean divides Americans today as much as, or more than, ever before. Few if any recent cases in the US Supreme Court have aroused as much public heat as the case of the Christian bakery owner in Colorado who declined, on religious grounds, to provide a wedding cake for a homosexual wedding, and was held to be in violation of anti-discrimination law – and ordered to provide the cake – by a Colorado State tribunal; or the case of the family-owned sporting goods stores that sought exemption from a new federal requirement, imposed by administrative directive under President Obama's Affordable Care Act, to provide for contraceptive (and arguably abortive) drugs for employees in violation of the employer's religious beliefs. In both cases the Supreme Court ruled that the Government had intruded improperly on religious freedom, but in the one case on narrow grounds (hence a narrow and uncertain precedent) and in the other by a bare 5:4 majority.[2]

[1] *Constitution* (US), Amendment I ('Congress shall make no law respecting an establishment of religion, or prohibiting the free exercise thereof'). Religious toleration, and the cognate idea of religious freedom, has long been a fundamental element of liberal theory and of Enlightenment principle. See generally P Zagorin, *How the Idea of Religious Toleration Came to the West* (Princeton, NJ, Princeton University Press, 2003); J Marshall, *John Locke, Toleration and Early Enlightenment Culture: Religious Toleration and Arguments for Religious Toleration in Early Modern and Early Enlightenment Europe* (New York, Cambridge University Press, 2006).

[2] *Masterpiece Cakeshop v Colorado Civil Rights Commission*, 584 US ___; 138 SCt 1719 (2018) (reversing the Colorado Civil Rights Commission on the ground that it acted with hostility to the bakery owner's Christian religion, hence without considering whether 'free exercise' would require a religious exemption from the anti-discrimination law in the absence of such improper hostility);

Should religious people and institutions receive special exemption from otherwise applicable laws when compliance with such laws is claimed to be inconsistent with religious obligation or belief? The question is not new in American life, although it may be arising more frequently and more divisively as American government grows, laying down the law in more and more areas of life, and as religion becomes ever more a proxy or a field of contention for the country's political and cultural divisions.

It is fairly obvious that without some special accommodation or exemption from various laws, it would be difficult for religious communities or even individuals to live religious lives. If public law forbids employment discrimination on the basis of religion, for example, religious groups have an obvious claim for exemption when choosing their clergy and deciding who qualifies to be priest, pastor, imam or rabbi.

But there are almost limitless situations in which the question of religious exemption might arise. Should Native American or Rastafarian sects be exempted from drugs laws that forbid peyote or marijuana? Should Muslims or Mormons be exempted from laws against polygamy? Should Sikhs be exempted from laws prohibiting the carrying of knives in public? Should observant Jewish or Sikh soldiers or officers be exempted from military uniform rules that would not permit the wearing of religious head covering? Should Christian Science devotees be exempted from laws requiring parents to provide medical treatment for sick children? Should religious individuals be exempted from duties that would otherwise be required on the job – a Sabbath-observer who will not work on the Sabbath, a nurse who refuses to assist in abortion or the administration of contraceptives, a police constable who refuses to arrest anti-war or anti-abortion protesters, or a postal worker who refuses to deliver mail that he or she considers blasphemous?

II. Are Religious Exemptions a Constitutional Right?

A. 'Establishment' and 'Free Exercise'

In the United States these questions, as with so many things in American life, are often framed as constitutional issues. The First Amendment provides that 'Congress shall make no law respecting an establishment of religion, or prohibiting the free exercise thereof'. So perhaps some or all of the claims for religious exemption must be granted in order to satisfy 'free exercise'. But if they are granted, whilst people who might want to smoke peyote, marry polygamously and/or carry ceremonial but sharp knives in public for non-religious reasons are prohibited from

Burwell v Hobby Lobby Stores, 573 US ___; 134 SCt 2751 (2014) (holding by a 5:4 majority that imposing an administrative 'contraceptive mandate' on a private company over the owners' religious objection violated the federal Religious Freedom Restoration Act (RFRA)).

doing so, this can be criticised as an 'establishment of religion': it would certainly discriminate in favour of religion and against people who might want exemption from the law for secular – but perhaps for serious or conscientious – reasons. 'Free exercise' and 'establishment', especially if each is construed broadly, threaten to collide with one another.

The 'establishment' clause itself has been a source of sharp contention at least since 1947, when the US Supreme Court suggested for the first time that the Constitution's prohibition on an 'establishment' of religion might require a 'wall of separation' between government and religion, forbidding any state subsidy of religion – even subsidies impartially available to all religions – or non-denominational endorsement of religion in general.[3] Although in America's founding era Thomas Jefferson strongly opposed any state-established church, and coined the phrase 'wall of separation' in a letter he published in 1802,[4] the 'original intent' and 'original understanding' of the establishment clause may well have been simply that no church or denomination should have official standing comparable to the Church of England (or the Church of Scotland or the Lutheran Church in the Scandinavian countries). In recent years the dispute over 'establishment' has mostly been between those who would bar any, or almost any, state endorsement or invocation or aid to religion, however impartial, and 'non-preferentialists' who would merely bar state preference or discrimination as between sects or denominations and, as to state aid, would not object to including religious groups on an equal footing with others receiving public largesse. Decisions of the US Supreme Court have wavered somewhat between these two understandings of the 'establishment clause'.[5] Meanwhile, the question of religious exemptions seems to be, at least more immediately, a question of 'free exercise' rather than of 'establishment': whether exemptions are necessary or appropriate to enable people freely to practise their religious faiths.

Are religious exemptions, then, a constitutional right in the United States? And to the extent that they are not, how broadly are religious exemptions nonetheless available, and what are their future prospects?

[3] *Everson v Board of Education*, 330 US 1 (1947).

[4] Thomas Jefferson's Letter to the Danbury Baptists, 1 January 1802, at https://www.loc.gov/loc/lcib/9806/danpre.html.

[5] See eg *Lee v Weisman*, 505 US 577 (1992), holding that a non-denominational benediction by a rabbi at a state school graduation ceremony violated the establishment clause; but cf *Rosenberger v Rector*, 515 US 819 (1995), holding that a public college did not violate the establishment clause by including a religious magazine amongst the student activities it subsidised. See generally JH Choper, 'The Religion Clauses of the First Amendment: Reconciling the Conflict (1980) 41 *University of Pittsburgh Law Review* 673 (urging a moderate interpretation of the establishment clause that would forbid only government action whose purpose is solely religious and that is likely to impair religious freedom). There is even something of an academic debate about whether the First Amendment prohibition of 'establishment' and guarantee of 'free exercise' constitute two constitutional clauses or one. See, eg, P Kurland, 'Of Church and State and the Supreme Court' (1961) 29 *University of Chicago Law Review* 1 (arguing that the freedom and separation clauses should be read as a 'single precept' that the Government may neither benefit nor burden religion).

B. The Fitful Evolution of Exemption as a Right

In the late eighteenth century era when the United States Constitution came into force, the presence in the country of a wide variety of Christian denominations and sects ensured that religious liberty was of great concern to Americans, as was reflected in the guarantees in the very first words of the Bill of Rights. The question whether religious freedom should mean a constitutional right to exemption from civil laws was in the air at the time: it was understood, for example, that pacifist sects such as Quakers might want exemption from military conscription, and even from taxation to support the armed forces.[6] One legal scholar in recent decades has argued that in the founding era, 'free exercise' did imply a right to exemption, at least so long as religious non-compliance would be peaceable and not inimical to important government interests.[7] But the weight of historical research suggests that while support for freedom of religious conscience was broad and deep among eighteenth-century Americans, this did not extend to a generalised right to religious exemption from civil laws. Sectarian leaders themselves mostly disclaimed any such right, insisting that religious freedom was consistent with obedience to civil law: what they opposed was the 'establishment' of state religion, as in Britain, which would threaten the liberty of religious dissenters. The idea that minority sects would demand such a right was seen as a smear launched by their religious opponents.[8]

Yet if a wholesale right to religious exemptions was not understood in the founding era to be entailed by 'free exercise', certainly not as a matter of entrenched constitutional right, specific exemptions or accommodations were granted in that era. The Constitution itself provided for 'affirmation' as an alternative to oaths, wherever oaths were otherwise called for, as in the Presidential oath, or the oath required of all federal and State officers to support the Constitution.[9] This was a deliberate concession to Quakers and a few other sects that forbade the taking of oaths. States which had established churches usually exempted religious dissenters from direct taxation in behalf of the established church – many American colonies had established churches before American independence, and the newly-adopted Constitution forbade only the national government, not the States, from

[6] See PA Hamburger, 'Religious Freedom in Philadelphia' (2005) 54 *Emory Law Journal* 1603 (showing that during the American Independence War it was mostly conceded in Pennsylvania that Quakers should be exempted from bearing arms, but there was deep resentment against Quakers' objections to paying for substitutes or otherwise contributing financially to the war).

[7] See MW McConnell, 'The Origins and Historical Understanding of Free Exercise of Religion' (1990) 103 *Harvard Law Review* 1409.

[8] See PA Hamburger, 'A Constitutional Right of Religious Exemption: An Historical Perspective' (1992) 60 *George Washington Law Review* 915 (offering extensive historical evidence against the proposition that the Constitution's framers, or the founding generation, considered constitutional 'free exercise' to entail a right to religious exemption).

[9] US Constitution Art II s 1 cl 8 (presidential oath or affirmation); Art VI cl 3 (oath or affirmation for public officers, 'but no religious Test shall ever be required as a Qualification to any Office or public Trust under the United States').

establishing religion. There were other exemptions as well. The State of Rhode Island exempted Jews from incest laws as to marriages 'within the degrees of affinity or consanguinity allowed by their religion'.[10] All these exemptions however, with the exception of the affirmation option in the national Constitution, were provided by statute – federal, or more often State – or in a State constitution, and all these are far more easily modified or repealed than the all-but-unchangeable federal Constitution.[11] These exemptions, then, were essentially a matter of grace and favour, granted in the course of democratic politics; and what majorities giveth, they can freely taketh away. There might be a more, or less, generous exemption policy at any given time and as to any particular law, but not a general entitlement or civil right.

In the nineteenth century, there were additional exemptions under various State laws: 'priest-penitent' testimonial privilege – an exemption from the legal obligation to give evidence, whereby religious clerics could refuse to disclose the content of penitential confession; exemptions in some States for sabbatarians from Sunday-closing laws; and sacramental wine exceptions from State-level prohibitions of alcohol.[12] These too, however, were granted by ordinary statute or by common law adjudication, and did not have the force of entrenched constitutional right.

The US Supreme Court's first encounter with a constitutional free exercise claim for religious exemption was in 1878, in *Reynolds v United States*, a criminal prosecution for bigamy against a member – actually the secretary to the Church's president – of the Church of Jesus Christ of Latter Day Saints (the Mormon Church).[13] Reynolds' defence to the criminal charge was that plural marriage was a religious duty in the Mormon faith. The Supreme Court unanimously rejected the defence and upheld the conviction. 'Laws are made for the government of actions', said the Court, 'and while they cannot interfere with mere religious belief and opinions, they may with practices'; there can be no religious exemption from laws as to 'actions which [are] in violation of social duties or subversive of good order'.[14] To hold otherwise, warned the Court, 'would be to make the professed doctrines of religious belief superior to the law of the land, and in effect to permit every citizen to become a law unto himself'.[15]

[10] An Act Regulating Marriage and Divorce § 7 (1798), reprinted in 2 *The First Laws of the State of Rhode Island* 481, 483 (John D Cushing ed, 1983); see D Laycock, 'Regulatory Exemptions of Religious Behavior and the Original Understanding of the Establishment Clause' (2006) 81 *Notre Dame Law Review* 1793, 1806.

[11] See *Constitution* (US) Art V (requiring supermajorities for Constitutional amendments).

[12] See RJ Colombo, 'Forgive Us Our Sins: The Inadequacies of the Clergy-Penitent Privilege' (1998) 73 *New York University Law Review* 225, 231 (reviewing 19th-century state priest-penitent testimonial privilege); M Newsom, 'Some Kind of Religious Freedom: National Prohibition and the Volstead Act's Exemption for the Religious Use of Wine' (2005) 70 *Brooklyn Law Review* 739, 796 (reviewing 19th-century state exemptions for sacramental wine).

[13] *Reynolds v United States*, 98 US 145 (1878).

[14] ibid 166–67.

[15] ibid.

In the years and decades after *Reynolds*, lawmakers chose to provide religious exemptions from certain legal obligations. The federal Volstead Act of 1919, for example, which enforced national prohibition of alcoholic beverages, had an exception for wine 'for sacramental purposes, or like religious rites'.[16]

Both the First and Second World War military conscription laws provided an exemption for religious conscientious objectors.[17] These were matters of legislative grace. Beginning in the 1940s, however, there were hints from the Supreme Court that exemptions might be constitutionally required in some circumstances. In 1943, for example, the Court upheld the right of Jehovah's Witness schoolchildren to abstain from saluting the flag, a daily exercise at the time in many public schools: the Court's ruling was on free-speech grounds, however, and not as a question of religious exemption.[18] The decision – impressively libertarian in wartime – meant that anyone, religious or not, was free to decline to salute. Justice William Brennan, on the other hand, appointed to the Supreme Court by President Eisenhower in 1956, consistently urged that religious exemptions are constitutionally required by First Amendment 'free exercise of religion'. In 1961, Brennan thus dissented from a decision upholding a Pennsylvania Sunday-closing law which provided no exemption for Orthodox Jewish merchants, who closed their shops on the Jewish Sabbath and were at an economic disadvantage, unable to do business both Saturday and Sunday, vis-à-vis competitors doing business six days a week.[19]

A constitutional right to religious exemptions from generally applicable laws was actually announced for the first time by the Supreme Court in two famous cases decided in 1963 and 1972. The first case, *Sherbert v Verner*, a decision written by Justice Brennan, involved a Seventh Day Adventist who wanted exemption from a requirement to be available for work on Saturdays as a condition of receiving unemployment benefit; the second, *Wisconsin v Yoder*, involved an Amish community that wanted its children excused from compulsory school attendance past the eighth grade.[20] The Court held that the free exercise clause of the First Amendment required a religious exemption in both cases. These two decisions proclaimed that, in principle, exemption must be available from any law, for persons whose religious beliefs or practices are substantially burdened by the law, unless a 'compelling state interest' justifies refusal of exemption.

[16] Public Law 66-66, Title II Section 6.

[17] See F Heisler, 'The Law Versus the Conscientious Objector' (1953) 20 *University of Chicago Law Review* 441 (reviewing the limited exemptions for conscientious objectors in the 1917 and 1940 military conscription laws).

[18] *West Virginia State Board of Education v Barnette*, 319 US 624 (1943).

[19] *Braunfeld v Brown*, 366 US 599 (1961). Justice Brennan, in dissent, characterised the issue as 'whether a State may put an individual to a choice between his business and his religion'; 366 US 599, 611 (Brennan J dissenting).

[20] *Sherbert v Verner*, 374 US 398 (1963); *Wisconsin v Yoder*, 406 US 205 (1972).

C. The Court Reverses Course and Legislation Takes Up the Cause

The Supreme Court reversed course in 1990 when it decided *Employment Division v Smith* and held that the free exercise clause does not, after all, require religious exemptions from generally applicable laws enacted for secular purposes.[21] Even in the years between 1963 and 1990, religious exemptions were by no means granted as readily as *Sherbert* and *Yoder* might seem to imply. The Supreme Court rejected all religious claims for exemption from tax laws; it rejected all claims arising from prisons and from the military; it rejected a claim for exemption from the Fair Labor Standards Act. Virtually the only claims the Court accepted were – like *Sherbert* – for religious exemption from requirements to be available for Sabbath work under unemployment benefit laws.[22]

Yet the 1990 decision in *Employment Division v Smith*, explicitly cutting back the constitutional right to exemption, aroused intense political opposition. An unusually broad coalition, ranging from the religious Right through the political centre to the multi-cultural Left on the American political spectrum, led Congress to enact the Religious Freedom Restoration Act (RFRA) in 1993 by unanimous vote in the House of Representatives and by nearly unanimous vote in the Senate.[23] The Act restored the *Sherbert* and *Yoder* principle that exemption should presumptively be available from any law – federal or State – if compliance with the law would substantially burden someone's free exercise of religion, unless there is a 'compelling state interest' in not offering an exemption.

In another turn, the Supreme Court soon struck down RFRA as unconstitutional – as applied to State laws but not as to religious exemptions from federal laws – in *City of Boerne v Flores*, decided in 1997.[24] In one sense this was a federalism decision, shielding State governments from Congress, but the decision also dwelt on the idea that only the Supreme Court, not Congress, can authoritatively interpret the Constitution. The Congressional attempt to countermand the effects of *Employment Division v Smith*, and to restore a presumptive right to religious exemptions nationwide, plainly did not go down well at the Supreme Court. No doubt it was tactless for Congress to call it the Religious Freedom Restoration Act.

Nonetheless, RFRA remains in force as to federal laws: a statutory grant of religious exemption from any federal law unless a compelling State interest precludes the exemption.[25] Many State legislatures enacted similar measures,

[21] *Employment Division, Department of Human Resources of Oregon v Smith*, 494 US 872 (1990).

[22] See WP Marshall, 'Smith, Ballard, and the Religious Inquiry Exception to the Criminal Law' (2011) 44 *Texas Tech Law Review* 239, 244–45 (summarising the Supreme Court decisions, mostly against exemptions).

[23] Religious Freedom Restoration Act 1993 (US), Pub L No 103-141, 107 Stat 1488, codified at 42 USC 2000bb to 2000bb-4 (2006).

[24] *City of Boerne v Flores*, 521 US 507 (1997).

[25] See *Gonzales v O Centro Espirita Beneficente Uniao do Vegetal*, 546 US 418 (2006) (confirming that RFRA continues to apply to the federal Government and its laws).

whereby religious exemptions are presumptively available from any of the States' laws unless there is compelling cause to the contrary.[26] It might seem, then, that religious exemptions are now broadly guaranteed – guaranteed by statute, to be sure, not by constitutional right; nonetheless, not merely by grace and favour on a case-by-case or law-by-law basis, but as a general policy both for federal laws and in many States as well.

In fact, however, any legal and public consensus for religious exemptions has eroded dramatically in recent years. It is increasingly uncertain whether religious Americans can rely on the idea that religious exemptions will be generously available when faith and public law conflict. What could prompt such a turnabout, given that the religious exemption statutes were passed by such enthusiastic and overwhelming majorities not so long ago, in Congress and in many State legislatures as well?

D. The Eroding Consensus for Religious Exemptions

Three broad developments in recent decades tend to make religious exemptions an uncertain haven in a secular America.

First, the sheer growth of government and the greater presence of government regulation in American life. The growth of the 'administrative state' is widely recognised in the United States. The Code of Federal Regulations ran to about 10,000 pages in 1950, 71,000 pages in 1975 and 175,000 pages in 2014.[27] The federal Government's share of the national economy was approximately 15 per cent in 1950. It is about 30 per cent today.[28] State and local government have grown as well.[29] It is not just the quantity of regulation but also the character of regulation that is more likely than in the past to impinge on religious people. Federal statutes and regulations touch upon ever more, and ever more intimate, aspects of American life: healthcare, including questions of death and dying;[30] education, once virtually entirely a State or local affair;[31] family life and sexuality, including

[26] Twenty-one States have enacted RFRA-like statutes. See National Conference of State Legislatures, State Religious Freedom Restoration Acts (2017) at http://www.ncsl.org/research/civil-and-criminal-justice/state-rfra-statutes.aspx.

[27] See Federal Register, Code of Federal Regulations Total Pages and Volumes 1938–2014 at https://www.federalregister.gov/uploads/2015/05/Code-of-Federal-Regulations-Total-Pages-and-Volumes-1938-2014.pdf.

[28] CW Crews Jr, *Ten Thousand Commandments* (Washington DC, Competitive Enterprise Institute, 2019) 26 at https://cei.org/sites/default/files/10KC2019.pdf.

[29] There were roughly 6.4 million State and local government employees in 1960; by 2017, there were more than 19 million. State and Local Government Employment: Monthly Data (2018) at http://www.governing.com/gov-data/public-workforce-salaries/monthly-government-employment-changes-totals.html.

[30] See The Patient Protection and Affordable Care Act, Public Law 111-148, 124 Stat 119 *through* 124 Stat 1025 (2010) (906 pages).

[31] For an overview of the US Department of Education's budget, and hence of the scope of its activities and powers, see the Budget Homepage of the Department of Education at http://www2.ed.gov/about/overview/budget/index.html?src=ct.

marriage, contraception and abortion, and child-rearing.[32] Food and drugs are regulated, including substances that might be sacramental.[33] There is extensive regulation of finance and many other economic questions, as well as environmental matters, with inevitable implications for – and the potential to clash with – religious social doctrine. Federal social welfare policy has expanded dramatically in scope and importance: means-tested welfare programmes alone now absorb 21 per cent of the federal budget, and federal spending on the leading welfare programmes has nearly quadrupled in real terms over the past three decades.[34] Welfare spending, inevitably, comes with rules, regulations and conditions: these too may impinge on religious practice.

The second development is the diversification or fragmentation of religious life in the United States. American religion has always come in a variety of denominations and sects, even in colonial times and in the decades after American independence, although in those eras the overwhelming majority of religious people and groups in America were Christian and Protestant. In 1943, according to Supreme Court Justice Felix Frankfurter, there were 'more than 250 distinctive established religious denominations in the United States'.[35] Yet the sociology of American religion in the mid-twentieth century was substantially reflected in Will Herberg's 1955 best-seller, *Protestant-Catholic-Jew* (with a pinch of kosher salt, perhaps, for Jews, who even then were only about 3 per cent of the population).[36] The 'Mainline churches', a relatively small number of well-established historic Protestant denominations, were strong numerically and institutionally: a majority of all churchgoers attended Mainline Protestant churches until the mid-twentieth century, and as late as 1970 their members, together with Roman Catholics, made up more than two-thirds of Americans.[37] Adherents to non-Judeo-Christian religions were numerically few and culturally almost invisible at the time. In the

[32] See, eg, IRS Revenue Ruling 2013–17 (2013) (recognising same-sex marriages for federal tax purposes).
For the Final Rule requiring health insurers to cover elective abortions under the Patient Protection and Affordable Care Act, see 'Patient Protection and Affordable Care Act; Establishment of Exchanges and Qualified Health Plans; Exchange Standards for Employers' at 77 *Federal Register* 18310–18475 (27 March 2012) at www.gpo.gov/fdsys/pkg/FR-2012-03-27/pdf/2012-6125.pdf. For an assessment of the impact of welfare-state policy on child-rearing in the United States and western Europe, see KJ Morgan, *Working Mothers and the Welfare State* (Stanford, CA, Stanford University Press, 2006).

[33] See Federal Food, Drug, and Cosmetic Act, 21 USC Sec 301 et seq.

[34] United States Senate Budget Committee, *CRS Report: Welfare Spending the Largest Item in the Federal Budget* (Jeff Sessions, Ranking Minority Member) at https://www.budget.senate.gov/imo/media/doc/CRS%20Report%20-%20Welfare%20Spending%20The%20Largest%20Item%20In%20The%20Federal%20Budget.pdf.

[35] *West Virginia State Board of Education v Barnette*, 319 US 624, 658 (1943) (Frankfurter J dissenting).

[36] W Herberg, *Protestant-Catholic-Jew* (Chicago, IL, University of Chicago Press, 1955). For Jewish population statistics at the time, see A Chenkin, 'Jewish Population of the United States 1955' in *American Jewish Yearbook* 119 (1956) (estimating the Jewish population in 1955, the year of publication of Herberg's book, as approximately 5 million, or 3% of the total approximate US population of 167 million).

[37] http://www.ropercenter.uconn.edu/public-perspective/ppscan/43/43003.pdf; see also JD Davidson and RE Pyle, *Ranking Faiths: Religious Stratification in America* (Lanham, MD, Rowman & Littlefield, 2011).

decades since the 1960s – and hence since the time that religious exemptions were introduced by the Supreme Court in the *Sherbert* and *Yoder* decisions – membership in the Mainline churches declined dramatically. The Episcopal Church, the American branch of the Anglican Communion, had nearly 3.5 million members in the mid-1960s: it has fewer than 2 million today, although the population of the country was less than 200 million then and is more than 300 million now.[38] There were more than 4 million Presbyterians in 1960; there are fewer than 2 million today.[39] The liberal United Church of Christ lost some 60 per cent of its membership between 1957 and 2017.[40]

A majority of church-going American Protestants today attend Evangelical, fundamentalist or charismatic churches, whose doctrines and practices are more varied than those of the older Mainline churches.[41] The number of Muslims in America, although they are still probably only about 1 per cent of the population, has grown, along with their visibility in American life and culture;[42] so likewise with Hindus, Buddhists and followers of other Eastern religions. The popularity of New Age and non-Christian religious or quasi-religious beliefs has grown.[43] A respected survey of American religious life reports that the religiously unaffiliated – those who say they have no particular religious affiliation – increased in just seven years from slightly more than 16 per cent of American adults in 2007 to slightly under 23 per cent in 2014.[44] The unaffiliated are by no means all determinedly irreligious however: more than half of them describe themselves either as 'religious persons' (18 per cent) or as 'spiritual but not religious' (37 per cent). A quarter of them believe in astrology; a quarter of them believe in reincarnation; 30 per cent of them say they believe in spiritual energy in physical things such as crystals, trees or mountains.[45] Today's array of religious groups, doctrines, notions and practices could easily give rise to far more varied claims for religious exemptions than was the case when the Mainline churches enjoyed more ascendancy, and when the religious landscape of the country could plausibly be described in a book entitled *Protestant-Catholic-Jew*.

[38] See Hartford Institute for Religion Research, Facts About American Religion at http://hirr.hartsem.edu/research/fastfacts/fast_facts.html#growlose.

[39] See PR Kincaid, '2012 Statistics Show Dramatic Decrease in PCUSA Membership, Congregations' at http://www.layman.org/2012-statistics-show-dramatic-decrease-in-pcusa-membership-congregations.

[40] See G Smith, 'Six Decades of Decline in the United Church of Christ' at http://sowhatfaith.com/2018/10/28/6-decades-of-decline-in-the-united-church-of-christ/.

[41] Pew Research Center, *America's Changing Religious Landscape* (2015) (of the 46.5% of Americans identifying as Protestant Christians in 2014, 25.4% affiliated with Evangelical churches, 14.7% with Mainline churches and 6.5% with historically Black churches). See at http://www.pewforum.org/2015/05/12/americas-changing-religious-landscape/.

[42] ibid.

[43] In American prisons, for example, there has been a sharp growth in adherence to a variety of sects, including the Nation of Islam ('Black Muslims'), pagan groups such as Wicca, Odinism, Asatru and Druidism (often associated with White Supremacists among the prisoners) and 'Native American Spirituality'. See United States Commission on Civil Rights, *Enforcing Religious Freedom in Prison* (2008).

[44] Pew Forum on Religion & Public Life, '"Nones" on the Rise: One-in-Five Adults Have No Religious Affiliation' 22 (2012).

[45] ibid 24.

The third development is the sharpening of political and cultural divisions in American society, with the question of religious exemptions increasingly drawn into these divisions. The major American political parties, which in the past overlapped ideologically to a considerable degree, are increasingly polarised, with many politically active Americans bitterly at odds with Americans of the opposite persuasion over such matters as abortion, sexuality and marriage, racial and ethnic identity, and more. Some speak seriously of a 'cold civil war' and an end to any political and social self-restraint, particularly when it comes to imposing one party's way of life on Americans of the other party.[46] Many if not most of the issues in contention have implications for religious belief and practice, with religious ideas and principles about sexuality, marriage and family life often confronted with opposing but equally fervently-held secular views. When such secular views become public law – for example about abortion or homosexual marriage – whether by majority vote or by judicial fiat, the advocates of these secular policies increasingly take offence at religious exemptions from the new legal regimes. A growing number of secular liberals condemn religious exemptions as an affront to the human dignity of those whose 'non-traditional' practices are felt to be validated by liberal secular policies.[47]

A shift in attitude about religious exemptions was already manifest at the time of the Supreme Court's *Hobby Lobby* decision in 2014, which granted religious exemption under RFRA to a family-owned company from federal mandates to provide insurance coverage for contraception and (arguably) for abortion on behalf of employees.[48] The decision by a closely-divided Supreme Court was met with angry dismay from political and opinion leaders who favoured the mandatory requirements.[49] Restrictive amendments to RFRA and even amendments to the Constitution were demanded by many in politics, in the media and in the academy who not long before were among the enthusiasts for RFRA and religious exemptions.[50] By the time the Supreme Court decided the *Masterpiece Cakeshop*

[46] See A Codevilla, 'The Cold Civil War', 17 *Claremont Review of Books* (Spring 2017) at https://www.claremont.org/crb/article/the-cold-civil-war/.

[47] See MO Degirolami, 'Free Exercise By Moonlight' (2016) 53 *San Diego Law Review* 105, 134: 'If perceived affronts or injuries to one's personal dignity constitute a significant or material harm … then it is difficult to see how many permissive religious accommodations could survive.'

[48] *Burwell v Hobby Lobby Stores* 573 US _; 138 S Ct 1719 (2014).

[49] See B McDonnell, 'The Liberal Case for Hobby Lobby' (2015) *University of Minnesota Law School Research Paper No 14-39*, 2 ('The case received a huge amount of media attention, more than any case of that term for the court. Reaction to the decision was intense and highly polarized. Conservatives celebrated, while liberals expressed outrage.')

[50] S Stein, 'White House, Democrats, Plot Response to Supreme Court Hobby Lobby Ruling' *Huffington Post Politics* (posted 30 June 2014, updated 28 August 2014) at http://www.huffingtonpost.com/2014/06/30/white-house-hobby-lobby_n_5544287.html. See also E Newlin Carney, 'Hobby Lobby Ruling Fuels Amendment Push' *Roll Call Beltway Insiders* (posted 2 July 2014) on proposed constitutional amendment to reverse the decision, at http://blogs.rollcall.com/beltway-insiders/hobby-lobby-ruling-fuels-amendment-push/?dcz=; K Pollitt, 'Why It's Time to Repeal the Religious Freedom Restoration Act' *The Nation* (30 July 2014) ('The law, passed in 1993 with near-unanimous support, has become an excuse for bigotry, superstition and sectarianism').

case on narrow grounds in 2018, overturning the Colorado ruling against the Christian bakery owner who declined to make a cake for a homosexual wedding, there was already a substantial body of academic and public opinion vehemently critical of religious exemptions, at least when religious scruples run up against laws couched as anti-discrimination measures.[51] Support for exemptions is plainly more fragile than it seemed not long ago, if it breaks down whenever exemption is sought, especially on behalf of a major Christian body of belief, from any law or administrative regulation whose supporters feel strongly about enforcing it.

When government's rules were fewer, in short, and its regulatory ambitions more narrow – and when the range of the country's religious diversity was narrower as well, so the kinds of exemptions likely to be sought were fewer and more predictable – it was easier to be generous in offering religious exemptions and accommodations. With more regulation, especially federal social regulation meant to shape or re-shape the country's way of life, the very purposes of such regulation may be threatened if exemptions are available to an ever-wider array of people and interests. Tolerance for religious objectors is in shorter supply, moreover, when Americans feel locked in a struggle over what the fundamental character of the country ought to be.

III. The Outlook for Religious Exemptions

What are the implications, then, for the future of religious exemptions in America, and for religious persons and groups who might seek them? It is not that many Americans, even those most critical of the *Hobby Lobby* and *Masterpiece Cakeshop* decisions, have turned against religious exemptions wholesale. The federal RFRA statute remains in force, calling for religious exemptions from federal laws whenever there is no compelling interest to the contrary; many States have similar statutes in force for their own State laws. There is, as yet, no concerted effort to repeal these statutes, although some left-leaning voices now call for repeal, and it is imaginable that the laws might be amended or modified. Religious exemptions for small or unconventional sects, especially sects whose history or whose ethnic character bespeak authenticity, are relatively uncontroversial. Exemptions that do not challenge secular passions, even exemptions for more mainstream Judeo-Christian groups, may (and probably will) continue to be accepted under the law and by most Americans without too much controversy.

On the other hand, there are, in a sense, two somewhat contradictory traditions in America about religious exemptions. One tradition is to grant exemptions generously out of respect for religious conviction. This tradition dates back to the

[51] See Degirolami (n 47) 108–09 (noting that the 'low esteem of academics' for religious exemptions is 'palpable' and '[e]xamples of hostility to religious accommodation in the academic literature are legion' (ibid fn 13)).

founding era, and to the exemptions from oaths and from military service for pacifist sects. But there is a counter-tradition, taking a more limited or intolerant view, based on a concern that laws, once enacted, should apply to everyone: that the laws, and perhaps the Rule of Law itself, might be undermined by too many or too-readily-granted exemptions.

The first tradition seemed to be ascendant, especially in politically liberal circles, since the 1950s and Justice Brennan's advocacy for the idea that exemptions are a constitutional right, and in the era of the Supreme Court's *Sherbert* and *Yoder* decisions, and with the subsequent near-unanimous passage of the federal RFRA statute. Even in the *Sherbert* and *Yoder* era, to be sure, the Supreme Court rejected more claims for exemption than it accepted, and the triumph of the idea that exemptions were a virtually unconditional right may have been more nominal than real.

The second view, more cautious or sometimes overtly hostile towards religious claims, has had a new lease on life in recent years, particularly in politically liberal and left-wing circles. To some degree, this might be seen as a reversion to the historical norm. For most of American history, after all, exemptions were generally viewed as concessions within the discretion of the lawmakers, not as unconditional rights entailed in the Constitution's guarantee of 'free exercise of religion'.

Religious Americans can reasonably expect, therefore, that some exemptions from otherwise applicable laws will continue to be granted in future. This will be true both for non-mainstream faiths and for Judeo-Christian denominations as well, at least when the exemptions in question are not felt to conflict with anti-discrimination or civil rights measures, or with other laws with impassioned secular support.

That said, relying on the prospect of exemptions, especially from laws and regulations that engage the passions of the 'culture wars' in the United States, is apt to be an unwise and ultimately perhaps a futile strategy. Emphasis on exemptions almost inevitably diverts the political energy of religious Americans from persuading their fellow citizens not to enact laws from which religious exemptions would be wanted or needed. The question of exemption arises most often, after all, when government grows in its reach and ambition. If most aspects of life, including those that touch on religious life, are left to people's private arrangement then not much special accommodation will be needed. When government assumes command and control over more areas of life, regulating who shall do what, under what rules and regulations, then clashes with one or other religious way of life are almost inevitable. To take an obvious example, with a relatively open market in healthcare and private health insurance, religious institutions needed no special exemptions to adopt their own approaches on questions of abortion and end-of-life issues, as on other matters. But greatly increased government regulation or takeover of healthcare implies more uniform standards and rules, and hence more controversy over whether there should be religious exemptions and if so, for whom, to what degree and on what terms.

Religious Americans, therefore, belonging to many faiths and denominations, have reason to be especially concerned about over-reach of government, since the more regulation – particularly federal regulation, with its nationwide command and, often, its secularist cultural bent – the more likely it is to impinge on religious practice and belief. Religious Americans, however, are numerous: depending on one's criteria of 'religious', probably a majority of Americans, notwithstanding the decline in religious affiliation in recent years and decades.[52] Moreover, many non-religious Americans, for entirely secular reasons, are also wary of the growth or over-growth of government. Religious people should seldom be without political allies in seeking to modify or defeat unjust or over-reaching regulatory propositions.

Nevertheless, political energy and resources are not unlimited. To the extent that these resources are devoted to seeking special accommodations and exemptions, they are not devoted to mitigating or opposing the enactment of over-intrusive rules and regulations.

The emphasis on religious exemptions thus represents a withdrawal, at least to some extent, from public debate and political action over the merits of things: a withdrawal, as religious people sometimes say, from the 'public square'. As such, it even implies acceptance, at least as a practical matter, of the idea that religious arguments are illegitimate in the sphere of public debate. When religious people do join in public debate on the merits, some of their arguments might be couched in religious terms or might invoke religious principles. The idea that religious arguments, or 'comprehensive doctrines', are alien to 'public reason' as a matter of liberal theory, and hence should not be introduced into public debate, has been a favourite of various secularist writers and publicists.[53] But it is an idea that many if not most religious people would reject in principle.

Seeking frequent exemptions and accommodations puts religious people in the invidious position of demanding special privileges. This is almost always a dubious demand, especially in an egalitarian liberal society where a core idea is rejection of special privilege. It is probably not sustainable beyond a limited number of exemptions, for a limited number of religious bodies, in a modestly regulated and generally consensus-minded polity. In an ever-more-minutely regulated yet sharply divided polity, religious people cannot keep demanding exemptions: they will not be granted. It is a well-known military axiom that armies in retreat are at their most vulnerable.[54] Religious Americans need not retreat from robust political action merely to plead for special indulgence. It will not avail them, at least not when political and cultural passions are engaged, if they do.

[52] See Pew Research Center, *America's Changing Religious Landscape* (n 41) 3 ('To be sure, the United States remains home to more Christians than any other country in the world, and a large majority of Americans – roughly seven-in-ten – continue to identify with some branch of the Christian faith').

[53] See eg J Rawls, *Political Liberalism* (New York, Columbia University Press, 1993) and 'The Idea of Public Sphere Revisited' (1997) 64 *University of Chicago Law Review* 765; R Audi, 'Liberal Democracy and Religion in Politics' in R Audi and N Wolterstorff, *Religion in the Public Square: The Place of Religious Convictions in the Political Debate* (Lanham, MD, Rowman & Littlefield, 1997) 25.

[54] See JA Keegan, *A History of Warfare* (London, Hutchinson, 1993) 271: 'It was from the example of Cannae [the defeat of the Romans, and the massacre of retreating Roman soldiers, by Hannibal's Carthaginian army] that the nineteenth-century French tactical analyst Ardant du Picq first proposed the important perception that it is in retreating that an army exposes itself to disabling losses.'

10

Whose Conscience? Which Complicity? Reconciling Burdens and Interests in the Law of Religious Liberty

CHAD FLANDERS AND SEAN OLIVEIRA

I. Introduction

Near the very end of their article on 'Conscience Wars', about the clash between religious conservatives and liberal antidiscrimination laws,[1] Douglas NeJaime and Reva Siegal move from the ostensibly descriptive to the harshly evaluative. Those who make conscience-based complicity claims – the plaintiffs in *Hobby Lobby* or in *Little Sisters*, and now, we might add, *Masterpiece Cakeshop*[2] – are not all that interested in accommodation, it turns out. Rather, they are trying to 'integrate' us all into their vision of 'community' – a 'legal order shaped by their underlying religious convictions'.[3] They are not pluralists, who are willing to live and let live, but 'evangelists', with religious liberty as a pretext for their 'evangelizing' mission.[4]

But could not the alleged evangelists say the same thing in almost exactly the same way? Those in favour of the contraceptive mandate use anti-discrimination or women's health as their pretext – *they* want a legal order shaped by their underlying secular convictions, which includes robust protections against discrimination. *They* have claims about how to 'live in community' with those who do not share their beliefs on 'contested questions of sexual morality'. They are not pluralists, either. They too are evangelists, just on the other side of the debate.

This seems to be the state of things, unfortunately, so it is appropriate that NeJaime and Siegal call this situation a kind of *war* over conscience. And if this is

[1] D Nejaime and RB Siegel, 'Conscience Wars: Complicity-Based Conscience Claims in Religion and Politics' (2015) 124 *Yale Law Journal* 2516.

[2] The cases are: *Burwell v Hobby Lobby Stores, Inc*, 573 US _; 134 S Ct 2751 (2014); *Zubik v Burwell*, 136 S Ct 1557 (2016) (per curiam); *Masterpiece Cakeshop, Ltd v Colorado Civil Rights Commission*, 584 US _; 138 S Ct 1719 (2018).

[3] Nejaime and Siegel (n 1) 2590–91.

[4] ibid.

where things stand, then the idea of religious accommodation – which has always held itself out as a way to get to a truce in the religious wars – is in real trouble. Bill Clinton, when it became clear in the Lewinsky affair that he could not come clean with the American people, that he could not admit that he had an affair and ask forgiveness without getting impeached or without having to resign, is reported to have said to Dick Morris, 'We'll just have to win, then'.[5] In Nejaime's and Siegel's telling, accommodating religious beliefs *is* letting the other side win. It is not a truce, a way to get along; it is a defeat. And so, we have to stop them; *we'll have to win, then*. The evangelists on the other side (the *religious* evangelists) may also think they have to win, or at least not lose as much. They will want to keep exemptions for religious believers. But then who really believes in pluralism anymore? Pluralism still seems defensible in principle, but the Religious Freedom Restoration Act and the Free Exercise clause of the First Amendment (generally, we refer throughout the chapter to both as 'RFRA') are looking more and more like poor vehicles for pluralism. That is, RFRA looks more and more like religious believers winning and antidiscrimination proponents losing. The result is that, in each case, it is not a matter of some principle being established, or some accommodation being made; it is always a matter of *winning* and *losing*. In the recent cases of the United States (US) Supreme Court, much of the response from secular liberals was exactly like this: each case was just another in a series of instances of a majoritarian religion winning on an ever more attenuated claim of complicity.[6]

This chapter squarely situates itself within US First Amendment jurisprudence. Specifically, the law with regard to a citizen's free exercise of religion. As can be seen from the above, of central importance is the tension in US law between the equality rights of citizens to be free from discrimination, and the freedom of religious believers to exercise beliefs that may be (illusory or not) at odds with those equality rights. That tension, however, is not tethered to the US alone. It is a global concern.[7] For the truth of the matter is as simple as this: pluralism values equally *both* the exercise of a person's religious beliefs *and* a person's ability to be free from discrimination. The tension arises because we are not so naive as to believe that there will be a way to accommodate every exercise of religious belief without

[5] Howard Kurtz, 'Dick Morris, High on the Critical List' *Washington Post* (3 February 1999) C1, at https://www.washingtonpost.com/wp-srv/politics/special/clinton/stories/morris020399.htm.

[6] See, eg, L Griffin, *Symposium: Workers remain at risk post-Zubik v Burwell, SCOTUSblog*, 17 May 2016, 12:06 pm, at https://www.scotusblog.com/2016/05/symposium-workers-remain-at-risk-post-zubik-v-burwell/ ('It should be unseemly that powerful religious leaders and the government continue to bargain away employees' rights in the name of religious freedom. But that is what the non-profits' dangerous exemption theory, the Court's order, and RFRA all encourage'); but, going the other way, see R Garnett, *Symposium: The Future of Accommodation, SCOTUSBlog*, 17 May 2016, at https://www.scotusblog.com/2016/05/symposium-the-future-of-accommodation/ ('There is no denying, though, that to the extent the right to religious freedom is regarded as a luxury good, a license to do wrong, or as special pleading by the culture war's losers, it is increasingly vulnerable').

[7] See, eg, Owen Bowcott, 'UK Supreme Court Backs Bakery that Refused to Make Gay Marriage Cake' *The Guardian* (10 October 2018) at https://www.theguardian.com/uk-news/2018/oct/10/uk-supreme-court-backs-bakery-that-refused-to-make-gay-wedding-cake.

allowing some discrimination, or vice versa. One side always prevails. Whoever loses, we think, it is a loss for that value. And therein lies the rub.

Where the end result is no solution, however, we look to the process. In US jurisprudence, for many constitutional rights, including free exercise rights, where the rights are at odds with laws, courts engage in varying forms of balancing called 'scrutiny'.[8] If the law does not pass the scrutiny then it is rendered unconstitutional. If it does, then so go the spoils. No matter the level of scrutiny, though, the balance is always the interest behind the law against the burden on the constitutional right. Both are to be given consideration. Most important, behind both interests are *people* with hurts, harms and hang-ups. Thus, at bottom, win or lose, the process of scrutiny requires the balancing and consideration of *peoples'* losses. And this may be more important than winning or losing.

Thus, if RFRA can be rehabilitated in the eyes of those on the side of anti-discrimination, which is what we propose to look at in this chapter, that project has to have two aspects to it. The first, which is pro-religion, is establishing that RFRA really is, in its own way, an *anti-discrimination* statute. That means that the claims really are claims against discrimination of a sort, and not just religious special pleading. Religious believers want fair treatment, too, and sometimes fair treatment requires an accommodation. Here we disagree with Fred Gedicks,[9] and argue for a rather expansive version of when religious believers are 'burdened' under RFRA.

But the second aspect to this rehabilitation is pro-anti-discrimination. Anti-discrimination *is* a compelling governmental interest, and it should win out in a lot of cases, maybe even the majority.[10] In fact, many missed that a lot of RFRA advocates were saying, regularly and forthrightly, that the private businesses would probably lose a lot of cases when anti-discrimination was in the balance and that

[8] Roughly, there are three types of scrutiny (with tweaks and twists given the case or right). We list them in the order in which they protect a constitutional right. Strict scrutiny requires a law to be narrowly tailored and necessary to further a compelling government interest. See *Trinity Lutheran Church of Columbia, Inc v Comer*, 582 US _; 137 S Ct 2012, 2024–25 (2017) (First Amendment free exercise case utilising strict scrutiny and holding the state does not have a compelling interest in violating the constitutional right). Intermediate scrutiny requires that the law furthers an important government interest through means that are substantially related to that interest. See *Craig v Boren*, 429 US 190, 200 (1976) (equal protection case utilising intermediate scrutiny and holding that the state's law focusing on gender does not further and is not substantially related to the important government interest of traffic safety). And finally, rational basis scrutiny, which requires a law be rationally related to a legitimate government interest. See *Nordlinger v Hahn*, 505 US 1, 17 (1992) (equal protection case utilising rational basis scrutiny to uphold a property tax assessment that made a distinction between longer-lasting property owners and relatively new ones). For a good, but brief, history of the emergence of strict scrutiny and thereby the other scrutiny types, see RH Fallon, Jr, 'Strict Judicial Scrutiny' (2007) 54 *UCLA Law Review* 1267.

[9] FM Gedicks, '"Substantial" Burdens: How Courts May (and Why They Must) Judge Burdens on Religion Under RFRA' (2017) 85 *George Washington Law Review* 94, 98.

[10] For example, as Justice Kennedy is at pains to point out in his concurrence in *Hobby Lobby*, that decision is not against anti-discrimination (in the form of women's health) as a compelling interest, but only against the means devised to further that interest *in this case*. *Hobby Lobby Stores, Inc* (n 2) 2785–86.

they probably *should* lose.[11] Here we try to bridge the gap between us and NeJaime and Siegel.

In these clashes one side wins and the other side loses. That is the way law usually works. Religion is accommodated or it is not; the government's compelling interest trumps or it does not. Someone is helped and someone is hurt. But there is a way in which, if both sides' values are at least acknowledged, pluralism wins – and so, in a way, do both sides. Religious believers should not be told that their religion is not burdened when they sincerely think that it is; but at the same time, we should not say that accommodations have 'precisely zero'[12] effect on the government's interest when this is probably false. After all, the government's compelling interest in these cases is also someone's interest, in getting healthcare or in getting a job. That interest should win in a lot of cases, but what the Court owes us above all is a fair and honest accounting of that interest. Our point is a simple one really: process matters, and getting the process right matters. It matters, when you are helping people avoid a hurt, that you recognise you might be hurting other people at the same time. Quite aside from winning or losing, both hurts can simultaneously be both real and unavoidable, and so *both* hurts need to be addressed.

II. How RFRA Helps Religious Believers, Sometimes

Start with this picture (a sort of parallel version of the NeJaime and Siegel article): religious believers who assert not just that they do not *like* contraception but who want their organisation to be free of the obligation to provide contraception were (and are) called various names by opponents – bigots, anti-women, etc. Or consider the 2015 controversy in Indiana over its State RFRA.[13] There was name-calling there, too. The language got extreme and harsh. At its most extreme, it was said that the businesses that supported the exemption from anti-discrimination

[11] Religious Liberty Protection Act of 1998 [RLPA]: Hearings on HR 4019 before the Subcommittee on the Constitution of the House Committee on the Judiciary, 105th Congress 236–38 (1998) (statement of Professor Douglas Laycock); Brief for Christian Legal Society et al as Amici Curiae Supporting Hobby Lobby and Conestoga Wood, et al, *Burwell v Hobby Lobby Stores, Inc* (Nos.13-354 & 13-356), 2014 WL 411294 at 16 and note 16 (Professor Laycock sums up the witnesses who agreed with him in the hearings on the RLPA, that believe the anti-discrimination claims should and would win most of the time in this context).

[12] As, for example, Justice Alito does in *Hobby Lobby*. *Hobby Lobby Stores, Inc* (n 2) 2760.

[13] See Justin Wm Moyer, 'Indiana Pizza Shop Won't Cater Gay Wedding, Gets Over $50K From Supporters' *Washington Post* (2 April 2015) at https://www.washingtonpost.com/news/morning-mix/wp/2015/04/02/indianas-memories-pizza-wouldnt-cater-gay-wedding-gets-40k-in-crowdfunding/?utm_term=.50e9b74c6ff8 (describing the fallout for a pizzeria that admitted it would not cater gay weddings in the middle of the Indiana RFRA debate); J Scott Trubey, 'Indiana Still Healing from Scars of RFRA' *Atlanta Journal-Constitution* (2 April 2016) at https://www.ajc.com/news/state – regional-govt – politics/indiana-still-healing-from-scars-rfra/f0lRpukhR4iD1XznoNkZYN/ (explaining the general timeline of events surrounding the passage and amendment of Indiana's RFRA, as well as the fallout).

laws were at best homophobic and at worst Nazis because of their religious convictions, sincerely held.[14] If there are dignitary harms in being considered 'sinners', there are dignitary harms in being called 'Nazis', too. We assume, also, that we can consider the dignitary harm as swinging more or less freely of the underlying truth of the matter being debated. Even if we are morally in the wrong on this or that issue, we can still be treated in ways we do not deserve, and that includes being called names.[15]

NeJaime and Siegel are right that there are real-world harms to being denied contraceptive coverage. But consider the real-world harms if religious organisations were denied an accommodation. Presumably, Hobby Lobby would choose not to violate its religious convictions – and so it would drop coverage altogether, or would have to pay huge fines (or both). Perhaps this is not a *huge* deal, but Hobby Lobby runs a rather progressive company (in terms of wages, time off, etc) and its workers would suffer if it went out of business. And then we perhaps get to more serious harms. Some hospitals, if denied an accommodation, would close; adoption services would have to shut down if they had to approve adoption to gay couples.[16] Other charities would probably follow suit. We can call such things churlish and maybe hope that things were different. But the facts do not change – or more appropriately, the convictions that would prompt these actions will not change. We either accommodate them, or we do not. But if we do not accommodate them, there are real-world consequences to this.

So, we could re-write 'Conscience Wars' in this parallel mode, pointing out how religious believers can face dignitary and concrete harms if they and their beliefs are not accommodated. Even here we may not get to the heart of the matter, which is that religious believers in general should have a right to pursue and practise their religious convictions. They should do so more or less free of insult. It is nice that religious believers do some good in the world, even in the business world, but, at bottom, religious believers have a right not to be discriminated against. Freedom from discrimination on the basis of religious belief really is a civil right. We assume that the same is (obviously) true of the anti-discrimination right on the other side of this debate: gays and lesbians should be able to live in the world without being discriminated against. That they are able to live in the world without being insulted and to engage in projects that help others – these are great things, but they are not at the root of the right. The root of the right is a norm against discrimination and for fair treatment.

[14] See Moyer (n 13); Trubey (n 13).

[15] Although compare S Girgis, 'Nervous Victors, Illiberal Measures: A Response to Douglas Nejaime and Reva Siegel' (2016) 125 *Yale Law Journal Forum* 399, 413 ('Moral stigma is a real cost. But tolerating it is a fair price for freedom with dividends of its own: an open society, rich in dissent. We cannot advance these goals while rejecting otherwise justified civil liberties simply because they give offense').

[16] Indeed, see Maggie Gallagher, 'Banned in Boston' *Weekly Standard* (15 May 2006) at https://www.weeklystandard.com/maggie-gallagher/banned-in-boston-13329 (describing the shutdown of adoption agency Catholic Charities of Boston when they were not given a religious exemption to anti-discrimination law).

The fact that the religious beliefs that get protected are majoritarian (ie Christian) is not quite to the point. Even those in the majority have the right to free speech and privacy, etc. Rights are not just for groups in the minority. Or perhaps better: it is not the case that those in the majority *are in the majority in all facets of their lives*. We may be majorities with regard to one facet of our lives, but minorities in another. We may be part of a majority religion but physically disabled – so we may not have to worry too much about our religion being persecuted, but do worry about access to buildings, etc. If we need to assert a right, it is usually because some majority – perhaps a permanent majority, perhaps a shifting coalition that just happens to be the majority at the time – is pressuring us, and risks violating that right.

What about the problem of attenuation? One major theme of 'Conscience Wars' is that the burden asserted by religious organisations is becoming ever more attenuated. Fred Gedicks in his essay argues that there *is* a problem here, and that courts should be more aggressive in policing when a burden on the believer is or is not 'substantial'.[17] But there *are* substantial costs to not complying with the mandate absent an accommodation: fines for those businesses or organisations that do not comply. And if the question is whether the violation of their religion is substantial or not, here we disagree with Gedicks. We should not import standards of tort law into determining how much someone is burdened by a secular law. Religious believers themselves are the best judges of this: when what the government is asking them to do goes too far, or whether it is something they can live with.

This sort of deference may seem exceptional, and to a certain extent it is, but must we not extend the same *kind* of deference on the other side. Do not question whether not having access to this or that contraceptive is really a burden – the point is a larger one, of principle. There is a real and perhaps significant deprivation, and that prevents full and equal treatment, even if the deprivation could be construed from a certain point of view as relatively minor. We should want to say, 'Who are you to say whether this access is really important. It's a denial of access, and I say it's important.' There has to be *some* objective basis to this, of course – the government has to be doing something to them, depriving them of something, but beyond that, we should pretty much take their word as to *how much* it hurts.

Let us close this section with what we hope is a sympathetic example, or at least let us try to draw it as sympathetically as possible. Take a prison inmate who has a 'strange', non-majority religious belief, held by a routinely despised group of people. He claims that his religious belief and practice is 'substantially burdened' by the prison's food policy, which requires him, at least once a week – and sometimes more, in cases when there is 'lockdown' of the prison – to forgo a meatless meal. Instead, his only option at those times is to go without food or eat the meals

[17] See Gedicks (n 9).

the prison provides, which means he violates his religious beliefs in what he says is a pretty substantial way. This kind of thing happens a lot.[18]

Should plaintiffs like this win on RFRA? In the end, perhaps not, but our point here is that it is important *how* they lose, if they lose. A lot of courts in this situation second guess the religious believer – they say missing one meal is *de minimis*, not enough to get to the level of a substantial burden. The prisoner should get over it. *But how*, we want to say, *do they know this is the case*? Even if our prisoner's beliefs were not shared by other members of his sect, that he was a minority of one, he could *still* be substantially burdened. If he loses (and we hasten to add that he probably should), we want to insist that there is a value in his losing in the right way, at a later point down the road, at the compelling interest stage. That is, his claim to be substantially burdened deserves to be validated even if the prison has a compelling interest in running its meal policy the way it does. Getting the process right matters, because recognising the values at every step of the way matters, and treating the parties involved with respect matters.

III. How RFRA Hurts Others, Sometimes: The Case of *Hobby Lobby*

The *Hobby Lobby* opinion has the strange distinction of being one that both affirms the compelling interest at stake (basically conceding the government has shown a compelling interest) but, at the same time, is open to fair accusations that it does not take the compelling interest seriously enough. The interest (broadly construed) is women's health, and the Court simply assumes (for the sake of argument) that promoting women's health is a very good thing and, moreover, that it is something that the Affordable Care Act promotes.[19] But the Court rules against that interest anyway, because it says that there are other means to get to that end, means that accommodate religion rather than run over it.[20] It is in saying that this 'means' is adequate that the Court suggests that it might not be taking the compelling interest all that seriously. Consider two things it does in this respect.

The first thing it did was to suggest, in passing, that the state might have an obligation to start a *wholly new* programme that would subsidise contraception for everybody.[21] If the government really did believe that contraception was so

[18] See eg Alyssa Mullins, 'Prison Refuses to Provide Buddhist Inmate with Vegetarian Meals' *Peta* (3 September 2013) at https://www.peta.org/blog/prison-refuses-vegetarian-meal/; Lizette Alvarez, 'You Don't Have to be Jewish to Love a Kosher Meal' *New York Times* (20 January 2014) at https://www.nytimes.com/2014/01/21/us/you-dont-have-to-be-jewish-to-love-a-kosher-prison-meal.html; N Moustafa, 'The Right to Free Exercise of Religion in Prisons: How Courts Should Determine Sincerity of Religious Belief Under RLUIPA' (2014) 20 *Michigan Journal of Race and Law* 213.

[19] *Hobby Lobby Stores, Inc* (n 2) 2780.

[20] ibid 2782.

[21] ibid 2780.

important to women's health then, the opinion seems to be asking, why not go whole hog? Why leave anything to the market and to employers? This is bizarre. It in theory upends a lot of free exercise jurisprudence – churches do not have to pay minimum wage, because the federal Government could subsidise it, etc.[22] More importantly, it is not obvious that such a programme *would* pass, and even if it did, there would be massive delays in getting it up and running. If utopia is the baseline[23] then it is not clear that there will ever be a regulation that meets the compelling interest/least restrictive means test. It will almost always be the case that the government could have done *something* instead of burdening the religion, especially if we are supposed to move heaven and earth in instituting that *something*.

And this gets us to the second thing that the Court did not sufficiently take into account when it says that there is another legitimate means for the government to use to get to its end of promoting women's health.[24] The 'other means' the Court eventually settled on is the one that the Obama administration proposed for religious non-profits (the one challenged in the *Little Sisters* litigation): that the insurance companies themselves pay for contraceptive coverage.[25] This is the one that the Court says would involve a 'precisely zero' cost to women.[26] But this is just not true. What *would* have had no ('zero') cost to women would be if the women were covered by their employer's insurance – they would have been covered *already* (that is, if they followed the mandate). By the time *Hobby Lobby* got to the Court, *some* women had already paid some cost.

Perhaps we do not count the time to litigation as part of the cost – we are just in a state of equipoise until the Court decides. Fine. But even after the *Hobby Lobby* decision was handed down, there was delay in women's getting contraceptive coverage.[27] Perhaps that is *de minimis*, but there is certainly *some point* where the delay would become something that would start affecting the government's compelling interest. If we regard an interest as compelling, there *has to be* such a point. For if we say that any period of delay, no matter how long, is permissible, we say that we do not think the interest is all that important. The 'precisely zero' remark glosses over this – it needs to be at the very least qualified. Because not only is it not true, it just cannot be true. The Court has to be assuming that some delay in getting coverage to women is perfectly OK – that is, that some delay is consistent with the government's compelling interest.[28]

[22] See *Tony & Susan Alamo Found v Secretary of Labor*, 471 US 290, 105 S Ct 1953 (1985) (holding that the FLSA applies to religious organisations and they have to pay minimum wages).

[23] That utopia, eg, would involve unlimited funds, congressional amity and zero transition costs.

[24] Again, see Gedicks (n 9).

[25] *Hobby Lobby Stores, Inc* (n 2) 2782.

[26] ibid 2760.

[27] See Cecile Richards, '6 Women Who Could Lose Their Contraception Coverage After the Hobby Lobby Decision' *Cosmopolitan* (9 July 2014) at https://www.cosmopolitan.com/politics/news/a28625/cecile-richards-hobby-lobby-contraception/.

[28] It is possible to give this phrase a more nuanced reading (which we owe to conversations with Chris Lund), that *when the reform is completed*, the costs to women will be, if not zero, nearly zero. Again, though, this simply brackets transition costs.

We think, in the end, it is clear that the opinion in *Hobby Lobby* does not count the costs fully – to show that helping hurts some of the parties involved, that the fit between means and ends is not perfect on the other means. The Court ends up being at least a little disingenuous in assuming the compelling interest, on the one hand, and then hiding the ball as to the costs to that interest by the alternative means, on the other. Perhaps Hobby Lobby still wins. There has to be some balancing of interests, and perhaps the means is good enough and the promotion of the compelling interest does not have to be *as good* as it would have been under the original means. It just has to be *very nearly* as good – and if it is, the protection of religious liberty wins out.[29] That would seem right, given that the point of RFRA is to tip the balance in favour of religious liberty.

But again, the balance should be *tipped* in favour of religious liberty; it should not always be a slam dunk in favour of religious liberty. The promotion of women's health and even the seamless running of the Affordable Care Act both seem to be good candidates for interests that are both *important and powerful* – in other words, interests that are compelling. The *Hobby Lobby* opinion did us no favours by punting on the question of what made the interest here compelling or compelling enough, because it just (sort of) assumed that it was – and shifted the question to the adequacy of the alternative means. It did say preventing racial discrimination was a compelling interest. But it did not say (because it did not have to) whether promoting women's health is more or less compelling than preventing racial discrimination. We do not know, in other words, whether this was a close case or not, because the Court does not say – does not have to say – how compelling the interest was, and if it was really a compelling interest.

The Indiana RFRA defenders were, on the whole, less cagey about what interests are compelling – in fact, they conceded that the anti-discrimination interest *would probably and should probably* win out in a lot of the cases about which opponents of RFRA are worried.[30] This was a point frequently lost in the debates.[31] The point was something like, 'Yes, there are really important state interests here, we just ask you to go through the balancing; we are not saying that we'll win, we're just saying that there's a burden on the believer and the courts have to go through the paces.' That this was a point so often lost is telling – because it collapses the difference between requesting an accommodation and losing, and not being able to request an accommodation in the first place. This sweeps away all cases

[29] After all, 'as good as' cannot mean 'exactly like' the means it replaces. If it did then there could never be another means, because no means is exactly like – down to the smallest detail – the programme it is replacing.

[30] See Jeff Guo, 'Here's How to Use Religious Freedom Laws to Fend off a Gay Discrimination Suit' *Washington Post* (3 April 2015) at https://www.washingtonpost.com/blogs/govbeat/wp/2015/04/03/heres-how-to-use-religious-freedom-laws-to-fend-off-a-gay-discrimination-suit/?utm_term=.caf543d0b02c.

[31] See Douglas Laycock, 'Letter Supporting Religions Freedom Act' (3 February 2015) at http://1stamendmentpartnership.s3.amazonaws.com/wp-content/uploads/Letter-Supporting-Religious-Freedom-Restoration-Act2.pdf ('Protecting Americans from discrimination is generally a compelling interest, and few claims to exemption from anti-discrimination laws are likely to succeed').

where an accommodation *should* be granted, because the government interest was not compelling, or because there was a least restrictive means. It classes them all under 'religious privilege'. This has the effect of making *every* government interest compelling, *no matter when* and *no matter how much* religion is burdened. We return to *Smith v Employment Division*[32] – if it is neutral and generally applicable, the government's interest wins, all the time and every time.

But if we lose the idea that plaintiffs should at least be able to ask for an accommodation, even when they do not get one, the policy of accommodation is really lost. We lose the idea of religious liberty as a species of liberty,[33] rather than as a mandate for evangelisation. And it may be that we have lost this sense because we do not believe we can count on courts to assess not only the compelling interests in each case, but also the effect on third parties. We hope not. Courts should not ignore real burdens – real hurt – on the side of religious believers, and not ignoring this is already a kind of help to those believers. They are recognised. But neither should courts ignore the real cost – the real hurt – to parties on the other side, which is not just the government but also those who stand to benefit from the government's efforts to help.

The point here is modest, and it is again a point about process, and about respecting the participants in the process. We have to see the *burdens* and *interests* on both sides before making a decision about accommodation. Courts should defer to plaintiffs who say that there is a burden, but courts should also not skimp on counting the costs to the government of accommodating that burden. We do not think we can say at the outset what interests are compelling, or for that matter what burdens are substantial.[34] But courts should do their best to acknowledge both of them in all of their fullness.

Of course, courts have not been doing this. In the next section, we give you two more recent examples of failure, in hopes of underlining what a success might look like.

IV. A Study in Contrasts: Two Recent Cases

Since 2013, there have been a number of cases of just the sort we have been talking about.[35] Each of these cases has the same basic pattern: business owners, on free

[32] See *Employment Division, Department of Human Resources of Oregon v Smith*, 494 US 872; 110 S Ct 1595, 1600 (1990).

[33] D Laycock, 'Religious Liberty as Liberty' (1996) 7 *Journal of Contemporary Legal Issues* 313, 353.

[34] C Flanders, 'Insubstantial Burdens' in K Vallier and M Weber (eds), *Religious Exemptions* (Oxford, Oxford University Press, 2018) 279.

[35] Note that these are in varying states of process. We cite them only to show the recent frequency with which these fact patterns are taking place. See *Elane Photography, LLC v Willock*, 309 P 3d 53 (NM 2013) (photographer brought free exercise action to overturn judgment against her for refusing to photograph same-sex wedding); *Masterpiece Cakeshop* (n 2) (baker brought free exercise action to overturn judgment against him for refusing to design and bake a cake for same-sex wedding);

exercise grounds, protest the enforcement against them of a State public accommodations anti-discrimination law protecting same-sex couples. Sometimes an RFRA is involved and sometimes the State constitution. But while a plethora of these cases exist, the various courts' recognitions of both parties' burdens and interests is of varying quality. Indeed, none of them succeed in giving full voice to the hurts, interests and burdens required to actually weigh a substantially religiously burdened individual's interests against the interests of those discriminated against.

One of the better opinions in this regard is *Arlene's Flowers*.[36] In Part II of the opinion, the factual background, the Superior Court of Washington lays out Barronelle Stutzman's religious beliefs, including the specific Southern Baptist tenets she follows as the president of Arlene's Flowers, Inc.[37] The background is important, because it casts her in the light of a long-time business owner and casts the business as an even longer-existing business in the community.[38] The court is careful to point out that Stutzman's religious beliefs are only in conflict when confronted by the creative act of arranging flowers for a same-sex wedding, and not in arranging flowers for same-sex couples for other holidays, such as Valentine's Day.[39] Indeed, Stutzman and the plaintiff, Robert Ingersoll, had long had a business relationship.[40] Stutzman knew Ingersoll's sexual orientation, and had often arranged flowers for him to give to his same-sex partner.[41] The court describes both party's concern and hurt when Ingersoll attempted to hire Stutzman to arrange flowers for his same-sex wedding.[42] Stutzman is described as having 'discussed the request with her husband', and, in denying Ingersoll, as having 'put [her] hands on his [hands] and told him that because of [her] relationship with Jesus Christ she couldn't do that, couldn't do his wedding'.[43] Ingersoll is described as leaving this meeting feeling hurt.[44] Ingersoll and his spouse, Curt Freed, had envisioned a traditional wedding and wanted Stutzman, whom they considered *their* florist, to do their floral arrangements.[45] Instead, after this letdown and the

State v Arlene's Flowers, Inc, 2015 WL 720213 (Washington Superior Court) (florist brought free exercise action to overturn judgment against her for refusing to provide floral arrangements for same-sex wedding); *Telescope Media Group v Lindsey*, 271 F Supp 3d 1090 (US District Court, District of Minnesota, 2017) (wedding videographers bring a pre-enforcement action based on their freedom to exercise their religion by refusing to film same-sex weddings); *Gifford v McCarthy*, 23 NYS 3d 422 (2016) (venue rental owners bring free exercise action to overturn judgment against them for refusing to provide rental space for a same-sex wedding); *Brush & Nib Studio, LC v City of Phoenix*, 418 P 3d 426 (Arizona Court of Appeal, 2018) (invitation and décor art makers bring pre-enforcement action based on their freedom to exercise their religion by refusing to provide art for same-sex weddings).

[36] *Arlene's Flowers, Inc* (n 35).

[37] ibid *3.

[38] ibid.

[39] ibid.

[40] ibid.

[41] ibid.

[42] ibid *4.

[43] ibid.

[44] ibid.

[45] ibid *3.

end of a nine-year business relationship with Stutzman, Ingersoll and Freed had a small wedding compared to their original plans.[46]

The court's highly detailed description of the background, including Stutzman's religious beliefs, her consideration of those in relation to Ingersoll and Freed's request, and Ingersoll and Freed's feelings and the ultimate loss of the wedding they had imagined, is important, because it lays the groundwork for the predicament the parties are in. It gives the truth to the burden Stutzman and her business are pinned down with. Indeed, the court says as much when it assumes she has a substantial burden based on case law. But this is where the opinion falls apart, at least insofar as recognising and truly weighing Stutzman's burden against the compelling interest of the state. For though the court agrees that Stutzman has a substantial burden, it does so begrudgingly, only for the 'purpose of analysis', and only to go on to point out that 'the [Attorney General] and the Individual Plaintiffs make a compelling case that the choice either to operate one's private business in a way inconsistent with one's religious beliefs, or forego 3% of gross profits is not the sort of "gross financial burden" that violates free exercise'.[47] But this ignores Stutzman's right to define what the burden means to her and her faith. And under the court's analysis, virtually any interest of the state would be compelling in comparison. While the court goes through the motions of weighing, they are, after all, only motions; we lose all sense of Stutzman's burden, and in the process never grasp just how compelling the state's anti-discrimination interest really is. When this happens, we argue, pluralism is undermined.

Probably the most well-known of these cases is now *Masterpiece Cakeshop*.[48] This decision, the majority opinion having been written by Justice Kennedy, was long awaited and could have been the perfect platform for the balancing of the interests of religious accommodation against the state's anti-discrimination interests.[49] In fact, Justice Kennedy said so himself in the opening of his opinion:

> The case presents difficult questions as to the proper reconciliation of at least two principles. The first is the authority of a State and its governmental entities to protect the rights and dignity of gay persons who are, or wish to be, married but who face discrimination when they seek goods or services. The second is the right of all persons to exercise fundamental freedoms under the First Amendment, as applied to the States through the Fourteenth Amendment.[50]

[46] ibid *3–*4.

[47] ibid *25.

[48] *Masterpiece Cakeshop* (n 2). Full disclosure – we have criticised this opinion for its incompleteness elsewhere, and indeed the present critique is a subset of that one. See C Flanders and S Oliveira, 'An Incomplete Masterpiece' (2019) 66 *UCLA Law Review Discourse* (arguing that *Masterpiece* is masking as a due process case and should have been remanded; or, alternatively, if it is a free exercise case, much of the central analysis is only implicit and all scrutiny application is missing).

[49] See, eg, E Volokh, 'The Masterpiece Cakeshop Decision Leaves Almost All the Big Questions Unanswered', *Reason: The Volokh Conspiracy* (4 June 2018) at https://reason.com/volokh/2018/06/04/the-masterpiece-cakeshop-decision-leaves, expressing dismay at the Court's refusal to take up the free expression issue and that the free exercise decision is narrow.

[50] *Masterpiece Cakeshop* (n 2).

Note that he might have just as well said that the case presents difficult questions as to the proper reconciliation between two groups. Instead of enacting this reconciliation, though, Justice Kennedy did one worse than the court in *Arlene's Flowers* – he promised a free exercise case,[51] guaranteeing we ought to see some balancing,[52] but that balancing never came, not even *pro forma*. The decision simply finds that the state showed some religious animus in its application of the anti-discrimination law (both toward other claims and in its adjudication of the baker's claim) and then finds for the baker.[53] Indeed, a word search over the opinion reveals that 'scrutiny' does not appear in the opinion once.[54] Worse yet, there is no explanation why.

If *Arlene's Flowers* represents failing to take the burden on the plaintiff seriously, the *Masterpiece Cakeshop* decision may represent a related but opposite failing: not taking the governmental interest seriously enough. At points, Justice Kennedy did talk about the problem of anti-discrimination, but in an abstract and hypothetical way. His Honour talked about – and seemed to fear – approving exemptions from anti-discrimination laws that might result in a large, social stigma against gays and lesbians.[55] But in Justice Kennedy's telling, *that* concern (however real) is not one that is present really at all in this case. His Honour did not quite explain why, and we might wonder whether the very fact that the Court was deciding a high-profile case in a way antithetical to the civil rights of gays and lesbians might itself implicate the very society-wide stigma that Kennedy himself speculated would be a problem.[56] If the case was a missed opportunity for the Court to defend, broadly, the religious rights of the baker, it was at the same time a missed opportunity to articulate the nature of the compelling interest in this case – and to specify a threshold for when an interest in anti-discrimination does become compelling. We did not get that.

Because of the failure to go through all of the test in *Masterpiece* – saying why the interest was not, in this case compelling – the Court was destined to go through the whole thing over again. Indeed, the parties found themselves right back in court over virtually the same issues.[57] Within days of the Court's opinion,

[51] ibid 1723–24.

[52] *Church of the Lukumi Babalu Aye, Inc v City of Hialeah*, 508 US 520; 113 S Ct 2217, 2233–34 (1993) (passage, written by Justice Kennedy, guaranteeing strict scrutiny balancing, even in cases where a law is not generally applicable).

[53] *Masterpiece Cakeshop* (n 2) 1732.

[54] The only mentions of 'scrutiny' are in Justice Gorsuch's and Justice Thomas's concurrences.

[55] *Masterpiece Cakeshop* (n 2) 1727.

[56] And that leaves all the fundamental questions unanswered. As Ian Millhiser put it, 'The opinion reads as if the central matter at issue was not so much about resolving a conflict between religious bakers and same-sex couples as it was about an urgent need to police the tone of civil rights commissioners.' Paul Waldman, 'The Religious Right Didn't Get the Supreme Court Victory it Hoped for yet' *Washington Post* (4 June 2018) at https://www.washingtonpost.com/blogs/plum-line/wp/2018/06/04/the-religious-right-didnt-get-the-supreme-court-victory-it-hoped-for-yet/?utm_term=.bce3864c9be2.

[57] See Nic Garcia, 'Masterpiece Cakeshop Owner Sues Hickenlooper, Claiming Religious Persecution Despite Supreme Court Ruling: Colorado Civil Rights Agency Investigates Refusal to Make a Cake Commemorating a Gender Transition' *Denver Post* (15 August 2018) at https://www.denverpost.com/2018/08/15/masterpiece-cakeshop-hickenlooper-lawsuit/.

the Colorado Civil Rights Commission found probable cause against the baker for refusing to make a celebratory transition cake for a transgender woman.[58] The baker then sued the Commission and the Governor, alleging that they were targeting him.[59] Had Kennedy used any kind of scrutiny or ordered a remand for a fair balancing, giving voice to the hurts of both the baker and the gay couple, one imagines no need for either party to keep trying to be heard. But they do,[60] and in the United States, until they are heard, Kennedy himself put it best:

> The outcome of cases like this in other circumstances must await further elaboration in the courts, all in the context of recognizing that these disputes must be resolved with tolerance, without undue disrespect to sincere religious beliefs, and without subjecting gay persons to indignities when they seek goods and services in an open market.[61]

In other words, their hurts must be heard, balanced and treated with respect.

This is not to say that the Court's recognition of real ('substantial') burdens on religious exercise in these cases will somehow make those burdens not burdensome, or that this will satisfy all the plaintiffs in these cases. It does not mean an end to the conscience wars. But recognition does mean something: it shows that the conscience wars need not be zero-sum: that one side winning means the other side losing everything. And of course recognition is not accommodation; certainly not when the plaintiffs fail to win their preferred accommodation. It is, nonetheless, a space for pluralism, or at least the possibility of pluralism and the possibility of a kind of truce in the conscience wars. Sometimes how we play the game is as important as winning or losing.

V. Conclusion: What Next?

Our argument here is perhaps simply this: *courts should apply the relevant constitutional or statutory tests – and all the parts of them* – because this is the best way to balance help and hurt. They should treat the interests on both side as important and worth getting right. In the case of substantial burdens, this means largely deferring to the plaintiff as to what is 'substantial' – if the Court finds that the state is putting some pressure on the plaintiff to change or to violate his or her religious practice, this *should be enough* for the plaintiff to have met his or her burden of showing 'substantial burden'. In most cases, the check on false claims of religious beliefs will happen early on, viz, in the decision of the plaintiff not to take up the

[58] ibid.

[59] ibid.

[60] While the baker and Colorado just settled their dispute by dropping all charges against each other, they continue to talk as if the battle is not over. For party comments indicating this, see Kathleen Foody, 'Colorado and Masterpiece Cakeshop Baker Jack Phillips End Legal Battle', CBS Denver (5 March 2019) at https://denver.cbslocal.com/2019/03/05/colorado-and-masterpiece-cakeshop-baker-jack-phillips-end-legal-battle/.

[61] *Masterpiece Cakeshop* (n 2) 1732.

expense of litigation. It is of course true that courts have to make a *legal* determination of substantial burden, but that is trivially true: the question is, *within that legal analysis*, how much should courts defer to the plaintiff's understanding of what effect the law has on his or her religious practice? Here, the court is limited to testing whether the state is *burdening* that religious practice – that is required by the statute. The burden must be one 'of substance',[62] that is, it must involve something the state is doing, but beyond this, 'substantial' does not indicate any measure of *quantity* or *magnitude*.

If we worry about even this sort of deference – when plaintiffs assert that the government is pressuring them to do something that violates their religious beliefs – the response is *to apply the rest of the test*. It is not to require plaintiffs to show more as to their burden, nor to second- or third-guess their religious beliefs by some theory of tort law (which might be foreign to their system of belief). We trust the courts to make the right judgment as to when a compelling interest exists and is enough to trump the substantial burden. The cure for the problem of 'too much deference' is not less deference to the religious believers – for extended too far, this removes the point of the tests, the idea that you can ask for an accommodation and at least get a hearing. Nor should we adopt a sort of free-form balancing, which is what the invasive inquiry into 'substantial burdens' invites – if the burden on your religion is small then a smaller compelling interest is enough to beat it. Again, *who is to say what is small*? What courts can say is *what interest is big*. If that interest is big enough, the government should win. And many times the government should win – in those cases where helping hurts a compelling interest.

It is no answer to the problem of religious accommodations to deny that failing to make a religious accommodation can result in real damage to people's exercise of their religion. Of course, we should accommodate those hurting when possible. But it is also our obligation, even our first obligation, to hear the hurt even when we are unable to help.

[62] We owe this formulation to Sam Bray.

11

Sanctuary: Religion and Law in the United States

DOROTHY ROGERS

I. Introduction

The contemporary Sanctuary movement to harbour undocumented immigrants in the United States (US) was originally initiated in the 1980s by progressive Christian activists opposed to US foreign policy in Latin America. Disillusioned by cumbersome immigration laws that blocked refugees' access to asylum, activists defied laws against providing shelter, aid or transportation to undocumented immigrants, to help them stay in the country or find refuge in Canada. The activists were charged and found guilty of violating US immigration law, and the courts struck down their arguments based on human rights and religious freedom claims. Despite this legal defeat over three decades ago, the Sanctuary movement has re-emerged in recent years. Not only religious organisations, but also secular institutions and state and local governments have declared themselves sanctuaries for undocumented immigrants. This chapter traces the history of the sanctuary tradition in religion, recognises the legacy of US immigration law as a factor in sanctuary practices, and examines the interplay of the legal, ethical and religious arguments related to sanctuary in recent decades.

II. The Religious Roots of Sanctuary

To fully discuss the Sanctuary movement in the US today, we need an overview, first, of the religious roots of the sanctuary tradition and, second, of the political and legal history of immigration in the country.

The tradition of sanctuary in Jewish and Christian religious history has been thoroughly examined and discussed, so here I provide only the briefest of sketches.[1]

[1] See, eg, I Bau, *This Ground is Holy: Church sanctuary and Central American refugees* (Mahwah, NJ, Paulist Press, 1985); and, more recently, L Rabben, *Sanctuary and Asylum: A Social and Political History* (Seattle, WA, University of Washington Press, 2016).

In the ancient Hebrew world, two different types of sanctuary provisions were in place. Cities of Refuge provided a shield from the death penalty in what today are considered cases of manslaughter or negligence. Blood libel was common practice when a person was responsible for another's death: in the ancient mind, the loss of life had to be atoned; even in cases of unintended or accidental fatalities, family of the deceased had a right to take the life of an assailant. A person responsible for the loss of life could avoid the penalty of blood libel, however, by escaping to one of six ancient cities of refuge: Golan, Ramoth, Bosor, Kedesh, Shechem or Hebron.[2] There they were allowed to remain until a trial could be held. A similar practice, 'altar sanctuary', allowed any offender to find asylum in sacred venues.[3] As scholars have noted, these practices were not unique to the ancient Hebrew peoples, and were likely derived from similar provisions in other cultures in the Mediterranean and Middle East. Such sanctuary traditions were carried on in both Judaism and Christianity, however, and remained influential in the western world for centuries.

The Catholic Church asserted a right of asylum – *jus asyli* – at the Lateran Council in 1123 and re-affirmed it at the Council of Trent (1545–63). Later in a papal bull (1591), the Church affirmed sanctuary as 'a divinely instituted right of the church. … [C]hurch buildings were declared inviolable, and fugitives were not to be removed without the rector's permission.' While *jus asyli* was designed primarily to provide safe haven for Christians in Catholic-dominant territories in this period, there were moments along the way when Jews and Muslims received protection. For instance, Rudiger of Speyer provided safety for Jews exiled from Mainz in 1084, and his successor, John of Speyer reportedly housed Jewish fugitives at his castle to ensure their safety during an outbreak of anti-Semitism at the turn of the twelfth century. In another act of protection by officials, the Bishop of Toledo wilfully ignored a decree in 1219 that required Jews to wear identification badges, saying he would 'defend them, by God … in every possible way'.[4] Finally, mandates in the 1300s forbidding Christians from harbouring Jews and Muslims in churches are interpreted by some scholars as an indication that widespread sanctuary-style practices were known during this period. If Christians had not been providing refuge to people of other faiths, there would have been no need for such mandates.

By 1727, the right of asylum was considered so sacred that Pope Benedict XIII threatened secular officials with excommunication if they failed to recognise it.[5] *Jus asyli* was again reaffirmed after the comprehensive codification of canon law, unveiled by Pope Benedict XV in 1917. It remained in place until 1983, when canon law was again reviewed and updated by Pope John Paul II.

The closest parallel to *jus asyli* in Protestantism would be the practice of offering a safe haven to religious dissenters during and after the Reformation.

[2] Numbers 35:6–34, Deuteronomy 4:41–43, Deuteronomy 19:1–13, Joshua 20:1–9.
[3] Exodus 21:12–15, 1 Kings 1:50–53; 1 Kings 2:28–29.
[4] N Roth, 'Bishops and Jews in the Middle Ages' (1994) 80 *Catholic Historical Review* 1, 12.
[5] Rabben (n 1) 52–54.

For instance, the Brethren, Quaker and Mennonite sects found refuge in Bohemia and Moravia. Calvinism made its home in Geneva. Early Unitarians were safe in Hungary/Poland, which also issued the first decrees of religious tolerance in the modern era, recognising a qualified right to religious freedom for followers of Eastern Orthodoxy, Judaism and Islam.[6] The colonial US saw moments of religious persecution counteracted by attempts to secure freedom of conscience: John Wheelright, Anne Hutchinson and William Penn established new settlements to secure religious freedom for Quakers. Roger Williams did the same in Rhode Island, favouring the Baptist tradition. The Calvert family provided religious freedom for Catholics in Maryland. Jewish congregations began to appear in the middle of the seventeenth century, first in New Amsterdam (now New York City), then in Rhode Island. Yet it was not until the mid-nineteenth century that a more robust sense of religious diversity became acceptable, as State-sponsored churches faded into the past and an interest in world religions took hold among intellectuals. It was also at this point in American history that religion and politics allied to create the predecessor of today's Sanctuary movement, in the network known as the Underground Railroad to help African Americans escape slavery.

III. Immigration Policy in US History

The history of immigration in the US is a volley of competing ideals – inclusion and exclusion – through time. Within a decade of ratifying the Constitution, the young US Government passed the Alien and Sedition Acts. This was a time when a war with France was a very real possibility, and internal strife between the ruling party and its opposition was intense. The Acts increased residency requirements for US citizenship to 14 years (up from five) and allowed the Government to deport foreign-born residents suspected of plotting against it. Arguing for passage of the Acts, the legislator Harrison Gray Otis warned against inviting 'hordes of wild Irishmen [and] the turbulent and disorderly of all parts of the world, to come here with a view to disturb our tranquility'.[7] Within a few years, most provisions of the Acts had expired or been repealed, but they set a xenophobic precedent that would be followed in the future. Far more attention was paid to migration within the US than immigration from without in the early nineteenth century. The federal Government forced Native Americans to migrate westward in waves beginning in 1830s, and their lifeways were brutally suppressed well into the

[6] In 1557, Queen Isabella of Hungary allied with the Ottomans against Rome to declare Catholicism, Lutheranism, Calvinism and Unitarianism 'accepted' religions. Her son, John Sigismund, affirmed this decree and added three 'tolerated' religions in 1568: Eastern Orthodoxy, Judaism and Islam. See D Buttry, *Interfaith Heroes* (2008), cited in *Interfaith Peacemakers* at https://www.readthespirit.com/interfaith-peacemakers/john-sigismund-isabella-jagiellon.

[7] *Annals of Congress*, 5th Congress, vol 7, 430; quoted in EC Carter, II, 'A "Wild Irishman" under Every Federalist's Bed: Naturalization in Philadelphia, 1789–1806' *Proceedings of the American Philosophical Society*, vol 133, no 2 (June 1989) 180.

twentieth century. Also in this period, African Americans – those who were legally free as well as those held in slavery – sought freedom in northern States or in Canada. Given the oppressions African Americans faced, this pattern of migration continued into the twentieth century.

Concerns about immigration began to emerge in the US in the mid-1800s with the arrival of refugees from the Irish potato famine, Germans escaping political upheaval in Prussia and Chinese labourers hired to work on the railroads. These groups were followed by increasing numbers of immigrants from Eastern Europe and the Mediterranean in the last third of the nineteenth century. And, as has been well documented, the US had a mixed legacy on immigration policy – socially, politically and legally – as immigration continued to rise on the cusp of the twentieth century. An overview of this history will further inform our discussion.

A set of key statutes and case law in the 1870s and 1880s helped establish the contours of US immigration policy for the coming century: the Page Act (1875), *Henderson v Mayor of the City of New York* (1875), *Chy Lung v Freeman* (1876), the Chinese Exclusion Act (1882), and the Immigration Acts of 1882 and 1891. Until the *Henderson* case, immigration was considered an exercise of the 'police power' of large port cities, the aim of which was to monitor immigration into their own States. Policy makers unapologetically identified those they wished to keep out, such as the 'lewd and debaucherous', 'paupers' and the infirm or mentally ill. New York required ship captains to provide a complete list of all passengers onboard and to pay a per-passenger fee. In *Henderson*, the shipmaster objected to the fees and the matter went to court. The court reasoned that immigration is linked to international commerce, which is the domain of the federal Government, rather than to a local government's police power. It also asserted that the nation needs uniform and consistent immigration policies. Thus, the Court ruled that State laws governing immigration are unconstitutional.

Similar reasoning was used in *Chy Lung v Freeman*. Chy Lung, a Chinese woman, was detained in San Francisco under suspicion of being 'lewd and debauched', and was required to pay a large fee or return to China. California's discriminatory policies toward Chinese immigrants in the late nineteenth century are now rather infamous. Even at the time, the Supreme Court recognised the State's bias. In *Chy Lung*, the court determined that San Francisco's law permitting fees to be imposed on specific passengers was designed to inhibit or restrict immigration by one class of people – in this case, travellers from China – and was therefore unconstitutional. Affirming the *Henderson* decision and noting concern over the potential for erratic immigration policies to damage international relations, in *Chy Lung* the court asserted that 'The passage of laws which concern the admission of citizens and subjects of foreign nations to our shores belongs to Congress, and not to the states. … If it be otherwise, a single state can at her pleasure embroil us in disastrous quarrels with other nations'.[8]

[8] *Chy Lung v Freeman*, 92 US 275, 280 (1875).

Notably, the court demonstrated less concern for individual liberty in the *Chy Lung* case than for US–China relations. Less than a decade later, international relations took a back seat to racism. In 1882, Congress passed the Chinese Exclusion Act – which served as an endorsement of anti-Chinese sentiment on the west coast. This legislation severely restricted entry of any new Chinese immigrants into the US, male or female. The Scott Act that followed in 1888 forbade re-entry into the country by any Chinese workers who had left the US.

This family of legislation ushered in an era of immigration quotas based on a mix of factors – from cultural biases in American society, to economic concerns, to US foreign policy. Chinese and other Asian immigrants continued to be a targeted group for decades after the Exclusion Act, which was renewed for 10-year periods in 1892 and 1902, extended indefinitely in 1904 and followed by the Immigration Act of 1917. The last Act in 1917 created the 'Asiatic Barred Zone' – a region that at times was understood to include everything from the Arab peninsula to Papua New Guinea in the South Pacific.[9] By 1922, Japanese immigrants were identified as ineligible for citizenship. In 1923, the Supreme Court ruling in *United States v Bhagat Singh Thind* allowed the Government to ban immigrants from India, and even to rescind the citizenship of naturalised Indians.

IV. Asylum and Immigration in the Twentieth Century

This intense anti-immigration period in the early decades of the twentieth century in the US coincided with the recognition of long-standing religious sanctuary protections by Pope Benedict XV. While still a cardinal in 1904, Giacomo della Chiesa assumed leadership of a comprehensive review of Catholic canon law, which he unveiled as Pope in 1917: the new Code of Canon Law. Within it, the medieval right of asylum remained largely intact, minus previous threats of excommunication: 'The churches enjoy the right of refuge, so that a criminal who has fled into it may, except in urgent necessity, not be taken out of it without the permission of the Ordinary or at least of the rector of the church.'[10] Significantly, in the US the National Origins Act was passed and the Border Patrol created in 1924 to set regional immigration quotas and control the flow of immigrants. It was not until 1947 that the US passed the Displaced Persons Act – the first recognition of refugees as deserving of a haven from war and political strife. Critics

[9] See text from the Immigration Act (39 Stat 874) s 3: 'The following classes of aliens shall be excluded from admission to the US … persons who are natives of islands not possessed by the United States adjacent to the Continent of Asia, situated south of the 20th parallel latitude north, west of the 160th meridian of longitude east from Greenwich, and north of the 10th parallel of latitude south, or who are natives of any country, province, or dependency situated on the Continent of Asia west of the 110th meridian of longitude east from Greenwich and south of the 50th parallel of latitude north', as cited in *Roots in the Sand*, at http://www.pbs.org/rootsinthesand. See also J Cheng, *The Asiatic Barred Zone* at http://planet-mongo.com/2013/01/the-asiatic-barred-zone.

[10] S Woywod, *The New Canon Law: A Commentary and Summary* (New York, JF Wagner, 1918) 239.

have long noted that this Act was 'too little, too late' for would-be refugees from Nazi Germany. They have also noted the contradictions inherent in a policy that offered asylum from violence and oppression in Europe just after the internment of thousands of people of Japanese descent within our borders. The National Origins Act was followed by the Immigration and Nationality Act in 1952 and the Refugee Relief Act of 1953, both of which continued to favour immigration from Western Europe.

The Reed-Johnson Act of 1965 maintained recognition of refugees and shaped US policies in this arena for the remainder of the twentieth century. It was supplemented by the Refugee Act of 1980, which outlined detailed procedures for providing resettlement assistance. The Refugee Act also established a clear definition of a 'refugee', drawing on UN guidelines: victims of persecution based on race, religion, nationality or political opinion. But it was often interpreted to exclude 'economic refugees' who were escaping poverty, victims of domestic violence and those fleeing a climate of general violence. As we shall see, this had negative repercussions for Central Americans who wished to enter the US.[11]

Add to this the fact that US foreign policy throughout the Cold War was designed to support capitalistic democracies and defeat any form of communism or socialism around the globe. As a result, the US did not accept emerging democratic socialism in Central America as a legitimate form of governance. Instead, US officials attempted to set things aright in the region by providing military training and support to governments deemed democratic, and working to subvert governments thought to embrace socialism.

V. The Origins of Sanctuary in the US

Liberal and progressive activists on the southwestern border of the US took notice of government intervention in Central America and voiced opposition. But it was a series of human tragedies that prompted a core group of activists to invoke the religious tradition of sanctuary in defiance of government policies.

In March 1980, Archbishop Oscar Romero was assassinated while celebrating Catholic mass in San Salvador – an attack widely believed to have been orchestrated by right-wing extremists. In July 1980, 13 refugees fleeing the war in El Salvador died in the Sonoran Desert near the US border after being misled by a corrupt and incompetent 'coyote' who promised them safe passage to the US. At the close of the same year, four US-born Catholic missionaries in El Salvador, Maura Clarke, Ita Ford, Ursuline Dorothy Kazel and Jean Donovan, were brutally raped and murdered. The crime was thought to be the work of a US-trained militia in the war-torn nation. Events like these prompted activists along the US–Mexico border

[11] See M Tienda and S Sanchez, 'Latin American Immigration to the United States' (2013) 142(3), 48–64, published online 8 July 2013, doi: 10.1162/DAED_a_00218.

to actively support Central American migrants seeking refuge in the US. In their view, the Sanctuary network was one way to address human rights violations that were made worse by US foreign policy in the region.

The two most prominent centres of Sanctuary activity were Tucson, Arizona and San Benito, Texas. Based on their accounts, the activists' goal was simply to assist refugees from war-torn regions in Central America who had undergone horrifying experiences of persecution, abuse and even torture. Activists believed these individuals would be approved for asylum. They also believed their own deeply held religious beliefs obligated them to provide assistance.

Early on in their advocacy, religious activists found few barriers to assisting asylum seekers. Reportedly, when they began their work in 1980, Immigration and Naturalization Services (INS) 'release[d] detainees on their own recognizance if they had a letter on church stationery stating that the church would provide social services for them'. After President Reagan entered office in 1981, however, there was a shift to 'a policy of mass detention and aggressive deportation'.[12] Activists became disillusioned as they began to encounter a labyrinth of bureaucratic delays and barriers that seemed to make it all-but impossible for migrants to become legal residents. For instance, fees for posting bond for a detained asylum seeker would suddenly be doubled; access to detainees would be blocked without explanation; one judicial district routinely rejected applications, while another readily approved them. As time passed and barriers to legal asylum became more difficult to overcome, activists became more aggressive. Invoking the ancient religious sanctuary tradition, the Underground Railroad and the resistance to Nazism in Europe, they determined it was better to defy the law than to abandon desperate and needy people seeking asylum.

In Tucson, Presbyterian minister, John Fife, and a retired Quaker, James Corbett, took the lead in assisting refugees. Other religious progressives, like Darlene Nicgorski, a Catholic nun who had seen the horrors of war in Guatemala, joined the movement from Phoenix. They began building a network of volunteers who housed migrants in homes as well as church buildings. A Sanctuary network also emerged in San Benito, Texas, where Catholic progressives established Casa Oscar Romero, a shelter for asylum seekers named in memory of the assassinated Salvadoran priest. It opened in 1982 with the blessing of the Catholic Diocese of Brownsville. Casa Romero's director, Jack Elder, and a network of volunteers helped assist an estimated 10,000 asylum seekers before the shelter closed in 1986.[13] Sanctuary soon expanded throughout the southwest, with synagogues joining the movement, most notably Arizona's oldest and largest Reform temple Congregation Emanu-El in Tucson, led by Rabbi Joseph Weizenbaum. The movement extended to points north, with direct lines to cities like Berkeley, Chicago and Boston. Hundreds of houses of worship were in the network. As time passed,

[12] B Bezdek, 'Religious Outlaws: Narratives of Legality and the Politics of Citizenship Interpretation' (1995) 62 *Tennessee Law Review* 921.

[13] 'Church Shelter for Refugees in Texas is Closed', *Los Angeles Times* (31 October 1986).

activists began to help refugees go north to Canada, where they could more readily obtain asylum.[14]

Leaders of the Sanctuary movement were aware they were violating US immigration law, which forbids transporting, sheltering or providing assistance to undocumented immigrants. Yet they were convinced that US immigration policies were immoral and in violation of human rights. They became openly defiant. In Tucson, for instance, activists sent letters notifying INS that new immigrants had arrived and would receive 'ongoing assistance of Tucson Sanctuary volunteers to obtain legal status'.[15] Central figures in the movement, like John Fife and James Corbett, publicised their work and accepted requests for interviews. The news show *60 Minutes* featured Sanctuary workers and the migrants they assisted. It was only a matter of time before the movement was infiltrated by government informants and several of its leaders charged with violating US immigration laws. In court, Sanctuary leaders and the movement's most active volunteers were charged with conspiracy, transporting, harbouring and/or concealing undocumented immigrants: Jack Elder and Casa Romero volunteer, Stacey Lynn Merkt, were convicted in San Benito, Texas, as were eight activists in and near Tucson – Maria del Socorro Pardo Viuda De Aguilar, Anthony Clark, Darlene Nicgorski, Philip Willis-Conger, John Fife, Margaret Hutchison, Wendy LeWin and Ramon Dagoberto Quinones. Although deeply involved in the movement, James Corbett was acquitted, because there was little evidence against him. Ironically, he had been in Mexico networking when most of the Sanctuary meetings were recorded by a government infiltrator. Activists appealed their guilty verdicts, which were decided by the US Court of Appeals in two precedent-setting cases: *US v Stacey Lynn Merkt and John B Elder* (1986) and *US v Aguilar* (1989). Following the *Merkt/Elder* decisions, the Supreme Court declined to consider the case, putting an end to the movement's legal battle.[16] Though convicted, activists served little or no jail time, or were put on probation. As one official said, 'This prosecution was really for deterrence; it was not for punishment.'[17]

VI. Legal Arguments for Sanctuary

In both *Merkt/Elder* and *Aguilar*, the legal teams made human rights claims and religious freedom claims to make a case for Sanctuary workers' defiance of US immigration law. In *Merkt/Elder*, there was greater emphasis on religious

[14] See Bau (n 1). See also M Davidson, *Convictions of the Heart: Jim Corbett and the Sanctuary Movement* (Tucson, AZ, University of Arizona Press, 1988) 6–12, 25; and N Stoltz Chinchilla, N Hamilton and J Loucky, 'The Sanctuary Movement and Central American Activism in Los Angeles' (2009) 36 *Latin American Perspectives* 101.

[15] Bezdek (n 12) 943.

[16] Stuart Taylor Jr, 'Supreme Court Roundup' *New York Times* (31 March 1987) at https://www.nytimes.com/1987/03/31/us/supreme-court-roundup.

[17] Bezdek (n 12) 921.

expression. Lawyers in *Aguilar* three years later focused more on human rights justifications for Sanctuary activism. The courts were not convinced by either claim. The religious freedom claim was carefully argued in the *Merkt/Elder* decision, but summed up succinctly in a footnote: 'The appellants' assertion that they were entitled to a religious defense instruction has been foreclosed by our holding that they had no religious defense.'[18]

Similarly, in *Aguilar*, the appeals court upheld the trial court's decision not to take into account the persecution and violence that migrants had faced in their war-torn homelands. Neither court had any interest in endorsing the activists' political motivations: '[A] rule which would allow appellants essentially to put Reagan Administration foreign policy on trial would be foolish.'[19]

Given the resurgence of the Sanctuary movement in recent years, the court's reasoning is informative and merits attention.

A. Human Rights Claims

Lawyers in the *Merkt/Elder* case argued that the immigrants who received assistance should be considered bona fide refugees 'as nationals of a country [El Salvador] torn by internal conflict' and receive asylum in the US. As such, they deserved the right to 'reside' in the country, based on custom, on the US Refugee Act of 1980 and on the nation's agreement to the UN's Protocol Relating to the Status of Refugees. The court rejected this claim, referring to it as an 'inventive argument'.[20] Drawing on precedents set in *United States v Pereira-Pineda*, *INS v Stevic*, *Bertrand v Sava* and *Pierre v United States*, the *Merkt/Elder* court made two clarifications. Past practice of avoiding detection is not equivalent to a 'custom' that validates the presence of undocumented immigrants in the country. Furthermore, neither the US Refugee Act nor the UN Protocol were meant to reinterpret or supersede current US criteria for establishing 'refugee' status. The Protocol itself both recognised the sovereignty of each nation and affirmed its rights to establish its own boundaries and immigration policies. In short, the UN Protocol 'did not create new rights or substantially alter existing domestic immigration and refugee law'.[21]

In the *Aguilar* case, the court spent a good deal of time addressing activists' claims that they considered the immigrants they assisted to be 'refugees' as defined by humanitarian principles. Citing both case law and US policies related to international human rights provisions, the court noted that the only acceptable means of establishing refugee status is to petition the Government for asylum. Activists' claims, according to the court, were rather sophistic: 'Appellants' contention

[18] *United States v Stacey Lynn Merkt and John B Elder*, 794 F 2d 950, 965, fn 18 (1989).
[19] *United States v Aguilar*, 871 F 2d 1436, 1448 (1989).
[20] *Merkt/Elder*, 794 F 2d 950, 964 (1986).
[21] ibid.

that … undocumented aliens are legal residents until the government proves differently … has no support in logic or precedent, and we reject it.' Furthermore, the court mused that 'When they contend that they believed in the legality of the aliens, they mean only that they thought the aliens were *entitled* to refugee status.'[22]

The court also addressed activists' claims that the meanings of terms used in US immigration law are sometimes debatable. What is the meaning of terms like transport, shelter or harbour in a legal sense? Some immigration cases have implied that these terms include secret concealment, but many Sanctuary activists did their work out in the open; others claimed to have volunteered without explicit knowledge of a given migrant's immigration status. Both sets of activists interacted with immigrants openly and freely. In host churches (like the one I attended in Boston), the immigrants who were interested and able to do so offered lessons in Spanish, spoke at church services, and participated in social action workshops and projects to educate congregants and build bonds of compassion with members of the local community. Activists' lawyers argued that there was no effort to be subversive, to 'smuggle' immigrants into the country, to conceal them or to avoid detection. In addition, many Sanctuary volunteers were not aware of the immigration status of those they assisted. Therefore, charges of harbouring, transporting and providing aid to undocumented immigrants should have been dismissed. The court disagreed, of course. For instance, the court noted that two defendants in the *Aguilar* case 'instructed illegal aliens on how and where to cross the border and supplied them with sanctuary contacts in the United States … [and] facilitated the aliens' illegal entry'.[23] Another activist was reported to have torn up immigration documents and instructed a migrant to avoid INS. A third activist insisted that she did not know the immigration status of a migrant family she assisted. Yet evidence showed that she was present when the family was interviewed on television as refugees from Guatemala, and later drove them from Phoenix, Arizona to Santa Fe, New Mexico – a 14-hour trip, during which they shared many details of their life, their hardships and the horrors of war in their homeland.[24]

In *Aguilar*, the court was unmoved by activists' 'necessity defense'.[25] It rejected the claim that Sanctuary workers felt a dire need to help immigrants in crisis and believed they were forced to choose between one of two evils – ignoring their plight and letting them suffer, or providing them with assistance in violation of US law. The court noted, however, that there was no evidence activists made use of legal means to assist refugees. Activists cited lengthy, bureaucratic and ineffective legal mechanisms as a barrier to helping migrants obtain legal asylum. Yet they 'failed to appeal to the judiciary to correct any alleged improprieties by the INS

[22] *Aguilar* (n 19) 1464 (emphasis added).
[23] ibid 1459–60.
[24] ibid 1460.
[25] ibid 1467.

and the immigration courts'[26] – a procedure which, according to the court, had been employed with some success by Salvadorans in *Orantes-Hernandez v Smith*.

B. Religious Freedom Claims

The argument that was more central to the *Merkt/Elder* case was the activists' religious liberty claim. In the US, religious freedom has a twin character: it prevents the establishment of religion by governing bodies, and it safeguards the expression of religious belief by individuals and groups. Sanctuary activists appealed to the second element of religious liberty – free expression. Their lawyers argued that the tradition of sanctuary in the Jewish and Christian scriptures and in religious history amounted to faith-based obligations that they, as observant and deeply committed Christians, were simply required to fulfil.

Yet, citing a generous body of case law, the *Merkt/Elder* court struck down this claim as well. First, it made a distinction familiar in First Amendment discussions: between the freedom to believe and the freedom to act. 'The first', it said, 'is absolute, but, in the nature of things, the second [the freedom to act] cannot be'.[27] This is true when the curtailment of religious freedom causes negligible harm or is merely an inconvenience to individuals. It is also true when government priorities override religious liberty. In brief, laws that are unrelated to religion or are neutral in regard to religion may be in effect to 'regulate the health, safety, and general welfare of the public … even if individuals will thereby be penalized because the practice of their religious doctrines violates the law'.[28]

The court went on to consider the protections of religious freedom ensured by the decisions in *Wisconsin v Yoder*[29] (regarding compulsory public education) and *United States v Lee*[30] (regarding social security tax). In these cases, the court determined that laws limiting religious freedom may be justified, but only if there is a 'compelling state interest' and government employs the 'least restrictive means' to do so. The court underscored the fact that both the *Yoder* and *Lee* decisions were related to the role of religion in regard to social goods and services; neither of these cases addressed 'legislation governing the public safety, peace, and order'. Ultimately rejecting Sanctuary activists' religious expression claim, the *Merkt/Elder* court concluded that any limitations on the petitioners' religious beliefs were indeed necessary to accomplish an essential government function, that is, maintaining national borders and setting immigration policy. The court was also satisfied that the state had used the least burdensome means of achieving its policy goals.[31]

[26] ibid.
[27] *Merkt/Elder* (n 18) 954 (citing *Cantwell v Connecticut*, 310 US 296 (1940)).
[28] ibid.
[29] *Wisconsin v Yoder*, 406 US 205 (1972).
[30] *United States v Lee*, 455 US 252 (1982).
[31] *Merkt/Elder* (n 18) 955.

In its ruling, the *Merkt/Elder* court noted that there are myriad forms of assistance a person with deeply held convictions can provide to the needy in another country: sending funds or supplies to community service organisations, or travelling to serve as social service workers or missionaries, for instance. In the words of the court, 'petitioners could have assisted beleaguered El Salvadorans in many ways which did not affront [US] border control laws … [but they] chose confrontational, illegal means to practice their religious views'.[32]

The *Aguilar* court argued further that activists' claims to have been motivated by deeply held religious beliefs confused intent and motive: 'So long as appellants intended to directly or substantially further the alien's illegal presence, it is irrelevant that they did so with a religious motive'.[33] Citing *Merkt/Elder*, the court concluded that accommodating Sanctuary activists 'would reduce [the government's] efforts to a pitiful farce'.[34] In short, as the *Henderson* and *Chy Lung* cases had determined, only the federal Government has the authority to determine and enforce international boundaries and immigration policies. National borders are 'an essential feature of national sovereignty … the peace, order, and very existence of a society are bound up in its border control laws', and there is no justification for morally- or religiously-motivated activists to violate US immigration law.[35]

Significantly, the activists' attempt to establish a connection between religious freedom and privacy rights was also unsuccessful. Their legal team argued that, in this case, their First Amendment rights to freedom of religious expression and freedom of assembly were deeply connected to their Fourth Amendment privacy rights. The paid government informant who participated in church activities and programmes in order to infiltrate the Sanctuary movement violated their rights to privacy, religious freedom and assembly. It is reasonable for churchgoers, activists argued, to expect that they can 'meet and worship in church free from the scrutiny of federal agents'. They should not need to 'assume the risk that apparent fellow worshippers are present in church, not to offer homage to God, but rather to gain thirty pieces of silver'. Yet while their 'argument has superficial emotive appeal … [and] privacy, trustworthiness, and confidentiality are undoubtedly at the very heart of many instances of free association and religious expression', the court ruled that 'first amendment concerns do not require procedural protections for privacy rights over and above those provided by the fourth amendment'.[36]

The *Aguilar* court affirmed the conclusion in *Merkt/Elder* that immigration law is a component of national sovereignty: 'appellants … cannot escape the government's overriding interest in policing its borders'. The Court 'has long recognized the power to expel or exclude aliens as a fundamental sovereign

[32] ibid 956.
[33] *Aguilar* (n 19) 1462.
[34] ibid 1469 (making independent arguments, while also citing *Merkt*, 794 F 2d 950 (1986) (n 18)).
[35] *Merkt/Elder* (n 18) 955.
[36] *Aguilar* (n 19) 1473.

attribute exercised by the Government's political departments largely immune from judicial control'.[37]

VII. Competing Domains – Religious and Political Authority

The majority of Sanctuary activists in the 1980s were inspired and emboldened by religious ideals expressed in the Jewish and Christian scriptures, as well as by the religious/political history that emerged out of those sacred texts. Significantly, however, the provision in the 1917 Code of Canon Law that helped ground the religious commitments of Catholic activists were omitted from the Code that was unveiled by Pope John Paul in 1983, because the Church considered *jus asyli* unnecessary in the modern context.[38]

It is instructive, however, to keep in mind two additional Canon Law provisions that appeared in both the 1917 and 1983 versions, which help to anchor the concept of sanctuary and may help further explain this omission. One such provision appears in the same chapter as the *jus asyli* provision under discussion: 'Sacred places are exempt from the jurisdiction of the civil authorities and in them the legitimate ecclesiastical authority freely exercises its jurisdiction.'[39]

This provision, canon #1003 in the 1917 Code of Canon Law, can be understood to assert ecclesiastic authority on three levels. First, it establishes religious sites – historically understood to include Church-owned buildings, structures and grounds – as independent, beyond the reach of political authority. Second, it indicates that officials approved by the Church – and only they – may exercise authority within religious sites. Third, it bars political authorities from entering the ecclesiastic realm. In this sense, canon #1003 could be read as a strong affirmation of the right of asylum. At the same time, this provision is tempered by the term 'legitimate ecclesiastical authority'. One could also argue – and, no doubt, conservatives both then and now have argued – that the inclusion of this term tempers any claims to the right of asylum. The fact that the assertive rhetoric in canon #1003 was neutralised in the 1983 Code of Canon Law further supports this counter-argument: 'The ecclesiastical authority freely exercises its powers and functions in sacred places.'[40]

Given this recasting of ecclesiastical authority as rendered in 1983, it is clear that in the modern context, officials in Catholic Church hierarchy wished to significantly limit the religious domain. And, again, conservatives could argue

[37] ibid 1469 (citing *Shaughnessy v United States,* 345 US 206 (1953) and *United States v Moylan*, 417 F 2d 1002, 1004 (1969)).

[38] K Martens, 'Holy Places and Sacred Spaces', in MJ Breger, Y Reiter and L Hammer (eds), *Sacred Space in Israel and Palestine: Religion and Politics* (New York, Routledge, 2013).

[39] Canon #1003, in Woywod (n 10) 235.

[40] Canon #1213, 1983 Code of Canon Law at http://www.vatican.va/archive/ENG1104/__P4G.HTM.

that another provision in both the 1917 and 1983 Codes of Canon Law recognised that international governance may sometimes override religious authority. Furthermore, another provision, which appeared in the opening chapter of both versions of the Code of Canon Law, could be understood to have a directive, guiding authority:

> 1917: 'Special agreements or concordats made between certain nations and the Holy See are not changed by the Code.'[41]
>
> 1983: 'The canons of the Code neither abrogate nor derogate from the agreements entered into by the Apostolic See with nations or other political societies. These agreements therefore continue in force exactly as at present, notwithstanding contrary prescripts of this Code.'[42]

We can leave an examination of the full, doctrinal impact of these provisions to experts in Catholic canon law. For our purposes, it is fair to say that the Church's abandonment of the right of asylum in 1983 was a significant blow to Catholic liberals and progressives, and it led to the popular perception that all Christian activists were now disempowered. Yet only the formal closure of Church-owned immigration facilities, like Casa Oscar Romero in San Benito, Texas in 1986, directly affected the Sanctuary movement. Sanctuary was an interfaith movement, which was widely supported by activists from a number of Christian denominations as well as liberal Jewish congregations. The Emanu-El Reform synagogue in Tucson hosted the first Inter-American conference on immigrant rights, for instance – an event that drew a crowd of 1,200 and featured the well-known Holocaust survivor, Elie Wiesel. Even among Catholics who were aware of the omission of the right of asylum in canon law, there was a sense that justice would prevail. For many religious activists – Catholics, Protestants and Jews – the progressive ideals of the 1960s did not really end. They continued to work right through the 1970s for peace, environmental protection and disarmament. And as they moved into the 1980s they supported not only Sanctuary, but also a number of liberation movements throughout Latin America and Africa.

In fact, the Sanctuary Movement itself did not disappear. For instance, in 1989, shortly after the *Merkt/Elder* and *Aguilar* rulings, San Francisco declared itself a Sanctuary for undocumented immigrants. Throughout the 1990s, church-based assistance and education programmes were prevalent. In 2002, John Fife re-asserted his commitment to immigrant advocacy and support by establishing the Samaritan Patrol and No More Deaths, both of which provide humanitarian aid to asylum seekers. It is no coincidence that Fife's moves closely followed the US Patriot Act of 2001, a law that aimed to prevent terrorists from entering the country but, in effect, served to further curtail immigration by non-Europeans. Fife's shift to providing only humanitarian assistance was, no doubt, carefully crafted. Since he and fellow activists were no longer transporting, harbouring or

[41] Canon #2, in Woywod (n 10).
[42] Canon #3, 1983 Code of Canon Law at http://www.vatican.va/archive/ENG1104/__P2.HTM.

housing undocumented immigrants, they were able to help a vulnerable population in need, while also expressing disapproval of restrictive immigration *policies*, yet without violating immigration *law*.[43] In 2007, with immigration still a point of contention at the US–Mexico border, liberal and progressive religionists revived the Sanctuary movement, issuing a pledge, which reads in part:

> We covenant to take a public, moral stand for immigrants' rights; reveal, through education and advocacy, the actual suffering of immigrant workers and their families …; and protect immigrants against hate, workplace discrimination, and unjust deportation.[44]

Interest in the Sanctuary movement intensified in the aftermath of an executive order issued by President Obama in 2012: Deferred Action for Childhood Arrivals (DACA), which allowed a possible path to citizenship for undocumented foreign-born residents under 30 years old who arrived in the US before their sixteenth birthdays. As the 2016 US presidential campaign heated up, politicians opposed to Obama's order were emboldened and pledged to dismantle DACA. Sanctuary activists responded by becoming more vocal, more open and more defiant. As a result, the movement began to expand – one might even say exponentially.

By the eve of the election, the Sanctuary movement was embraced and is now thriving. In fact, Sanctuary churches and synagogues have been joined by colleges, universities, cities and towns around the nation. This despite the fact that the court struck down both the human rights and religious freedom claims of the 1980s. What has inspired the Sanctuary movement in its new incarnation, and will it succeed?

Hundreds of institutions and communities have declared themselves a Sanctuary since 2016. And this time, activists seem to be aware that there are generally three paths to pursue when making a Sanctuary declaration:

(a) State, county and municipal governments address Sanctuary as a jurisdictional issue, and any declaration they hand down must cover this.
(b) Local governments address only local issues, ordinances and policies; they do not serve as an extension of the federal Government by enforcing immigration law.
(c) Educational institutions recognise the limits of their jurisdiction, that is, the academic and financial concerns of the institution and the well-being of its constituents.

The Sanctuary statements issued by local governments and colleges/universities must address the realities they face – and in most cases they do. Voluntary organisations, primarily houses of worship, however, have no 'jurisdiction' as such. Their Sanctuary statements may invoke the right of asylum in religious history,

[43] Since this chapter was written, however, No More Deaths activists were arrested for providing humanitarian aid to refugees. When the case was tried, it resulted in a hung jury, with prosecutors pledging to retry the case.

[44] Groups responsible for reviving Sanctuary: Clergy and Laity United for Economic Justice of California, Interfaith Worker Justice and New York Sanctuary Coalition. See K Sharar, 'The New Sanctuary Movement' at https://annunciationhouse.org/2007/12/01/the-new-sanctuary-movement.

but members of their community need to recognise that *jus asyli* has no standing, legally speaking. Traditionally, they have received consideration and support in the communities they inhabit. Houses of worship, after all, are still considered sacred spaces. Religious Sanctuary activism attained a degree of success in the 1980s, in large part because the US Government was reticent to invade that sacred space to apprehend activists and the migrants they assisted.

One of the earliest and best-known Sanctuary statements came from San Francisco, and it pre-dates the New Sanctuary Movement. It was issued in 1989, and it advances some of the strongest protections by a municipal government in the nation:

> The Sanctuary Ordinance generally prohibits City employees from using City funds or resources to assist Immigration and Customs Enforcement (ICE) in the enforcement of Federal immigration law unless such assistance is required by federal or state law.[45]

Specifically, the city of San Francisco will not serve as an extension of federal power at the local level. As noted on the city's website, it will not facilitate ICE investigations, detentions or arrests related to violations of civil law (as opposed to criminal law). Nor will it inquire about immigration status, or limit city benefits or services to any person based on immigration status, unless required by State or federal law or by court order. Finally, it will not provide ICE with advance information about undocumented immigrants who are in local custody, or extend a person's detention, based on a federal immigration detainer.

Following a threat by the Trump administration in 2017 to withhold federal funds from Sanctuary cities – a threat that was thwarted by the courts – the city's mayor issued a statement:

> San Francisco's Sanctuary City laws are in compliance with federal law. If the federal government believes there is a need to detain a serious criminal, they can obtain a criminal warrant, which we will honor, as we always have.[46]

Some of the largest cities in the US, and over 100 counties in sixteen States have adopted similar Sanctuary provisions. San Francisco's city ordinance is backed up by California's statewide Sanctuary law, which also asserts that State funds and resources will not be employed to enforce immigration laws. The State law adds that government buildings and personnel will not be put to use for the sake of supporting federal immigration enforcement activity. A total of nine other US States – Colorado, Connecticut, Illinois, Massachusetts, New Jersey, New Mexico, New York, Oregon and Washington – have similarly declared Sanctuary status.[47]

[45] San Francisco, Office of Civic Engagement and Immigration Affairs at https://sfgov.org/oceia/sanctuary-city-ordinance-0.

[46] Office of Civic Engagement and Immigration Affairs at https://sfgov.org/oceia/sanctuary-city-ordinance-0.

[47] Source for current Sanctuary cities, counties and States, Center for Immigration Studies online at https://cis.org/Map-Sanctuary-Cities-Counties-and-States, as well as independent research in more recent news reports.

Other Sanctuary declarations carry less force – and understandably so, given what the *Merkt/Elder* and *Aguilar* cases have taught us. Close to 200 public universities have issued statements of support for undocumented students, and they follow a similar pattern: a university official affirms the campus's commitment to supporting all its members. The official openly recognises that a 'sanctuary' declaration would not provide any specific protections to undocumented students. The official then pledges to do everything within the parameters of the law to support undocumented students. Among the stronger statements by public colleges and universities, the official may assert: 'We hold firm that enforcement generally rests with US Immigration and Customs Enforcement (ICE) and not with state, local and university police.'[48] The statement then closes with details about types of support the institution can provide – which are generally already standard practice in higher education: maintaining student privacy, securing the safety of student records, providing counselling and health services, and offering confidential assistance related to international travel. Many institutions have enhanced or more clearly articulated the services they provide to immigrant students. A number have also instituted training programmes to ensure that faculty and staff can provide effective support to students not born in the US, regardless of immigration status.[49]

Unlike Sanctuary cities, however, public colleges and universities are generally reticent to take the next step and pledge non-compliance with federal authorities, because their 'jurisdiction', as such, is limited to the academic or financial life of the institution. Like any private individual, a college or university administrator might feel *personally* compelled to take action to defy a repressive law to protect the university's students, but he or she cannot direct staff to do so. As one university administrator said, half-joking, 'What would we do? Command our campus police officers, *who are sworn to uphold the law*, to keep out the feds?'[50] In theory, leaders of a private college or university have more leeway in this regard, since private institutions do not have formal ties to the Government. With the extent to which all institutions of higher education are dependent on government funding and financial aid in the US, however, private college and university leaders also have limited non-academic decision-making power.

Due to concerns similar to the typical college or university president, many cities and towns have chosen not to issue a Sanctuary declaration. In fact, in some locations State law prohibits any form of non-compliance at the local level with State and federal law. Therefore, rather than issue a 'sanctuary' declaration, several local municipalities have passed a 'welcoming community' resolution. This approach makes sense from a moral standpoint. A declaration of sanctuary

[48] This selection is from the statement regarding Sanctuary at Northern Illinois University at https://www.niu.edu/undocumented/resources/sanctuary-campus.shtml.

[49] To review statements of Sanctuary to see their commonalities as well as their variations, see the American Public and Land-Grant Universities site at http://www.aplu.org/members/councils/strategic-communications/immigration-actions/index.html.

[50] This perspective was shared with me at an academic gathering and is included here with permission. Given the informal nature of the discussion, I have chosen not to identify the speaker.

in the fullest sense is a pledge to protect the most vulnerable members of our society by refusing to submit to an overly zealous federal Government. But if it cannot be enforced, sanctuary is little more than an empty promise to those whom a community aims to protect. A 'welcoming community' resolution, on the other hand, while a less forceful statement of support, is a more realistic one for communities that are constrained by State law and/or have no authority to enforce policies of their own. There is a deeply humanitarian impulse behind both sanctuary declarations and 'welcoming community' resolutions. But in some cases, declaring Sanctuary can be imprudent. Legally speaking, a sanctuary declaration is effective only if it does more than express strong moral convictions. Hundreds of liberal and progressive communities and institutions have affirmed their support of undocumented immigrants. But only those that have a structure in place for harbouring immigrants, and volunteers who are willing to defy the law, will serve as genuine Sanctuary sites.

VIII. Conclusion

To the liberal or progressive, Sanctuary provisions are inspiring. To moderates and conservatives, they are infuriating. How can a nation function, the second group will say, if there is not cooperation among law enforcement agencies at the local, State and federal levels? Economics and national security are central to conservative arguments against Sanctuary: open border policies, as the argument goes, would allow in migrants who will take jobs away from native-born citizens and/or take advantage of the many benefits we offer in American society, namely education, healthcare and social welfare. Additionally, our current immigration policies have created a haven not only for the undocumented immigrant who is otherwise law-abiding, but for dangerous criminals, gang members and terrorists as well. Global realities today tell us that there are a number of forces around the world that despise America and Westernisation. This is no time to forget that US policy makers must be 'wily as serpents' not simply 'innocent as doves'.[51] Conservatives might add that, in relation to other issues, liberals and progressives in the US have argued for legal uniformity across the nation – civil rights for African Americans in the mid-twentieth century, for instance, and gay and transgender rights today. If we cannot have a nation divided over the civil rights of minority groups, how can we live in a nation with a patchwork of immigration laws that apply to different people in different times and places?

The response from liberals and progressives, however, is this: We did need a uniform approach to civil rights in the past, and we need a uniform approach to LGBTQ rights now … We may also need a uniform approach to immigration law, but … The difference for liberals and progressives is this: Today's immigration

[51] Matthew 10:16.

laws are unjust. First, individuals now being targeted for deportation have lived within US borders for years, many of them since they were small children. Second, the vast majority of undocumented immigrants have been law-abiding and embrace American ideals and values. There is no need to target and punish them for their immigration status alone. Third, our immigration policies continue to strongly favour western Europeans and thus discriminate against people from Latin America, Africa, the Middle East and Asia – many of whom are the most in need of a safe haven from dire poverty, from civil and political discord, or from outright war. If local governments, educational institutions and religious organisations support and assist with enforcing these immigration policies, they become complicit in advancing injustice.

Regardless of political persuasion, it is not difficult to see that if our national Government tried to accommodate the wide variety in beliefs and values about immigration that exist in the US, its 'efforts would result in no immigration policy at all … [or would allow] individuals to form personal immigration policies'.[52] Of course this is untenable. However, Sanctuary activists have cited the US institution of slavery prior to the Civil War as well as the 'final solution' in Nazi Germany as prime examples of how and why defying national immigration laws may be justifiable. Just as there were laws in place to dehumanise and delegitimise both African Americans and Jews in those historical periods, Sanctuary proponents say, so too have we created legal categories today that attempt to dehumanise and delegitimise people based on immigration status. Yet people who live as migrants among us are deserving of equal consideration and human rights. Today, we are outraged by stories of fugitive slave catchers who returned people to the horrors of slavery before the US Civil War. We are sickened by reports that local police forces in Poland and the Ukraine accepted assignments to round up and slaughter innocent villagers en masse during the Holocaust. In contrast, we now laud as heroes the resisters who helped to harbour, assist and transport slaves along the Underground Railroad in the US before our Civil War and Jews throughout Europe before and during the Second World War. Yet these people we now celebrate as champions of freedom could not have done what they did if they had complied with the national mandates in place at the time. At nearly every turn, these activists disobeyed the law: by publishing educational tracts designed to counteract racist propaganda, by teaching a child to read or allowing an elder to pray, by driving past a checkpoint with human beings hidden in the back, by pretending not to notice when a fugitive disembarked from a ship to find long-awaited freedom. Sanctuary activists maintain that each of these acts was illegal before wars were fought to bring an end to untold abuse and injustice. From the liberal and progressive perspectives, resistance was necessary then and it is necessary now. At core, Sanctuary is resistance to a government that places more value on political power than on human rights.

[52] *Aguilar* (n 19) 1470.

12

Exorcism: Faith versus Fraud

The Balance Struck between Freedom of Religion and Protecting the Vulnerable from Exploitation

JAVIER GARCÍA OLIVA AND HELEN HALL

I. Introduction

In common with many Western societies in the twenty-first century, the United Kingdom (UK) is an extremely diverse context in terms of both religion and culture,[1] and as Weller demonstrates, this gives rise to debates around clashes of views and priorities.[2] Whilst the nature, categorisation and optimal management of this stranded tapestry of belief is set to remain the subject of sociological debate for the foreseeable future,[3] lawyers are, in the present moment, left to manage its complex out-workings. This chapter focuses on 'exorcism' as one particular area that continues to generate both legal and social debate,[4] much of which is born from the convergence of different world views within a single national and social paradigm.

For some people, the very word 'exorcism' conjures up images of either horror films or the Middle Ages.[5] However, defined as 'any rite or practice aimed at freeing a person, place or object from a negative, external spiritual influence',[6]

[1] Office for National Statistics, *Religion in England and Wales 2011* at https://www.ons.gov.uk/peoplepopulationandcommunity/culturalidentity/religion/articles/religioninenglandandwales2011/2012-12-11.

[2] P Weller, Religious Diversity in the United Kingdom: Contours and Issues (New York, Continuum, 2008).

[3] H Berking, S Steets and J Schwenk (eds), *Religious Pluralism and the City: Enquiries into Post-Secular Urbanism* (London, Bloomsbury, 2018).

[4] See, eg, E Stobart, *Child Abuse Linked to Accusations of 'Possession' and 'Witchcraft'* (Department for Education and Skills, 2006).

[5] M Cuneo, 'Of Demons and Hollywood: Exorcism in American Culture' (1998) 27 *Studies in Religion* 455.

[6] J García Oliva and H Hall, 'Exorcism and the Law: Are Ghosts of the Reformation Haunting Contemporary Debates on Safeguarding Versus Autonomy?' (2018) 180 *Law and Justice* 52.

the label encompasses a vast array of diverse but related practices, which range from the dramatic to the low key. For example, words spoken in the course of a Church of England baptism service are in fact the residual traces of the exorcism that accompanied the christening prior to the Reformation,[7] but for many participants the moment slips by almost unnoticed. In contrast, some forms of exorcism are communal, public and impossible to miss, for instance a number of the rituals associated with Chinese New Year are aimed at driving out evil spirits.[8] Dramatically different again are the prayers of a Muslim healer endeavouring to free an individual from a jinn,[9] or a Pentecostal minister attempting to drive a demon out of a believer.[10] In these cases, the recipient may writhe, cry, scream or even snarl in response to impassioned shouting from the person conducting the exorcism, perhaps mirroring more closely some of the popular stereotypes from Hollywood and literature.[11]

These are just three examples of the numerous practices of exorcism present in contemporary Britain, and some forms of it take place at the convergence of different social streams, where currents from traditional, organised religion swirl together with new religious movements,[12] popular culture[13] and even the commercial world.[14] For example, businesses and individuals can and do offer commercial spiritual house-cleaning or 'ghost-busting' services for a fee.[15]

As with every other sphere of human activity, it is the responsibility of the state to balance conflicting interests and provide an adequate legal framework to mediate between them. Most of the academic legal commentators on this topic, such as Hall,[16] hitherto have focused on the role of the criminal law in this regard. This is unsurprising, given that exorcisms in the UK and elsewhere have resulted in prosecution following the death of the recipients,[17] and there have been some

[7] 'May almighty God deliver you from the powers of darkness, and lead you in the light and obedience of Christ', *Church of England, Common Worship, Holy Baptism* at https://www.churchofengland.org/prayer-and-worship/worship-texts-and-resources/common-worship/christian-initiation/holy-baptism-accessible-language/holy-baptism#p16, accessed 20 July 2018.

[8] G Ferraro and S Andreatta, *Cultural Anthropology: An Applied Perspective* (Belmont, CA, Wadsworth, 2012) 30.

[9] M Maarouf, *Jinn Eviction as a Discourse of Power: A Multidisciplinary Approach to Moroccan Magical Beliefs and Practices* (Leiden, Brill, 2007) 159.

[10] G Giordan and A Possamai, *Sociology of Exorcism in Late Modernity* (Melbourne, Palgrave, 2018) 107.

[11] F Goodman, *The Exorcism of Anneliese Michel* (Eugene, OR, Resource, 2005) 122.

[12] A Bradney, 'New Religious Movements: The Legal Dimension' in B Wilson and J Cresswell (eds), *New Religious Movements: Challenge and Response* (Routledge, London, 1999) 81.

[13] C Olson and C Reinhard, *Possessed Women, Haunted States: Cultural Tension in Exorcism Cinema* (London, Lexington, 2017).

[14] B Duivenvoorde, *Consumer Benchmarks in the Unfair Commercial Practices Directive* (Amsterdam, Springer, 2015).

[15] See, eg, 'Your Spiritual Evolution' at https://www.rachelkeene.co.uk/my-services/house-cleansings-blessings-exorcism/; and Spirit Knights: Paranormal Investigators at http://www.skpi.co.uk/.

[16] H Hall, 'Exorcism, religious freedom and consent: the devil in the detail' (2016) 80 *The Journal of Criminal Law* 241.

[17] *R v Rabiya Patel and Others* [1995] 16 Cr App R (S) 827; *R v Lee* (2006) 5 LRC 216 (New Zealand).

high-profile tragedies as a result of the abuse and murder of young children in the course of such practices.[18] Undoubtedly, the human-rights-based imperative upon the state to protect the vulnerable from this kind of treatment is unquestionable[19] but, as outlined above, by no means all forms of exorcism involve practices of this nature.

Criminal law is the most coercive imposition of state authority in the lives of citizens, and it is accepted that it should only be applied where necessary to satisfy an extremely weighty societal need.[20] Nevertheless, there are many circumstances in which civil law provides parties with a means of privately seeking redress against their neighbour, even though the wrong complained of will not cause the criminal law machinery to swing into action.

As Mitchell eloquently demonstrates, achieving a definition on English tort law is by no means straightforward, neither is succinctly setting out its purpose,[21] but this is not a quagmire through which the present discussion needs to trek. Suffice it to say that the principles of tort may be relevant to many situations involving exorcism, independently of whether or not criminal liability is also triggered,[22] and it is also the case that contract law and consumer protection legislation may have relevance in certain situations.

This chapter aims to address the scope of the civil law regulation of exorcism, particularly from the perspective of those who are the recipients of such rituals. This is of interest in its own right, given the breadth of such practices as outlined above, as well as the number of individuals and groups involved in them, but it is also important in demonstrating the role that civil law has in terms of both embodying and vindicating human rights. As the UK's Supreme Court reiterated in *R (UNISON) v Lord Chancellor*,[23] common law has evolved to protect fundamental rights in a manner that is independent from, but supportive of, the framework imposed by the ECHR via the Human Rights Act 1998.[24]

Furthermore, the malleability of common law allows judges to interpret it in a way that gives Convention rights what commentators like Phillipson have termed 'weak horizontal direct effect'.[25] In other words, even though it is not

[18] *The Victoria Climbe Report: Key Findings from the self-audits of NHS organisations, social services departments and police forces* at https://www.justiceinspectorates.gov.uk/hmicfrs/media/victoria-climbie-inquiry-report-key-findings-20031009.pdf.

[19] Art 3 of the European Convention on Human Rights (ECHR) guarantees all people, including children, freedom from inhuman and degrading treatment. It is not sufficient for the state itself to refrain from inflicting such treatment, it must effectively protect individuals from being subject to such abuse by third parties. See, eg, *MC v Bulgaria* [2003] ECHR 651; HM Government, *Child abuse linked to faith or belief: national action plan* (Department for Education, 2012).

[20] M Allen, *Criminal Law* (Oxford, Oxford University Press, 2013) 4.

[21] P Mitchell, *A History of Tort Law: 1900–1950* (Cambridge, Cambridge University Press, 2015) 13–17.

[22] R Stevens, 'Private Rights and Public Wrongs' in M Dyson (ed), *Unravelling Tort and Crime* (Cambridge, Cambridge University Press, 2014) 111.

[23] *R (UNISON) v Lord Chancellor* [2017] UKSC 51.

[24] ibid [89] (Lord Reed).

[25] G Phillipson, 'The Human Rights Act, "Horizontal Effect" and the Common Law: A Bang or a Whimper?' (1999) 62 *Modern Law Review* 824.

possible for individuals to use their Convention rights as weapons in litigation with private parties, the suffusion of these rights through the juridical framework as a whole moulds the way in which legal concepts and provisions are interpreted in *all* proceedings.[26] Consequently, the way in which civil law deals with exorcism has important wider implications, both for liberty of religion and conscience, and for human rights more widely. This discussion will focus in particular on the following areas:

(a) *Tort and negligence.* What duty of care, if any, is owed by those carrying out exorcisms to the recipients and/or third parties who may suffer harm as a result?
(b) *Tort – privacy and reputation.* To what extent does the law provide protection to the recipients of exorcism, in light of the intense public and media fascination with these practices? Is the weight attached to individual rights and wider societal interests correctly calibrated?
(c) *Tort and contract – financial exploitation.* Are the mechanisms in place to provide individuals with redress in the event of fraudulent practices sufficiently robust to meet this aim? Do they achieve it without unduly limiting the religious and ideological freedom of both recipients and practitioners?

We shall then reflect on the common threads that can be discerned across these contexts, and consider what we can learn more generally about systemic approaches to faith, belief liberty and other interests in the current paradigm.[27]

II. Tort and Negligence

It is well established that the tort of negligence provides a cause of action where, due to the carelessness of the defendant, a claimant suffers a form of legally recognised harm;[28] but as Lunney and Oliphant correctly observe, English law allows for a different approach, depending upon whether the damage suffered is personal injury, property damage or pure economic loss.[29] In this context, we are primarily concerned with personal injury (which may be bodily or psychiatric, although the latter must be objectively verifiable by a doctor).[30] In short, if the recipient of an exorcism ritual goes on to harm himself or herself or a third party, is the person carrying out the ritual legally responsible for the consequences, particularly if it

[26] M Hunt, 'The Horizontal Effect of the Human Rights Act' [1998] *Public Law* 423.

[27] In relation to most private and criminal law matters, the Scots legal system is distinct from that of England and Wales, hence our reference at times in these sections to 'English law' when we are addressing examples drawn from that context.

[28] *Donoghue v Stevenson* [1932] UKHL 100, [1932] AC 562; *Caparo Industries PLC v Dickman* [1990] UKHL 2, [1990] 2 AC 605.

[29] M Lunney and K Oliphant, *Tort Law* (Oxford, Oxford University Press, 2013) 122.

[30] *Page v Smith* [1995] UKHL 7.

becomes apparent that medical, rather than spiritual, intervention might have resulted in a less regrettable outcome?

This question is by no means hypothetical, as the notorious episode of the Michael Taylor exorcism in Ossett, Yorkshire demonstrates.[31] Taylor underwent an all-night exorcism, carried out by an Anglican priest with the assistance of a Methodist minister, and when he returned home afterwards, he murdered his wife and the family dog with his bare hands, in an exceptionally savage attack. The incident was the catalyst for the Church of England to introduce strict modern guidelines on 'deliverance ministry', the branch of Anglican pastoral care that includes exorcism.[32]

It should be noted, nevertheless, that not all exorcism practices are carried out by religious ministers, as many are undertaken by friends or family members of the subject.[33] In such cases, where no special authority or expertise is being held out, it is extremely unlikely that legal liability will attach for failure to correctly diagnose and understand the nature of the problem (although note the complexity of the position in relation to faith communities and representatives for the purposes of vicarious liability). However, where the exorcist was acting in his or her capacity as an expert adviser, it seems reasonable at least to explore the possibility of this giving rise to a cause of action. In essence, the claim being put forward would be a species of professional negligence or, as it has been termed in the United States (US), 'clergy malpractice'.[34]

It must be acknowledged from the outset that clergy malpractice in the sense of professional negligence (as opposed to vicarious liability for deliberate torts committed by clergy during sexual assaults)[35] has not been widely discussed in the UK. Furthermore, whilst the issues have been aired in the US, this potential branch of tort failed to get off the ground. In the test case of *Nally v Grace Community Church of the Valley*,[36] the parents of a college student attempted to sue religious ministers for malpractice after their son committed suicide. The plaintiffs complained about many aspects of the ministers' handling of his pastoral care, including a refusal to state that taking his own life would endanger his salvation, when challenged on that specific point by the young man. The court refused the claim on First Amendment grounds, and in relation to the operation of both fiduciary duty and negligence.

Of course, in a phrase that has been described as 'beloved of lawyers', each case turns on its own facts.[37] It cannot have helped the parents' case in *Nally* that the ministers had done everything that could reasonably have been expected,

[31] L Watkins, *The Real Exorcists* (York, Methuen, 1983) 143.

[32] M Perry, *Deliverance* (London, SPCK, 2012) 1–3.

[33] Stobart (n 4).

[34] M Weitz, *Clergy Malpractice in America* (Lawrence, KS, University of Kansas Press, 2001).

[35] See, eg, *JGC v Portsmouth Roman Catholic Diocese* [2012] EWCA Civ 938; and *John Doe v Bennett* [2004] SCJ No 17.

[36] *Nally v Grace Community Church of the Valley*, 763 P 2d 948 (1988).

[37] J Hodgson and J Leithwaite, *Tort Law* (Oxford, Oxford University Press, 2007) 292.

including attempting to persuade the young man to accept secular medical treatment, whilst his family had actively and vociferously opposed his admission to a mental health facility. Although his parents claimed that it was inappropriate to tell Nally that people who committed suicide were not excluded from heaven, it is hard to see how that argument could ever have succeeded. This logic would have applied even if the line taken might have appeared outlandish or irresponsible to citizens in general, although in this particular case the approach appears to have been compassionate and in step with contemporary social attitudes to mental health and suicide.

Undoubtedly, the idea of a court's weighing the appropriateness of spiritual advice given by a minister would have an anathema to the First Amendment[38] (and would be highly likely to infringe Article 9 ECHR in a UK context), but regardless of this, it is very difficult to imagine any court ruling that any counsellor or advisor, religious or secular, should try to deter a person from suicide by threatening consequences in the afterlife. Attempts to try to frighten a vulnerable individual in the depths of a mental health crisis away from self-harm would be unethical, and in most cases ineffective.

However, *Nally* has been affirmed in other decisions where it might have been easier to prove a claim had one been allowed: for instance, in *White v Blackburn*,[39] where a minister failed to refer the plaintiff on to a secular counsellor. Loue has criticised this outcome, arguing that if clergy offer what is effectively secular counselling, they should be held to the same standards as other professionals in the field, and that separating out the religious and non-spiritual elements of their advice, whilst allowing claims only in relation to harm from the latter, was possible.[40]

Loue is not an entirely lone voice. Lund also suggests that there is scope in some areas to expand the civil liability of religious groups, without having courts trespass on sacred ground, although he is cautious about the difficulties,[41] and it should not be underestimated that in the US at least, such arguments are swimming against the general tide.[42] Consider in contrast the decision in *Kubala v Hartford Roman Catholic Diocese Corp*,[43] in which a woman attending a Charismatic Roman Catholic service fell over 'in the spirit' and nobody caught her, meaning that she sustained injury. The courts were not prepared to rule on what they considered would have been the appropriate manner to run a healing

[38] The US Constitution, First Amendment states that 'Congress shall make no law respecting an establishment of religion, or prohibiting the free exercise thereof; or abridging the freedom of speech, or of the press; or the right of the people peaceably to assemble, and to petition the Government for a redress of grievance.'

[39] *White v Blackburn*, 787 P2d 1315 (1990).

[40] S Loue, 'Faith based mental health treatment of minors: A call for legislative reform' (2010) 31 *Journal of Legal Medicine* 171.

[41] CC Lund, 'Free Exercise Reconceived: The logic and limits of Hosanna-Tabor' (2014) 108 *Northwestern University Law Review* 1184.

[42] SE Ericsson, *Clergy Malpractice: An Illegal Legal Theory* (Springfield, VA, Christian Legal Society, 1981).

[43] *Kubala v Harford Roman Catholic Diocese Corporation*, 41 A 3d 351 (2011).

service, so the claim failed. Equally, in *Franco v Church of Christ of the Latter Day Saints*,[44] a 14-year-old girl disclosed that she had been sexually assaulted at the age of 7 years by an older boy in the congregation. The Church advised her and her parents to forgive, forget and seek atonement. Although the family tried to do this, they were unable to cope, and eventually they went to the police, a decision that angered the Church and led to their being ostracised. The family attempted to sue for the distress caused by the delay in going to the police and the pain of being rejected by the Church community, but once again, First Amendment considerations meant that they were unsuccessful. In fact, the court refused to rule on the appropriateness of religious teachings about forgiveness, or responding to others who rejected the advice of leaders.

For our purposes, needless to say, it must be acknowledged that these decisions were made in a different legal and cultural context, and it should not be overlooked that US judges, at least in some states, are fiercely protective of the First Amendment, as well as being concerned about respecting the practice of exorcism in particular. In *Pleasant Glade Assembly of God v Schubert*,[45] a Texan court refused to allow a vulnerable young woman an action in trespass when she was held down and exorcised against her will, in a manner traumatic enough to cause serious psychiatric injury. The justification was that she had consented to such practices by becoming a member of the Church in question, and could not withdraw her consent without leaving the community. In the view of the Supreme Court of Texas, allowing her to bring an action would have meant regulating the internal affairs of a religious group.

Koploy[46] criticises this decision from a US stance, as being out of step with judgments in leading rulings on free exercise, such as *Boerne*[47] and *Smith*.[48] In Koploy's analysis, the position that has emerged from previous case law is that facially neutral laws will be applicable in religious contexts, and free exercise cannot be used as a cover to justify harm to third parties, especially physical harm. She suggests that there were three considerations underlying the court's conclusion here:

(a) The Texan court regarded exorcism as a religious practice worth protecting, and feared an unconstitutional chilling of religious freedom if a church in this situation was found to be liable.
(b) The judges regarded themselves as having generous scope to adapt and develop case law.
(c) The plaintiff had in fact given consent, by virtue of her voluntary membership of this particular Church.[49]

[44] *Franco v Church of Christ of the Latter Day Saints*, 21 P 3d 198 (2001).
[45] *Pleasant Glade Assembly of God v Schubert* 264 SW 3d 1 (2008).
[46] C Koploy, 'Free Exorcise Clause? Whether Exorcism Can Survive America's "New Neutrality"' (2010) 104 *Northwestern University Law Review* 363.
[47] *City of Boerne v Flores*, 521 US 507 (1997).
[48] *Employment Division v Smith*, 494 US 872 (1990).
[49] Koploy (n 46) 400–06.

Despite the fact that Koploy makes a highly persuasive case, her analysis does not alter the conclusion of the appellate court in this instance, and for our present purposes, we are left to speculate how all of this might play out in a UK context. How much of this reasoning would hold good on the opposite side of the Atlantic? To start with, there is a stark difference, as the wall of separation between Church and State, which was so critical to judicial reasoning in all of these American cases, does not exist for English and Welsh courts. In fact, in *Shergil v Khaira*,[50] the UK Supreme Court indicated that in recent decades judges had been unduly reticent about adjudicating in religious contexts but, unlike in the US, the British court was willing to draw a distinction between disputes in a faith-based setting and disputes that turned on faith-based questions. Whilst the latter were clearly outside of the constitutional remit of secular courts, the former were not. The refusal of the court to accept jurisdiction of a defamation claim in a religious context in *Blake v Associated Newspapers*[51] had been sharply criticised, on the basis that the ruling in *Wachmann v Chief Rabbi*[52] had been misunderstood. It had been assumed in *Blake*, and indeed by academic commentators like Cranmer,[53] that *Wachmann* outlined a principle that secular courts would not involve themselves in disputes relating to religion, but in fairness to both judges and authors, the Supreme Court's reinterpretation of *Wachmann*, as turning on the scope of judicial review in respect of public interest, came rather as a bolt out of the blue.[54] Does this new-found willingness to enter sacred space, at least for certain purposes, make professional negligence for clergy more plausible? If so, is there greater scope for possible actions arising from exorcism?

The truth is that, even in the absence of a line as decisive as that drawn in the US between the sacred and secular, there are still formidable obstacles that would have to be overcome before a religious minister could be held liable for a form of professional negligence. First, it should be emphasised that in *Shergil v Khaira*, the Supreme Court did not suggest that it would ever be appropriate for a state court to enter into an evaluation of the merits or correctness of religious doctrine, and given that this is the exact field in which religious ministers are claiming expertise, it is difficult to see how their professional practice could be assessed without judges' entering into theological discussion. The problem here is not simply a lack

[50] *Shergill v Khaira* [2014] UKSC 33.

[51] *Blake v Associated Newspapers Ltd* [2003] EWHC 1960.

[52] *R v Chief Rabbi of the United Hebrew Congregations of Great Britain and the Commonwealth, ex parte Wachmann* [1992] 1 WLR 1036.

[53] F Cranmer, 'Beating People is Wrong: Campbell, Cousins, Williamson and their aftermath' in M Hunter-Henin (ed), *Law, Religious Freedom and Education in Europe* (London, Ashgate, 2011) 283, 291.

[54] In short, the Supreme Court read Simon Brown in *Wachmann* as declining to extend the (at the time, still controversial) *Datafin* principle, namely that a private body exercising public law functions may be susceptible to judicial review in this regard. In order to be subject to judicial review the Chief Rabbi's decision would have to have had a public law element, not merely a 'public' element, and some connection to governmental functions/activities. Given that the Chief Rabbi was not regulating any area of public life, such that the State would have had to take on the task in his absence, there was no justification for judicial review.

of technical knowledge (although as Dwyer eloquently demonstrates, judicial assessment of expert evidence is a field of study in itself[55]) but a fundamental one of religious freedom. When considering beliefs protected by Article 9 ECHR, in *R (Williamson) v Secretary of State for Education and Employment*,[56] the House of Lords was clear that once the sincerity of a religious belief has been established, it is neither possible nor appropriate to demand that it be susceptible to objective, logic-based analysis.

The belief must relate to matters more than merely trivial. It must possess an adequate degree of seriousness and importance. As has been said, it must be a belief on a fundamental problem. With religious belief this requisite is readily satisfied. The belief must also be coherent in the sense of being intelligible and capable of being understood. But, again, too much should not be demanded in this regard. Typically, religion involves belief in the supernatural. It is not always susceptible to lucid exposition or, still less, rational justification. The language used is often the language of allegory, symbol and metaphor. Depending on the subject matter, individuals cannot always be expected to express themselves with cogency or precision.[57]

Given that Article 9 clearly affords protection to beliefs, which in Lord Nicholl's phrase are not susceptible to 'rational justification', how could a court adjudicate between different doctrinal positions without making value judgements between them and favouring some beliefs over others? Moreover, many spiritual pathways demand suffering, stoicism, detachment or other behaviours that run counter to objective best interests, and English law explicitly recognises and protects this, for instance in the 'religious mortification' exception to the general prohibition on inflicting actual bodily harm or more serious harms, regardless of consent.[58] Consequently, there is express acknowledgement that practising a religious faith or following a spiritual pathway may lead to physical or mental suffering; were it otherwise, faith groups would not be free to teach that parties to an unhappy marriage should try to honour vows which they now regret,[59] or that homosexuals should remain celibate.[60] Unquestionably, any external observers might consider such messages unwise and even dangerous, but to make them subject to civil law challenge would render it impossible to hold to mainstream views within Roman Catholicism, conservative evangelical Christianity or Islam, whilst the threat of litigation would hang over practitioners like the sword of Damocles and have a chilling effect upon teaching and practice. Therefore, any form of professional negligence for clergy around doctrinal advice would be incompatible with

[55] D Dwyer, *The Judicial Assessment of Expert Evidence* (Cambridge, Cambridge University Press, 2008).

[56] *R (Williamson) v Secretary of State for Education and Employment* [2005] UKHL 15.

[57] ibid [23] (Lord Nicholls).

[58] *R v Brown* [1994] 1 AC 212.

[59] K Vann, *What God Has Joined: A Catholic Teaching on Marriage* (Charlotte, NC, Basilica Press, 2008).

[60] E Shaw, *Same-Sex Attraction and the Church: The Surprising Plausibility of the Celibate Life* (Downers Grove, IL, Intervarsity, 2015).

religious freedom and, this being the case, it is difficult to envisage any legal action ensuing from a minister's labelling an individual as possessed or otherwise troubled by evil spirits.

However, what about liability for pastoral care not directly related to doctrines of the faith, for example a failure to encourage someone to seek medical help, even though that person appeared to be in the grip of a mental health crisis? Loue argues that the secular part of clergy counselling could be hived off from the sacred,[61] but this assertion would be problematic in the eyes of many religious ministers, who would see the two as inextricably linked, or perhaps even as mutually suffusing.[62] Certainly, the theologically troubling nature of this division would not necessarily prevent courts in the UK from attempting to make it, and some parallels could be drawn with the realm of vicarious liability, in which the courts have been happy to classify Roman Catholic priests and other religious ministers as being in a position 'akin to employment'.[63] The motivation behind such categorisation, namely to enable victims of heinous and criminal acts to secure compensation from an insured or solvent organisation, is fully understandable, but it has left the law in utter disarray when it comes to other elements of vicarious liability. In order to attach, a claimant must demonstrate not only that the defendant's relationship to the tortfeasor is one to which the doctrine should apply, but also that there is a 'close connection' between the tort and the relationship.[64] This position had evolved from the classic conception of vicarious liability as arising out of a tort committed by an employee acting in the course of his or her employment,[65] and establishing any real clarity about what a close connection might mean, despite dogged attempts to refine the definition,[66] has been very challenging. Furthermore, the general chaos is compounded in a religious context, where the 'job' is in fact a commitment to a way of life. The court acknowledged this problem in *Maga*, when imposing vicarious liability on a Roman Catholic diocese for acts of sexual abuse committed by a priest, where the victim was neither a member of the congregation nor even a Roman Catholic,[67] but it did not propose any tangible mechanism for addressing it.

The above reflection on vicarious liability is relevant for exorcism and professional negligence in two principal respects. First, as noted, it is a clear demonstration that the incoherence of sieving out the secular elements of pastoral care from the sacred ones, as far as faith communities are concerned, would not necessarily deter state courts from pursuing this line. Second, it also reveals another disturbing

[61] Loue (n 40)190–91.

[62] M Jensen, 'Life Histories and Narrative Theology' in D Streere (ed), *The Supervision of Pastoral Care* (Eugene, OR, Wipf and Stock, 2002) 114, 119; M Ramsey, *The Christian Priest Today Care* (Eugene, OR, Wipf and Stock, 2012).

[63] *JGE v Trustees of the Portsmouth Roman Catholic Diocesan Trust* [2012] EWCA Civ 938.

[64] *Lister v Hesley Hall* [2002] 1 AC 215; *Mohamud v Morrisons* [2016] UKSC 11.

[65] *Rose v Plenty* [1976] 1 WLR 141.

[66] *Cox v Ministry of Justice* [2016] UKSC 10.

[67] *Maga v Birmingham Roman Catholic Diocese* [2010] EWCA Civ 256.

element of 'professional' negligence in a religious setting: many of the individuals with positions of responsibility are in fact volunteers, and not all faiths' traditions have the same clear line between clergy and laity found in Anglicanism or Roman Catholicism, for example, nor the same divisions of responsibility within the community.[68] Role expectations and mechanisms for accountability vary from religion to religion, a factor that has already yielded some surprising results where vicarious liability is concerned. For instance, in *A v Trustees of the Watchtower Bible and Tract Society*,[69] a faith group was made liable for the acts of a 'ministerial servant', an unpaid lay-person, who had certain special duties related to Bible studies in homes of the congregation and mission more generally on weekday evenings.

Against this backdrop, exorcism is potentially a concerning area of activity for faith communities, given that it covers a wide range of practices and is not necessarily the exclusive province of accountable individuals within a hierarchy. As discussed, vicarious liability attaches by virtue of the *relationship* between the second defendant and the tortfeasor, not any fault on the part of the second defendant, and this fascinating discussion opens up questions about legal exposure for acts carried out privately by members of faith communities in other contexts (eg exorcism), now that vicarious liability clearly applies beyond paid ministers.

The complexities of this, however, lead us back to another fundamental stumbling block to making clergy professional negligence a workable premise. As was flagged up in *Nally*, there are major questions about how the standard of care should be determined,[70] and in most instances of exorcism-related claims, the issue would be similar to that which arose in *Nally*, namely accusations of mishandling a situation where an individual was experiencing some form of mental health crisis. Religious ministers are not purporting to have medical training or expertise, and as a result, it seems unreasonable to assert that they could be professionally expected to diagnose mental illness. Furthermore, they do not have legal powers of the kind vested in the police to compel a person to accept help and intervention.[71]

With regard to expertise and legal powers, most religious ministers are in reality not in a materially different position from any other member of the general public in dealing with someone suffering from mental illness. Given that there is no obligation to act as a Good Samaritan where the welfare of third parties is concerned, ministers would not be responsible to ensure that a person sought medical help, *unless* they had somehow or other assumed responsibility.

As Kortmann demonstrates, there is no overarching duty to act in English law, as well as a systemic reluctance to impose liability for non-feasance as opposed to misfeasance,[72] and consequently, in practical terms, it is unlikely that there would be scope for liability in tort, unless the exorcist had somehow assumed control of

[68] I Tomlinson, *Clergy, Culture and Ministry* (London, SCM, 2017) 162.
[69] *A v Trustees of the Watchtower Bible and Tract Society* [2015] EWHC 1722.
[70] *Nally* (n 36).
[71] Mental Health Act 1983 (UK), s 135.
[72] J Kortmann, *Altruism in Private Law* (Oxford, Oxford University Press, 2005).

the claimant's environment, such that he or she had a duty to care for the claimant. For instance, in the tragic Canadian case of *Mejia Lopez*,[73] the defendants forcibly restrained the victim and failed to ensure that he was properly hydrated, resulting in his death. Of course, this was a criminal matter, but if, hypothetically, an individual in England consented to being tied up in the course of an exorcism (so that there was no issue of false imprisonment), the exorcist would have an obligation to ensure that the individual received appropriate physical and, if necessary, medical care.

Nevertheless, liability in general terms for failing to encourage or facilitate an individual to see a doctor is very different from that kind of situation of physical control and risk, and for all of the reasons set out above, establishing a claim in English law on the basis that a competent and reasonable religious minister should have ascribed a clinical, rather than spiritual, cause to an individual's symptoms would be an uphill struggle. Extrapolating from this, the possibility is even more remote with regard to third parties' successfully claiming in the event that the recipient of an exorcism goes on to harm them whilst in the throes of an untreated mental health episode.

This debate is really not new. In fact, the desirability of counsellors and therapists having a duty to warn has been high profile in the US, even since the notorious *Tarasoff case*[74] in the mid-1970s, in which a student confessed to a university counsellor that he was having fantasies about murdering a young woman with whom he was infatuated. Tragically, he ultimately acted upon these ideations and murdered her. The Supreme Court of California found, by majority, that the knowledge that a specific, identified individual was at risk triggered a duty to warn that person, and since then a number of US States have placed such an obligation on a legislative footing.[75] Although English law to date has not developed along these lines, Young argues that such a duty would be compatible with its principles.[76] He puts forward, by analogy, the celebrated case of *Home Office v Dorset Yacht Co*,[77] in which a group of young offenders escaped during a residential trip, due to the negligence of custodians, and once on the loose did a huge amount of damage to neighbouring property. In finding the Home Office liable for this, Lord Diplock concluded that there was a 'special relationship' between the prison officers, the young offenders and the distinct group of people who were their potential victims.

Young maintains that this decision provides scope to argue that there could be a duty of care as between a psychiatrist and third parties harmed by a patient,

[73] *R v Mejia Lopez* Ontario Court of Justice, Docket No 30-3008 (2003).

[74] *Tarasoff v Regents of the University of California*, 17 Cal 3d 425, 551 P 2d 334, 131 Cal Rptr 14 (1976).

[75] See generally R Johnson, G Persad and D Sisti, 'The Tarasoff Rule: The Implications of Interstate Variation and Gaps in Professional Training' (2014) 42 *Journal of the American Academy of Psychiatry and the Law* 469, 469.

[76] A Young, 'In the Arms of the Infinite: The Liability of Mental Health Professionals for the Violent Acts of their Patients' (2011) *Mental Health and Learning Disabilities Research and Practice* 3, 6.

[77] *Home Office v Dorset Yacht Co* [1970] AC 1004.

and draws on the case of *W v Egdell* for further support.[78] This case concerned a doctor who was asked to provide a report by the plaintiff, who had been detained in a secure hospital after shooting and killing a number of people but was hoping to demonstrate that he was now not a risk to others. In the event, however, the doctor was so concerned about the potential danger posed by the patient that he felt obliged to share his conclusions with the authority. The aggrieved plaintiff then attempted to sue the doctor for breach of confidence. This background is relevant because Young attempts to use this case to support the contention that the doctor owed a duty to the public at large, as well as his patient,[79] but it must be acknowledged that putting forward a duty as a shield against liability is very different from contending that there exists a duty imposing liability. Some duties have this double-nature, but by no means all. For instance, in the Scottish case of *Moss v Howdle*, it was affirmed that a hypothetical driver might successfully put forward a defence of necessity in relation to dangerous driving, were he or she rushing a passenger suffering from a heart-attack to hospital,[80] but the question of whether a driver would be liable in negligence for *not* driving at high speed would be an entirely distinct legal question. If one adult stranger were to stagger to another's car in a remote location with no mobile coverage, suffering from chest pains and begging for help, a driver might be legally *justified, but not legally obliged* to speed in order to get medical treatment for that person as quickly as possible.

Therefore, using *Egdell* as authority for a positive duty to disclose cannot really be endorsed, and even at the very furthest stretch the case is obiter on the point. Furthermore, as Young acknowledges,[81] case law in relation to public authorities is not promising in relation to demonstrating a duty to protect members of society in general from the acts of an individual, or even a broad category of persons who may be under threat. So, in *Hill v Chief Constable of West Yorkshire*,[82] an action in negligence against the police by the estate of one of the later victims of the Yorkshire Ripper, who might have been saved if the criminal investigation had been carried out more effectively, failed on this basis. Given that the deceased was no more at risk than any other woman, there was no special relationship between her and the police, and no duty of care upon which a negligence claim could be hung. Similarly, in *Palmer v Tees Health Authority*,[83] a psychiatric patient under the care of the health authority had expressed an intention to murder a child and was known to have a history of violence. Unfortunately, he did indeed go on to abduct, abuse and murder a little girl, but once again a claim in negligence foundered upon the duty of care, as no special duty was owed to either the child or her mother.

[78] *W v Egdell* [1990] 1 All ER 835.
[79] Young (n 76) 6.
[80] *Moss v Howdle* 1997 SLT 782 (HCJ).
[81] Young (n 76) 7.
[82] *Hill v Chief Constable of West Yorkshire* [1989] AC 53.
[83] *Palmer v Tees Health Authority and Hartlepool and East Durham NHS Trust* (1999) Lloyd's Rep Med 351.

Osman v Ferguson[84] could be contrasted from these cases. In this instance, a teacher developed an obsessional attachment towards a pupil; he began stalking and harassing the boy and his family; and after a number of disturbing incidents, including criminal ones, the teacher's behaviour culminated in his shooting the boy and killing his father. Given that in this case the link to the known and very specific target family was clear, it was possible to establish a special relationship, but the UK courts followed *Hill* and found the police to have a blanket immunity in these circumstances, citing public policy reasons and the need to avoid an unduly litigation-driven and defensive approach to law enforcement. The European Court of Human Rights (ECtHR) took a different view and ruled that a general protection from action breached Article 6 ECHR and the right to a fair hearing.[85]

The truth is that the ECtHR judgment has been controversial, and widely criticised, for example by Gearty[86] and Davies;[87] as Fulbrook notes, the more plausible reading of the case law is that *Hill* has frequently been misunderstood: the police do not in fact enjoy a blanket immunity from suit – it is simply that in many of these cases, claimants will be unable to satisfy the general criteria for negligence, including those imposed for reasons of public policy.[88] If this logic is followed, *Osman* is simply distinguishable on the facts from *Hill*. For present purposes, however, it is not helpful to engage in a lengthy and tangential discussion about the merits and implications of the decision with regard to police forces and health authorities. In our discussion about negligence and exorcism, the points of interest are as follows: first, it is clear that establishing a duty of care to third parties where the risk posed by an individual is to society at large, is an extremely difficult, if not doomed, endeavour. Second, even where a specific victim is in peril, claimants will be swimming against the tide in attempting to establish a successful claim. And, third, and for this discussion most significantly, the strongest arguments available in such circumstances come from professional or public duties of a kind almost certainly absent in cases relating to exorcism.

For example, in *Home Office v Dorset Yacht Co*,[89] the defendants had a public duty and also legal powers to keep the young offenders securely and under control, and in the cases around psychiatric patients, both doctors and health authorities had professional expertise and legal powers of detention at their disposal, but all of these elements will be missing for most people carrying out an exorcism. Once again, we are back to the same rocks on which much of the potential for actions against exorcists by recipients ran aground. Fundamentally, the absence of any claims of specialist clinical knowledge and/or legal powers to compel an individual

[84] *Osman v Ferguson* [1993] 4 All ER 344.

[85] *Osman v UK* Case no 87/1997/871/1083 (ECtHR, 28 October 1998).

[86] C Gearty, 'Unravelling Osman' (2001) 64 *MLR* 159.

[87] A Davies, 'The European Convention and Negligence Actions: Osman "Reviewed"' (2001) 117 *LQR* 521.

[88] J Fulbrook, 'Robinson v Chief Constable of West Yorkshire' [2018] *Journal of Personal Injury Law* C65.

[89] *Home Office v Dorset Yacht Co* (n 77).

to be detained, submit to assessment or seek help, makes constructing a claim exceedingly difficult, and when this is coupled with the challenge of demonstrating a duty of care towards third party victims, the barriers to a successful claim are demonstrably very high.

Added into the mix is the need to respect religious freedom pursuant to Article 9 ECHR, and the implications of forcing ministers and others to practise their faith with half an eye towards litigation. This discussion should not be interpreted as a suggestion that a successful claim could never ever arise, but we have been at pains to stress that it would be very difficult. However, if events as dramatic and extreme as those in the Ossett situation were to arise again, and on this occasion the recipient of the exorcism was expressing a clear and direct intention to go and attack a named individual, there might be an arguable case for negligence if the defendant exorcist declined to act or seek help.

In essence, where the tort of negligence is concerned, a duty of care to others will generally only be imposed where the defendant has done something proactive to assume it. In circumstances where a minister or other person is only promising to offer spiritual advice or assistance, it will be difficult to interpret this as an undertaking to safeguard mental or physical well-being. Any alternative position might make religious advisers reluctant to offer spiritual care to individuals known or suspected to be suffering from mental illness, a conclusion that would harm, rather than further, the protection of the vulnerable.

Having assessed the position in relation to negligence, we shall now go on to consider how the law might balance competing interests in regard to privacy and reputation.

III. Privacy and Reputation

The press appetite for stories around exorcism seems to be insatiable, and reports of such rituals regularly appear on television, in newspapers and on the Internet.[90] As indicated in section I, however, exorcism in reality covers a wide range of different practices and ideas, and it cannot be assumed that everyone undergoing such a rite is necessarily lacking the capacity to consent, or is otherwise vulnerable. Nevertheless, there are legitimate questions about how civil law might seek to balance, on the one hand, the Article 8 ECHR rights of participants in these rituals (ie the protection of respect for private and family life, as well as privacy and personal reputation) and, on the other, the right to freedom of expression of journalists (under Article 10 ECHR).

[90] For example, recent stories include: 'Unholy row in Italy after ministry of education offers teachers exorcism courses' *The Telegraph* (15 February 2019) at htps://www.telegraph.co.uk/news/2019/02/15/unholy-row-italy-education-ministry-offers-teachers-exorcism/; 'Family accused of killing man during apparent exorcism believed a demon was in him, court told' *The Independent* (12 February 2019) at https://www.independent.co.uk/news/uk/crime/family-exorcism-demon-kenny-ife-enfield-north-london-a8775321.html.

In relation to privacy, this is an area in which English common law has seen substantial developments in the last two decades.[91] Fertilised by Article 8 ECHR, breach of confidence has grown into a more robust form of protection, and although it has not yet quite produced the fruit of a new tort for breach of privacy in a general sense, disclosing confidential information without informed consent by the subject will result in civil liability, unless this can be justified on the basis of public interest.

In this context, the recent case of *Ali v Channel 5*[92] is particularly informative, and sets out how the current balance is struck. The programme, *Can't Pay? We'll Take It Away*, featured a family who were unexpectedly evicted from their home. The father of the family did eventually give some form of reluctant consent to talk and tell his side of the story, but only after pleas for the filming to stop had been repeatedly ignored, and when it became apparent that this was his best hope of reputational damage limitation. As a result, his consent could not be relied upon, and the question became whether, in the circumstances, it was lawful for the confidential information to have been disclosed without his consent. The litigation that followed saw a direct clash between the Article 8 rights of Mr Ali and his family, and the Article 10 freedoms and public interest arguments put forward by Channel 5.

As Steyn[93] argues, the arguments of Channel 5 in this case failed to prevail because there was little real focus on the public interest upon which the broadcaster was purporting to rely, namely, demonstrating that eviction can lawfully take place without prior notice in the UK; instead the programme focused on the conflict, drama and appealed to the voyeuristic lure of so-called 'poverty-porn'.

This decision gives a very useful insight into how a court might respond to the reporting of an exorcism, without the free and informed consent of one or all of the participants. In order to escape liability, those responsible for the article or feature would have to demonstrate that there was a public interest in sharing the information, and that their presentation was meeting the interest in a way that outweighed the Article 8 rights of those whose private information had been shared. Clearly, this would be fact specific, depending on the kind of exorcism rite, where it had taken place, and the manner and purpose of its presentation, but given the tendency for the press to sensationalise stories with this theme, *Ali v Channel 5* provides a salutary shot across the bow for those hoping to capitalise on widespread curiosity and love of the 'reality TV' genre.

Furthermore, in addition to the question of privacy, there is the capacity of English law to protect reputation through the tort of defamation.[94] Could there be liability for asserting that a person is in need of exorcism or has undergone such a ritual? Conversely, what about accusations that an exorcist has acted

[91] *Campbell v Mirror Group Newspapers Ltd* [2004] UKHL 22; *Douglas v Hello! Ltd* [2005] EWCA Civ 595; *Wainwright v Home Office* [2003] UKHL 53.

[92] *Ali v Channel 5 Broadcast Ltd* [2018] EWHC 298 (Ch).

[93] E Steyn, 'Channel 5 Ordered to Compensate Couple Evicted on "Can't Pay? We'll Take it Away!"' (2018) 29 *Entertainment Law Review* 147.

[94] P Mitchell, *The Making of the Modern Law of Defamation* (Oxford, Hart Publishing, 2005).

inappropriately or cynically in performing a rite? Whilst cases are not impossible here, this avenue is less promising for claimants than that of breach of confidence, because of the nature and structure of the tort of defamation.

It should be noted at the outset that there are two forms of defamation, libel and slander, depending upon whether the material has been published in a permanent form or not.[95] This is significant, because libel has historically been actionable per se, whereas slander usually requires some damage (although this position has now been modified by statute to some degree, as a 'body which trades for profit' must effectively suffer serious financial loss before a claim for defamation can be brought, whether libel or slander is involved).[96]

One of the important caveats to slander's requiring damage is relevant for our purposes. Slander is actionable per se if the statement complained of is an imputation reflecting negatively on a person in his or her office, profession, trade or business.[97] Therefore, where religious ministers are concerned, or individuals offering commercial services of deliverance or spiritual healing are involved, there may be an argument for slander being actionable per se. The first issue that would need to be established by any potential claimant would be that the statement[98] was both defamatory and met the threshold of having caused or been likely to cause 'serious harm'.[99] The test provided at common law in *Sim v Stretch* is still helpful in discerning whether the content of a statement can be properly construed as defamatory, or in other words whether the message conveyed would 'tend to lower the [claimant] in the estimation of right thinking members of society'.[100]

Any potential claimants objecting to being labelled as possessed, or as otherwise in need of exorcism, would be required to demonstrate that this imputation would lower them in the estimation not just of a particular group, but of 'right thinking members of society' at large. This, as Whelan observes, is not straightforward, because in reality there is often no objectively discernible consensus amongst 'right thinking' people.[101]

Whilst speculating in the abstract about the defamatory statements is difficult, it is unlikely that right thinking people would judge a person negatively because a religious minister considered that person to be in need of exorcism. Presumably, the likely conclusions would either be that he or she was suffering from some form of organic disease with a scientific explanation, or that he or she was the victim of spiritual attack, depending on the worldview of the person in question. In either case, there is no reason to suppose that the individual would be regarded less favourably as a result. A third possibility, of course, would be to conclude that the

[95] *Cairns v Modi* [2012] EWCA 1382.

[96] Defamation Act 2013 (UK), s 1(2).

[97] Defamation Act 1952 (UK), s 2; *McManus v Beckham* [2002] 1 WLR 2982.

[98] Statement is defined by statute to include 'words, pictures, visual images, gestures or any other method of signifying meaning' (Defamation Act 2013 (UK), s 15).

[99] Defamation Act 2013 (UK), s 1.

[100] *Sim v Stretch* [1936] 2 All ER 1237, 1240 (Lord Atkin).

[101] R Whelan, 'Case Comment: *Cowan v Bennett*' [2013] *Juridical Review* 557, 558.

person asserting the need for exorcism was either malicious or misguided, but in those circumstances, whilst the victim might find the statement upsetting, there would be no cause of action. This is illustrated well by the Scottish decision in *Cowan v Bennett.*[102] In this case, the defender repeatedly referred to the pursuer as that 'gay painter' in a networking group, made childish jokes about 'bum-chums' and distributed pink versions of the pursuer's business cards. The action for defamation failed because it was self-evident that this kind of comment would actually lower the *defender*, rather than the pursuer, in the eyes of right thinking people, as it is not generally considered desirable in our society to be bigoted and puerile.

This is relevant for our purposes, because it is a powerful reminder that defamation protects reputation but it does not safeguard individuals from distress or harassment, and consequently, as a general proposition, asserting that someone needed exorcism would not be defamatory. There might be scope, however, for claims founded on an accusation that an individual, particularly a religious minister, was carrying out exorcisms in a fraudulent manner with a view towards personal gain. Given that the Supreme Court[103] strongly criticised the refusal of the court in *Blake v Associated Newspapers*[104] to allow a claim for defamation, purely because the factual backdrop was faith-based, there is no reason why a successful claim could not be brought in this context. Whilst secular courts will not investigate questions of religious doctrine, accusing a minister of dishonesty is professionally damaging, and arguably no different from making a similar allegation about a grocer or a school-teacher. Provided that the other requisite elements of the tort are satisfied, barring a claim is not possible.

IV. Financial Exploitation

This brings us to our third and final area for consideration: what is the position if the accusations of financial exploitation are not in fact unjust? Clearly, this will not be a consideration in cases where there is no element of financial gain on the part of the exorcist. Nevertheless, what would be the position, in civil as opposed to criminal law, if an individual holding no genuine belief to this effect, deliberately set out to convince a victim that he or she was in need of exorcism and charged him or her for the service?

There has been no case law or relevant academic discussion exactly on point, but Greenfield, Osborn and Roberts[105] have addressed some parallel issues where the practice of mediumship is concerned, following the repeal of legislation that specifically dealt with this field.[106] They suggest that the Consumer Protection

[102] *Cowan v Bennett* (2012) GWD 37-738 (Sh Ct (Tayside) (Dunfermline)).
[103] *Shergill v Khaira* [2014] UKSC 33.
[104] *Blake v Associated Newspapers Ltd* [2003] EWHC 1960.
[105] S Greenfield, G Osborn and S Roberts, 'From beyond the grave: the legal regulation of mediumship' (2012) 8 *International Journal of Law in Context* 97.
[106] Fraudulent Mediums Act 1951.

from Unfair Trading Regulations 2008 (UK) (SI 2008/1277) could only bite in respect of mediums who were charging for their services in contacting the dead and deliberately acting dishonestly.[107] This would trigger criminal liability, but also the interest and protection of Trading Standards. The stumbling block in many cases would be the need to prove dishonest intent, as in practical terms, this would be very difficult to achieve.

The same is applicable to the other obvious avenue, in terms of the common law: the tort of deceit. Whilst it is undeniable that, as Murphy demonstrates, the nature and application of deceit is highly complex and not infrequently misunderstood,[108] it is clear that at its heart there is a requirement for *deliberate* deception.[109] A claimant must be able to show that he or she was induced by fraudulent representations to enter into a contract, and suffered a financial detriment as a result, and as Weaver's analysis shows, this is a high hurdle to clear, even on the civil law test of the balance of probabilities.[110] Given that claims around spiritual matters are of their very nature highly subjective and not easily verifiable, demonstrating a lack of sincerity will not be an easy task in most instances.

Of course, the issue will only arise in the first place if the recipient of the exorcism, or more accurately the party who has paid for it and entered into the contract, becomes sceptical about the service he or she has received. One positive glimmer for claimants in such circumstances comes from the law of undue influence, and the specific and long-standing acknowledgement that individuals are in a disempowered position vis-à-vis their spiritual advisors.[111] Where the person carrying out the exorcism might be deemed the 'spiritual advisor' of the other party, there will be a presumed relationship of influence, and unless the defendant can show that this was not exercised improperly, there will be the possibility of escaping the contract and recovering any money paid over, if a transaction had taken place that required explanation.[112]

The complicating factor would lie in the claimant having presumably received whatever 'service' he or she had paid for from the defendant, for example a 'smudging' of a house to rid it of evil spirits. There would not be a question of the defendant having received something for nothing, and unless the fee demanded was unreasonably high, it is difficult to see what justification there could be for asserting that it should be set aside. Also, in cases where, for example, the claimant had simply found the defendant online, contacted him or her and agreed to pay for a service, it is arguable that there would be no relationship of spiritual advisor/advisee in any case. In that instance, it would need to be proved that there was a relationship of trust and confidence on the facts, a contention that seems unlikely as between virtual strangers. Certainly, the paradigm is very different from that of the Mother Superior and postulant in a convent in *Allcard v Skinner*.

[107] Greenfield, Osborn and Roberts (n 105) 107.
[108] J Murphy, 'Misleading appearances in the tort of deceit' (2016) 75 *CLJ* 301.
[109] *Derry v Peek* (1889) LR 14 App Cas 337.
[110] M Weaver, 'The Mane Lane' (2013) 163 *NLJ* 223.
[111] *Allcard v Skinner* (1887) 36 Ch D 145.
[112] *Barclays Bank v O Brien* [1994] 1 AC 180.

Thus, whilst the doctrine of undue influence might be quite properly applied with regard to some contracts involving exorcism services, it will not be an appropriate or suitable avenue for most of them. As in every area we have considered, it is instructive to note what kind of interests English law will and will not protect, and also who it deems responsible for protecting them.

V. Conclusion

As was the outlined intention of this piece, the discussion has encompassed three types of civil law dilemmas arising out of the provision of exorcism. No apology is made for having devoted the lion's share of our attention to the assessment of negligence, given the implications this tort has where the claimant has suffered a catastrophic outcome. Despite the scope for tragedy in this area, as the Ossett case all too graphically demonstrates, the possibilities for actions against religious ministers or other individuals performing exorcisms are relatively remote. This is the result of the reluctance of our legal framework to impose a proactive duty to safeguard the welfare of third parties, in the absence of the capacity to fulfil it and some positive step to have embraced it in the first instance. In offering spiritual help, individuals are generally not purporting to have medical expertise, nor do they have any special legal powers to require others to seek or accept help. As a consequence, it would be neither reasonable nor appropriate to render them liable for harm that recipients of exorcism have inflicted on themselves or others.

When it comes to privacy, modern law will respect the rights of individuals not to have confidential and intimate information shared without their permission, unless there are weighty public interest reasons that demand otherwise. Therefore, those involved in exorcisms can expect some shelter from frivolous exploitation by the press and others. Securing reputational protection in relation to these matters via the tort of defamation is more complex, however, as in general terms, involvement in an exorcism will not damage a person's standing in the eyes of society at large.

Finally, in situations where money changes hands in the performance of exorcism rituals, the position is more complicated. Where there is deliberate fraud, as would be expected, the law will step in to provide redress. Nevertheless, the subjective nature and value of the services being offered makes fraud hard to prove, and establishing a fair balance between the parties is a complex endeavour. If all contracts relating to exorcism could be readily undone, those who seek to make a living in this field would be placed in an impossibly precarious position.

In general terms, the legal framework prioritises religious freedom and personal choice in this area, over and above paternalistic protection or regulation. Provided that individuals do not attract the notice of criminal provisions, civil law in general terms is content to allow them wide latitude, a position that is in keeping with the values of a liberal democracy, which does not prioritise one worldview over another.

13

Sacred Sites and State Failures: A Case Study of the Babri Masjid/Ram Temple Dispute in Ayodhya

PETER W EDGE AND MC RAJAN

I. Introduction

Sacred sites are powerful sites. Often this power is seen as an opportunity, for instance when a sacred site is seen as generator of social capital to combat disadvantage, or a nexus for the delivery of public goods such as aid. Other times, this power is seen as a threat, for instance when a sacred site is seen as a centre for radicalisation in the context of counter-terrorism, or a location for denial of state values such as non-discrimination on the grounds of gender. They can also have a potent symbolic power for members of those communities that see them as sacred, as well as others.

Sacred sites are complex sites. As Hayes has demonstrated, the 'religious precinct' goes well beyond a particular numinous space or a 'place for worship'.[1] A sacred site may be limited to, say, a chapel, but it may cover open spaces, community spaces and commercial spaces, the understanding of which is shaped by the association with the place for worship.

Sacred sites are human sites. Within a particular religious worldview, a sacred space may exist without human agency or knowledge. We are going to privilege a rather different perspective, which treats sacredness as a human construct. From this perspective, 'This space is sacred' is shorthand for 'This space is sacred to …'. A space may be sacred to an individual alone, but law is more frequently engaged in relation to spaces that are sacred to a community – perhaps a small community or family, but in any case a plurality of individuals.

Sacred sites are shared sites. To some extent, every sacred site is a shared site, unless it has meaning only for one other person who does not have to share it

[1] S Hayes, 'The religious precinct: Setting the scene for equality law in action?' in B Scharffs, JA Maoz and A Wooley (eds), *Freedom from Religion: The Emerging Context* (New York, Springer, forthcoming).

with other interests. Members of a single, cohesive religious community may need to share it with one another. Many of the best-known controversies over sacred sites involve sites claimed by different religious communities – for instance the long-going controversies in Israel over the Noble Sanctuary/Temple Mount.[2] Controversies can also arise over non-religious sharing – for instance over the religious and heritage uses of Stonehenge in England. Given the involvement of the state in the use of any space within its territorial jurisdiction, the state also shares in these sacred sites.

In this chapter, we focus on the legal aspects of one extremely long-running controversy, albeit not one that has become an international icon:[3] the dispute over the Babri Masjid/Ram Temple in Ayodhya, India. In section II we discuss the context, and history, of the dispute. In section III we focus on the litigation aspect of the dispute, including discussion of the twenty-first-century judgments by the High Court and Supreme Court of India. In our conclusion, section IV, we reflect on broader lessons to be drawn from this case study.

II. Context and History

Ayodhya is a North Indian town situated in the Faizabad district in the State of Uttar Pradesh (UP). It has some connection with every major religion in India.[4] However, the important affiliations for our purposes are those that Hindus and Muslims have with the place.[5]

For Hindus, Ayodhya existed as a Saivic centre for many centuries, and in the eighteenth century it became a dominant Vaishnavite centre.[6] In particular, Ayodhya is seen by Hindus as the birthplace of Hindu god Ram, who went on to rule the kingdom.[7] These events in the age of *Treta*[8] – the distant past – were followed by a period during which Ayodhya had disappeared. In the present age,

[2] See more generally RE Hassner, *War on Sacred Grounds* (New York, Cornell University Press, 2009).

[3] D Viejo-Rose, 'Destruction and reconstruction of heritage: Impacts on memory and identity' in H Anheier and YR Istar (eds), *Heritage Memory and Identity* (New York, Sage, 2011).

[4] KN Panikkar, 'A Historical Overview' in S Gopal (ed), *Anatomy of a Confrontation: The Babri Masjid-Ramjanmabhumi Issue* (New Delhi, Viking, 1991) 25–26; H Bakker, *Ayodhya* (Groningen, Institute of Indian Studies, 1984) 38.

[5] For more information on Ayodhya, see S Gopal (ed), *Anatomy of Confrontation: Ayodhya and the Rise of Communal Politics in India* (London, Zed, 1993); and for a contrasting view, K Elst, *Ram Janmabhoomi vs Babri Masjid* (New Delhi, Voice of India, 1990).

[6] S Gopal et al, 'The Political Abuse of History: Babri Masjid-Ramjanmabhumi Dispute – An Analysis by Twenty-Five Historians' in AG Noorani (ed), *The Babri Masjid Question 1528–2003: 'A Matter of National Honour'*, vol I (New Delhi, Tulika Books, 2003) 30.

[7] P van der Veer, 'Riots and Rituals: The Construction of Violence and Public Space in Hindu Nationalism' in PR Brass (ed), *Riots and Pogroms* (London, Macmillan, 1996) 160.

[8] In Hindu cosmology, the cosmos passes through cycles within cycles for eternity. The basic cycle is the *Kalpa*, formed by 1,000 *Mahayugas*. Each *Mahayuga* is divided into four *yugas* or ages, called *Krta*, *Treta*, *Dvapara* and *Kali*. Their lengths are respectively 4,800, 3,600, 2,400 and 1,200 'years of the Gods', and each year equals 360 human years. According to Hindu mythology, Rama spent his youth in

the site was located by King Vikramaditya.[9] Within Hindu traditional accounts, although not necessarily archaeological or secular historical accounts, he constructed a huge temple on the birth site of Ram,[10] which was then destroyed to allow Muslims to construct Babri Masjid in 1528, thus giving Hindu claims over the site temporal priority.[11] From the eighteenth century, Ayodhya was established as a major pilgrim centre in North India,[12] and by 1991, Bawa estimated there were 6,000 Hindu temples in the area, with most of the trade and employment opportunities serving pilgrims.[13]

As with the Hindu narrative, the Islamic narrative of the history of Ayodhya stresses the antiquity of the connection between religion and the site, long before conventional history might do so. Muslims argue that their attachment to Ayodhya dates back to the pre-Islamic period, with the burial of Seth, one of the children of Adam and Eve, at Ayodhya, as well as Noah.[14] Both burial sites continue to attract a substantial number of religious visitors.[15] Ayodhya was ruled by Muslim kingdoms from, it is likely, the eleventh century. The first Mughal Emperor defeated the ruler of Ayodhya in battle, and his governor built a mosque in Ayodhya in 1528.[16] Ayodhya is considered a '*Khurd Mecca*' (small Mecca), because of the large number of Muslim holy persons, including sufi saints and other revered religious figures, who are believed to be buried there.

The pre-1528 history of the site, then, differs considerably between the two communities. This is reflected in how they see the year 1528. Hindu groups, particularly *Sangh Parivar*,[17] allege that the first Mughal Emperor destroyed a magnificent and ancient Ram temple in order to build his Babri Masjid. The Muslim view is that the mosque was built on an empty space, and that there was no evidence of the demolition of a Hindu temple.[18] With the beginning of the direct

Ayodhya and was king during the *Treta-yuga*, thousands of years before our present age, the *Kali-yuga*. For details, see AL Basham, *The Wonder that was India*, Sidgwick & Jackson Great Civilizations Series, 3rd rev edn, (London, Sidgwick & Jackson, 1967) 320–21.

[9] A Copley, 'Indian Secularism Reconsidered: From Gandhi to Ayodhya' (1993) 2 *Contemporary South Asia* 47, 57.

[10] R Friedland and R Hecht, 'The Bodies of Nations: A Comparative Study of Religious Violence in Jerusalem and Ayodhya' (1998) 38 *History of Religions* 101, 106.

[11] P van der Veer, 'God Must be Liberated!: A Hindu Liberation Movement in Ayodhya' (1987) 21 *Modern Asian Studies* 285; *Vishwa Hindu Parishad* Publication, New Delhi, at http://www.vhp.org/englishsite/e.Special_Movements/dRanjanambhumi%20Muti/historical_legalperspective.htm, accessed 8 March 2018.

[12] P van der Veer, *Gods on Earth: The Management of Religious Experience and Identity in a North Indian Pilgrimage Centre* (London, Athlone, 1988) 36.

[13] M Bawa, 'Scenes From Ayodhya' *The Sunday Times of India* (New Delhi, 3 November 1991) 18.

[14] MJ Akhtar, *Babri Masjid: A Tale Untold* (New Delhi, Genuine, 1997) 10.

[15] T Mahmood, 'Ayodhya, Ram and Islam' in VN Mishra (ed), *Ramjanambhoomi Babri Masjid: Historical Documents, Legal Opinions and Judgements* (New Delhi, The Bar Council of India Trust, 1991) 24.

[16] MJ Akhtar, *Babri Masjid: A Tale Untold* (New Delhi, Genuine, 1997)11.

[17] *Sangh* means organisations and *Parivar* means family. *Sangh Parivar* means 'Family of Hindu Nationalist Organisations', which is an umbrella organisation of Hindu nationalist groups.

[18] RS Sharma et al, *Ramjanmabhumi-Babari Masjid: A Historians Report to the Nation* (New Delhi, People's Publishing House, 1991) 6–7.

rule of the area by the British Crown in 1856, the stage was set for these and other community differences to begin to be worked out by litigation.

III. Litigation, 1856–2018

Panikkar traces organisation of the two communities around litigation to the beginning of British rule.[19] In 1857, a Hindu priest took a part of the Babri Masjid compound and constructed a *chabutra*, a raised platform for idols. This was opposed by local Muslims, and the dispute was resolved by agreement to build a wall between the mosque and the *chabutra*, which was later called *Janmastan* temple. However, Muslims made a petition to the local magistrate on 30 November 1858, objecting to the construction of a clay *chabutra*. The Babri Masjid was officially registered in 1860 as a place of worship for Muslims.[20] Between 1883 and 1885, petitions to allow the priest of *Janmastan* to erect a temple over the *chabutra* were denied.[21] In 1886, the dispute reached the District Court. The judge dismissed the petition on three grounds. First, while it was unfortunate that in 1528 a masjid had been built on land specially held sacred by the Hindus, as the event occurred 356 years ago it was too late to remedy the grievance. Second, any change could cause more harm and derangement of order than benefit. Third, there were no documents to support the claim of the Hindu priest to be the land owner.[22] The decision of the District Court was affirmed by the Judicial Commissioner of Avadh, who, in his judgment dated 1 November 1886, noted that it was a very wise and proper procedure on the part of the executive and the civil courts to have promptly dismissed the plaintiff's claim. The pleas on appeal were wholly unsupported by the facts in the case or by any arguments that appear to be weighty. In addition, there was nothing on the record to show that the plaintiff was the proprietor of the land in question. Hence the appeal was dismissed, and both parties were requested to maintain the status quo.[23]

An internal dispute between Muslims in 1943–45 was similarly swiftly resolved, with a statutory enquiry finding that the Babri Masjid was established by a Sunni Muslim,[24] and a later court decision finding that the site was used by both Sunni and Shia Muslims but was Sunni waqf property.[25]

[19] KN Panikkar, 'A Historical Overview' in S Gopal (ed), *Anatomy of a Confrontation* (Delhi, Viking, 1992) 31.

[20] MJ Akhtar, *Babri Masjid: A Tale Untold* (New Delhi, Genuine, 1997) 181.

[21] Mahant Raghubar Das, *Mahant of Janmastan, Ayodhya v The Secretary of State for India in Council*, Plaint dated 29 January 1885 – no 61/280 of 1885.

[22] Judgment by FEA Chamier, District Judge, Faizabad dated 26 March 1886.

[23] Judgment by Judicial Commissioner W Young, Oudh, dated 1 November 1886 in no 1221 K/1886, cited in Noorani (ed) (n 6) 188.

[24] The report of Faizabad District *Waqf* Commissioner, dated 8 February 1941.

[25] *Shia Central Board of UP Waqf v Sunni Central Board of UP Waqf* (1945) Regular Suit no 29/1945. A waqf is a Muslim endowment for a religious, educational or charitable purpose.

In 1949, the controversy took a new turn. During the final months of 1949, a group of *sadhus* occupied a Muslim cemetery near the mosque, and ignited sacred fires to emphasise their claim that the area was originally a Hindu religious site.[26] Some days later, idols of Ram, Lakshman and Sita were discovered inside the mosque, which Hindus claimed were placed there by miraculous means.[27] As Gould observes, 'this miracle story created a local sensation. Hindus and Muslims flocked to the *Janmastan*, the former to bear witness to the miracle, the latter to defend the Babri Masjid against desecration and seizure by the Hindus'.[28]

As the dispute exacerbated local tensions, the local authorities ordered the gates of Babri Masjid to be locked,[29] and prohibited both communities from its use, on the basis that the dispute was likely to lead to a breach of the peace. A receiver was appointed to arrange for the care of the property in dispute, and took charge of the disputed property on 5 January 1950.[30] A plethora of suits and counter-suits followed, being consolidated into a single suit in 1964, with the lead suit being a 1961 suit brought by The Sunni Central Board of Waqfs, UP, for declaration and recovery of possession of the mosque and graveyard after removing the idols and other articles.[31] A date was set for the final hearing, but the death of the Receiver in 1970 created a fresh dispute, which was only resolved in 1987.[32]

By the time the substantive action was returned to, however, Ayodhya had begun the process of transformation into a national controversy.[33] In 1984, *Vishwa Hindu Parishad*, (VHP),[34] a Hindu nationalist organisation, initiated a movement

[26] C Jaffrelot, *The Hindu Nationalist Movement and Politics 1925 to the 1990s* (London, Hurst & Co, 1996) 93.

[27] However, the First Information Report stated: 'At about 9.00 in the morning around fifty to sixty persons entered the Babri Masjid after breaking open the locks. They did not care when Hans Raj, the constable No 70, stopped them from entering. Provincial Armed Constabulary (PAC) guards were called for help but by then the mob had already entered the *masjid*.' Regarding the offenders, Mata Prasad points out that 'Ram Das, Shukla Das, Sudharsan Das with 50 to 60 persons desecrated the mosque by trespassing the mosque through rioting and placing idols in it'. AG Noorani, 'Legal Aspects to the Issue' in S Gopal (ed), *Anatomy of a Confrontation: The Babri Masjid-Ramjanmabhumi Issue* (New Delhi, Viking, 1991) 70.

[28] HA Gould, *Grass Roots Politics in India: A Century of Political Evolution in Faizabad District* (Oxford, IBH Publishing Co, 1994) 181–96.

[29] Criminal Procedure Code 1973 (CrPC) (Act No 2 of 1974), s 145 contains an entire chapter on 'Disputes as to immovable property'.

[30] SK Tripati 'One Hundred Years of Litigation' in AA Engineer (ed), *Babri Masjid/Ramjanmabhoomi Controversy* (New Delhi, Ajanta, 1990) 20.

[31] Regular Suit no 12 of 1961 in the Court of Civil Judge, Faizabad.

[32] From the averments of Writ Petition no 746/86 in the Allahabad High Court. For more details, see K Prasad et al, *Report: Citizen's Tribunal on Ayodhya* (New Delhi, The Secretariat, 1993) 97–98.

[33] DS Burlet, *Challenging Ethnic Conflict: Hindu-Muslims Relations in India 1977–1993* (PhD thesis, Department of Peace Studies, University of Bradford, 1997) 191.

[34] Vishwa Hindu Parishad (VHP) literally means 'World Hindu Council'. As a major component of Sangh Parivar, VHP was founded in 1964. In Hinduism, there existed several sects that represented innumerable rival schools of thought, and this division was perceived as the root cause of the weaknesses of Hinduism. The VHP was therefore created to endow Hinduism with a church-like centralised structure and to use this new ecclesiastical apparatus to counter Christian proselyte activities. VHP worked in close association with former rulers, businessmen, respectable politicians, and the religious heads of several Hindu sects and monasteries. From 1984, VHP conducted campaigns to liberate sacred sites where Muslim mosques were built in the previous centuries. Particularly, they took up the Babri Masjid–Ramjanmabhumi dispute, and claimed the ownership of it to build a Ram temple in its place.

to 'liberate' the *Ram Janmabhumi* and rebuild a magnificent Ram temple at Ayodhya. In 1986, a Hindu intervener who was not a part in any of the main suits secured an order allowing him free entry into the building for prayer, which was not permitted under the interim order of 1950. In his order, Judge KM Pandey stated:

> After having heard the parties it is clear that the members of the other community, namely Muslims, are not going to be affected by any stretch of imagination if the locks of the gates are opened and the idols inside the premises are allowed to be seen and worshipped by pilgrims and devotees. It is an undisputed fact that the premises are presently in the Court's possession and for the last 35 years Hindus have an unrestricted right of worship as a result of the Court orders of 1950 and 1951 (19.1.50 and 3.3.51). The District Magistrate has stated before me today that members of the Muslim community are not allowed to offer any prayer at the disputed site. If this is the state of affairs, then there is no occasion for law and order problem arising as a result of the removal of locks. It is absolutely an affair inside the premises.[35]

The tension among Hindus and Muslims in Ayodhya accelerated when the UP State government acquired 2.77 acres of disputed land on 7 October 1991.[36] The government argued that this was to promote tourism and provide amenities for pilgrims. The acquisition was challenged on the basis that the land was waqf property, and so could not be acquired under the relevant legislation; and that the exercise of power was colourable[37] in as much as the real purpose of acquisition was to destroy the mosque and to transfer the land to some Hindu organisation to construct a temple thereon.[38] An interim order by the High Court Bench allowed the State to take possession of the land, but ordered that no permanent structure could be erected, and prohibited transfer of the land to any other party. However, through a Deed of Lease on 20 March 1992 between the State government and the *Shri Ramjanmabhumi* Trust, the land was transferred to the trust against the order of the High Court. In defiance of the court order, the *kar sevaks*[39] started building a platform on the acquired land, after demolishing existing buildings and temples, which clearly violated the status quo order. This was challenged by the Muslims before the court, and on 15 July 1992 the Lucknow Bench passed an order stopping any construction activity on the disputed site. On 16 July 1992, the Chief Secretary

[35] *Umesh Chandra Pandey v State of UP and Others* (1986) Civil Appeal no 66/1986.

[36] The Places of Worship (Special Provisions) Act (Act No 42 of 1991) passed in September 1991, would have prevented this, but s 5 explicitly excluded Babri Masjid from its purview.

[37] Justice Krishna Iyer defines colourable legislation as follows: 'In the jurisprudence of power, colourable exercise of or fraud on legislative power or, more frightfully, fraud on the Constitution, are expressions which merely mean that the legislature is incompetent to enact a particular law, although the label of competency is stuck on it, and then it is colourable legislation.' *RS Joshi and others v Ajit Mills Ltd and another; RS Joshi and others v Idar Taluka Sahakari and others* (Civil Appeals no 533, 1004, 1410 and 1671–1685 of 1975) AIR 1977 SC 2279.

[38] Writ Petition no 3540 (M/B) of 1991 (Civil Miscellaneous Application no 22799 (W) of 1991 and Civil Miscellaneous Application no 22810 (W) 1991.

[39] *Kar sevak* means 'voluntary labourer', usually in pursuit of a religious objective such as the construction or renovation of a sacred site.

directed the District Magistrate to ensure compliance with the High Court orders that had been defied by the VHP leaders.[40]

On 31 October 1992, the *Daram Sansad*, a religious Parliament of Hindu priests, announced the resumption of *kar seva* from 6 December 1992.[41] The Prime Minister, PV Narasimha Rao, tried to counter the increasing communal tension by making an appeal to the Supreme Court to intervene.[42] Subsequently, on 27 November, through an affidavit, the UP State government assured the Court that they would protect the mosque. The High Court appointed a District Judge as an observer who would report periodically.[43] Despite objections by opposing counsel, the Supreme Court, in its order of 28 November 1992, permitted *Kar Seva* as 'a symbolic occasion', while it disallowed any construction work on the acquired 2.77 acres of land. On 30 November 1992, the Supreme Court asked the UP State government to improve the inadequate security arrangements. However, despite all the assurances from the State government, the Babri Masjid was demolished by the members of *Sangh Parivar* on 6 December 1992, who built an ad hoc Ram temple on the site where Babri Masjid had stood.

After the Babri Masjid had been demolished, the Court delivered its judgment in relation to the acquisition of land challenge. The Court found against the UP government on a number of grounds, most significantly because the action by the State gave advantage to one party in litigation over the other, contrary to Article 14 of the Constitution, and gave more favourable treatment to one religious group than another, contrary to Article 15(1).[44]

After the demolition, a Writ Petition was filed before the High Court by a lesser-known forum called the World Hindu Lawyers Association, praying for the *darshan*, or image of the deity, in the makeshift Hindu temple. They requested the court to allow them to exercise their constitutional right to worship,[45] and to remove the hurdles for *darshan* and worship. In their judgment, Justices HN Tilhari and AN Gupta ordered the relaxation of the orders that were imposed under section 144 CrPC[46] after the demolition. The judges also directed that the State officials allow the petitioners, the Hindus and devotees of Ram to have *darshan* in the makeshift temple at Ayodhya.[47] The judges made their decision in part because an illustrated copy of the Constitution signed by members of India's

[40] Prasad et al (n 32) 62.

[41] 'Nothing Can Stop Kar Seva' *The Hindu* (New Delhi, 1 November 1992).

[42] 'Ayodhya: PM Favours Court Arbitration' *The Hindu* (New Delhi, 15 November 1992).

[43] 'Observer for Ayodhya' *The Hindu* (New Delhi, 30 November 1992).

[44] Judgment dated on 11 December 1992 in 'Acquisition of the Land Case'.

[45] Indian Constitution Art 25.

[46] CrPC (n 29), s 144 grants power to a magistrate to issue orders in urgent cases of nuisance or apprehended danger to life, health or safety, or on a disturbance of the public tranquillity, a riot or an affray.

[47] Judgment delivered on 1 January 1993 by Justice HN Tilhari and AN Gupta in *Vishwa Hindu Parishad v Union of India*, case cited in AG Noorani (ed), *The Babri Masjid Question 1528–2003: 'A Matter of National Honour'*, vol II (New Delhi, Tulika Books, 2003) 247–48.

Constituent Assembly in 1949 contained a picture of the Hindu God Ram.[48] The judges found that Ram was therefore 'a constitutional entity' and a 'figure constitutionally accepted as the Lord by the builders of this nation and its culture'.[49] The High Court's *darshan* order was challenged in the Supreme Court, which refused to pass any order on the pleas of Muslim organisations to stay the High Court order, and directed maintenance of the status quo.[50]

Although Babri Mosque had now been demolished, in pursuance of the Supreme Court judgment on 24 October 1994, proceedings in the High Court were re-started in January 1996, and continued until judgment by the Allahabad High Court in September 2010. The protracted hearing resulted in three judgments totalling more than 8,000 pages.[51]

All three judges noted the undesirability of the very long period that had passed before the unlocking order of 1986 could be resolved. There was also a willingness to make findings of fact as to the history of the site: Justice Khan, for instance, found that the constructed portion of the premises under dispute had been erected as a mosque under orders of Babar,[52] and that no temple was demolished for its construction.[53] Justice Sharma, on the other hand, found that such a temple had existed, that it had been destroyed in order to build a mosque and that, under Islamic law, 'the disputed structure could not be a mosque as it was raised by force of arms on land belonging to the plaintiff deities'.[54]

The majority of the Court ruled that the site should be partitioned into three parts – roughly two-thirds Hindu, one-third Muslim. Justice Khan stressed sharing of the site between Hindu and Muslim worshippers since pre-1855, and from this found that both communities were in joint possession of the entire premises in dispute, although for convenience they were using and occupying different parts. The three parties (Muslims, Hindus and a named Hindu sect) were declared joint holders until formal partition. Proposals for partition were required within three months, but some areas were set aside for the non-Muslim parties. Justice Khan was joined by Justice Argawal, who endorsed the tripartite division, but who was more specific about areas set aside for the Hindus. He also stressed the role of the Government of India in making their land available to allow 'separate entry … of the people without disturbing each other's rights'. The dissenting justice, Justice Sharma, found that the building was not, under Shariah, a mosque, and that the land remained owned by the Hindu deities in the (pre-existing) Temple. Government attempts to extinguish the sacredness of the place were beyond its competence.

[48] H McDonald, 'India: Backlash in Bombay' (1993) 21 *Far Eastern Economic Review* 16, 18.

[49] MJ Akhtar, *Babri Masjid: A Tale Untold* (New Delhi, Genuine, 1997) 173.

[50] S Ahmad, 'Judicial Complicity with Communal Violence in India' (1996) 17 *Northwestern Journal of International Law and Business* 320, 334.

[51] For a fuller analysis of the decision, see G Arcot Srikantan, 'Re-examining secularism: The Ayodhya Dispute and the equal treatment of religions' (2017) 5 *Journal of Law Religion and State* 117.

[52] ibid 227.

[53] ibid 242.

[54] ibid 202.

Immediately after the judgment, the Indian Prime Minister appealed for peace, and suggested that the status quo would be maintained until the Supreme Court took up the case. In May 2011, the Supreme Court stayed the verdict, describing it as 'strange and surprising'. It noted in particular that the High Court had granted a relief – partition – that had not been sought by any of the parties. Instead, all parties had sought exclusive rights over the entire precinct. The Supreme Court ordered the status quo, until the case was resolved by the Supreme Court.

In December 2017, the Supreme Court announced that it would begin to hear the civil appeals against the Allahabad High Court judgment in February 2018. In February 2018, the Supreme Court made it clear it would approach the case as a pure land dispute, and accordingly, in March 2018, rejected the applications of a significant number of persons wishing to intervene in the case. The Supreme Court began to hear the substance of the case on 23 March 2018.

IV. Analysis

A. The Significance of Delay

A key feature of the dispute is the judicial failure to provide a speedy legal resolution to a dispute over the rights to a particular section of space. In particular, for 35 years (1950–85) the Ayodhya dispute remained a local dispute between a few members of two religious communities. There was no final legal resolution of the dispute before the 1992 demolition, and indeed the Supreme Court did not begin substantive hearings on the case until 2018.

Delay has been described as the 'pathology of the Indian legal system',[55] and has been a longstanding cause of concern. Chodosh has suggested that the adversarial model is poorly designed to meet the needs of a rural population with widespread poverty, illiteracy and unfamiliarity with formal legal procedure, particularly since most of it is conducted in the English language,[56] while Deshpande suggest that it creates the opportunity for parties with a weak case to delay resolution against them.[57] Average delays in the civil process have been calculated at between

[55] O Mendelsohn, 'The Pathology of the Indian Legal System' (1981) 15 *Modern Asian Studies* 824.

[56] HE Chodosh et al, 'Indian Civil Justice System Reform: Limitation and Preservation of the Adversarial Process' (1997–1998) 30 *New York University of International Law and Politics* 1, 29; see also R Moog, 'Delays in the Indian Courts: Why the Judges Don't Take Control' (1992) 16 *Justice System Journal* 19, 22.

[57] VS Deshpande, 'Civil Procedure' in J Minattur (ed), *The Indian Legal System* (Bombay, Tripati NM, 1978) 201. Some of the critical factors involved in delay are: objections to pecuniary or territorial jurisdiction; applications for transfer; pleas of facts; framing of issues; preparation of decrees; failure to scrutinise plaint and appeal; revision; death of defendants or respondents; filing of suits and appeals for the sole purpose of delay; multiplicity of appeals; and stays and temporary injunctions.

10 and 15 years,[58] and a similar level of delay can be found in cases before the higher judiciary.[59]

Although delay has been an ever-present factor in the Indian legal system, it does not usually exceed 10 to 15 years. However, in the Ayodhya dispute the delay extended to 42 years (1950–92) without even a preliminary trial. The protracted litigation period means that interim relief is especially important – interim relief in this case has, literally, spanned generations. The 1950–51 interim relief barred Muslims from Babri Masjid; the 1986 opening of the locks turned the space into a place of Hindu public worship.

Thus, this dispute demonstrates how failure to provide a speedy resolution to sacred site disputes can result in exacerbation of communal conflict and denial of human rights. Had the Ayodhya dispute been settled in 1950, it is likely that much of the violence and many of the human rights violations would have been averted. The delay by the courts to adjudicate the title suits for 42 years led to the demolition of the mosque. The post-demolition period, particularly between 6 and 13 December 1992, witnessed serious communal riots, which according to the official records claimed 1,200 lives.[60]

B. The Importance of the Rule of Law

A recurring feature of the dispute is the unwillingness, or inability, of the executive to enforce the orders of the courts against non-state actors; or indeed a willingness to contravene such orders itself.[61] The clearest example of the latter happened in March 1992. The State government leased out about 42 acres of land in the vicinity of the Babri Masjid complex to the *Ram Janmabhumi Nyas* (Trust), on perpetual lease, for the implementation of the Ram Story Park project.[62] This was in contravention of the court order, which stated that the acquired land should not be transferred or alienated.[63]

The Indian Constitution created a federal system, based upon a strong Union Government with State governments that are not sovereign but which have

[58] Chodosh et al (n 56) 29. Chodosh et al indicate that the time period between the filing of the complaint and the written statement and the framing of the issues by the court averages six to nine months, the taking of evidence takes an average of five years. In the case of appeals, the current backlog is 12 years for interim orders and longer for final dispositions. This may add up to a time period exceeding 20 years for much litigation.

[59] M Kachwaha, *The Judiciary in India: Determinants of its Independence and Impartiality* (Leiden, PIOOM,1998) 38.

[60] C Jaffrelot, *The Hindu Nationalist Movement and Politics 1925 to the 1990s* (London, Hurst & Co, 1996) 458–64.

[61] In Contempt Petition no 97 of 1992 in Writ Petition no 977 and no 972 of 1991.

[62] 'The deed of Lease dated 20 March 1992 between the UP Government and the *Shri Ramjanmabhumi* Trust' cited in Noorani (ed) (n 47) 352–61.

[63] The Supreme Court order on 15 November 1991 in Writ Petition (C) no 1000/91 with Writ Petition (C) no 977 and no 972 of 1991.

constitutionally enumerated powers.[64] If the constituent States fail to adhere to the constitutional authority or suffer from internal disturbances, the Union Government is empowered to use its authority to re-establish democratic rule within those States under Article 356 of the Constitution.[65] When the State government of UP violated the provisions of the Indian Constitution, it was open to the Union Government to implement President's Rule under Article 356 to maintain public order and restore constitutional democracy, which includes the rule of law and the protection of secularism.[66] As the 1992 events approached their climax, 'a contingency plan for a take-over of the complex and imposition of President's rule was kept ready but there was no clear view within the government on whether the union should get fully involved'.[67]

Even on 6 December 1992, the Union Government could have acted and averted the destruction of the mosque. According to the official account, the Home Ministry received information at 12.00 noon about the attack on the Babri Masjid, yet despite this, a Cabinet meeting was only convened at 6.00 pm and President's Rule was proclaimed only at 21.10 pm.[68] The delay in convening the Cabinet meeting and taking a decision on imposing President's Rule was crucial. The breakdown in the law and order situation allowed for the continued assault and destruction of the Masjid, the clearing of its debris, and work on the building of a platform for the installation of the Ram and other idols. The *kar sevaks* were therefore given vital time to complete their assault on the Babri Masjid, and to give a wholly new dimension to the problem by building the foundation of the proposed *sanctum sanctorum* of a Ram Temple.

The Indian Constitution grants unambiguous legal rights to religious communities, reinforced by specific provisions in relation to places of worship in the Indian Penal Code and the 1991 Protection of Places of Worship Act. Generally, legal rights granted to a religious community become insufficient if the state organs are unwilling to use their power to enforce them – either as a party in relation to public law rights, or as the guarantor of the rule of law more generally, such as in relation to enforcement of private law rights. Failure of the state organs in enforcing them makes the sacred sites vulnerable to attacks and destruction. For example, the Ayodhya dispute is particularly sobering for the range of state organs that failed to effectively implement legal guarantees. On 6 December 1992, the day of the demolition of the mosque, the Supreme Court itself observed that a

[64] Part XI (Arts 245–263) of the Indian Constitution delineates the relations between the Union and States.

[65] The Indian Constitution, Art 356 confers powers on the President of India to dismiss the duly elected State government if he is satisfied 'on receipt of a report from the Governor of a state or otherwise' that there is a breakdown of constitutional machinery in that State. In the exercise of the emergency powers, however, the role of the governor is crucial.

[66] *SR Bommai v Union of India* AIR 1994 SC 1918.

[67] M Godbole, *Unfinished Innings: Recollections and Reflections of a Civil Servant* (New Delhi, Orient Longman, 1996) 347.

[68] Prasad et al (n 32) 84.

grave situation had emerged, where a constitutionally elected government could not discharge sensitive duties in a matter of this magnitude.[69] The statement of VP Singh, the former Prime Minister of India, that 'the fall of the three domes of the Babri Masjid were in fact the collapse of the three pillars – Legislature, Judiciary and Executive – of Indian democracy',[70] emphasises that legal rights granted to a religious community are rendered insufficient if the state organs are unwilling to use their power to enforce them.

C. The Importance and Complexity of Histories

A significant form of legitimation of claims by parties competing over Ayodhya has been an appeal to historical fact. As Mehta puts it, 'Each of the contending parties, and there are at least four, evokes the status quo to establish the legitimacy of its claims.'[71] The status quo is a particular statement of how the site was being used at a particular moment, and clearly had an important function in relation to interim relief. Given the duration of interim relief in this dispute, judicial understanding of the status quo has been of considerable practical significance.

The dispute involves broader entanglements between law and history, however. Writing in 1990, Gopal found that the historical claims by the Muslim and Hindu communities 'can find no sanction from history', and stressed that while appropriation of history is a continual process in any society, 'in a multi-religious society like ours, appropriations which draw exclusively on communal identities engender endless communal conflicts'.[72] History, and archaeology, has played a central role in the framing of the legal dispute over ownership and use of the site.[73]

The appropriation of history, including debates over historical fact in order to shape contemporary legal and political realities, is by no means restricted to debates with a religious dimension.[74] The religious dimension in Ayodhya, however, adds to the complexity. As Mehta puts it, 'two temporal registers, asymmetric and incommensurate, are entangled with each other – historic time and mythic time. The first is based on rules of evidence drawn from empirical detail, while the second provides a kind of habit within which belief and faith are mobilised.'[75]

[69] Legal Correspondent, 'UP Government did not discharge its duties' *The Hindu* (New Delhi, 7 December 1992).

[70] MJ Akhtar, *Babri Masjid: A Tale Untold* (New Delhi, Genuine, 1997) 202.

[71] D Metha, 'The Ayodhya Dispute: Law's Imagination and the Functions of the Status Quo' in D Mehta and R Roy (eds), *Violence and the quest for justice in South Asia* (New Delhi, Sage, 2018) 293.

[72] S Gopal et al, 'The political abuse of history: Babri Masjid-Rama Janmabhumi Dispute' (1990) 18 *Social Scientist* 76, 80–81.

[73] See S Ratnagar, 'Archaeology at the heart of a political confrontation: The case of Ayodhya' (2004) 45 *Current Anthropology* 239.

[74] U Belavusau and A Gliszczynska-Grabias (eds), *Law and Memory: Towards Legal Governance of History* (Cambridge, Cambridge University Press, 2017).

[75] D Mehta, 'The Ayodhya Dispute: The absent mosque, state of emergency and the jural deity' (2015) 20 *Journal of Material Culture* 397, 398.

D. The Difficulty of State Neutrality in Clashes between Minority and Majority Communities

The Preamble to the Indian Constitution defines India as 'a Sovereign, Socialist, Secular, Democratic, Republic'.[76] The framers recognised that in a multi-religious, multi-ethnic country like India, it was essential for religious harmony and for the social fabric of the society that independent India was governed by secular principles. These secular principles were the basis on which the fundamental human rights of all Indian citizens were to be protected, especially those of the minority groups. Protection of minority rights is embedded in the Constitution and delineated in Articles 29[77] and 30.[78] The Supreme Court in various cases[79] has held that the protection of minorities was supported by the principles of secularism.

In India, the Gandhian understanding of secularism, that all religions should have equal respect, came to dominate legal and political thought in the country.[80] The meaning of secularism, as contemplated by the Constitution, did not preclude religious protection; rather, it sought to promote religious harmony.[81] One distinguishing feature of constitutional secularism in India is the state's promise that it will not identify itself with or be controlled by any single religion. Jacobsohn has defined Indian secularism as 'ameliorative secularism', because it tried to heal some of the inequalities existing in Indian society.[82]

The legal dispute in Ayodhya centred on the question of property rights over the site, but became inextricably linked with the differing religious claims that led to continual conflict. Parikh observed that the principle of constitutional secularism permeates the Ayodhya situation, where the religious dispute culminated in a legal action brought by a few Hindus challenging property rights over the disputed site in Ayodhya.[83] The judicial enthusiasm for resolving the case as a property rights case, rather than a human rights or group rights case, may in part be a strategy to frame the issues in a way that facilitates performative neutrality.

[76] The word 'Secular' was substituted by the Constitution (Forty-second Amendment) Act 1976.

[77] The Indian Constitution, Art 29: '(1) Any section of the citizens residing in the territory of India or any part thereof having a distinct language, script or culture of its own shall have the right to conserve the same. (2) No citizen shall be denied admission into any educational institution maintained by the State or receiving aid out of State funds on grounds of religion, race, caste, language or any of them.'

[78] The Indian Constitution, Art 30: 'All minorities, whether based on religion or language, shall have the right to establish and administer educational institutions of their choice.'

[79] *In Re Kerala Education Bill* AIR 1958 SC 956, 976–77; *Shri Krishna v Gujarat University* AIR 1962 Guj 88; *DAV College v State of Punjab* AIR 1971 SC 1731, 1744.

[80] AA Engineer, 'Secularism in India: Theory and Practice' in RC Heredia and E Mathias (eds), *Secularism and Liberation* (New Delhi, Indian Social Institute, 1995) 40.

[81] MV Pylee, *India's Constitution* (London, Asia Publishing House, 1962) 123.

[82] GJ Jacobsohn, *The Wheel of Law: India's Secularism in Comparative Constitutional Context* (Princeton, NJ, Princeton University Press, 2003) 94. Jacobsohn defines it as ameliorative, since it seeks an amelioration of the social conditions of people long burdened by the inequities of religiously based hierarchies, while embodying a vision of inter-group comity whose fulfilment necessitates cautious deliberation in the pursuit of abstract justice.

[83] S Parikh, 'Enshrining a Secular Idol: A Judicial Response to the Violent Aftermath of Ayodhya' (2005) 37 *Case Western Reserve Journal of International Law* 85, 89.

Subsequently to the *Faruqui* case,[84] the Court failed to strike down section 7 of the Acquisition of Certain Lands in Ayodhya Act. The majority of judges in this case rejected the argument that section 7, which in effect permitted the continuance of the worship of the idols, favoured the Hindu community and was anti-secular. Though the majority in the Supreme Court said that the demolition was a 'national shame', it continued to allow worship in the makeshift temple. In this case, the minority judgment rightly held that 'to condone the acquisition of a place of worship in circumstances in which it was demolished is to efface the principle from the Constitution'.[85] The Supreme Court also noted that 'the perpetrators of this deed, struck not only against a place of worship, but also at the principles of secularism, democracy and the rule of law enshrined in the Constitution'.[86] Yet despite this recognition, the Supreme Court, and for that matter the High Court, also failed to restore the site, or make it accessible by the minority community. Parikh argued that the court's definition of secularism contradicted the Indian definition of secularism as 'treating all religions equally'.[87]

McHugh stated that the disconnection between the language of secularism set out by the Supreme Court and the action actually taken was a result of the Court's own biases.[88] He further alleged that 'one aspect of this problem is the continued, practical dominance [by] members of upper castes within the political, social, economic, and legal institutions of India'.[89] Jacobsohn argued in the same manner when he observed that 'secularism appears in the form of a radical majoritarian in the service of an assimilationist agenda'.[90]

V. Conclusion

Thus religiously based dispute over a sacred site can be simply one facet of a broader dispute based around community identities.[91] Communal violence resulting from the Ayodhya dispute proved to be a turning point in Indian politics, which has led to each community's having deeply entrenched, polarised political views. The tragedy of the Ayodhya dispute is that it has eroded the belief of communities in the federalist, secular principles enshrined in the Constitution. The political confrontation encouraged religious-cultural confrontation, and that in turn strengthens

[84] *Ismail Faruqui v Union of India and Others* AIR 1995 SC 605.
[85] Noorani (ed) (n 47) 271.
[86] *Ismail Faruqui v Union of India and Others* AIR 1995 SC 605.
[87] Parikh (n 83) 98.
[88] JT McHugh, *Comparative Constitutional Traditions* (Oxford, Peter Lang, 2002) 105.
[89] ibid.
[90] Jacobsohn (n 82) 97.
[91] A Ahmad, 'Somnath to Gandhinagar: A Night of Long Knives' in KN Panikkar and S Muralidharan (eds), *Communalism, Civil Society and the State: Reflections on a Decade of Turbulence* (New Delhi, SAHMAT, 2002) 27.

the former.[92] Since sacred sites are tied up with the identity of particular communities, any attack on them is seen as an attack on the community, and will naturally be defended vigorously. This was demonstrated in the ensuing violence that took place all over India and in the region after the demolition.[93]

Additionally, if a constitutional order uses secular values to protect minorities, undermining secular values can lead to the erosion of the minority rights. In the Ayodhya dispute, it has been shown that the courts continued to support the majoritarian religious community by allowing the Hindus to worship in the Babri Masjid. Throughout the dispute, the judiciary neglected the principles of secularism and protection of minority rights. Minority communities still view secularism as a guarantee of their fundamental rights; while, more broadly, the secularism enshrined in the Constitution is seen as the linchpin that binds together all the diverse groups of people within India. As secularism is basic to the Constitution, any attack on a sacred place could be construed as an attack on secularism as established by the Supreme Court in the *Bommai* case.[94] A similar opinion was expressed by Justice Sawanth, as 'the concept of secularism as religious tolerance and equal treatment of all religious groups includes an assurance of the protection of life, property, and places of worship for all religious groups'.[95] A failure to deliver these guarantees may, as Justice Ramaswamy points out, result in 'social disunity [that] is bound to corrupt leading to national disintegration'.[96]

[92] AA Engineer (ed), *Communalism and Communal Violence in India: An Analytical Approach to Hindu-Muslim Conflict* (New Delhi, Ajanta, 1989) 94–95.
[93] Post-Babri Masjid demolition saw Hindu temples being demolished in Pakistan, Bangladesh and in various Arab countries. M Mahmood, 'Backlash to the Destruction at Ayodhya: A View from Pakistan' (1993) 33 *Asian Survey* 711.
[94] *SR Bommai v Union of India* (1994) 3 SCC [1].
[95] ibid [149].
[96] ibid [208].

14

The Place of Shari'a in Australia

MD JAHID HOSSAIN BHUIYAN

I. Introduction

Australia, being a multicultural country, has seen increasing differences within its population with respect to birth country, spoken languages, Aboriginal or Torres Strait Islander descent, and religious belief and practice (or lack of religious belief). According to the 2016 Census, 67 per cent of the population was Australian-born; almost 49 per cent were either born outside the country, or one or both of their parents were born outside.[1] Western democracies started recognising and accommodating diversity by adopting multiculturalism policies (MCPs) and minority rights from the 1970s to the mid-1990s. Some states, as well as international organisations, sanctioned these policies, and the previous ideas of uniform nationhood were dismissed.[2] However, multiculturalism started facing criticism and withdrawal from the mid-1990s, and the concepts of nation building, shared identity and beliefs, and unified citizenship were reasserted.[3]

The issue of legal pluralism is at the centre of the discussions on Australian Muslims,[4] and whether the secular legal system should formally recognise Shari'a is considered from time to time.[5] This prompts the question: how much can a liberal country's legal system tolerate a minority group having autonomy in a given area of law? Should Muslims be allowed to resolve their family disputes in a Shari'a tribunal? The prospects of having legal pluralism is, according to Bryan S Turner, a significant means of testing the limitations of multiculturalism or how

[1] Available at https://www.abs.gov.au/ausstats/abs@.nsf/lookup/Media%20Release3 (accessed 16 July 2019).

[2] W Kymlicka, *Multiculturalism: Success, Failure, and the Future* (Washington, DC, Migration Policy Institute, 2012) 3.

[3] ibid.

[4] B Nagra and I Peng, 'Has Multiculturalism Really Failed? A Canadian Muslim Perspective' (2013) 4 *Religions* 603, 604.

[5] JM Roose and A Possamai, 'Between Rhetoric and Reality: Shari'a and the Shift Towards Neoliberal Multiculturalism in Australia' in F Mansouri (ed), *Cultural, Religious and Political Contestations: The Multicultural Challenge* (Heidelberg, Springer, 2015) 91, 92.

much it is backed by the public.[6] Legal pluralism is explained by legal anthropologist John Griffith as 'the presence in a social field of more than one legal order'.[7] It is seen as 'a critical response to the ideology of legal centralism that inextricably binds law to the structures and processes of the modern nation-state'.[8] Legal centralism, by contrast, is an ideology that law is bound to the structures and procedures of contemporary nation state, and it should be the same for all individuals and applied by a unitary body of state institutions. Other normative authorities like the church, the family, and other voluntary and economic organisations, while they may have a great deal of autonomy from the state in respect of their internal affairs, are generally required to obey state institutions and relevant secular law.[9]

William Twining anticipated that the degree to which the norms and beliefs of different cultures, religions or traditions should be recognised, or even enforced, by the state would be a matter of disputation in Western societies.[10] Between 2003 and 2005, the relevance of Shari'a-based family law arbitration was debated in the Canadian province of Ontario. The *Arbitration Act 1991* had allowed for religious and non-religious arbitration in family matters to address the backlog of cases in provincial courts. In November 2003, a press conference was held by Syed Mumtaz Ali, the ex-head of the Institute for Islamic Civil Justice, to declare that the Institute would provide religious-based arbitration to Muslims.[11] According to Irfan Syed, chairman of the Toronto-based Muslim Lawyers Association, such provision is normal in multicultural countries and is a legal way of offering a certain degree of autonomy to religious communities. He asserted that it was possible for the two systems to co-exist because the final supervisory capacity is with the Canadian courts.[12] Critics asserted that patriarchal norms were allegedly present in Shari'a, and this would be detrimental for Muslim women when it was used in family law arbitration.[13] A review was carried out by an ex-Attorney General, Marion Boyd, and the report she presented in 2004 suggested that the Shari'a should be adopted. The report led to further debate, both for and against the introduction of Shari'a.[14] A policy statement was presented on the religious arbitration debate by Ontario Premier Dalton McGuinty on 11 September 2005, in which it was stated, '[T]here will be no sharia law … [and] no religious arbitration in Ontario. There will be

[6] BS Turner, *Religion and Modern Society: Citizenship, Secularisation and the State* (Cambridge, Cambridge University Press, 2011) 174. Cited in Roose and Possamai (n 5) 92.

[7] J Griffiths, 'What is Legal Pluralism?' (1986) 24 *Journal of Legal Pluralism* 1, 2.

[8] ibid 1.

[9] ibid 3.

[10] W Twining, *Globalisation and Legal Theory* (London, Butterworths, 2000) 51.

[11] JA Selby, '"The Diamond Ring Now Is the Thing" Young Muslim Torontonian Women Negotiating *Mahr* on the Web' in A Masquelier and BF Soares (eds), *Muslim Youth and the 9/11 Generation* (Albuquerque, NM, University of New Mexico Press, 2016) 189, 191.

[12] J Sturcke, 'Sharia law in Canada, Almost' (8 February 2008) at https://www.theguardian.com/news/blog/2008/feb/08/sharialawincanadaalmost (accessed 1 August 2019).

[13] Selby (n 11) 191.

[14] Sturcke (n 12).

one law for all Ontarians.'[15] This policy was later enacted as the Family Statute Law Amendment Act 2006.

In London, on 7 February 2008, a speech entitled 'Civil and Religious Law in England: a Religious Perspective' was delivered by the Archbishop of Canterbury, Dr Rowan Williams. The Archbishop claimed that it was not possible to avoid the inclusion of certain aspects of the Shari'a in Britain. The Prime Minister's Office, the Conservative Party and the Chairman of the Government's Equalities and Human Rights Commission criticised the speech. On the same day, Archbishop Williams told the British Broadcasting Corporation (BBC) that British law already recognised certain aspects of Shari'a and that Orthodox Jews were even using their own courts based on religious law to resolve certain disputes.[16] Even before Archbishop Williams had presented his proposal, Shari'a was already applicable in Britain through councils that provide rulings on Islamic civil justice. Disagreements among British Muslims on issues such as child custody, housing, property and employment are arbitrated by these councils. However, criminal law or any civil issue that would create a direct conflict between Shari'a and British statutory law are not handled by these councils. The Shari'a judges were offered official authority to make rulings on divorce and financial disagreements between couples by Britain in the latter part of 2008.[17] Decisions taken by tribunals using Shari'a as per the Arbitration Act 1996 are legally valid,[18] and are enforceable, yet reviewable, in the county courts and High Court in Britain.[19]

In 2011, the Australian Federation of Islamic Councils asserted that Muslims should be provided 'legal pluralism'. Sheik Mohamadu Nawas Saleem, a prominent Muslim leader in Australia, has shown support to introduce Shari'a in Australia, which could be a part of family law system. However, then-Attorney-General, Robert McClelland stated that Shari'a could not operate within the multicultural policy of Australia.[20] Shari'a is frequently viewed in a negative light by Australians. Nevertheless, the Government endorses Islamic finance, apparently on the basis that it is a potential source of foreign investment.[21] This chapter examines the extent to which Shari'a can be and has been accommodated in Australia's legal system, and searches for an explanation as to why Islamic finance law has been welcomed while Shari'a in family matters have so far been rejected.

[15] A McIlroy, 'One law to rule them all' (14 September 2005) at https://www.theguardian.com/world/2005/sep/14/worlddispatch.annemcilroy (accessed 1 August 2019).

[16] MM Keshavjee, *Islam, Sharia & Alternative Dispute Resolution: Mechanisms for Legal Redress in the Muslim Community* (London, IB Tauris & Co Ltd, 2003) 192.

[17] RL Miller and FB Cross, *The Legal Environment Today: Business in its Ethical, Regulatory, E-commerce, and Global Setting* (Mason, OH, South-Western Cengage Learning, 2010) 65.

[18] See CR Lepore, 'Asserting State Sovereignty over National Communities of Islam in the United States and Britain: Sharia Courts as a Tool of Muslim Accommodation and Integration' (2012) 11(3) *Washington University Global Studies Review* 669, 669.

[19] See A Black and K Sadiq, 'Good and Bad Sharia: Australia's Mixed Response to Islamic Law' (2011) 34 *University of New South Wales Law Journal* 383.

[20] Patricia Karvelas, 'Imam wants sharia law here, but A-G says no way' *The Australian* (18 May 2011) at https://www.theaustralian.com.au/national-affairs/imam-wants-sharia-law-here-but-a-g-says-no-way/news-story/27b2b125adc9561b92b4319b9cf89422 (accessed 13 September 2019).

[21] Black and Sadiq (n 19) 389.

II. Muslim Communities in Australia

Macassan fishermen were the earliest Muslims to visit Australia, arriving from 1750 onwards, prior to European settlement. Fishermen from Macassan located in Sulawesi, part of present-day Indonesia, would make yearly visits to the northern Australian coast to catch the trepang, a specific kind of 'sea slug'.[22] These fishermen came in contact with Aboriginal people from northern Australia during their visits.[23] In general, there were peaceful and cordial interactions between them.[24] This may have been the earliest inter-religious contact in Australia.[25] These Muslims made visits to Australia for more than 150 years; however, restrictions were placed on Macassans coming into Australian territorial waters after Europeans gained control of the island continent. The yearly visits of the Macassans had ceased by 1907 after heavy custom duties were imposed, the enactment of the *Immigration Restriction Act* in 1901 and the restriction of entry of Macassans in certain ports in the north.[26]

In the nineteenth century, Australia brought Afghan Cameleers to assist in transportation in and exploration of the Australian desert. It was in June 1860 that the first Muslim cameleers reached Port Melbourne to take part in the Burke and Wills expedition.[27] The Victorian Exploration Expedition Committee claimed that the camels would be of no use without their native drivers, which is why these cameleers were brought to Australia.[28] Samuel Stuckey visited Karachi, Pakistan in 1866, with the intention of importing camels to Australia. He managed to bring over 100 camels and their drivers from Afghanistan and the Indian subcontinent. Subsequently, cameleers from various ethnic groups and locations, such as Baluchistan, Kashmir, Sind, Punjab, Turkey and Persia, came to Australia, and were together referred to as 'Afghans'.[29] The most significant religious structure for Muslims – mosques – were developed by these Muslim cameleers.[30] Surveys, carrier tasks and construction were also carried out from 1870 to 1872 by the Afghan Cameleers for the Overland Telegraph Line. Starting from 1880, the demand for Afghan camel drivers increased. Employment of Afghans became common following the discovery of gold in Western Australia and other minerals

[22] A Saeed, *Islam in Australia* (Sydney, Allen & Unwin, 2003) 3.
[23] ibid 4.
[24] ibid.
[25] See N Amath, '"We're serving the community, in whichever form it may be": Muslim Community Building in Australia' in M Peucker and R Ceylan (eds), *Muslim Community Organizations in the West: History, Developments and Future Perspectives* (Wiesbaden, Springer, 2017) 93, 94.
[26] Saeed (n 22) 4.
[27] A Kenny, 'Australia's early Muslim settlements' in P Jones and A Kenny (eds), *Australia's Muslim Cameleers: Pioneers of the Inland, 1860s–1930s* (Adelaide, Wakefield Press, 2010) 19, 19.
[28] VEE Committee minutes, 19 May 1859 (SLV); quoted by Kenny, ibid.
[29] N Faris and M Abdalla, *Leadership in Islam: Thoughts, Processes and Solutions in Australian Organizations* (Cham, Switzerland, Palgrave Macmillan, 2018) 29.
[30] ibid 30.

in Queensland in the early part of the 1890s. Employers believed that they could pay lower wages to the Afghan camel drivers. In addition, their camels were considered to be more robust and effective for transportation.[31]

Following the federation of Australia in 1901, a restriction was imposed on non-white immigration and citizenship through the 1901 *Immigration Restriction Act*.[32] According to the Act, all the non-whites coming to Australia would have to complete a medical assessment and a dictation test in any European language. Most Muslims could not pass the language test. In addition, resident non-whites who wished to move from one State to another had to obtain a special certificate. This meant the abolition of unrestrained crossing of State borders, which was vital for the inland trade of the Afghan cameleers. The 1902 *Roads Act* made it compulsory to get a licence for operating a camel carrying-business, along with the payment of a registration fee.[33] The camel transport industry stopped operating in the 1920s, and new transportation means emerged, such as the automobile. Many Afghans were forced to depart from Australia due to the combined impact of racism, the White Australia Policy and the annihilation of the camel transport industry.[34]

The new Muslim community developed in Australia during the economic expansion following the Second World War. In the new world of the United Nations and de-colonisation, the preceding restrictive policies became invalid. Because of the high labour requirements, Cypriot Turks, Albanians, Bosnians, and then mainland Turks and Lebanese were welcomed.[35] Muslim communities were able to restore their presence in Australia after almost three-quarters of a century following this friendly policy towards immigrants and refugees from different parts of the world, alongside the establishment of a national multicultural policy framework.[36] Currently, nearly 40 per cent of Australian Muslims are Australian-born, having parents or grandparents who migrated to Australia. There is ethnic, linguistic and geographic diversity among the Australian Muslims.[37]

III. Definition of Shari'a

Literally, Shari'a refers to the path to attain salvation and felicity.[38] Religiously, Shari'a refers to a path to achieve a noble life filled with religious values that are

[31] NA Kabir, *Muslims in Australia: Immigration, Race Relations and Cultural History* (Abingdon, Routledge, 2010) 42.

[32] Saeed (n 22) 6.

[33] B Cleland, 'The History of Muslims in Australia' in A Saeed and S Akbarzadeh (eds), *Muslim Communities in Australia* (Randwick, University of New South Wales Press, 2001) 12, 18.

[34] Saeed (n 22) 6–7.

[35] Cleland (n 33) 29.

[36] ibid 29–30.

[37] Department of Immigration and Citizenship, Australian Government, *The Australian Journey – Muslim communities* (2009) 8.

[38] MH Kamali, *Shari'ah Law: An Introduction* (Oxford, Oneworld Publications, 2008) 1.

applicable to social behaviour in addition to individual morality.[39] Shari'a, being a path towards religion, is mainly related to values that are essential to Islam, and how they can be best protected. The five pillars of Islam (*al-arkan al-khamash*) are faith in God, prayers, fasting, giving a share of wealth annually for the support of the poor (*zakat*) and the pilgrimage (*hajjj*). Hence, the essence of Shari'a is having faith in God, worshipping him and observing these five pillars.[40]

Shari'a is confused with *fiqh* by many people; however, they are different from each other. Shari'a is essentially presented through divine revelation (*wahy*) that is part of Qur'an and authentic hadith. However, *fiqh* signifies primarily 'the *corpus juris* that is developed by the legal schools (*madhhabs*), individual jurists and judges by recourse to legal reasoning (*ijtihad*) and issuing of a legal verdict (*fatwa*)'.[41] Following the Prophet's migration from Mecca to Medina, Shari'a rulings became evident with the establishment of a new Muslim community and government. The Prophet was involved in propagating the belief and principles of Islam and its moral virtue in the initial years of his campaign. It was during the 10 years that the Prophet spent in Medina that the focus shifted to the adoption of legal rules given in the Qur'an.[42] The Qur'an was considered by the Prophet as an authoritative source, and he started referring to his own teachings and examples (*Sunna*) to direct conduct only in his final years in Medina. The terms Shari'a and *fiqh* do not have their typical meanings in the *Sunna*.[43] It seems that the Pious Caliphs (*Khulafa' Rashidun*) did not use the word Shari'a, nor the word *fiqh* to refer to a legal code. It was only after a long time that these terms developed their juristic meanings.[44]

Mohammad Hashim Kamali stressed that while it has commonly been thought that Shari'a is a legal code that is the defining aspect of an Islamic state, the source evidence does not provide a powerful basis for this. The significance of Islam is as a religion and a moral code that is based on its five pillars, and the adoption of a legal code is secondary to the actual message of Islam.[45] Abdullah Saeed also argues that Shari'a and *fiqh* should be differentiated from one another. There is a linguistic relationship between Shari'a and terms like 'the road' or 'the path'. Hence, it is believed to be a path that has been established by God and which provides salvation to Muslims. It is the divine guidance that is part of what was revealed to the Prophet through the Qur'anic verses, and additionally highlighted through the sayings and actions of the Prophet (*Sunna*). Shari'a, in terms of Islamic law, signifies the guidance mentioned in the Qur'an and *Sunna* and typically expressed as

[39] WM Zalewski, *The Crucible of Religion: Culture, Civilization, and Affirmation of Life* (Eugene, OR, Wipf & Stock Publishers, 2012) 275.

[40] Kamali (n 38) 2.

[41] ibid 2.

[42] ibid 2–3.

[43] ibid 4.

[44] ibid.

[45] ibid.

instructions and prohibitions. Such instructions are sometimes specific, such as those relating to dietary matters as well as certain penal laws, or they are ideals that should be inculcated in the believers, for example the persistent reminders to act impartially in one's dealings and exhibit honest and just actions.[46] To summarise, the instructions and limitations presented in the Qur'an and *Sunna* constitute the Shari'a.[47] In contrast, *fiqh* signifies the particular rulings that are acquired as a result of the comprehension and interpretation of the Shari'a acquired from other sources, such as *Ijma* (consensus), *Qiyas* (analogy), *urf* (customs), *ra'y* (opinion or reason) and *Ijithad* (effort). Hence, for Muslims, Shari'a is based on God and the divine, while humans are the source of *fiqh*.[48] These terms are briefly discussed below.

Ijma means 'consensus'. It refers to following a particular ruling that is determined by a group of Muslims regarding what is allowed and what is not permissible following the Prophet's demise. In general, *Ijma* is considered to be unanimous consensus achieved by Muslim scholars (jurists) or the overall Muslim community on a given issue. An agreement is typically attained on a legal issue, but at times theological issues may also be addressed.[49] *Qiyas* means 'analogy'. The issues that are not provided for by any rulings in the Qur'an or the *Sunna* are dealt with through *Qiyas*. Scholars make use of analogical deduction based on the teachings of the Qur'an and *Sunna* to come up with rulings on a certain issue.[50] For example, in one of the Qur'anic verses, wine consumption is strictly prohibited. A majority of the jurists believe that this prohibition is made because alcohol has a strong effect on the mind. Hence, according to the principles of *Qiyas*, when this justification is used, any product that creates similar effects may be prohibited. Accordingly, the rule for wine is also applicable to narcotics, even though the Qur'an and *Sunna* have not specifically prohibited them.[51] The root word of *urf* is 'a-ra-fa', meaning 'to know'. Hence, *urf* is something that is known. In juristic terms, it refers to the combined practice carried out by a large number of people and which has been made customary, or certain words that have acquired a distinct meaning, such that the other meanings are no longer used and one interprets only the special meaning. *Urf* is a tradition that people acknowledge and practise, though there are no express pronouncements on it. However, it does not defy logic, nature or Islamic values.[52] *Ijtihad* means 'effort' or 'trying'. It signifies the greatest possible effort expended by a trained jurist to identify a ruling for a given scenario.[53]

[46] A Saeed, *Islamic Thought: An Introduction* (Abingdon, Routledge, 2006) 43.
[47] ibid 44.
[48] ibid.
[49] ibid 49.
[50] N Alam, L Gupta and B Shanmugam, *Islamic Finance: A Practical Perspective* (Cham, Switzerland, Palgrave Macmillan/Springer Nature, 2017) 27.
[51] Saeed (n 46) 49.
[52] R Dogan, *Usul al-Fiqh: Methodology of Islamic Jurisprudence* (Clifton, NJ, Tugra Books, 2013) ch 7.
[53] IA Khan Nyazee, *Theories of Islamic Law* (New Delhi, Adam Publishers & Distributors, 2006) 9.

IV. The Issue of Shari'a in Australia

In Australia, the Muslim communities have various community-based dispute procedures for resolving family disputes. In most cases, these practices are unofficial and unenforceable.[54] Hence, demands have been put forward by some in the Muslim community that the decisions and settlements made in these community forums should have legal recognition.[55] For example, former Islamic Council of Victoria (ICV) president and lawyer Hyder Gulam has called for the 'recognition of Sharia in terms of dispute resolution (similar to what the Jewish community has in relation to the Beth Din courts, or similar to the reconciliation hearings at the Koori Courts in Victoria)'.[56] Hyder contended that until 1992, 'the Muslim communities of Christmas and Cocos (Keeling) Islands successfully managed their religious affairs and regulations using their Muslim personal and customary laws without any conflict with Australian Family Law of 1975'.[57]

In April 2011, the Australian federal Government sought submissions from the public, community groups and representative organisations, to play a part in formulating the multicultural policy of Australia. Iqbal Patel, President of Australian Federation of Islamic Councils (AFIC), submitted that 'multiculturalism should lead to legal pluralism, arguing that conflicts should be resolved according to the law and traditions of one's own religion'.[58] In response to this submission, the then-Minister for Immigration, Chris Bowen, said that 'Anybody who calls for Sharia law is not doing so in the name of multiculturalism. They are doing so as extremists and extremists need to be dealt with, whatever their creed.'[59]

The Director of the Islamic Women's Council of Victoria, Joumanah El Matrah, opposed the establishment of a separate Shari'a tribunal or court because she thought that it would bring about 'legal ghettoization of Muslims', and that 'establishing a parallel system for Muslims' would not necessarily bring about a culturally relevant reaction to justice but would essentially restrict 'Muslims from

[54] G Krayem and F Ahmed, 'Islamic Community Processes in Australia: An Introduction' in S Bano (ed), *Gender and Justice in Family Law Disputes: Women, Mediation, and Religious Arbitration* (Waltham, MA, Brandeis University Press, 2017) 246, 246.

[55] ibid.

[56] Gulam Hyder, 'Shariah and English Law' *Al-Wasat* (September 2012) 72. Cited in M Abdalla, 'Sacred Law in a Secular Land: To What Extent Should Shari'a Law be Followed in Australia?' (2012) 21 *Griffith Law Review* 657, 659.

[57] Gulam Hyder, 'The Historical Application of Shariah in Australia' *Al-Wasat* (October 2012) 26. Cited in Abdalla, (n 56).

[58] Australia Federation of Islamic Councils; Submission 81: 'Embracing Australia Values – Maintaining the Right to be Different'. Cited in A Black, 'Colonial legacies: family laws in Singapore and Australia' in N Hosen (ed), *Research Handbook on Islamic Law and Society* (Cheltenham, Edward Elgar Publishing, 2018) 13, 33.

[59] Sabra Lane, 'Multiculturalism is Back', ABC News *AM Program* (17 February 2011) at http://www.abc.net.au/am/content/2011/s3141073.htm (accessed 27 September 2019).

services they as citizens have a right to access'.[60] The Joint Standing Committee on Migration, in its report in March 2013, asserted that it was not essential or desirable to legally recognise Islamic practices.[61] In addition, legal pluralism was not supported by the Committee.[62]

Muslims give special importance to family law, no matter whether they are citizens of a traditional Muslim country or of the secular West. First, Islamic family law has a firm grounding because it originates directly from God's revelations to the Prophet Muhammad, as there are various verses (*ayat*) in the Qur'an that present the laws for family associations, marriage and divorce. Second, cultural and sociological factors play a part, as family law is directly linked to 'individual identity within a shared identity of the family' and encompasses a shared belongingness towards the global Muslim community (*ummah*).[63] Often, Islamic family law is promoted as a stronghold against secular society. It has been asserted by the governments of Muslim countries, and by the Muslim minorities in non-Muslim countries, that families are kept safe from getting influenced by impermissible (*haram*) activities (for example, child abuse, prostitution, extra-marital affairs, alcohol and drug abuse, etc) by following Islamic family law. When this value system is adopted, a greater degree of security is awarded to families, and the economic, political and social implications of family disruption in Western societies can be avoided.[64] Apart from certain exceptions, particularly Turkey, some kind of Islamic family law is followed by all Muslim majority countries, while several other countries, such as Singapore, India, Thailand, Israel and the Philippines, have established a distinct mechanism of Islamic courts, as well as policies to enable the administration of Islamic family law for their Muslim residents. For instance, a statute called the *Administration of Muslim Law Act 1966* has been enacted in Singapore, which has authorised the use of family law for the Muslim minority within the country, with distinct Shari'a courts funded by the Government, in addition to the Islamic Religious Council. In the past few decades, there have been extensive migrations of Muslims to Western countries, as a result of which there are people who support the provision of Muslim autonomy on such personal status issues in North America, Europe and Australia.[65]

[60] J El Matrah, 'A Sharia Tribunal is a Contradiction of Islam' *The Age* (20 October 2009). Cited in Black (n 58) 34.

[61] Parliament of the Commonwealth of Australia: Joint Standing Committee on Migration, *Inquiry into Migration and Multiculturalism in Australia*, March 2013, at https://www.aph.gov.au › committees › house_of_representatives_committees (accessed 27 September 2019) 85. Cited in Krayem and Ahmed (n 54) 247.

[62] Parliament of the Commonwealth of Australia: Joint Standing Committee on Migration, *Inquiry into Migration and Multiculturalism in Australia* (n 61).

[63] A Black, H Esmaeili and N Hosen, *Modern Perspectives on Islamic Law* (Cheltenham, Edward Elgar, 2013) 107.

[64] ibid 109.

[65] ibid.

V. Shari'a and Financial Opportunity

While the Australian Government seems to have adopted the stance that the Australian legal system would not incorporate any aspect of Shari'a, an extensive document entitled *Islamic Finance* presented by an Australian Federal Agency, the Australian Trade Commission (Austrade), in January 2010[66] asserted that Islamic finance was a rapidly developing field of the financial services industry of the world. In addition, it asserted that the last 10 years has seen more than a 10 per cent annual increase in Shari'a-compliant financial assets. Furthermore, it was estimated that the worth of the international Islamic finance industry was almost US$822 billion in 2009, as calculated by Shari'a-compliant assets of financial institutions.[67] Austrade reports estimated that international Shari'a-compliant assets would attain US$1 trillion by 2010 and US$1.6 trillion by 2012.[68] It asserted that there are four factors that determine the rapid development of Islamic finance:

(a) increasing oil revenue and robust economic progress in the Gulf;
(b) demand from Muslim and non-Muslim investors;
(c) limited levels of penetration; and
(d) the ethical nature and financial consistency of products.[69]

In relation to the first factor, Austrade reported that almost half of the oil reserves all over the world are held by the Gulf Cooperation Council (GCC), while oil earnings constitute almost 70 per cent of the exports and revenues of the GCC. Because of the high liquidity of the petrodollar in the Gulf countries, investment in offshore assets is sought by petrodollar investors, some of which is as Shari'a-compliant financial assets.[70] In relation to the second factor, Austrade reported that higher investments are sought by investors from Middle East and Asia in products consistent with their religious views. When offered a competitive substitute for traditional services, 50 per cent of Muslims all over the world would choose Islamic finance. Diversification of the investment base is sought by conventional buyers, especially when there is limited access to wholesale funding sources following GCC.[71] In relation to the third factor, the Austrade reported that although the Islamic banking and finance industry experienced growth, asset classes and products continued to have insufficient depth, which implied unexploited potential. Although countries like Indonesia, India and Pakistan that have the highest population of Muslims in the world, the Islamic banking and finance industries in these

[66] The Australian Trade Commission (Austrade), *Islamic Finance*, at http://www.crescentsofbrisbane.org/00%20Files%20&%20Images/CCN278/Islamic-Finance-Publication.pdf (accessed 27 September 2019).
[67] ibid 5.
[68] ibid 11.
[69] ibid 15.
[70] ibid.
[71] ibid.

countries is not well-established.[72] In relation to the fourth factor, the Austrade reported that in a world of corporate social responsibility, a greater degree of attention is drawn by Islamic finance. No investments are made by Islamic finance in weak asset categories, which has impeded the financial performance of various conventional banks.[73]

Islamic finance is an industry worth $2.2 trillion in 2018, present in more than 60 countries, while the majority of it is found in limited markets. Only 10 countries account for 95 per cent of the international Shari'a-compliant assets, as determined by the research department of the Union of Arab Banks. These include Iran (30 per cent of the worldwide total), Saudi Arabia (24 per cent), Malaysia (11 per cent), the United Arab Emirates (10 per cent), Qatar (6 per cent), Kuwait (5 per cent), Bahrain (4 per cent), Bangladesh (1.8 per cent), Indonesia (1.6 per cent) and Pakistan (1 per cent).[74] It is in these countries that industry standards are established, Islamic finance development is brought about and innovation is encouraged. The yearly growth of Islamic finance was 10–12 per cent in the previous decade.[75] In a report by Thompson Reuters' Islamic Finance Development entitled *Resilient Growth* (2016), Islamic assets were expected to amount to $3.5 trillion by 2021, depending on whether these 10 markets remain economically stable.[76]

On 26 March 2010, after Austrade's publication of *Islamic Finance*, Senator the Honourable Nick Sherry, then Assistant Treasurer, told Australian funds managers that plans were being made by the Australian Government to develop Islamic finance in Australia to turn the country into a dominant international hub of financial services. Thereafter, Sherry made visits to Qatar, the United Arab Emirates and Bahrain in April 2010, to carry out discussions on the promotion, export and regulation of Islamic finance, insurance and banking.[77] On 26 April 2010, Senator Sherry declared that a comprehensive assessment would be carried out on the tax laws of Australia, to make sure that they did not prevent the extension of Islamic banking, insurance and finance products.[78] In May 2010, he launched a book entitled *Demystifying Islamic Finance – Correcting Misconceptions, Advancing Value.* At the book launch, Senator Sherry claimed that although the number of Muslims in Australia is small, the geographical location of Australia is such that it provides a critical overview of the Islamic finance sector. Indonesia, the immediate neighbour of Australia, has the highest number of Muslims (207 million), while the

[72] ibid.

[73] ibid.

[74] C Domat, 'Islamic Finance: Just For Muslim-Majority Nations?' (25 July 2018) at https://www.gfmag.com/topics/blogs/islamic-finance-just-muslim-majority-nations (accessed 27 September 2019).

[75] ibid.

[76] ibid.

[77] See at https://chironthebusinessdoctor.com/islamic-finance-system-a-primer/ (accessed 27 September 2019).

[78] See The Board of Taxation, *Review of the Taxation Treatment of Islamic Finance: A Report to the Assistant Treasure* (June 2011) vii.

wider south East Asia region is home to 40 million Muslims. In addition, Senator Sherry asserted that the Australian Financial Centre Forum had been formulated by the Government the preceding year to provide global endorsement for the financial services sector in Australia. The Forum had also discussed Islamic finance as providing significant opportunities in the field of financial services. Furthermore, he claimed that the increasing awareness in the community and among law makers of the opportunities for Islamic finance in Australia had been emphasised by Australian bankers. The Government was keen to make certain that the growth of Islamic finance in the country did not face any hurdles, which is consistent with its commitment to encourage a free and competitive financial system, as well as a socially inclusive setting. Furthermore, it was acknowledged that job creation and development is encouraged by Islamic finance.[79]

Senator Sherry received negative reactions from certain community members following his visits to the Middle East and the Government's show of interest in Islamic finance. Senator Sherry stressed the need to have further discussions. He said that some of the criticisms were open assertions that terrorism is spread by Islamic finance, that Islamic finance is a means of advancing the dominance of Islam over other religions and that it is intended to take the place of conventional financing. Hence, Sherry claimed that the challenge was to continue with community discussions in order to spread awareness of the actual facts.[80]

The terms of reference for a review were presented on 12 May 2010 by the Assistant Treasurer. The Board of Taxation was asked to determine the factors in the existing Australian tax laws that made it difficult to develop and offer Islamic finance products.[81] The financial report was presented by the Board of Taxation in 2012, but the Government did not issue a comprehensive response to it.[82] The Honourable Bernie Ripoll MP, Parliamentary Secretary to the Treasurer & Parliamentary Secretary for Small Business, stated, while addressing the Amanie Australia Islamic Finance Forum in April 2013, that by incorporating Islamic finance products in local markets, the Australian Government hoped to provide new growth opportunities to the financial services sector as well as to the economy.[83] A total of 44 recommendations were presented in the Financial System Inquiry Report (2014) based on 237 submissions. No references were made to Islamic finance in this report.[84] Even so, a Memorandum of Understanding (MoU) was signed by the Australian Prudential Regulatory Authority with the Dubai

[79] Cited in MK Hassan and M Mahlknecht, *Islamic Capital Markets: Products and Strategies* (Chichester, John Wiley & Sons Ltd, 2011) 348.

[80] G Segal, 'The Islamic Finance System: What's It Got to do with Australia; What's It Got to do with Me?' at https://www.moneymanagement.com.au/news/financial-planning/sherry-launches-islamic-finance-booklet-dispel-misconceptions (accessed 27 September 2019).

[81] See The Board of Taxation (n 78) 3.

[82] M Tucker, *Student Banking Behaviour in Australia: A Mixed Methods Study of Muslims and Non-Muslims*, PhD Thesis, Faculty of Business and Law, Swinburne University Australia, 2017, 216.

[83] Cited in Segal (n 80).

[84] Tucker (n 82) 217.

Financial Services Authority in July 2015, regarding collaboration in the monitoring of the banking and insurance sector, including Islamic finance.[85]

VI. Shari'a and Australia's Move to Neoliberal Multiculturalism

A persistent aspect of societies is ethnic differentiation. Typically, ethnicity signifies the distinguishing of social groups based on five different criteria. First, a critical aspect is the idea of a 'homeland' or place of shared origin that is connected with the notion of a diaspora in which migration of an ethnic group has occurred from that area to develop communities in another area similar to their place of origin. Second, a key aspect of creation of an emotional connection to a group is a common language, which may be itself be distinct, or a distinct dialect of a language spoken in common with other groups. A core element of various ethnic groups may be the association with a distinctive religious, such as Sikhism, or a religion in common with others. Other criteria employed to differentiate ethnic groups are a shared culture with unique social institutions and behaviour, dress and diet, and a shared tradition or history of one's own 'people' or community.[86]

A relatively new concept is the adoption of policies by the state to affirm and provide protection to ethnic minorities. Nation states have always shown a lack of trust towards 'minority ethnic mobilization', calling the mobilising groups 'disloyal, backward, and balkanizing'.[87] Consistent pressure was created by the history of state–minority relationships across the nineteenth and twentieth centuries for integration, together with hostility towards minority political mobilisation.[88] Nonetheless, a more liberal multicultural outlook towards state–minority relationships was observed beginning in the 1960s.[89] In countries that have a significant immigrant population, multiculturalism serves as a significant national account of coherence and unity. Difference is the foundation of a nation, and the potential to merge these distinctions into a single project, which is the establishment of nation, is thought to offer the state strength and legitimacy. This project is carried out by the state by means of its laws on individual as well as (meticulously defined) group rights, for example those demonstrated by the philosophy and practice of multiculturalism.[90]

[85] ibid 218.

[86] I Law, *Racism and Ethnicity: Global Debates, Dilemmas, Directions* (Abingdon, Routledge, 2013) 78.

[87] W Kymlicka, 'Neoliberal Multiculturalism' in PA Hall and M Lamont (eds), *Social Resilience in the Neoliberal Era* (Cambridge, Cambridge University Press, 2013) 99, 101.

[88] ibid.

[89] ibid.

[90] K Mitchell, 'Educating the national citizen in neoliberal times: from the multicultural self to the strategic cosmopolitan' (2003) 28(4) *Transactions of the Institute of British Geographers* 387, 391.

Tariq Modood puts forward three different levels on which the term 'multiculturalism' is functional. The sociological level is the foremost, where the fact that 'racial and ethnic groups' are prevalent in society is recognised. As a result, minorities are informed that they are unique and are also awarded their individual identity. Often, 'multicultural society' is used to signify this social recognition so as to differentiate it from political notions. The political level is the second aspect, which belongs to a more extensive debate regarding the most appropriate reaction to social reality, consisting of assimilation on the basis of respect for individuals (without 'political recognition of groups'). Another reaction is multiculturalism that is based on the 'equal dignity of individuals' as well as the 'political assimilation of group identities', with the intention of nurturing 'respect and inclusion' for disadvantaged groups, while defying 'exclusionary racisms and practices'. The third level may be known as the 'imaginative level', on which a positive perspective is put forward for the overall society that has been reconstructed so that those who were left out or marginalised earlier based on belonging or equality are integrated. It calls for extending the focus on exclusion and minorities to a point at which 'multicultural integration' or 'multicultural citizenship' can be referred to.[91] Modood correctly argues that the least attention has been given to this third level, which includes the sociological fact of 'diversity, groupness and exclusion' and extends further than the idea of 'individual rights and political accommodation'. This may be the reason why multiculturalism has been comprehended by many as just pertaining to fostering minority difference, in the absence of a counteracting stress on 'cross-cutting commonalities' and the idea of a larger good. As a result, multiculturalism has been considered by many authors and politicians to be disruptive.[92]

Instead of being a threat to the state, political movements and the public expression of minority ethnic identities began to be acknowledged as a normal and lawful aspect of a democratic society. There has been an increasing trend towards accepting minority rights within Western democracies, such as in the case of 'land claims and treaty rights for indigenous persons', enhanced 'language rights and regional autonomy for substate national minorities' and 'accommodation rights for immigrant-origin ethnic groups'. These are all referred to by Will Kymlicka as 'multicultural policies' (MCPs).[93] Kymlicka argues that a number of policies are included in this term; however, the common factor in all of them is that they extend further than protecting the fundamental civil and political rights of all individuals in a liberal-democratic state. This is done by offering 'public recognition and support for minorities' to some extent, so that they can voice their 'distinct identities and practices'.[94] Making sure of fair background environments is the

[91] T Modood, 'Multiculturalism, Britishness, and Muslims' (27 January 2011) at https://www.opendemocracy.net/en/multiculturalism-britishness-and-muslims/ (accessed 8 October 2019).
[92] ibid.
[93] Kymlicka (n 87).
[94] ibid.

responsibility of the state, such as the institutional conditions that are pertinent to the public recognition of linguistic and cultural aspects; however, individuals can perform cost and benefit analysis of the different alternatives in the background before making a choice of their own free will. Hence, instead of imposing any obligations to maintain any given identity or path of life, the focus of liberal multiculturalism is on providing fair opportunities to 'pursue culture-related interests' without any limitations.[95]

A strong force surfaced in the initial part of 1980s, which is often referred to as 'neoliberalism'.[96] It was in the 1930s that a German economist, Alexander Rüstow, coined the term 'neoliberalism' to explain the development of novel and refreshed liberal concepts that were against 'state intervention and collectivism', extensively prevalent in the initial years of the twentieth century.[97] David Harvey argues that neoliberalism pertains to political economic activities, and he suggests that the maximisation of entrepreneurial independence as part of an institutional framework can most appropriately foster human welfare. This framework includes individual freedom, private property rights, free trade and agile markets.[98] Harvey argues that the state is responsible for the development and maintenance of an institutional framework that is relevant for these practices. For instance, the quality and integrity of money should be the responsibility of the state. In addition, it is also responsible for providing protection to private property rights and endorsing freely operating markets by establishing military, juridical and defence functions. Similarly, if there is a lack of markets (such as in the fields of healthcare, education, environmental pollution or social security) then it is imperative for the state to take action, if required, to develop these markets. However, the state should not interfere further than this. After markets have been developed, state intervention should be very limited, as it is not possible for the state to have sufficient information to predict market signals and because state interventions will certainly become disrupted and biased (specially in democracies) towards personal benefits due to dominant interests.[99] Neoliberalism is considered by Gerald Dumenil and Dominique Levy as 'the ideology of the markets and private interests' in contrast to state intervention.[100] According to Robert W McChesney, 'neoliberalism' refers to the policies and procedures in which social life can be regulated as much as possible by a small number of private interests so as to achieve their personal benefits.[101] Though neoliberalism has been described by Graham Harrison as the

[95] W Kymlicka, 'Liberal Multiculturalism as a Political Theory of State-Minority Relations' (2018) 46(1) *Political Theory* 81, 81.

[96] Kymlicka (n 87) 107.

[97] JA Scholte and R Robertson, *Encyclopedia of Globalization*, vol 3 (New York, Routledge, 2007) 865.

[98] D Harvey, 'Neoliberalism as Creative Destruction' (2007) 610 *The Annals of the American Academy* 22, 22.

[99] ibid 22–23.

[100] G Dumenil and D Levy, 'The Neoliberal (Counter-) Revolution' in A Saad-Fiho and D Johnson (eds), *Neoliberalism: A Critical Reader* (London, Pluto Press, 2005) 9.

[101] RW McChesney, 'Introduction' in N Chomsky, *Profit over People: Neoliberalism and Global Order* (New Delhi, Madhyam Books, 1999) 7.

basic political good, which is individual freedom, 'which is best secured through a competitive market society', this is only applicable in states where interference in the economy is restricted to only as much as is needed 'to ensure the second condition'. Hence, neoliberalism is synonymous with 'terms such as laissez-faire, marketization or rolling back the state'.[102]

In the first years of the 1980s, neoliberalism developed in societies that were being shifted towards multiculturalism.[103] Multiculturalism was criticised by neoliberals in Canada, the United Kingdom, the United States and Australia.[104] For example, Margaret Thatcher stated during the 2001 election campaign that she was against 'a multicultural society', as it would 'never be a united society'.[105] In Canada, the Brighton Report recommended that issues be faced in providing direct funds to ethno-cultural organisations. The Report used the concept of 'special interests' (a term often used in neoliberal discussions for groups such as minorities and women) to assert that in its current form, 'the funding of ethno-specific organizations' should be curtailed. It had been reinforced in the previous funding practices that multiculturalism was not a programme for all Canadians, rather it was a 'program for special interests'. The Report then stated that 'the *Minister should make clear that all Canadians – rather than sub-groupings of Canadians – are the recipients of the benefits of multiculturalism*'.[106] Kymlicka argues that multiculturalism was opposed by neoliberalism in both an institutional and a symbolic form. In the institutional sense, the relationship of the state with the progressive advocacy groups was attacked by these neoliberals, and these groups received reduced financing and political access. In the symbolic sense, a comparison between 'ordinary' diligent taxpaying residents and the 'special interests' signified by 'ethnic lobbies' was carried out by neoliberals, thus delegitimising multiculturalism.[107] As Matt James states, discourses were entered into by neoliberals that valorised what was known as the 'ordinary Canadian', considered as a consumer and taxpayer, leading to civic discussions delegitimising group experiences and characteristics as positive concerns.[108]

Charles Hale examines neoliberal multiculturalism as a developing field of governance through the cultural variations that are shaped and created instead

[102] G Harrison, *Neoliberal Africa: The Impact of Global Social Engineering* (New York, Zed Books, 2013) 19.

[103] Kymlicka (n 87) 107.

[104] ibid.

[105] Quoted in Andrew Sparrow, 'Is it safe for Tories to attack multiculturalism?' (27 February 2008) at https://www.theguardian.com/politics/blog/2008/feb/27/camerononmulticulturalism (accessed 8 October 2019).

[106] Brighton Report, *Strategic Evaluation of Multiculturalism Programs* (1996) (Ottawa, Corporate Review Branch, Department of Canadian Heritage, Government of Canada) 76, cited in Y Abu-Laban and C Gabriel, *Selling Diversity: Immigration, Multiculturalism, Employment Equity, and Globalization* (Ontario, Broadview Press, 2012) 114 (emphasis in original).

[107] Kymlicka (n 87) 107.

[108] M James, 'Neoliberal Heritage Redress' in J Henderson and P Wakeham (eds), *Recognising Canada: Critical Perspectives on the Culture of Readers* (Toronto, University of Toronto Press, 2013) 31, 32.

of being inhibited.[109] Hale argues that ethnic rights have been accepted by national elites following 'encouragement of multicultural institutions', meticulously describing them in the realm of politics and programmes so as to avoid any deflection to the development of a neoliberal paradigm. He further argues that 'elite development interests' may be considered while describing cultural rights; however, a counter-argument may be made by using the 'discourses inserted on participation'.[110] Neoliberal multiculturalism is considered by cultural theorists, such as Jodi Melamed, as a group of dominant normative differences between 'globalizing cosmopolitans and parochial traditionalism', which separates legitimate diversity from illegitimate diversity.[111]

Nonetheless, the possibility of multiculturalism's including minorities in international markets and the role they can perform in economic competitiveness has recently been discovered by neoliberal thinkers.[112] Kymlicka states that ethnicity has finally been legitimised by neoliberals, while explaining MCPs that provide protection to those ethnic projects and integrating these policies into the fundamental concepts of neoliberalism (encouraging decentralisation, improving economic competitiveness and innovation, transferring responsibility from the state to civil society, placing lesser stress on national solidarity and, instead, concentrating on local or translational relations, and considering cultural diversity as an economic asset or international commodity).[113]

The definition of multiculturalism has undergone evident changes in the process. Kymlicka argues that the root of multiculturalism was present in social liberalism (focused on alleviating drawbacks) as well as nationalism (creating good citizens who are capable of working across disparities for the good of the state). The inherent notion of 'citizenization' was shaped by both of these ideas. On the other hand, the neoliberal view of multiculturalism is deeply unconcerned about the continuing equality-seeking element of multiculturalism as well as its national boundaries. Neoliberal multiculturalism sought to develop cosmopolitan market players who were able to successfully compete over state borders, instead of tolerant national citizens who were apprehensive about the less privileged in their own society.[114]

James P Walsh has argued that an important case is put forward in Australia for registering the relationship of multiculturalism with neoliberal government.[115] Its founding regulations have had a significant impact on nation and citizen

[109] C Hale, 'Neoliberal multiculturalism: The remaking of cultural rights and racial dominance in Central America' (2005) 28(1) *Political and Legal Anthropology Review* 10, 12–13.
[110] ibid 13.
[111] J Melamed, 'The Spirit of Neoliberalism: From Racial Liberalism to Neoliberal Multiculturalism' (2006) 24(4) *Social Text* 1. Cited in James (n 108).
[112] Kymlicka (n 87) 109.
[113] ibid 110–11.
[114] ibid 111.
[115] JP Walsh, 'The marketization of multiculturalism: neoliberal restructuring and cultural difference in Australia' (2013) 37 *Ethnic and Racial Studies* 1, 2.

development. Furthermore, Australia has transformed from an insular British society into a poly-ethnic country because of post-war immigration. To address this diversity, a significant role has been played by the state in developing policies to monitor integration and deal with the impact of diversity on communal identity and relationships. To appease the prevailing anxiety and adhere to novel administrative mechanisms and developmental plans, multiculturalism was reconstituted in the mid-1980s. There was a shift in the policy of John Howard, Prime Minister of Australia from 1996 to 2007, from a domestic reaction to the needs and shortcomings of minority populations to a kind of moral and market discipline developed to supplement the socio-economic and cultural requirements of neoliberal reorganisation.[116] Australia is against the introduction of Shari'a in family matters, but it endorses Shari'a for financial matters and gains; hence, it may be asserted that Australia practices neoliberal multiculturalism.[117]

It is noted that there are certain practices of the Shari'a family matters that lack coherence with Australian law. For instance, since colonial times, polygamy has been strictly prohibited in Australia, which was then substantiated in more recent criminal law and family law statutes and cases.[118] Second marriages carried out in other countries are not accepted in Australia, though polygamists are offered a certain degree of social welfare. Speaking of Australia, John Witte Jr argues that it is difficult to rely on the human rights case for polygamy in Australia because a national bill of rights[119] is absent and the international human rights instruments to which Australia is a party have not been interpreted to support a right to practise polygamy.[120] Australia should not recognise a practice that is not consistent with its law.

VII. Conclusion

Even though some Muslims in Australia want to use Shari'a to resolve family issues, the stance adopted by the Government has been that Shari'a will not have any place in Australian society. Yet there is apparent support for it in financial matters. Australian Muslims may thus experience confusion because of the Government's acceptance of Shari'a in some instances and its rejection in others. In addition, the media give a lot of attention to the use of Shari'a in family issues,

[116] ibid 2–3.

[117] See Roose and Possamai (n 5) 101–02.

[118] See *Marriage Act 1969* (Cth), s 94, with discussion in *Dohm v Acton* [2008] FamCA 482 and *Wold v Kleppir* [2009] FamCA 178.

[119] See P Babie and N Rochow (eds), *Freedom of Religion Under Bill of Rights* (Adelaide, University of Adelaide Press, 2012).

[120] J Witte, Jr, *The Western Case for Monogamy Over Polygamy* (Cambridge, Cambridge University Press, 2015) 10.

with most Australians criticising it. Hence, Australian governments need to do more to explain to Australian Muslim communities why Australia does not support Shari'a in family issues. If this does not happen, Australian Muslims will feel like they are not part of Australian society and are unable to participate in policy discussions in the country. Such participation in public discussions is a key element of citizenship.[121]

[121] C Calhoun, 'Secularism, Citizenship, and the Public Sphere' in C Calhoun, M Juergensmeyer and J Van Antwerpen (eds), *Rethinking Secularism* (Oxford, Oxford University Press, 2011) 75, 75.

INDEX